Politics and Economics in Northeast Asia

Politics and Economics in Northeast Asia

Nationalism and Regionalism in Contention

Edited by
Tsuneo Akaha

St. Martin's Press
New York

#40996233

POLITICS AND ECONOMICS IN NORTHEAST ASIA

Copyright © Tsuneo Akaha, 1999. All rights reserved. Printed in the United States of America. No part of this book may be used or reproduced in any manner whatsoever without written permission except in the case of brief quotations embodied in critical articles and reviews. For information, St. Martin's Press, 175 Fifth Avenue, New York, N.Y. 10010.

ISBN 0-312-22288-2

Library of Congress Cataloging-in-Publication Data
Politics and economics in northeast Asia:nationalism and regionalism
   in contention / edited by Tsuneo Akaha.
      p. cm.
   ISBN 0-312-22288-2 (cloth)
   1. East Asia—Politics and government—20th century.   2. East
Asia—Foreign economic relations.   3. East Asia—Military relations.
4. East Asia—Relations—Russia—Russian Far East.   5. Russian Far
East (Russia)—Relations—East Asia.   6. East Asia—Relations-
-Mongolia.   7. Mongolia—Relations—East Asia.8. Regionalism
(International organization)   I. Akaha, Tsuneo, 1949-.
DS518.1P62   1999
320.95—dc21
                                                          99–25809
                                                              CIP

Designed by Letra Libre, Inc.
First published: September 1999
10 9 8 7 6 5 4 3 2 1

CONTENTS

LIST OF ACRONYMS

APEC	Asia-Pacific Economic Cooperation
ARF	ASEAN Regional Forum
ASEAN	Association of Southeast Asian Nations
CCP	Chinese Communist Party
CINCPAC	Commander-in-Chief, U. S. Pacific Command
CIS	Commonwealth of Independent States
CMEA	Council of Mutual Economic Assistance
CSCE	Conference on Security and Cooperation in Europe
DMZ	Demilitarized Zone
DPRK	Democratic People's Republic of Korea
ERINA	Economic Research Institute for Northeast Asia
ESENA	Energy, Security, and Environment in Northeast Asia
HKSAR	Hong Kong Special Administrative Region
ICSEAD	International Centre for the Study of East Asian Development
IAEA	International Atomic Energy Agency
KEDO	Korean Peninsula Energy Development Organization
LDP	Liberal Democratic Party
MFN	Most Favored Nation
MITI	Ministry of International Trade and Industry
MOFA	Ministry of Foreign Affairs
MPR	Mongolian People's Republic
NAFTA	North American Free Trade Agreement
NEA	Northeast Asia
NEACD	Northeast Asia Cooperation Dialogue
NEADeC	Northeast Asia Development Center

NEAEF	"Northeast Asian Economic Forum" Project:
NEAEI	"Northeast Asia Economic Cooperation Initiative: Capacity Building Toward Improved Policy Research and Development Management" Project
NET	natural economic territory
NFP	New Frontier Party
NIEs	Newly Industrialized Economies
ODA	official development assistance
PBEC	Pacific Basin Economic Council
PECC	Pacific Economic Cooperation Council
PRC	People's Republic of China
RF	Russian Federation
RFE	"Russian Far East Economic Yearbook" Project
RTAs	regional trade agreements
ROK	Republic of Korea
SDF	Self-Defense Forces
SEZs	Special Economic Zones
SPF	Sasakawa Peace Foundation
TRDP	Tumen River Area Development Program
TREDA	Tumen River Economic Development Area
UNDP	United Nations Development Program
WTO	World Trade Organization

NORTHEAST ASIA AT A HISTORICAL TURNING POINT

Robert Scalapino[*]

Global and Regional Trends

THERE ARE TWO GLOBAL TRENDS that are shaping our times and will continue to be critical in the decades ahead. One is the dominance of economics in domestic and foreign affairs today. Irrespective of system, irrespective of historical background, almost every leadership in the world has been drawn to the tasks of economic development and is judged thereby. This is also a pervasive factor in international relations. We are seeing the economic interdependence of countries and regions steadily grow. We are also seeing manifestations of nations skipping stages of economic development. This is a powerful force.

---

[*]Originally given as a keynote speech at the Monterey Institute of International Studies, Monterey, California, June 19, 1997.

The second factor, somewhat less recognized than the first, is the simultaneous rise of three somewhat conflictual forces: internationalism, nationalism, and communalism. Internationalism is in a variant stage—economic, strategic—but we are experimenting widely, in Asia with such organizations as APEC, and on the global level with the WTO. Equally important, perhaps more important, is the emergence of what I call natural economic territories (NETs). These are economic entities that cut across political boundaries, combining resources, manpower, technology, and capital to form optimal economic units. Hong Kong–Guangdong Province was an early NET. South Korea–Shangdong today, efforts to establish a Tumen River NET in Northeast Asia, a Sea of Japan or Eastern Sea NET that would bring Western Japan, the Russian Far East, the Korean peninsula, and portions of China into a working economic relationship—these are all a form of internationalism in the economic sphere that is non-institutional, but absolutely vital.

But alongside the emergence of internationalism we are also seeing the resurgence of nationalism, and nowhere more so than in Northeast Asia. The nationalist movement that has blossomed in China is well known. Its sources are varied. For one thing, as the appeal of Marxism-Leninism goes down, the need to find some appeal is by no means gone. This leads to an effort to recreate a sense of loyalty based on China's 5,000-year history, and on a certain Middle Kingdom complex. But we are also seeing a resurgence in Japan, and here, too, is perhaps the feeling that Japan has been slighted in the international sphere, that it has been given too little credit and too much blame for the historical legacy of the past. All of these factors are encouraging a younger generation of Japanese to reconsider their position vis-à-vis the United States and other countries. Korea has always had a strong nationalist thrust, manifesting itself in diverse ways—North and South. This is not to imply that nationalism has only ascended in Northeast Asia, or in Asia. It is also a conflictual force of sorts in the United States and in Europe, partly as a response to grave apprehension about internationalism in its diverse forms.

Then, there is the emergence of communalism. There is a certain growth in identification with one's ethnic group, with one's religious affiliation, with one's regional identity. We are seeing this in diverse forms partly because people's moorings are being shaken by the scope and the rapidity of the scientific-technological revolution. Old values are being challenged. Such institutions as the family are being shaken. The result is a search for community, and sometimes that is localist in nature, or at least it may have ethnic and religious roots.

These three forces—internationalism, nationalism, and communalism—in their interaction, in their partial conflict, will be very critical forces as we move into the next century.

Economic Appraisal

Now let us go from the general to the more specific, and start with some appraisal of where the economies of Northeast Asia are going. Japan, South Korea, and Taiwan are success stories, broadly speaking. That is to say, at an earlier point, these three societies, with Japan in the lead, combined neomercantilist policies—that is to say strong government regulation, control, and support—with the advantages of high educational standards, peace and stability, and the opening of markets in the United States and elsewhere, to create a really remarkable economic revolution over the last three decades. The rise in productivity in these societies, their growing economic internationalization, and the corresponding improvements in living standards for their people all deserve praise. But these are societies that also demonstrate a lesson: no economic strategy, however successful, is good for all time. Japan and South Korea in particular are facing a need today for structural adjustments, for deregulation or regulatory changes. The system has become too inflexible to adjust to the rapid changes in the international economic atmosphere. People like Hashimoto and his successor Obuchi, like Kim Young Sam and his successor Kim Dae Jung, like President Lee in Taiwan, are going to be judged in very considerable measure by whether they can carry through the kind of reforms that will increase flexibility, and that will also put a higher premium upon creativity in the scientific-technological sense. Nonetheless, these societies will continue, on balance, to be successful economically and to set the pattern for others in the region.

Now, in this area there are also certain societies that have in some degree or other left Stalinist economics and are out on a path that may be quasi-socialist but where the market is playing an increasing role, and China is a prime example. As we try to draw up a balance sheet on the Chinese economic situation, we can put the following factors on the plus side. Since Deng Xiaoping's reforms began nearly twenty years ago, there has been an almost incredible per annum increase in productivity of 10 percent plus—leading Asia. There also has been a remarkable influx of foreign investment, and with it science and technology pouring in, in certain select fields. Inflation has been kept under reasonable control, particularly in recent years. The standard of living of hundreds of millions of Chinese has gone up, particularly in coastal and eastern China. These are accomplishments, among others, that certainly warrant admiration. However, China also faces huge problems in the years ahead. One problem that the Chinese leadership is trying to face at the moment is the plight of state-owned enterprises, which still contribute nearly 40 percent of China's industrial productivity. That is the socialist part. Many of these state enterprises, probably 50 percent of them, are losing money, constituting a very great drain on China's banking and financial institutions, as well as the federal treasury. Why? The sources of difficulty vary—inadequate, old-fashioned management that is used to meeting quotas but is not concerned with quality or profits; inadequate, obsolescent machinery, and surplus labor. And here one of the ironies is that China does not have an adequate social security system at the state level, despite its socialist antecedents. Thus, the plant has been responsible for not just the wages, but the educational facilities for the children, housing—almost everything that goes into life. If you dismiss a worker, therefore, problems ensue, including social difficulties. This is an aspect of the old order that is very difficult to change.

Another problem is the huge number of under- and unemployed rural workers, maybe 125–150 million surplus laborers in rural China. And every year some 15–20 million of those workers pour into China's cities, creating social problems even though their purpose is to stay temporarily and send money back home. China has tried to handle this difficulty by expanding its township industries, but that has not been easy. And the township industries themselves, in addition to being heavy polluters, most using soft coal, are also in many cases producing items of fairly inferior quality. But the point is that the task of modernizing 1.3 billion people, of bringing them into some degree of convergence in developmental terms, is enormously difficult. No continental society can be expected to develop uniformly. The United States did not—the South was backward until after World War II in many economic senses. But the West–East gap in China is huge, and it produces problems, especially since the rural population is so large.

Then there is the problem of corruption. Though broad cultural generalizations are very suspect, there is one that has some merit and ought to be looked at carefully. After centuries of travail, Western politics is essentially based on legalism. Asian politics to a very considerable degree remains based on reciprocity. You do this for me, and I'll do that for you. There is an effort to move toward legalism in China and elsewhere, but it is still faltering. Reciprocity is of course a way, an easy route, to what we call corruption—the interaction of politicians, business elements, privileged children of highly-placed families, or princelings, as they are called in China. All of these factors that breed cynicism and indifference to politics, along with the decline in ideology that has taken place, are very powerful forces. The legal institutions to control corruption are still very, very weak in a country like China, and corruption goes on in a multiplying fashion. Though the Hong Kong business community is generally optimistic, or at least so they say, there are three issues that concern them: Will the rule of law continue as under the British? Will the judiciary be independent? And will corruption be controlled? These are the issues that reflect the China problem in some respects.

In the twenty-first century China will be a major power with major problems. How it handles its domestic problems will have a great deal to do with precisely how it operates in the region and in the world.

There are also some other societies in Northeast Asia that are struggling to come out from under the Stalinist economic past, and those would include the Russian Far East and Mongolia. Both of these territories are still very much behind in trying to institute reforms, even though there are some signs of progress. Certainly there is a commitment to development of a more open nature in these societies, but the problems have yet to be solved.

Then there is one failing society, and that is North Korea. North Koreans blame their problem on the collapse of the Soviet Union, which accounted for about 70 percent of their trade and the overwhelming percentage of their aid, and on the floods. But of course, the North has not yet given up the highly autarkic economic system that has separated it almost completely from the scientific-technological revolution. Only now is it beginning to explore turning outward, through a special economic zone in the northeast, through invitations to various entrepreneurs. But it lacks a legal structure, it has no infrastructure, and it is not very competitive with others who are seeking foreign assistance. And thus the crisis. North and South Korea come from a similar culture and a similar history, but they are diametrically different today in economic and political terms.

Political Appraisal

Let us turn from the economic picture to the political picture. There is no question that the scandals and the recent economic malaise in Japan have affected the stability of the Japanese political system. The one-and-a-half-party system that dominated Japan from 1955 to the early 1990s is gone, or at least for the moment it seems gone. Japan has entered coalition politics with a certain degree of uncertainty about the political fortunes of the various parties. The left, at least the socialist left, has gone down precipitously in popularity. The communists have done a little better, partly because they are perceived as honest and not very communist in Japan. But it is symbolic of the concerns of the Japanese electorate that not so long ago two TV comedians were elected as heads of government in Tokyo and Osaka, Japan's most important cities. This shows that there are no political heroes in Japan today. Maybe there are very few in the world, and politics is now at a fairly low ebb. Yet, the situation in Japan is not a regime threat. This is not the 1930s. This is not a situation where the whole parliamentary structure is at risk. The system will go on and two-party and coalition politics may continue for a longer period, or a return to the one-and-a-half-party politics may even take place. Meanwhile, however, the issue of political ethics in a democratic society is one that all democratic societies in Asia and out of Asia are going to have to take more seriously.

In Korea there is a similar problem, doubled in spades. President Kim Young Sam was under great siege, his son in jail, ex-presidents in jail, and scandals breaking one after another that tied politicians to business in self-interest terms. Once again, however, this was not regime threatening. There was not and there is not any evidence in South Korea of another military coup. The military are strongly under civilian control in the South. But again there is a question of attitudes, philosophy, and whether democracy can satisfy the people. No system, including democracy, is immune to periodic tests and travails, and no system is guaranteed permanence.

When one looks to the old Leninist societies, however, the problems are at least equally serious. In China, power has moved from a first- and second-generation to a third- and fourth-generation leadership. The individuals who are currently in power are better educated, they are more technically inclined, they have had much more local administrative experience than the old revolutionaries—the Maos and the Dengs—ever had. But they do not in any single case have a real reach into total power. Jiang Zemin, who denominated the core of the leadership in China, is not regarded as a strong man by knowing Chinese. The question is, can more collective leadership now work? At the height of his power, Mao could make decisions alone, and he did, some of them very bad. Deng had to consult, but he consulted with a very small group, usually of veteran revolutionaries like himself. Jiang Zemin and his colleagues have to consult with interest groups—military, civil, business regional—and the putting together of policy has become very complex. Can collective leadership work in China? It does not run in accord with Chinese political culture. Someone was always needed at the top to symbolize ultimate power. But this is a new age, with new challenges.

Also, can China establish an institutionalized federal system? As with all continental societies, the issue of power at the center versus power in the regions is an ongoing issue of utmost significance. And unless a federal system is institutionalized, it is going to be highly dependent upon personalities, and that is not necessarily good. The question now is what will substitute for a waning ideology? Will nationalism suffice? The average younger Chinese, particularly in urban coastal China—Shanghai, Beijing, Guangzhou—is not very interested in politics. He is interested in making money, and politics does not attract him. The question of how to keep in this huge, diverse society allegiance, loyalty, and support is going to be a continuing challenge.

There are some who say China may very well disintegrate, or break into regional unions. That seemed a much more likely prospect at the time of the Cultural Revolution. There is no evidence that the military are aloof or separated from the party or in serious disunion. And the party does exercise control through centralized appointments and the moving of people around regions. Furthermore, the ethnic minorities, though they are troublesome, constitute less than 8 percent of the population of this vast area. They create difficulties, as they have recently, in Xinjiang in western China, and of course in Tibet. But these will not threaten the regime; they will be put down militarily, if necessary, as they have been.

However troublesome, cultural differences are not regime threatening. It seems that China's broad move will be from Leninism to what I call authoritarian pluralism, a movement already underway. Politics will remain authoritarian; I do not see democracy as we define it on the horizon or in the foreseeable future for this vast, heterogeneous, complex society. Stability will be a cry whenever democracy threatens. But at the same time, there is a certain looseness—freedom to talk, if you know with whom you are talking, freedom to move about, more decentralization, now village elections—all controlled by the party, but nonetheless some degree of flexibility. And meanwhile the civil society apart from the state is emerging with varying degrees of autonomy. And the economy is becoming more mixed, with the private sector increasingly important. In this respect, China is moving the way that South Korea and Taiwan moved in earlier times before these societies began their experimentation with democracy, into an authoritarian pluralist structure.

The other point to be made about China politically is that China is increasingly being brought into the region, first through its economic interactions but gradually, sometimes reluctantly, through multilateral security arrangements—ARF (the ASEAN Regional Forum), of course the United Nations, and other bodies of a similar type. And our gamble—a legitimate gamble—is to involve China in a variety of institutions, structures, and mechanisms. It is the best way to try to institute a more moderate approach in the international realm. It is more meaningful than any attempt at containment in a pure sense.

Security Issues

Let me say just a word about North Korea. I have been to North Korea four times, on four very brief trips. The last time was in the summer of 1995 just before the floods. This is not a revolutionary society; this is a very traditional society—worship of leaders, limited mobility, simple lifestyle, a high level of isolation. All values and characteristics of traditional Korea still seem to prevail, except two or three borrowings from Stalinism: mass mobilization, cradle-to-grave indoctrination, and of course a very large and important military. No one can predict the future of North Korea because there are many variables, and what the regime itself does in the next few months and years will be crucial. There are at least five scenarios. One is rapid collapse. The second is gradual and irreversible disintegration with factional struggles and some turning out for assistance, perhaps to China or even the South. The third scenario is hunkering down, Albanian-style—military control with minimal change. The fourth is conflict, a desperate regime striking out. And the fifth is a gradual, evolutionary process, whereby the North begins to undergo some of the reforms that China has attempted in the last few decades.

Immediate collapse—not likely. I see no evidence of sufficient disunity of the elite. Support for Kim Jong Il seems to be strong. How can you oppose the Son of God? Kim Il Sung has been reborn in his son. This is the theme. The Father, the Son, the only thing missing is the Holy Ghost. This structure is not yet disabled.

Gradual disintegration—far more possible. Unless there are serious economic changes, this scenario is perhaps quite likely, and it is a very dangerous scenario because it could be regionalized. It would present the Chinese with the greatest dilemma if they were asked to come in and save this regime. They do not want a unified Korea on the Yalu River. China has 700,000 ethnic Koreans living on Chinese soil, and Korean nationalism might become a real threat as far as China is concerned. But at the same time, China does not want to become involved in another Korean War, and it would be extremely cautious if faced with this choice.

Hunkering down—not for the long run. Korea is not Albania in the 1950s. It is surrounded by dynamic societies; it cannot hold onto the past very much longer.

Conflict—doubtful, because the political elite will not knowingly commit suicide on behalf of itself and its people. And the Northern leaders today know that the United States is credible, as they had no reason to know in 1950. Of course, conflicts by accident, incidents that mushroom, that is more possible. But the likelihood is that it would be controlled.

Finally, an evolutionary prospect—this is possible. I hope it is possible; at least it seems the way we ought to try to shape American policy with respect to North Korea. Working with the South Koreans and with the other powers as well represents the path of the future in regional terms at least at this moment; namely, ad hoc coalitions, not permanent fixed regional institutions—we are not yet ready for that unfortunately in the security realm—but ad hoc coalitions that try to work together around the problem with their own national interests clearly in mind. That is precisely what is happening. China is cooperating on the Korean issue today, and so are Japan, South Korea, and Russia. We have differences, but they are surmountable.

Now the other security issue of an immediate nature is Taiwan, and I am somewhat more worried about Taiwan than I am about the Korean peninsula, because the Taiwan situation is one where there is no clear path to the future. The PRC insists on one country, two systems. In my opinion, that will never be acceptable to the Taiwanese people. Meanwhile, the Kuomintang, which has been in power in Taiwan for a very considerable time—ever since Taiwan became again independent in 1947–48—is faltering, and after Lee Teng-Hui, it is possible that the DPP, the so-called Independence Party, will come to power. It is possible, by no means certain. This is a party that in the past has proclaimed that it stands for independence. In fact, Taiwan has been independent for nearly a century, or rather separate from China. It was not independent as a part of the Japanese empire, but it was separate from China. Consequently, though economic and cultural interaction is growing, there is no evidence yet of political reforms. And unless Beijing is prepared at some point to offer confederation or some system that will set sovereignty aside for the moment and enable a political dialogue, I find it very difficult to see a resolution or even a containment, because Taiwan nudges this issue by seeking greater international recognition in a variety of ways.

And this is the kind of issue that could involve the United States. American policy toward Korea and Taiwan are quite different: toward Korea, firm assertion of commitment; toward Taiwan, calculated ambiguity. We do not want to say we will support Taiwan, because if we do we aid the independence movement; if we say we will not, in the event of a conflict, we might aid the hard-liners in Beijing. These are the two security issues.

Let me conclude by mentioning a longer-term security/economic issue that is likely to be the most critical in the twenty-first century, and that is the combined issue of population, energy, food, and water. Most of these countries, Japan being a prominent exception, are going to increase in population for the next three or four decades at least. China will triple its energy needs by the year 2015. And food is already a problem in some regions. How these issues—environmental issues, resource issues—are handled, either cooperatively or through greater friction, is going to be a telling aspect of the twenty-first century.

Conclusion

Let me close by saying that I am optimistic. I am cautiously optimistic. And the reason is as follows: first, the combination of domestic drive for economic development and growing economic interdependence will be conducive to working out solutions short of conflict. Every major state involved in this region, including the United States and Russia—peripheral states—has an enormous stake in keeping negotiatory formulae developing. And we are moving in that direction, haltingly perhaps, slowly, but there are increasing mechanisms to negotiate disputes of all sorts—economic through the WTO, security through ad hoc coalitions and ARF and similar agencies. I also think that with the decline of ideology, the barriers to intercourse are lessened, and we will have more and more dialogue at nonofficial as well as official levels. Thus it seems that our chances are reasonably good for a peaceful, developing Northeast Asia. There will be crises, there will be regime threats in countries like North Korea, but these are not likely to lead to an all-regional or all-global struggle.

INTRODUCTION

Tsuneo Akaha

Northeast Asia as a Region

NORTHEAST ASIA IS LARGELY A GEOGRAPHICAL referent rather than a political entity or an economic unit. The countries in the region remain suspicious of each other politically and unintegrated economically. China, Japan, North and South Korea, Mongolia, and Pacific Russia share neither a common cultural identity nor a unifying world view. They have little or no experience in collective problem solving or in developing institutions for multilateral cooperation. Interdependencies, to the extent they exist among Northeast Asian economies, are based largely on bilateral ties, some nurtured by policy, as between Japan and China, and others driven by market forces, as between Japan and South Korea. The political and security consultations that do exist in this subregion are conducted bilaterally.

The international relations of Northeast Asia are complex, and obstacles to multilateral cooperation are numerous. The legacies of prewar, wartime, and Cold War conflicts weigh heavily on the contemporary relationship among China, Japan, Korea, Mongolia, and Russia. The United States also continues to have extensive political, economic, and security links to the countries of the region. During the Cold War Washington's strategic interests in this part of the world favored bilateralism over multilateralism, and the United States continues to prefer bilateral approaches to policy cooperation with Northeast Asian powers, the only visible exception being the "four-powers talks" over the Korean armistice. Moreover, the combination of diverse cultural, political, and economic systems, the disparate levels of economic development, and the widely varied degrees of integration with economies outside of Northeast Asia pose formidable challenges to regional cooperation over economic issues.

There are contradictory forces at play in Northeast Asia. On the one hand, there is plenty of evidence that demonstrates the growing interest among the national and local leaders in this region in promoting multilateral regional cooperation over economic matters. Proponents of Northeast Asia regionalism have been encouraged by the integrative efforts at the global level, such as by the World Trade Organization (WTO), and at the regional level, such as by the European Union (EU), North American Free Trade Agreement (NAFTA), Asia-Pacific Economic Cooperation (APEC), and by the Association of Southeast Asian Nations (ASEAN). On the other hand, suspicions continue, particularly in Japan's relations with its neighbors and in Sino-Russian relations, over a history that predates the current century. As a result, the habit of cooperation is rare among Northeast Asian countries, and institutions of cooperation among them are virtually non-existent. There are also emerging issues of increasing concern to the leaders in this part of the world. Among them are the changing balance of power, which is raising concerns about regional rivalry and stability, and the potentially destabilizing effects of growing cross-border flows of goods, money, people, information, and pollution.

There are clear indications that the current pattern of development in the region's economies is not sustainable, domestically or internationally. Population growth and lack of economic opportunities are imposing unsustainable pressures on the environment and natural resources in northeast China. The disintegrative forces of post-Soviet Russia and lack of indigenous sources of development, particularly of capital and markets, are seriously constraining the economic development of the Russian Far East. North Korea's international isolation and dysfunctional economic system are moving that country down a dangerous spiral of economic crisis and possible political disintegration. Mongolia's nascent democracy is struggling to survive the devastating impact of the dissolution of its ties with the former Soviet Union. The unforgiving forces of global finance and transnational production are testing the limits of the hitherto successful Japanese and South Koreans, forcing them to liberalize their domestic systems at the risk of major dislocations among their members. National and local governments in Japan, China, South Korea, and Russia often pursue competing, even conflicting priorities, central authorities often overriding local initiatives. All countries of Northeast Asia are preoccupied with the short-term benefits of economic development, to the neglect of its long-term social, environmental, and health consequences. There are significant numbers of ethnic minorities, but their social and economic needs are often under-represented or ignored in public policies. The situation is further compounded by the growing presence in every Northeast Asian country except North Korea of foreign agents engaged in cross-border trade, direct investment, labor migration, and international tourism. The foreign presence is not always seen as positively contributing to the development of local economies. It is even seen by some as a threat to their identity or their economic survival. If unchecked, these developments could generate suspicions and animosities among the regional neighbors, where there are already mutual apprehensions and hostilities of historical origin.

From the perspective of "regionalists"—those who foresee great potential gains from expanded transnational interaction—the need for international cooperation and regional order in Northeast Asia is obvious. They in fact see no alternative for the regional powers but to cooperate, to respond to the challenges just noted. Where they disagree is over which country should lead the cooperative efforts and what role the state should play relative to the private sector. On the other hand, "nationalists"—those who emphasize national unity and national independence—argue in favor of national control and management of transnational forces. They remind their compatriots of the legacies of the past, when their lives were exposed to the forces of imperialism and foreign intervention, of their losses in territory and dignity to foreign aggressors.

In this collection of essays, we examine the ongoing debate in each of the Northeast Asian countries regarding the management of international relations in post–Cold War Northeast Asia. The authors particularly note the various shades of nationalist and regionalist argument in their analyses. In order to put the contemporary debate in perspective, some authors provide insightful analyses of the historical sources of current views and the political and cultural contexts of the contemporary debate.

Focus and Organization of the Book

As Scalapino points out in the preface, the two broad trends sweeping the globe today are the dominance of economics in domestic and foreign affairs and the simultaneous rise of the conflictual forces of internationalism, nationalism, and communalism. The purpose of this collection of essays is to examine how these trends are changing the political and economic landscape of Northeast Asia, and whether the growing importance of economic factors is conducive to international cooperation and the establishment of a stable regional order in Northeast Asia, the region that presents the greatest challenge to post–Cold War multilateral cooperation.

In order to explore the prospects for regional cooperation in Northeast Asia, it is necessary to understand the historical sources and contemporary patterns of cooperation and conflict in the region. How will the fluid balance of centripetal and centrifugal forces in Northeast Asia shape the regional order? What can and should the Northeast Asian countries do, individually or collectively, to ensure sustainable development of the region's economies and to promote regional cooperation that is politically sustainable and economically viable? Is it necessary for the Northeast Asian countries to develop a regional identity to overcome the legacies of nationalism and imperialism of the past? Is it possible? Short of sharing a common civilizational or cultural identity, what measures can or will the national leaders in Northeast Asia take to manage the potentially destabilizing effects of international interdependence? Can they contain nationalist sentiments and rivalries in favor of regional cooperation? Will multilateralism overcome bilateralism? These are the central questions of this book.

Earlier versions of all but this introduction, Chapter 9, and the book's conclusion were first presented at the international conference "International Cooperation in Establishing a Regional Order in Northeast Asia," held in Monterey, California on June 20–22, 1997.[1] The introduction, Chapter 9, and the conclusion were prepared after the conference. All contributions were revised to reflect major developments since mid-1997 up through late 1998.

The preface and the two chapters in Part 1 provide an overview of Northeast Asia, capturing the present-day region in its historical evolution, highlighting the impact of the past on contemporary relations among the regional powers, and dissecting the unstable mutual perceptions among the great powers of Northeast Asia. Scalapino points out that Northeast Asia is experiencing the primacy of economic dynamism over political-ideological rationale in the aftermath of the Cold War but that the region's powers have yet to forge stable long-term relationships to take advantage of the great potential regional cooperation offers. Buszynski, in Chapter 1, provides an overview of the complex layers of conflict, some of them of historical origin and others of more recent vintage. His analysis of the historical evolution of major power relations and their rivalry over the Korean peninsula reveals that civilizational and cultural conflicts overlay state-to-state conflicts. He notes that some conflicts defy common culture. He adds, however, that the past does not necessarily have to determine the shape of the future regional relations. This observation leads to the analysis by Rozman in Chapter 2, in which the sociologist focuses on the evolution of mutual perceptions among China, Russia, and Japan since the end of the Cold War. He observes shifting bilateral perceptions that affect and are affected by each country's perception of a third major power in the region. The instability in these mutual perceptions reflects the uncertain shape of great power relations in Northeast Asia.

The instability of great power relations in the post–Cold War era is the focus of Part 2. In Chapter 3, I review the impact of the end of the Cold War on Russo-Japanese relations, noting a visible shift in Japan's approach to the issue that has dogged the bilateral relationship throughout the Cold War period, the dispute over the Northern Territories (the southern Kuriles). I explain the change in Japan's policy as a result of important changes in the domestic, bilateral, regional, and global contexts. Chapter 4 by Anderson

examines Japan's views on international cooperation in Northeast
Asia and identifies a conflict between status-quo "bilateralists"
and optimistic "multilateralists." Conflict in national perspectives
is also found in China, the focus of Hu's analysis in Chapter 5.
According to the Chinese analyst, his country faces a serious challenge. The real and potential benefits of the policy of opening to
the world are accompanied by the fear of loss of control over its
own destiny under the constraints of growing economic interdependence. Meyer, in Chapter 6, examines this issue more closely
when she looks at evolving Sino-Japanese relations. She observes
that there are both reasons to expect closer bilateral relations and
signs of future trouble. She notes that China appears more interested in the economic benefits of closer ties with Japan, while
Japan is more interested in gaining influence over China's political future but finds the task very difficult.

Part 3 is devoted to an examination of the interests and perspectives of the smaller powers in Northeast Asia. Jeong and Mo in
Chapter 7 identify political and economic factors promoting the
idea of regional cooperation in South Korea as well as a number of
obstacles to greater regional cooperation, both domestically and internationally. The analysis by Moon and Ko in Chapter 8 casts a
theoretical light on the debate between realists and neorealists and
liberals and neoliberals in South Korea. They identify various strains
of the two theoretical understandings of the costs and benefits of international cooperation and conclude that for now realist views are
more dominant among the governing elite. Batbayar's analysis of
the Mongolian perspective in Chapter 9 posits a much simpler calculation of costs and benefits of regional cooperation for his country. With the disappearance of the Soviet Union and continuing
political and economic turmoil in Russia, Mongolia is free to pursue
an independent course of foreign policy but is seriously constrained
by the limited resources it has at its disposal.

Part 4 presents analyses of three very different sources of instability in Northeast Asia, the economic reform in Russia, the North
Korean situation, and demographic changes in Northeast Asia.
Chapter 10 by Ivanov examines the devastating short-term impact
of Russia's economic reform on the economy of its Far Eastern

provinces and territories and points out that their long-term development will depend critically on Russia's ability to further develop trade, investment, and other ties with the Northeast Asian economies, as well as with the United States. In Chapter 11, Mansourov maintains that North Korea's current economic crisis is indeed a result of the failed economic system under the dictatorship of Kim Il Sung and his son Kim Jong Il but argues that the international community's unwillingness to pursue a more active policy of engagement, including massive humanitarian assistance, is also to blame for the suffering that is gripping the people of the beleaguered nation. Chapter 12 by Van Arsdol discusses the possible long-term implications of changing demographic patterns in Northeast Asian countries, noting that the dramatically unbalanced population growth and immigration pressures in the region need to be monitored carefully for their possible destabilizing effects on regional international relations.

Finally, Part 5 examines the oft-overlooked role of nongovernmental institutions and processes in the transnational interactions in Northeast Asia and their potentials and limitations as catalysts for regional cooperation. Chapter 13 examines the Northeast Asia Economic Forum, one of the most visible multilateral fora in the region. Valencia, one of the key participants in the forum from its very inception, discusses the evolution of the forum and its future prospects. Chapter 14 by Shirasu and Lau of the Sasakawa Peace Foundation provides an assessment of their own organization's initiatives to develop intellectual dialogue and direct contact among research communities in the Northeast Asian countries. They note both some progress and certain limitations in their nongovernmental efforts.

Acknowledgments

As editor, I wish to thank each author for his/her expert knowledge and perceptive observations, which have made this book a rich source of information and ideas for further advancing our understanding of the current problems and future possibilities in Northeast

Asia. On behalf of the participants in this collaborative effort, I want to thank the institutions with which we are associated for their support. I also acknowledge with appreciation the funding support provided for this endeavor by the Asia Research Fund of Yonsei University, the Sasakawa Peace Foundation, the Japan Foundation, Mr. and Mrs. Sakaguchi of Sakaguchi Electric Heaters, Tokyo, and the Monterey Institute of International Studies. Thanks also go to the following graduate assistants of the Center for East Asian Studies for their tireless assistance during the Monterey conference (see endnote), from which this book has been developed, as well as for their help in the editing of earlier drafts of the chapters: Mari Felton, (Stuart) Kenzo Kimura, Katsuko Kuroiwa, Karen Mattison, Judy Norton, and Philip Chou. Finally, last but not least, I wish to thank Amy Reading and Ruth Mannes of St. Martin's Press for their expert editorial assistance.

Notes

1. International Seminar "International Cooperation in Establishing A Regional Order in Northeast Asia," June 20–22, 1997, Monterey, California, organized by the Monterey Institute of International Studies' Center for East Asian Studies.

PART 1

OVERVIEW OF NORTHEAST ASIA

CHAPTER 1

HISTORICAL PERSPECTIVES OF RELATIONS WITHIN NORTHEAST ASIA

Leszek Buszynski

Introduction

NORTHEAST ASIA HAS BEEN A REGION in which historical rivalries and animosities have been strongly marked. Indeed, unlike other regions of the world Northeast Asia has not yet developed a regional consciousness that would facilitate regional cooperation, or that would provide a foundation for the kind of regional order that could ensure long-lasting stability. Unlike Europe, the region cannot be regarded as a cultural or civilizational entity; neither has it developed a sense of unity derived from shared experience as has been the case in Southeast Asia. In contrast, Northeast Asia has been an arena for the competitive interaction of rivals and clashing interests, which has created the conditions for conflict. Underlying historical rivalries stimulate and provoke nationalist responses that militate against attempts to construct a viable basis for regional order, and for this reason this paper will explore the historical background to

Northeast Asian relations. It will identify areas of past conflict and present tension as well as examining proposals for overcoming the negative legacy of the past.

The Notion of a Region

There are two basic ways in which regions may be viewed. The first or static approach would identify regions according to their unchanging cultural or civilizational characteristics. Regions are by definition areas of common culture, civilization or ethnicity that create shared perceptions of commonality. Regions are, according to this approach, identified in terms of relatively durable and static factors that then determine the extent to which a regional consciousness may be forged. Europe's common Christian heritage as well as its collective historical experience has created a unique consciousness of a European identity that has served as the basis for an impressive level of regional integration. Similarly, the Arab world and South Asia have demonstrated a regional consciousness based on cultural or religious commonality without, however, transcending subregional divisions arising from communal and confessional differences. Samuel Huntington has popularized the idea of culture or civilization as fundamental to our understanding of state or national behavior in international relations. The assumptions outlined in his work will be examined in this paper to identify the role of culture and civilization in Northeast Asia.[1]

The terms *culture* and *civilization* have been the subject of much discussion by historians, particularly those from the nineteenth-century German tradition, and require definition. Toynbee regarded civilizations as "units of historical study" and thought that societies of "kindred species" constituted civilizations. According to Toynbee civilizations are groups of societies that lend themselves to being studied in isolation.[2] Culture on the other hand was the literary, artistic or philosophical product of a civilization, which was its material manifestation. Fernand Braudel in his study of the Mediterranean of the sixteenth century claimed that "civilizations are regions" and that "a civilization exists in geographic area which has been structured by men and history."[3] Braudel used the term *culture* to refer to the art form of a civilization, while Oswald Spengler used the word culture in preference to *civilization*.[4] Huntington defines civilization as the "highest cultural grouping of people and the broadest level of cultural identity," which embodies the Toynbean understanding of the term *culture*.[5] For the purposes of the following discussion the term *civilization* can be defined as an area of cultural affinity in which the focus of the analysis is on the impact of patterns of cultural affinity upon contemporary international politics.

The second or dynamic approach examines regions from the perspective of an evolutionary process that follows an integrative path. According to the dynamic approach a region is simply a stage on a particular albeit complex path of integration. The particular stages in the development of a region can be depicted as follows: 1. A geographic unit defined by physical characteristics. 2. An interactive political, economic, and social system. 3. An organizational region that allows for cooperation in various dimensions, security as well as economic. 4. A regional civil society when the organizational region encourages the development of shared or congruent values. 5. A "region state" or a comprehensive level of regional activity and integration.[6] Regions, therefore, may develop over time and are not necessarily fated to remain fixed for all time.

Regions develop according to the experience of political and economic interaction, which may override primeval cultural loyalties or civilizational identities. Culture and civilization from this perspective cannot be regarded as enduring determinants of patterns of relations in international affairs but are shaped by economic and political interactive processes. What becomes important in the development of regions is not the cultural or civilizational legacy but the political commitment of the governments concerned in promoting cooperative relations. Also important is the operation of the market in stimulating the interactive processes that draw communities together. The tendency to view culture and civilization as static realities in international relations, which is characteristic of Samuel Huntington's thinking, is one that results in a certain political fatalism. Moreover, it fails to account for the process of cultural change and development.

In many respects, the contemporary history of Southeast Asian international relations reveals the importance of political and economic factors in overcoming cultural or civilizational divisions. Southeast Asia is probably the most culturally diverse region of the world, as a crossroads for the interaction of four major civilizations: Hindu/Buddhist, Sinic/Confucian, Islamic, and Western/Christian.[7] The ethnic and cultural divisions that characterize the region could have resulted in a state of regional conflict similar to that of the Middle East today, but Southeast Asia has avoided that path. One reason may be that the strong Hindu/Buddhist influences, which emanated from India over the course of a thousand years, have created a culture of tolerance that serves as a ready basis for regional accommodation. Another and more salient reason has been the political commitment of the regional leadership to overcoming divisive ethnic and cultural influences. Southeast Asian leaders have understood that conflict and destruction would be the result of an invocation of ethnic or culturally based nationalism and have acted to curb such potentially damaging influences through regional association in ASEAN. Indeed, Southeast Asia regionalism has had a significant impact in defining a regional consciousness that otherwise may not have been formed. To a considerable degree the process of regionalism has shaped the idea of region in Southeast Asia. The assumption of common culture is not necessarily useful in identifying regions or in assessing the ability of states to overcome conflicts. Culture and civilization have been important factors in international relations in identifying patterns of affinity between peoples and states. To leap to the conclusion that these factors can determine attitudes and govern political behavior in a particular way would be unjustified given the well-attested observation that politics has shaped culture. Indeed, cultural affinity and proximity can provoke conflict and rivalry, and ethnically related peoples may be prompted to organize themselves into separate and competitive states. Cultural affinity then becomes a stimulus or a focal point for the development of nationalism, which underpins the division into separate states. Political will and commitment may, on the other hand, override cultural and civilizational divisions, and shared aspirations among disparate cultural entities can promote regional association. That commitment is strengthened by the recognition of the dangers that could arise if cultural and ethnic disputes and misunderstandings were allowed to influence the conduct of international relations.

Northeast Asia as a Region

There are several historical features of Northeast Asia that should be taken into account in any discussion relating to the region's future and its potential for cooperation. Huntington notes that East Asia is an area where the "core states" of four civilizations interact: they are the United States, China, Japan, and Russia. A "core state" is one that has contributed extensively to the evolution of its civilization and epitomizes its values and achievements today. Huntington concludes that "the seeds of conflict among states are plentiful in East Asia." This is a somewhat pessimistic assessment.[8] Certain major conflict areas in the region have their origins in clashes of civilization as younger and more dynamic cultures have attempted to extend their influence beyond existing borders. In this context Russia's encounter with China and Japan can be understood as a struggle over the definition of civilizational borders and areas of influence.

There are also conflicts within cultures and civilizations that have shaped the region's history. The Korean peninsula is one example of a violent inter-national conflict that has had and will continue to have a significant impact upon regional events. Cold War politics intruded into the Korean peninsula to divide a nation into two separate states that have competed for national legitimacy. The virulence of the conflict has been fueled by the sense of common ethnicity, bearing testimony to the observation that cultural and ethnic proximity may exacerbate conflict. Japan's relations with both China and Korea, however, present problems of definition for the theorists of culturally determined conflict in international relations. Huntington's unsatisfactory definition of Japan as a separate civilization belies the extensive cultural linkages that have existed between that country and China and also Korea. Japan may be regarded as a derivative Sinic culture and not necessarily a separate civilization, just as Russia may be viewed as a derivative Christian culture. Shared culture provided the background for a Japanese lunge for hegemony within the Sinic world civilization in what could be described as an intra-civilizational clash of nationalism.

Northeast Asia may be examined in terms of its history to identify the areas of conflict and to discuss the ways in which they may be overcome. First, there are the conflicts that have been cultural or civilizational by nature and relatively long lasting. In these areas historical enmities may stimulate underlying tensions between states, but they are not predestined to erupt into violence unless invoked by populist nationalists. Accommodation is possible between the leaderships of states representing different civilizations if the core values of communities and peoples are not threatened, contrary to what Huntington has argued. The obvious differences in this case may facilitate agreement between political leaderships over the demarcation of spheres of influence and the avoidance of provocative actions. Russia's relations with China may be examined in this context of mutual accommodation between two different civilizations. Secondly, there are troublesome clashes of nationalism that have occurred within a particular context of cultural affinity that may have been stimulated by a contest for hegemony or supremacy within a particular civilizational grouping. Japan's difficulties with both China and Korea display the characteristics of a clash of nationalism within a broadly shared civilization, one that was provoked by a Japanese effort to dominate that civilization in modern times. In such cases outbreaks of popular nationalism can impede attempts at resolution between governing elites. Thirdly, some conflicts have been a product of the clash of state interests alone, which may be more venomous in the short term but are more easily resolved once the underlying cause is removed—the Korean Peninsula is an example. Common culture or nationhood can serve as a means for conflict resolution once the exacerbating division is surmounted.

Russia and China

Russia's intrusion into Northeast Asia in the late nineteenth century was an example of a young and then vigorous Orthodox Christian culture pushing against the boundaries of older and more established Sinic cultures. The European imperialists were maritime powers, and their presence in the region was limited and temporary at best. Russia was the only imperialist land power with vaulting ambitions for territorial acquisition whose presence was an immediate threat to the regional states. Russia's imperial ambitions were stimulated during the time of Ivan the Terrible (1532–1594) when Muscovy conquered the Khanate of Kazan in 1552. This event prompted expansion eastward when the Stroganov merchants, Cossacks and runaway peasants moved beyond the Urals into Siberia and eventually reached the Sea of Okhotsk in 1647. Russia's encounter with China and Japan soon followed, an event that was to shape the history of the region during subsequent centuries.

In relation to the Qing Dynasty Russia's penetration of the Amur region in the 1640s immediately brought into focus the need to demarcate areas of influence and to establish a border. The result was the Treaty of Nerchinsk of September 1689, which was the first treaty signed by the Qing Dynasty with a European power. For the Manchu Qing Dynasty the intention was to preserve the Amur region and to keep the intruders away from Manchu areas of influence. The Russians, however, regarded the treaty as a stage for further expansion eastward but at that time were in a militarily disadvantageous position in relation to the Manchus. As Russia was deflected from the Amur basin its expansion was directed toward the Sea of Okhotsk. When Qing Dynasty power weakened considerably in the nineteenth century the stage was set for a renewal of Russian territorial expansion toward the Manchu homeland.[9]

The Qing Dynasty was tottering as a consequence of defeat at the hands of the British during the Opium Wars of 1839–42, 1856–60. Russia exploited China's weakness to acquire additional territory during the years 1858–1924; an area at least one third the size of the United States was obtained by Russia then.[10] Under the Treaty of Aigun of 1858 Russia obtained the northern bank of the Amur River, which established the Manchurian boundary along the Amur and Ussuri Rivers.[11] Under the Treaty of Beijing in 1860 Russia obtained territory east of the Ussuri River, which gave her a common frontier with Korea. Russia continued to take advantage of

Manchu frailty to seize territory in excess of that permitted by these treaties. After the Boxer Rebellion of 1900 Russia expelled Chinese from the northern bank of the Amur, which was a violation of the treaty of Aigun. In the same vein Russia's seizure of the Liaotung peninsula in order to deny the territory to Japan went against an 1896 treaty with China.[12]

Russia's absorption of territory that was previously linked with the Qing Dynasty occurred on an unprecedented scale. The Chinese subsequently claimed that the territory in question was sovereign, which was a modern interpretation of past tributary relations. The territory obtained by Russia was for the most part uninhabited by Han Chinese but instead belonged to indigenous tribes of the area, which had to varying degrees engaged in tributary relations with the Manchus.[13] The Qing Dynasty was compelled by its own impotence to witness Russia's absorption of territory that had been previously under its influence. The myth of "lost territories" was exploited to the full by the Chinese communist party during the Sino-Soviet split and it still continues to circulate among Chinese.

Russia's pressure upon Manchuria was another matter, however, as here Russia threatened the homeland of the ruling Qing Dynasty. Russia had designs on Manchuria, and Chief of the General Staff Nikolai Obruchev argued in 1894 that all territory south of the Amur including northern Manchuria should be incorporated into Russia to protect her position in the Far East.[14] A combination of factors, including Japanese power after the 1904–05 war and the difficulty of controlling a hostile population, prevented Russia from absorbing Manchuria, and Russia's expansion reached its limits. Nonetheless, Russia managed to detach Mongolia from China when the formation of the People's Republic of Mongolia was proclaimed in September 1924. When Mao Zedong in October 1949 accepted Mongolian independence as a necessary preparation for negotiations with Stalin, many Chinese were angered by what they regarded as a "sell out of national interests."[15]

What impact will these historical events have upon future Russian-Chinese relations? Chinese today may allege that the loss of territory to Russia was a "gross dereliction of filial duty" at a time when China was weak and Russia strong. Russia was in the ascendant at that stage, but the power relationship between the two countries has been reversed since the collapse of the Soviet Union. As China becomes economically more powerful the situation may change, and Chinese historical grievances may be openly expressed and territorial claims raised. After the return of Hong Kong to China Russia's territorial gains will be the only remaining legacy of European imperialism in China.[16] How a strong China will regard a weakened Russia that has been demonstrably unable to enforce its will in Chechnya is a question for the future.

Both Russia and China are well aware of their fragility, and both are compelled by mutual vulnerability to establish a framework for an extensive cooperative relationship. A mutual concern about the West is an additional factor. Russia's apprehension concerning the expansion of NATO eastward is matched by a similar Chinese distress about the so-called "hegemonial" aspirations of the United States in the Asia Pacific region. The legacy of the past has prompted Russia and China to conclude a border agreement that was negotiated with the Soviet Union in May 1991. Problems remain as local politicians in the Russian Far East have protested against the return of some territory to China, but Moscow is committed to making the agreement work. When Jiang Zemin visited Moscow in April 1997 mutual reductions of forces along the common border with Russia, Kazakhstan, Tajikistan, and Kyrgyzstan were agreed, and this will bring greater stability to the border areas.[17]

Russia and Japan

The Russia-Japan relationship may also be depicted as a civilizational clash, as both in the past regarded each other as natural enemies. Both, indeed, were expansionist imperial powers at similar stages in their history, and a major conflict of strategic interests was the inevitable result. On the continent Russia and Japan struggled for influence over Manchuria and Korea, and each regarded the other as a rival. Moreover, Russian expansionism in the Far East came close to the Japanese homeland as the Russians moved down the Kurile Islands in the early 1700s and awakened a Japanese sense of vulnerability. In the modern era, it was Russian penetration of the area to the north of Hokkaido that first aroused a sense of external danger among the Japanese.

Russia's interest in Manchuria was stimulated by a fear of Japan, whose presence in the Korean peninsula had become disturbing. Russia wanted to limit Japanese influence on Korea and prevent Japan from penetrating further into Manchuria, which would place the security of the Russian Far East at risk. The construction of the Trans-Siberian Railway, which began in 1891, was related to the need to constrain Japan by allowing Russia to deploy military power in the area. Japan's defeat of China in the 1894–95 war alarmed the Russians, who understood that they too could become a Japanese target.[18] The concessions that Russia wrested from China subsequently were dictated by strategic rivalry with Japan. The Chinese Eastern Railway, which was the largest concession ever obtained from China by any imperialist power, made it possible for Russia to avoid the difficult Amur region in the construction of the Trans-Siberian Railway. A direct route could be constructed linking Chita with Vladivostok across Manchuria. For similar reasons Russia occupied the Liaotung peninsula in 1898 and obtained the South Manchurian Railway concession.[19]

Under the Treaty of Shimonoseki of April 17, 1895, which concluded the 1894–95 Sino-Japanese War, Japan was given Taiwan, Southern Manchuria, and the Liaotung peninsula. Japan was compelled to surrender the Liaotung peninsula after Russia joined Germany and France to place pressure upon Japan in the Triple Intervention of 1895. This denial of the fruits of victory kindled Japanese resentments, which were directed toward Russia. Conflict in one way or another became inevitable as Russia attempted to wield influence in Korea, which the Japanese regarded as their own sphere of influence. It was Russia's refusal to accept Korea as an exclusive Japanese area of influence that provoked the 1904–1905 war, which resulted in Russia's humiliation. The consequence of this war was the establishment of Japan as the major power in Northeast Asia and Japanese dominance over Manchuria, Korea, and the Sea of Okhotsk. Another result was a Russian desire for revenge, which was to find satisfaction in a later era.

Russian-Japanese rivalry over these areas was possible only in the presence of a fragmented China and a weak Korea. The establishment of the People's Republic of China in October 1949 and separate Korean regimes in the north and south of the peninsula removed the basis for this rivalry on the Northeast Asian mainland. Russia and Japan have withdrawn from this area and are unlikely to come into contact here again as a strong China is likely to be accompanied by a united and nationalistic Korea at some point in the future. Nonetheless, in the Kurile Islands/Sea of Okhotsk area neither Russia nor Japan can easily withdraw since their national territories are contiguous. Here, competing territorial claims relate to the borders of what is considered to be the national homeland of the respective peoples and can become an issue of nationalism between Russians and Japanese.

The Northern/Kurile Islands dispute is a consequence of the failure to establish an acceptable boundary between two vastly different cultures.[20] In Huntington's terminology the dispute has the features of a clash of civilizations around a fault line that divides them. As far back as the time of Peter the Great (1672–1725) Russia's movement into this area was initiated with the intention of opening trade with China, Japan, and India through the Pacific. When Commander Martin Spanberg, who was employed by the Russians, ventured down the Kurile Islands to land on Honshu in 1739 the Japanese were alarmed. Concern about Russian penetration from the north stimulated a Japanese landing on the island of Kunashiri in 1754, the first such recorded case. Russian activity increased in the area, and in 1786 Catherine the Great incorporated the islands into the Russian Empire by imperial decree. The Shogunate attempted to forestall further Russian advances by staking a claim to the island of Etorofu, and by establishing direct rule over Hokkaido and Sakhalin in 1807. A natural demarcation was reached when the Russians settled for Urup and the islands to the north and the Japanese claimed Etorofu and the islands to the south. This demarcation was the basis of the Treaty of Shimoda, which was concluded in 1855 with the intention of establishing a formal boundary between the two countries.[21]

The boundary was subsequently adjusted according to events. Russia surrendered its claim to all 18 Kurile Islands as a consequence of the Treaty of St. Petersburg of 1875 but gained the island of Sakhalin. After Russia's defeat in the 1904–1905 war Sakhalin was partitioned at the 50th parallel as Japan was prevented from obtaining the entire island by the mediation of Theodore Roosevelt. Thereafter the Russians awaited a more favorable time when they could exact revenge on the Japanese. Well before the Pacific war had erupted, the Soviet Union had the intention of wresting the Kurile Islands from Japan. In negotiations with the Japanese ambassador general Tatekawa, Soviet foreign minister Molotov requested that Japan make a "present" of the Kurile Islands as consideration for Soviet good faith.[22] Stalin took advantage of Japan's weakness during the closing stages of the Pacific war to occupy the Kurile Islands in a campaign that began on August 18, 1945 and ended on September 5. In his famous victory speech of September 2 Stalin betrayed a characteristic view of Russia's rivalry with Japan by describing it as a blood feud. With the humiliation of the 1904–1905 war in mind, Stalin declared that "for 40 years we Russians of the older generation have been waiting for this day."[23] Stalin had designs on Hokkaido as well, and in his memorandum to President Truman on August 16, 1945, he pressed for a Soviet occupation zone there. Commander in chief of Soviet naval forces in the Far East Vassilevsky reportedly issued an order on August 19, 1945 for the occupation of northern Hokkaido. President Truman was willing to accept Soviet occupation of the Kuriles but deflected Stalin's demands for the division of Hokkaido.[24]

The Russians have regarded the four island groups, which the Japanese call the Hoppo ryodo, as having been obtained by right of conquest as the final act in a complicated drama of prolonged struggle with the Japanese. Russian government representatives have relied on the Yalta agreements of February 1945, which they claim amounted to endorsement of a Soviet right of conquest over these islands. The Japanese position is that the San Francisco conference of September 1951 was the higher authority in determining the outcome of the Pacific war and that the Yalta agreements only had the authority to endorse temporary occupation zones. Under the terms of the San Francisco Treaty Japan was to surrender all territory obtained by imperial conquest, and Prime Minister Yoshida Shigeru insisted at the conference that this stipulation excluded the four northern islands. Yoshida argued that the treaties of Shimoda and St. Petersburg had determined the fate of the islands, in which case they could not be regarded as conquered territory for the purposes of the San Francisco Peace Treaty. Yoshida also argued that the islands claimed by Japan were not part of the Kuriles anyway, in which case the Yalta agreements would not apply to them.[25]

The dispute has aroused nationalist feelings on both sides as it involves attachment to homeland territory, which is not easily receptive to rational bargaining and compromise. The Russian government attempted a solution to this dispute in 1992 when President Yeltsin aborted his planned visit to Japan in September. While the Russian government is prevented by nationalist opinion from displaying flexibility on this issue, it is compelled to endorse the Soviet position based on a right of conquest. On the Japanese side other issues have been linked with the territorial problem, including the treatment of Japanese POWs in Siberia in 1945–46, the Soviet abrogation of the April 1941 Neutrality Pact, and the continuing detainment of Japanese fishermen around the disputed islands.[26] For Japan there can be no improvement of relations with Russia unless the territorial issue is resolved.

Despite the weight of history, which impels both countries toward an impasse over this issue, the deadlock need not be enduring. Democratic opinion within Russia generally concedes that the right of conquest as invoked by the Soviet Union cannot legitimize the occupation of the islands and that the problem has to be eventually resolved. A resolution of the issue cannot be expected while Russia is internally weak, however, and while nationalist forces are able to blackmail the Moscow government. Nonetheless, there has been an improvement in Russian-Japanese relations since the Hashimoto-Yeltsin meeting in Krasnoyarsk in November 1997. At that meeting Japan agreed to sponsor Russia's membership in APEC and both sides declared their intention to sign a peace treaty by the year 2000 that would demand a resolution of the territorial issue. A fishing agreement was signed in February 1998 that allowed Japanese vessels to fish around the disputed islands and that removed an area of past friction. Japan has been motivated to improve relations with Russia to ensure that it would not find common cause with China against Japan, particularly after the promulgation of the revised defense guidelines between the United States and Japan in September 1997. Under more favorable circumstances, when the Moscow government is in a stronger position internally, a resolution of the issue and a peace treaty would indeed be conceivable.

Japan and Its Neighbors

Japan is a fusion of various cultural influences and may be regarded as a derivative culture within the general umbrella of Sinic civilization. There are too many cultural linkages with Korea and China for Japan to be separated from its neighbors, and yet the many differences indicate that Japan cannot be simply classified with them. Japan's complex relationship with her neighbors may be regarded as intra-civilizational in the broadest sense of the term. Japan's past efforts to colonize and dominate her neighbors demonstrate that civilizational ties do not necessarily avert or prevent conflict and that the most lethal of struggles have often been conducted among members of the same civilization. The burden of history in Russia's relations with her Northeast Asian neighbors can be distinguished from the problems of Japan's relations with Korea and China. Whereas Russia never seized the Han Chinese homeland and failed to occupy Japan, the memories of Japanese acts in both Korea and China will continue to influence relations in Northeast Asia for some time to come.

The Japanese colonization of Korea from 1910–45 has left an indelible imprint upon the Korean national consciousness that will take centuries to erase. Peter Duus has examined the assumption of common ethnicity as a critical factor in Japanese attitudes toward Korea during this period. Public figures in Meiji Japan regarded the Koreans as members of the same *yamato minzoku* or

Japanese nation.[27] In the Japanese chronicles *Nihon shoki* the yamato gods were depicted as having ruled the Korean peninsula, which was conquered by Empress Jingu.[28] The assumption of common ancestry served to justify the coerced assimilation of the Korean people, and it was Japan's first governor general of its Korean colony Terauchi Masatake (1910–16) who declared publicly that this was the goal.[29]

The coerced assimilation of the Korean people was promoted with vigor in the 1930s as a response to the exigencies of empire. The invasion of Manchuria in September 1931 embroiled Japan in China, and Korea became a strategic base for the war effort on the Asian continent. Koreans then were conscripted into supporting the empire in a movement for the "imperialization of subject peoples," or *kominka*. This policy resulted in the enforced Japanization of subjugated peoples and their mobilization on behalf of the empire.[30] Under Governor General Ugaki Kazushige (1931–36) the teaching of Japanese was made compulsory in Korean schools. Under his successor Minami Jiro (1936–42) the slogan "Japan and Korea as one body" (*Nissen ittai*) was promulgated. The study of the Korean language in schools and for general instruction was prohibited. In 1935 Japan attempted to impose Shinto upon the Koreans by demanding that government employees and students attend Shinto ceremonies. In 1939 the Koreans were compelled to adopt Japanese names and in 1940 all Korean language newspapers were closed down. The Japanese intention was described as the "cultural extinction" of the Koreans.[31]

There is no doubt that Japanese colonization had contributed to Korea's economic development, though in a distorted way. Japan located industries in peripheral colonies and developed modern industry, transport, and communications. As colonialists the Japanese have been called "unusually development oriented" in the establishment of modern economic infrastructure and the introduction of industry and commerce.[32] Some historians claim that Japanese colonialism laid the foundations for the subsequent transformation of the South Korean economy through the construction of the railway system and the promotion of a textile industry.[33] Nonetheless, the memory of forced assimilation will not be easily forgotten by the Koreans, and this period of Korean history will be remembered as a time when "Japan fractured the Korean national psyche, pitting Korean against Korean."[34] "Hostility toward Japan," as one Korean author explained, "was deeply entwined with national identity, and post war Korean nationalism was imbued with anti-Japanese sentiment."[35]

Japan's problems with Korea are the consequence of the assumption of cultural and ethnic proximity. The premise of common civilizational origins was used to justify the Japanese drive to assimilate the Korean people and to obliterate their culture. This historical experience demonstrates that common culture may trigger the most bitter of conflicts, those that touch upon the identity and loyalties of peoples. There have been victim states in history that have suffered from attempts at assimilation on the part of larger neighbors, and intense patterns of animosity have been the result. Such instances include Russia's attempt to assimilate Poland and the Han Dynasty's attempt to turn Vietnam into a province of the empire. In both situations history has shaped present relationships, and the national identity of the victim state has been created as an act of rejection of the larger state. Korean nationalism is a product of resistance against Japan and has manifested itself in various ways: in delaying the establishment of diplomatic relations between South Korea and Japan until 1965, in the banning of Japanese popular culture in South Korea until 1998, and in the acute sensitivity that Koreans feel in relation to Japan.

Japan's relationship with China has been marked by a recognition of shared culture and civilization in a context of political rivalry. Chinese travelers to Japan in the 1870s regarded Japan as a "country sharing civilization," by which they meant sharing the universality of the Chinese world view. Subsequently, as Japan initiated its program of modernization under the impact of contact with the West, Chinese scholars regarded Japan in a different light. As a country that had "imitated" the ways of the barbarians Japan had abandoned civilization in Chinese eyes.[36] The Meiji reformers' view of China at that time was expressed by Fukuzawa Yukichi, who emphasized Western learning to the point where, according to him, all Chinese influences should be eliminated from Japan. According to

Fukuzawa no advance could be expected in China as long as the old civilization remained, as embodied in the Qing Dynasty.[37] The Meiji reformers set Japan on a path that was to change its relationship with and its views of the country that had been the source of its culture. Thereafter Japan and China diverged considerably.

Japan's attempt to colonize China in the 1930s and 40s was defended in terms of common culture, but the connections then were vague, loose, and patently unconvincing. The opportunity for gain and plunder was behind the Japanese move into China, and there was no attempt at assimilation as was the case in Korea. Japan's attempt to subdue China, which began in earnest with the invasion of Manchuria in September 1931, was a haphazard enterprise initiated by Kwangtung army officers with little guiding direction or control from Tokyo. In the phenomenon known as *gekokujo* junior officers created expectations in the name of nationalist sacrifice that their superiors felt compelled to fulfill and that governments in Tokyo felt obliged to endorse. One of the most influential of Kwangtung staff officers was Itagaki Seishiro, who had orchestrated the Mukden incident of September 1931 as a pretext for the invasion of Manchuria. Another was Ishiwara Kanji, who justified Japan's push into China in terms of a monumental struggle between Japan and the West. Ishiwara repeatedly embarrassed his superior officers with his blatant insubordination and yet managed to attract support for his views.[38] The Kwangtung army remained uncontrollable and untouchable in Japanese politics, a law unto itself, by way of the powerful hold it had established over the symbols of the extreme nationalism that prevailed during those times.[39] Kwangtung officers staged the Marco Polo bridge incident of July 1937, which was used as a justification for the invasion of China proper and which fully embroiled Japan in the Chinese civil war until 1945.

The Japanese presence in China that was initiated in the Meiji era had the characteristics of what Peter Duus described as an "informal empire." By this it was meant that a disadvantageous economic system was imposed upon a subjugated state without territorial control.[40] By the 1930s Japan's entanglement in China was the consequence of the reckless ambitions of particular and powerful personalities in the Kwangtung army who could invoke the frenzied nationalism of the time. These personalities operated within a fragmented and unstable decision-making system that gave leverage over policy to outspoken and aggressive nationalists. As Marius Jansen has noted, Japanese imperialism was not "a deliberate thought-out plan" but a "response to opportunities in the international setting and environment."[41] There were attempts to justify the move into China in terms of *dobun-doshu* (common culture, common race), but this quickly degenerated into a haphazard and savage drive for territorial conquest, in a struggle that Japan could not win.

The assumption of common civilization may have been vague and amorphous in Japan's effort to colonize and subdue China, but it was noticeable nonetheless. Ideologues of expansion such as Ishiwara Kanji argued in 1930 that "to save China, which has known no peace ... is the mission of Japan."[42] As the historian Ienaga Saburo has noted, the Japanese at that time adopted a posture of cultural superiority over the Chinese, who were regarded with popular contempt.[43] Cultural borrowing from China endowed the Japanese with an acute sense of rivalry with China, which in turn stimulated a Chinese feeling of resentment directed toward Japan.

The impact of the Japanese occupation of China on contemporary international relations has been momentous. The Japanese conquest has been regarded as the "midwife of modern Chinese nationalism" that has provided a "powerful impetus to political mobilization in 20th century China and greatly reshaped its history."[44] The Japanese Imperial Army severely weakened Chiang Kaishek's Kuomintang forces and may have established the conditions for the victory of Mao Zedong's communists in 1949. The Chinese saw how their internal divisions and conflicts were eagerly exploited by the Japanese and have been particularly sensitive to what they fear could be a "revival of Japanese militarism." National fragmentation after the collapse of the Qing Dynasty encouraged the Japanese in their adventure into China, and the present Chinese leadership has been particularly concerned to maintain unity lest the past be repeated. Moreover, the Chinese recall that between 1931 and 1945 the Japanese were responsible for the deaths of 3 to 8 million soldiers and for 18 million civilian casualties.[45] Ienaga Saburo has given several graphic accounts of Japanese atrocities in China during this period, which included trafficking in heroin and opium, the regular plundering of property, and rape as "accepted prerogative of the Imperial Army."[46]

The Chinese experience of modern history before the establishment of the PRC in 1949 was one of internal fragmentation and external intervention. The result has been a sense of national humiliation that strongly influences attitudes toward the outside world. That sense of humiliation is particularly keen in relation to Japan, which has been regarded by the Chinese as a product of their own culture and civilization. As a consequence, the Chinese are particularly vigilant in guarding against what they perceive to be any revival of militarism in Japan. Extreme views percolate among the Chinese suggesting that Japan will as a matter of course fall under the spell of militarism again. Various issues in relation to Japan's future trouble the Chinese, including the proposed expansion of Japan's security role under the terms of the revised defense guidelines developed with the United States in September 1997, or Japan's defense of its claims to the Senkaku/Diaoyu islands, or Diet members' visits to the Yasukuni Shrine.[47]

The Division of Korea

Conflicts between divided nations may be intense while they exist, but they heal relatively swiftly once the underlying divisions have been removed. Examples of such conflicts include those between West and East Germany, North and South Vietnam, and China and Taiwan. In all cases the division was a product of the Cold War, during which separate regimes or governments were established and supported by external great powers. The division was artificial and unnatural from the perspective of ethnicity, language, and culture and was maintained largely through military coercion. The divided states engage in a vehement struggle for international and domestic legitimacy in which the prize is the loyalty of the single nation. Once the coercion that maintains the division is lifted, or the underlying resolve behind it collapses, the divided nation is reunited again, which was the experience of Germany and Vietnam. Common ethnicity or culture then provides a basis for reconciliation and the establishment of institutions that can heal the wounds of the past.

The division of Korea was the result of Soviet engagement against Japan in the last act of the Pacific war. The Allies had agreed at the Cairo conference of December 1943 that there would be a four-power trusteeship over Korea, but at no stage was the permanent division of Korea accepted. In August 1945 Soviet forces occupied Korea down to the 38th parallel following the Potsdam agreements, which had allocated the task of receiving surrendering Japanese forces in this zone to the Soviets. Kim Il Sung (Kim Song-ju) was brought to Korea by the Soviet army and in 1946 promptly established a government at Pyongyang. As an anti-Japanese guerrilla fighter Kim had fought alongside the Chinese communists in Manchuria in the 1930s and sought refuge in the Soviet Union in 1941. He had spent the years 1941–45 in training camps near Khabarovsk and Vladivostok in the Soviet Far East, where he was awarded the rank of major in the Soviet Army.[48] At the outset it seemed that the Korean communist leader would be yet another Soviet puppet, which certainly was not the case.

The division of Korea differs from the case of Germany in that North Korea has developed an autonomous identity that has withstood the collapse of the Soviet Union. Kim Il Sung promulgated the Democratic People's Republic of Korea in September 1948, and the Soviet forces were withdrawn from the North. The Soviet occupying presence was maintained in East Germany until its collapse in 1989; thereafter Russian troops remained until August 1994 because they had nowhere else to go. Kim Il Sung was freed of the Soviet control that was the fate of Eastern European regimes, Rumania and Yugoslavia excepted. Moreover, the North Korean communist regime grew indigenous roots through the proclamation of *juche* ideology in December 1955.

The *juche* ideology of self reliance subsequently permeated all aspects of North Korean society, justifying militant nationalism and ethnocentrism.[49] It was a useful tool to mobilize the population for the task of economic reconstruction and the establishment of a self-sufficient economy. From 1967 a surrogate religion was developed in the form of the Kim Il Sung personality cult and the all embracing propaganda campaign behind it.[50] In 1972 *juche* replaced Marxism-Leninism in the party program and became a weapon in the North's competition for legitimacy with the South, which was then under military rule. After 1985 when Kim Il Sung sought the communist world's endorsement of his son Kim Jong Il as heir it became apparent that indigenous customs and traditions had surfaced beneath the facade of communism.

The North Korean regime could successfully resist the impact of the collapse of the Soviet Union and the communist East European states as its authority had been grounded in an indigenous mythology, recreated and adapted to the contemporary world. Nonetheless, the regime has not escaped the fact that *juche* has led it to its present situation of international isolation and famine. North Korea was a creation of the communist world and relied upon fuel and grain supplied at artificially determined prices by the Soviet Union and China. Without outside support the regime could not cope with market prices for its essential commodities as demanded by both Russia and China. *Juche* has pushed the country into a self-made disaster.

Conflict between divided nations may be intense in the short term, but the end of the division results in relatively rapid reconciliation. The symbols of national legitimacy, common language, ethnicity, traditions, and customs provide a basis for overcoming the hostilities of the past and for eventual reintegration into a reconstituted nation. Then, intra-national conflicts are likely to be replaced by extra-national tensions as the newly integrated nation takes stock of its situation. Reunification may boost national confidence, in which case there may be attempts to settle scores with historical adversaries or to use such enmities to strengthen national legitimacy. A reunited Vietnam, for example, came into conflict with its historical adversary, China, after 1975 when the Vietnamese leadership, in their moment of triumph, overestimated their strength and their ability to withstand Chinese pressure. A similar outcome may follow Korean reunification, in which case the likely target would be Japan. The region, indeed, should be prepared for this development.

Northeast Asian Regionalism

In what sense is it possible to envisage the emergence of a Northeast Asian region and an accompanying regionalism? The issue relates to the emergence of cooperative patterns of interaction that can transcend cultural and national divisions on the basis of a common regional consciousness. Northeast Asia is a region only in the geographic sense and has been included in the integrative processes of the wider Asia-Pacific region, where progress has been possible. Throughout its modern history it has been an arena of conflict between great powers, each struggling to expand its sphere of influence or to defend its position against others. There has been little interaction between these powers save that required by conventional diplomacy to foster a balance of power or to promote particular alignments. For the 40 years of the Cold War superpower rivalry froze existing historical conflicts and postponed the necessary process of indigenous region-building or regionalism that could overcome the legacies of the past. Northeast Asia, moreover, is a region of great power actors with proud national traditions, and their absence from Southeast Asia has greatly facilitated the success of regionalism there.

The past need not determine the future, however. The sections above have shown that Huntington's idea of civilizational conflicts may be captivating but does not accurately identify the impact of the past upon the present in all cases. According to civilizational analysis, the greatest points of conflict should be between Russia and its East Asian neighbors, since the cultural differences are greatest in these areas. There has been a strong element of civilizational conflict in the Russo-Japanese territorial dispute, as the outstanding issue is the negotiation of a mutually acceptable border between two distinctly different cultures. In Russian-Chinese relations another picture emerges where the current leaders of both countries realize very well the dangers of conflict and have initiated measures to stabilize their relationship. Recognition of these dangers impels the leadership to overcome the civilizational factor in their relations and to construct an enduring basis for future interaction. The civilizational differences have acted as barriers to the occupation of homeland territory and have prevented any attempt by one to assimilate the other so that inter-state relations need not be held hostage to aggrieved nationalism.

The most troublesome areas for the future will be those where a common civilizational factor was present to some degree, as in the case of the Japanese-Korean and Japanese-Chinese relationship. Indeed, the common civilizational factor justified the occupation of homeland territory and misguided assimilation policies that transformed state rivalries into acute conflicts of identity and nationalism. Japan's past behavior has become a nationalist issue for both Korea and China, and the issue has been strengthened by the Japanese unwillingness to come to terms with history. It would be premature to expect the political leadership to establish stable patterns of interaction while past injuries remain vivid in the national consciousness of China and Korea. In the absence of deeply rooted grievances, it may be possible for the political leadership of the countries concerned to establish a commitment to regionalism, as has been the case in Southeast Asia. In Northeast Asia the political leadership has been vulnerable to nationalist pressure over these animosities and on occasion has even attempted to exploit them for foreign policy advantage.

Various proposals for a Northeast Asia dialogue between Japan, Korea, and China have been aired in the past. In 1994 South Korean President Kim Young Sam proposed a regional forum to include the three countries, while Japan's foreign ministry (*gaimusho*) has called for an expansion of U.S.-security dialogue to include China as well. Separate dialogue processes have been initiated involving Northeast Asian military officers and other officials together with the United States but they stop short of the political leadership as yet. One way or another there can be no progress in terms of multilateral dialogue or security mechanisms unless there is a reconciliation between the peoples involved, and some attempt by Japan to atone for past wrongs. Franco-German reconciliation made progress toward a European community possible and served as the foundation for the most successful case of regionalism today. There has been some movement toward reconciliation in Northeast Asia. South Korean President Kim Dae Jung's visit to Tokyo in October 1998 elicited an apology from Japanese Prime Minister Keizo Obuchi and resulted in a declaration that the ban on Japanese culture in South Korea would be lifted. Chinese leader Jiang Zemin visited Tokyo the following November in what was a partial success. The Japanese prime minister offered an oral apology, which the Chinese regarded as insufficient, and the joint declaration remained unsigned. The Chinese effort to link the apology with the Taiwan issue irritated the Japanese side and demonstrated the difficulty of untangling history from present relations between the two countries.

Reconciliation between these countries would be facilitated if a framework for dialogue existed that involved all the regional actors including the United States. Without this incentive the Japanese political leadership would no doubt fear that historical injuries could be utilized by others to extract a never-ending series of concessions over a broad range of issues. The Japanese leadership would then be pushed by nationalist and conservative forces to resist the sacrifices required for reconciliation with neighbors. What is required is a Northeast Asian forum, which is separate from the ASEAN Regional Forum, that would involve China, the two Koreas, Russia, and the United States. With the involvement of the United States Japan's fear of becoming a victim of impossible demands would be reduced considerably, and the context for a much-postponed historical reconciliation would be in place. One way or another there can be no progress at the multilateral level without historical reconciliation, yet no reconciliation without the incentive and accompanying support of multilateralism. Both should develop together.

The future will bring a gradual easing of tensions between Japan and its neighbors as the political leaderships of China and South Korea are prompted for strategic and economic reasons to strengthen relations with Japan. Concern about the United States over the Taiwan issue, aside from economic interest, is enough to ensure that China will not alienate Japan, while South Koreans will require Japanese assistance to overcome the impact of their current economic crisis. There is the danger that a reunited Korea may turn hostile toward Japan, but reunification will occur in a prolonged series of stages that will absorb the attention of Koreans for at least a decade. Over time it can be expected that the conditions for effective multilateral dialogue will be established in the context of strategic and economic necessity. Then, the final steps in the process of historical reconciliation will be reached.

Notes

1. See Samuel P. Huntington, *The Clash of Civilizations and the Remaking of World Order,* New York: Simon and Schuster, 1996.
2. Arnold J. Toynbee, *A Study of History,* Abridged Edition, Vol. 2, Oxford: Oxford University Press, 1957, pp. 420–421.
3. Fernand Braudel, *The Mediterranean and the Mediterranean World in the Age of Philip II,* Vol. 2, Fontana, 1973, p. 773.
4. Oswald Spengler, *The Decline of the West,* New York: Alfred Knopf, 1930.
5. See Huntington, p. 43.
6. Bjorn Hettne and Andras Inotai, *The New Regionalism: Implications for Global Development and International Security,* Helsinki: United Nations University, 1994, p. 7.
7. On the relationship between history, culture, and the notion of a Southeast Asian region see O.W. Wolters, *History, Culture, and Region in Southeast Asian Perspectives,* Singapore: Institute of Southeast Asian Studies, 1982.
8. Huntington, p. 219.
9. On the Treaty of Nerchinsk see John J. Stephan, *The Russian Far East: A History,* Stanford, CA: Stanford University Press, 1994, pp. 31–32.
10. See S.C.M. Paine, *Imperial Rivals: China, Russia, and Their Disputed Frontier,* Armonk, NY: M. E. Sharpe, 1996, p. 343.
11. Paine, p. 3.
12. Ibid., p. 348.
13. Stephan, p. 26.
14. Paine, p. 183.
15. See Sergei N. Goncharov, John W. Lewis, and Xue Litai, *Uncertain Partners: Stalin, Mao, and the Korean War,* Stanford, CA: Stanford University Press, 1993, p. 81.
16. The boundary with Russia was "the physical incarnation of China's failure to fend off the predators of European civilization." (Paine, pp. 9 and 15–16.)

17. Itar-Tass, April 29, 1997.
18. Paine, p. 182.
19. Ibid., p. 187.
20. Saburo Okita and Minoru Takahashi, "The Northern Territories/Southern Kurile Islands Dispute," in James E. Goodby, Vladimir Ivanov, and Nobuo Shimoatami, eds., "Northern Territories" and Beyond: Russian, Japanese, and American Perspectives, Boulder, CO: Praeger, 1995, p. 7.
21. See John J. Stephan, The Kurile Islands: Russian-Japanese Frontier in the Pacific, Oxford: Clarendon, 1974, pp. 40–47.
22. David Rees, The Soviet Seizure of the Kuriles, Boulder, CO: Praeger, 1985, p. 33.
23. William F. Nimmo, Japan and Russia: A Reevaluation in the Post Soviet Era, Westport, CT: Greenwood Press, 1994, p. 28.
24. Rees, p. 76; Nimmo, p. 25.
25. Yoshida argued that two smaller island groups, Habomais and Shikotan, were part of Hokkaido and not part of the Kurile Island chain, though he did not specifically mention the other two islands, Kunashiri and Etorofu. (Rees, p. 96) Subsequently the Japanese government developed the position that all four islands were separate from the Kurile Islands on the basis that the Treaty of St. Petersburg of 1875, which gave the Kurile Islands to Japan, mentioned 18 islands (from Urup to Shimushu). This list did not include the four islands currently claimed by Japan. (See Japan's Northern Territories, Tokyo: Ministry of Foreign Affairs, 1987, pp. 7–9.)
26. Hiroshi Kimura, "Japanese Perceptions of Russia," in Goodby et al., p. 57.
27. Peter Duus, The Abacus and the Sword: The Japanese Penetration of Korea, 1895–1910, Berkeley: University of California Press, 1995, pp. 413–423.
28. Chong Sik-Lee, Japan and Korea, Stanford, CA: Hoover Institution Press, 1985, pp. 153–155.
29. Carter J. Eckert et al, Korea: Old and New History, Seoul: Ilchokak for Harvard University Press, 1990, p. 255.
30. Mark R. Peattie, "Japanese Attitudes toward Colonialism," in Ramon H. Myers and Mark R. Peattie, eds., The Japanese Colonial Empire 1895–1945, Princeton, NJ: Princeton University Press, 1984, p. 121.
31. Carter J. Eckert, pp. 314–320.

32. Samuel Pao-San Ho, "Colonialism and Development: Korea, Taiwan, and Kwangtung," in Myers and Peattie, *The Japanese Colonial Empire*, p. 385.

33. Carter J. Eckert, pp. 390–391.

34. Bruce Cumings, *Korea's Place in the Sun: A Modern History*, New York: Norton, 1997, p. 171.

35. Sung-Hwa Cheong, *The Politics of Anti-Japanese Sentiment: Japanese-South Korean Relations Under American Occupation, 1945–1952*, Westport, CT: Greenwood Press, 1991, p. xi.

36. D. R. Howard, *Borders of Chinese Civilization: Geography and History at Empire's End*, Durham, NC: Duke University Press, 1996, pp. 7 and 236.

37. Eiichi Kiyooka, *The Autobiography of Fukuzawa Yukichi*, Madison, Maryland, 1992, pp. 91 and 277.

38. Mark R. Peattie, *Ishiwara Kanji and Japan's Confrontation with the West*, Princeton, NJ: Princeton University Press, 1975, pp. 315–316.

39. Albert Feuerwerker, "Japanese Imperialism in China: A Commentary," in Peter Duus, Ramon H. Myers, and Mark R. Peattie, eds., *The Japanese Informal Empire in China 1895–1937*, Princeton, NJ: Princeton University Press, 1989, p. 433.

40. Peter Duus, "Japan's Informal Empire in China, 1895–1937," in ibid., p. xiv.

41. Marius B. Jansen, "Japanese Imperialism: Late Meiji Perspectives," in Myers and Peattie, eds., *The Japanese Colonial Empire*, pp. 76–77.

42. Peattie, *Ishiwara Kanji*, p. 69.

43. Saburo Ienaga, *The Pacific War, 1931–1945: A Critical Perspective on Japan's Role in World War II*, New York: Pantheon, 1978, p. 6.

44. Albert Feuerwerker, "Japanese Imperialism in China: A Commentary," in Duus, Myers, and Peattie, p. 435.

45. Ibid., pp. 431–432.

46. Saburo Ienaga, pp. 166–171.

47. The Chinese press attacked the visit by 150 diet members and two cabinet ministers to the Yasukuni shrine in April 1997. (See *Straits Times*, April 25, 1997.) The China Youth Daily recently criticized Japanese comic books as honoring "militarism" because of the violence depicted. Translations of these comic books are now spreading in China and have become a source of concern. (See *Straits Times*, May 5, 1997.)

48. On Kim Il Sung see Erik Van Ree, *Socialism in One Zone: Stalin's Policy in Korea, 1945–1947,* Oxford, New York, Munich: Berg, 1989, pp. 24–31.
49. On *Juche* see Han S. Park, "The Nature and Evolution of Juche Ideology," in Han S. Park, ed., *North Korea: Ideology, Politics, Economy,* Inglewood Cliffs, NJ: Prentice Hall, 1996, pp. 9–18.
50. Ingeborg Gothel, "*Juche* and the Issue of National Identity in the DPRK of the 1960s," in ibid., pp. 28 and 29.

CHAPTER 2

MUTUAL PERCEPTIONS AMONG THE GREAT POWERS IN NORTHEAST ASIA

Gilbert Rozman

Introduction

WHILE SOME IN THE WEST BASKED in the glow of a new world order that promised to end the danger of big wars and even to accelerate acceptance of a shared civilization along with a global market economy, others in the "East" dreaded the prospect of a lone superpower unfettered in its sponsorship of westernization and capitalism. China was the first great power in opposition. With its leadership committed to four cardinal principles of socialism and its state subject to lingering sanctions imposed after June 4, 1989, China adamantly objected to the proposed order from the start. Russia faced the challenge of reconciling itself to a diminished status as the Soviet Union's successor amidst rampant economic decline. By 1995 its leaders had come to identify with China in the struggle against unipolarity. Japan welcomed aspects of the new world order, but it sought a distinct role in Asia and maneuvering room among the great powers. In response to problems in its relations with China and Russia, by 1995 Japan was reassessing its prospects. Together, China, Russia, and Japan's images of each other and the shared regional order offer clues to how great power relations will take shape at the beginning of the twenty-first century.

After a transitional phase from 1992 to 1994 of learning to grasp the main lines of great power development, images in China, Russia, and Japan have grown clearer. These images are evolving interdependently. An overview of bilateral images and the fit among images can point to what otherwise might be missed if we only looked separately at each country's worldview.

Emerging Perceptions of the World Order

China awakened to the cataclysm in the world order of 1989 to 1991 with a single obsession: it must maneuver to limit the power of the United States by building a multipolar world as fast as possible. Yet, no matter how much its spokesmen protested that the international environment had become favorable,[1] at the moment of the collapse of the Soviet Union Chinese leaders shuddered at the prospect of a new world order integrating Russia, Japan, and the European Union as allies of the United States. Recognizing that Russia was the weak link in this chain, Beijing began to play great power politics in the hope that Russia would break loose and become an independent pole.

In 1992 and the start of 1993 Beijing took satisfaction in the turn of events when Moscow first announced in July that it was adopting an Eastern strategy to balance its Western strategy. Then Boris Yeltsin demonstrated in a series of Asian summits, after snubbing Japan, which was supposed to have been his first port of call, that Russia was ready to play the Asian card. In 1993 and the start of 1994 Beijing watched hopefully as nationalism roared to the front in Russia, and received Yeltsin's proposal to form a "constructive partnership." Meanwhile, Beijing's fervent wish that Japan would be stymied in its quest to translate economic great power status into political power was bolstered by encouraging news within Japan about the bursting of the bubble economy and the consequent setback to the postwar political order. By 1995 Chinese were confident that great power realignment was turning to their advantage. Their images confirmed a multipolar order offering Beijing increased flexibility, but some lingering fears could not be concealed.

Russia did not take long to sober to the seriousness of its falling global status. In need of leverage in great power relations, Russia found China an appealing partner. Despite the rise in 1994 of strong misgivings about Chinese immigration and cross-border trade,[2] locking arms with China became the preferred strategy for preventing the United States from forming a unipolar world. Having turned to China in the second half of 1992 after becoming angered by Japan, Moscow continued to regard Beijing rather than Tokyo as the gateway to the Asia-Pacific region.

If Chinese turned to Russia to buy time so that their country's overall national strength would not be overwhelmed by the strength of the United States, Russians usually had more short-term considerations. They reacted to the injustice or even deception that they accused the United States of causing in the late 1980s and early 1990s. They acted hurriedly to gain immediate leverage as the expansion of NATO and other decisions, some strictly domestic, loomed. Before long, however, Russian perceptions were solidifying against the West with the possibility of an enduring coalition at home and abroad in opposition.

While the United States, at least until 1996, mostly shrugged off the Sino-Russian partnership as little more than a nuisance, in Japan, on the contrary, alarm bells rang. Perhaps a distant superpower did not need to stoop to strategic triangle maneuvering to counteract Sino-Russian cooperation, but an island nation with doubts about its further development strategy could not be so nonchalant toward a nearby continental liaison of such dimensions. Japan was the third great power to be jolted into rethinking great power relations.

The temptation for many Japanese for some time after being snubbed by Yeltsin was to blame Russia and retaliate by cutting aid. Even after Yeltsin visited Tokyo in October 1993 many regarded the results as inconsequential and expected little improvement in bilateral relations for a long time to come. Yet others recognized the trauma Russia was facing and pushed forward. Before long they were joined by Japanese who were disturbed by tensions in relations with China.

Sino-Russian Mutual Perceptions

By the start of 1995 Chinese analysts had turned quite pessimistic about the Russian economy. Even taking into account a series of favorable assumptions—no further historical transformation, smooth presidential elections in 1996, and on-track economic reform—they projected that the GDP of Russia would not overtake England and Italy to become third in Europe until the 2020s.[3] Having largely rejected "shock therapy" in 1992 and privatization at one thrust in 1993–94, Chinese had little reason to find hope in Russian economic policies.

Assessments of Russia's political situation and social problems mostly reinforced Chinese pessimism, although analyses did not ignore a degree of political stabilization after the October 1993 Moscow showdown between Yeltsin and the parliament. A divided polity could not take the steps necessary for economic revitalization. Yet Chinese evaluations of the 1996 elections did not, on the whole, differentiate two contradictory approaches to economic development; they argued that whether Zyuganov or Yeltsin won the reform course would be largely the same.[4] Reform would continue, but the process would be slow. Meanwhile, crime, income polarization, and other social problems would complicate the transition.

The contradictory nature of Chinese evaluations had its origin in Chinese politics and Sino-Russian relations. On the one hand, good relations with the Russian government had the usual effect in communist-led countries of censorship suppressing outright criticism. After 1992 the tone in China changed from blanket condemnation of Yegor Gaidar's policies to no direct criticism of Boris Yeltsin, Viktor Chernomyrdin, or other leaders. On the other hand, sympathy with a communist-led opposition meant that the obstructionist policies of the State Duma toward some of the very measures that China had used to accelerate its economic growth—free economic zones, profitable arrangements for foreign investment, etc.—did not arouse criticism. It sufficed to blame a lack of political unity for indecision, implying that, by contrast, China's one-party system with political stability best meets the needs of our times.

Chinese praise concentrated on Russia's foreign policy. Assessing 1994, Chinese analyst Zheng Yu stressed the "full-scale unfolding of great power diplomacy."[5] If in 1992 Russia completely leaned to the West and in 1993 it still one-sidedly favored the West, at last in 1994 Russia based its international relations on its own national interests. Given Russia's strained relations with the West and its priority on integration in the former Soviet Union, close ties with China naturally had become a cornerstone of the new diplomacy. Chinese predicted that this shift would endure, regardless of political twists inside Russia.

While from late 1994, following Jiang Zemin's summit in Moscow and Chinese acceptance of the label "constructive partnership," to mid-1998 there had been no notable shift in Chinese perceptions of Russia, three topics in particular aroused an undertone of debate beneath the veneer of censorship: 1) Is Russia too weak to serve as a pole in a multipolar world? 2) Are Sino-Russian relations not secure enough to make this partnership the nucleus of China's great power relations? and 3) Is Russia's place in the world order changeable in a way that could limit its utility for China?

The fact that Chinese sources grasp for reasons that Russia remains a full-fledged great power should be a warning that they are countering doubts. The list of what makes Russia a great power includes: its territory, its natural resources, its nuclear capability, its conventional military forces, its science and technology, its permanent membership in the United Nations Security Council, and its sphere of influence in the CIS. This is a rather long list, and it seems to suffice to prove Russia's case. Nonetheless, territory and natural resources can best be described as latent sources of power, while science and technology appear more as a past source of strength that is rapidly dissipating.[6] Chinese struggle with the suspicion that Russia is becoming a weak pole that cannot hold up its share of a multipolar world. In the second half of 1998 such doubts were reinforced.

Sino-Russian relations offer Russia a way to maintain its national strength, according to the Chinese logic. The key word is "complementarity," although this is also a very sensitive notion that Chinese have stopped repeating. The two countries compensate for each other, beginning with the largest territory, sparsely settled and loaded with resources, and the largest population, densely packed and in need of more employment outlets and resources. After the uproar in the Russian Far East in 1994 about Chinese immigration and alleged designs for "quiet expansion," the focus of discussions about complementarity has shifted. Now Beijing proposes to Moscow that Russia's arms assembly lines can stay in operation through exports to China and that Russia's strength in science and technology can be applied through joint development zones in Russian cities. Moreover, by teaming together in the United Nations and elsewhere Moscow and Beijing can multiply their voice on security matters. As evidence that China really supports a rise in Russian national strength, Beijing also assures Moscow that it backs Russia's sphere of influence in the CIS, and it sponsors Russian entry in the Asia-Pacific region. Although Russia may be in danger of becoming a weak pole, China offers its assurance that it opposes that outcome and can make a difference in reviving Russia.

What bothers Chinese is that Moscow vigorously pursues the symbols and rhetoric of upgraded relations without taking many substantive steps. While Chinese exports skyrocketed to more than $40 billion to the United States and Japan, they hover at barely $1.5 billion to Russia. Despite the effusive mutual praise in summit communiqués, the Russian media more often takes an alarmist tone to China than a positive tone. Chinese proposals for closer economic ties do not conceal the fact that Russia is not yet taking the steps to develop such ties. Not only is the Russian Far East resistant to most such initiatives, but nationalists in Moscow fear to act at the same time as internationalists prefer to deal with the West and Japan. Worrisome to the Chinese was the campaign, launched from the Far East, against completing the border demarcation agreement of 1991 that was ratified by the Russian parliament in March 1992.[7] This agreement is nothing less than the cornerstone in bilateral relations separating past animosity and present-day pragmatism. If it were to have been rejected, especially by Russian refusal to transfer a plot of land along the Tumen river roughly ten miles from the Pacific Ocean, an enormous setback to relations could not have been avoided. Only after last-ditch negotiations were Yeltsin and Jiang able to announce in November 1997 that the demarcation was completed apart from three disputed islands set aside in 1991 for a later time. While closely following unofficial wavering in Russia on close partnership relations, Chinese rely on the Yeltsin administration to steer ties ever closer.

Finally, Beijing watches Russia's agreements with NATO, its negotiations with Japan, and its unofficial dealings with Taiwan with some uncertainty. China has emphatically identified Russian great power national interests, but does Moscow steadfastly recognize them itself? When Andrei Kozyrev was foreign minister, Chinese had doubts that he did. But Yevgeniy Primakov reassured China's leaders in a more convincing manner. As long as he runs foreign relations (prime minister since August 1998) with a keen eye to building a multipolar world order, Beijing should feel confident of its strategic partner. But if foreign economic relations begin to drive foreign policy, as some thought might have occurred when the presidential program for the development of the Russian Far East and Transbaikal appeared to rise to the forefront under the leadership of Deputy Prime Minister Boris Nemtsov, then China may not be satisfied with Russia's redefinition of its national interests.

Russian images of China are more complicated. From June 1989 to the end of Soviet rule the official position favored self-restraint. Since normalization had been so difficult to achieve, why risk it with criticisms of China? In 1992 the situation in Russia was changing so quickly that China was largely forgotten. A few voices, however, stressed the importance of China for Russian security, for Russian development, and even for Russia's position in the world. By 1994 such voices were largely in tune with official policy. They were beginning to elaborate a rationale for partnership in the face of dissenting voices in the academic community and political circles. The dissent has reverberated quite loudly through 1998. It accentuates three powerful arguments. First, critics of China point to the changing balance of power, drawing the conclusion that China, before long, will threaten Russian security. The principal threat may be territorial: unrelinquished claims to Russian lands, immigration that would fill the vacuum of sparsely settled Siberia and the Russian Far East, or border demarcation transferring land in the Tumen river delta that would give China access to the sea and make Russia's Pacific ports uncompetitive.[8] Less vocal are critics of accelerating arms sales and technology transfers who warn that China could turn its new strength to the north rather than the southeast.[9] Second, Russians express concern about China's rapid economic development from one of two perspectives. One group foresees an economic powerhouse that could use its weight to Russia's disadvantage. The other fears dysfunctional consequences from uneven development or resource shortages: food and energy shortages, regional inequalities coupled with overpopulation and leading to mass emigration, perhaps in the aftermath of civil disorder, etc. Third, Russians worry about China's rise as a great power, flexing its muscle in the global system. Russian interests will be left behind.

Official rationale for boosting relations with China reverses all of these dissenting opinions. Rather than being a threat to Russian security, China offers the only hope in a rapidly worsening security situation.[10] Sales to China will keep weapons assembly lines in operation. China promises to support Russia's sphere of influence in the CIS, especially in Central Asia. The border demarcation, rather than endangering security, signifies Beijing's abandonment of territorial claims. If some illegal immigration could not be controlled, China at least is cooperating fully to restrict it. As long as Moscow keeps control over its own local administrations in the Far East, it should dictate the terms of regionalism, not Beijing. Likewise, China's economic development serves Russia's interests. Needing to re-equip many factories built in the 1950s with Soviet aid and satisfied with lower technological requirements, China provides a potential market for Russian industrial exports, even for nuclear reactors.[11] Finally, as the foremost opponent of U.S. hegemony and Western civilization, China is Russia's natural partner on the global stage.

From January 1994, when Yeltsin sent a letter to Jiang Zemin suggesting a "constructive partnership," the official view might have been expected to eclipse the dissenting one. Yet at best it emerged as a countervailing perspective. To the consternation of Chinese officials, the Russian Far East led the way in focusing criticism on their country. If at first this seemed to be an aftereffect of the gyrations in cross-border trade that China admitted it had brought on itself with inadequate regulation of false and shoddy goods and rampant abuse of visa-free agreements, then soon it was ascribed to demagogic governors in the Far East playing on nationalism to curry favor among voters and exert pressure on the Yeltsin administration.[12] But even after these governors won their election campaigns handily and gave their support to Yeltsin in his reelection bid, the rhetoric did not abate. Chinese worry that public opinion in Russia is a weak prop for the strategic partnership.

Visits by Li Peng to Moscow in December 1996, Jiang Zemin to Moscow in April 1997 and November 1998, and Boris Yeltsin to Beijing in November 1997 punctuated proposals for close cooperation between the two governments to underpin relations in order to guarantee their long-term effectiveness. This meant expanding trade and economic cooperation, which would draw powerful interest groups in each country together. It also meant reaching out to young people, who showed little interest in studying the other country's language or admiring its culture. At first the immediate priority remained to change the tone of Russian writings on China. When Jiang Zemin devoted a day to visiting the writer Lev Tolstoy's home at Yasnaya Polyana during his 1997 visit, one goal was to impress Russians with civilizational congruence to counteract widespread anxiety over a civilizational divide.[13] At the same time, spokesmen were careful not to highlight the fact that most top Chinese leaders with whom Moscow dealt had studied in Russia, bantered in Russian, and waxed nostalgic with their Russian counterparts.[14] Such images could suggest that the Sino-Russian cultural bond was in fact a socialist bond. By 1998 as trade was declining and as Russia watched Sino-U.S. relations improve and Chinese watched Russo-Japanese relations improve, it had become a matter of urgency just to keep the strategic relationship from faltering.

Russian nationalism regards the United States and the West as the principal danger; therefore it is divided on how to treat China. For communists Chinese political stability under communist party authority and resistance to the West serve as a model. But the communists hesitate to proceed very far with this conclusion, since they themselves have mixed feelings about China and they object to much of China's economic reform strategy, including massive foreign investment through special economic zones. Although Chinese tend to oversimplify Russian reactions, blaming westernizers such as Yegor Gaidar for stirring anti-Chinese passions while hesitating to accuse nationalists opposed to both the West and China, they cannot equate Governor Yevgeny Nazdratenko of Primorsky Krai or other outspoken critics in the Russian Far East with the pro-Western group. As their tactic, the Chinese chose patience: to say little about the charges against their country, to acknowledge mistakes in 1992–93, to pledge cooperation, and above all to prevent criticisms of Russia that might degenerate into tit-for-tat accusations. Chinese forbearance helped to create a most benign environment for improving relations. But in 1997–98 the Chinese had lost some of their patience, they were openly blaming Russia for its own problems and its negative worldview, and relations were no longer improving.[15]

Sino-Japanese Mutual Perceptions

As Chinese relations with Russia were improving, relations with Japan were declining. This defies economic logic. In 1994 and 1995 Sino-Russian trade retreated sharply and then stagnated at $5 to $5.5 billion, while Sino-Japanese trade climbed sharply and continued in 1998 to equal well over ten times the level of Sino-Russian commerce. In four respects Japan met expectations that Russia could not: as a source of foreign assistance, especially in infrastructure; as a source of foreign investment, primarily in production; as a source of advanced technology; and as a market for Chinese exports. China showed little appreciation; its criticisms intensified through 1996 and ameliorated only partially as diplomatic relations stabilized in 1997–98.

The opening phase of the post–Cold War era came amidst intense Chinese alarm that Japan would be the primary beneficiary of the transformation in the world order. Three factors pointed to an advantage for Japan. First, a shift in global competition from military to economic strength would favor Japan, which was on target to surpass the United States in total GDP as it had already done in per capita GDP. Second, the rise of the Asia-Pacific region as the center of the global economy was coupled with Japan's strategy of a "flying geese formation" in which Japan led the pack and transferred technology only to the extent that its lead was not diminished. This strategy appeared to relegate China to the fourth tier after the four little dragons and the lead countries in ASEAN, leaving a huge gap with Japan that would be difficult to narrow. Third, the breakup of the Soviet Union left a vacuum in political and military leadership, which Japan, drawing on its strong economy, was intent on filling. Chinese publications repeatedly warned that Japan was bent on becoming first a political great power and then a military great power.

By 1995 Beijing was more confident that Japan's aspirations could be checked. The 50th anniversary of the end of World War II gave China an opportunity to remind its citizens and the world of Japan's infamous behavior and Japan's inability to properly acknowledge what horror had been inflicted on Chinese and other Asian peoples. Cooperating with South Korea and positioning itself to influence the outcome in the Korean peninsula as well as siding with Russia on the territorial dispute between it and Japan, China no longer worried about Japan's domination of Northeast Asian regionalism. The most worrisome development, however, was that instead of economic conflict intensifying between Tokyo and Washington, the two were drawing closer together as strategic allies. In 1996–97 Chinese sources harshly criticized the strengthened alliance between the two and the prospect that Tokyo would use it for great power advantage in Asia.[16]

All along Beijing had worried that Japan's quest for power would endanger peace and stability in the Asia-Pacific region. Despite Japan's economic slowdown, Chinese assessments saw ample room before 1998 for recovery through the release of free competition.[17]

They pointed to expanded naval development by Japan as a destabilizing element. Having set its sights on becoming the world's third pole along with the United States and the European Union, Japan was returning to Asia to consolidate its own rival economic sphere in an era of rising regionalism and protectionism. Chinese set their own sights on limiting Japan's return, guiding it to serve China's rise rather than its containment.

Northeast Asia was one front on which the struggle between China and Japan was beginning to take place. China feared that Japan would push for vertical relations through a division of labor favoring its own technology and capital, rather than horizontal relations or equality favoring mutual development and technological transfer. Chinese writers warned that Japan cannot reenter Asia on the basis of superior economy and technology alone.[18] According to this view, Asian countries will not accept interference in their internal affairs. Japan must separate itself from the U.S. strategy and forego political and military ambitions of its own to succeed in reentering Asia.

Chinese presented an image of a Japan unworthy of a normal great power status. Its historical atrocities were not a distant memory, but a flaw in national character readily revived. Many of its politicians were scarcely concealed nationalists, ready to reassert old tendencies that offended the Chinese people.[19] This negative image justified China's opposition to Japan becoming a permanent member of the Security Council. It explained also a double standard in Asia: China has the right to become an all-around great power, but Japan's role should stop at economic power or, in some generous versions, at a limited degree of political power.

Whereas Chinese analysts calculated ways to limit Japan's power, they stumbled when it came time to accommodate the effects of a backlash. First, they found a silver lining in the cloud of U.S.-Russian cooperation, which allegedly disrupted relations between the United States and Japan by raising trade deficits to the fore and focusing attention on their economic competition rather than on their security alliance. But Chinese satisfaction at building a partnership with Russia that exacerbated U.S.-Russian relations could not avoid regret that one effect was to solidify U.S.-Japanese ties. All of China's efforts to stymie or at least criticize Japan's plans contributed to a backlash in Japan, which began to see China itself as the greatest potential threat. It became harder to keep reasserting that the U.S.-Japanese alliance was built on a fragile foundation, and that as Japan pressed to become a political great power it would clash more seriously with the United States.[20]

Japanese views of China adjusted slowly to the new great power maneuvering. Despite the disappointment felt by much of the public at China's shift toward repression in 1989 to 1991, the Japanese government felt relieved that negative reactions had been kept quite under control. Japan became identified as the chief advocate in the G-7 countries for abandoning sanctions. In 1992 the emperor's visit went well enough and Japanese investment and trade began accelerating in a manner that suggested the onset of a new age. Many even expected a new balancing role for Japan between the United States and China, offering Tokyo the benefits of belonging to both the West and Asia and of becoming the swing country in the world's most important new strategic triangle.

By 1995, however, Japanese sensed that their problems with China were of a different order from the periodic trade disputes in U.S.-Japanese relations. China's turn toward Russia was but confirmation of this realization. Indeed, for Beijing Japan was but third in priority after the United States and Russia, and, apart from economic cooperation, Beijing's actions were matching its rhetoric in dismissing Japan. Japanese had expected something better. They wondered how it could be that after a quarter century of sustained contacts no warming could have occurred in Chinese attitudes toward their country.

Japanese could think of nothing new to add to their array of public relations tools in dealing with China. Such soft measures did not seem to make any imprint. According to Beijing, Tokyo was turning instead to hard measures. These included: collaborating with the United States to change Japan's security role in logistics and expanded defense of sea lanes far from Japan; possible cooperation to develop theater missile defenses; and new attitudes toward "splitting" Taiwan from China. Supposedly, Japan contemplated such actions in the hope that they would increase its leverage with China.

While economic linkages continued to expand, hopes for the transformation of relations as a whole were dimming. Chinese regarded Japanese investment as too narrow and self-serving, targeted at keeping China from becoming an economic competitor and a strong country. In turn, Japanese feared that too much was being transferred, with insufficient control to prevent China from "stealing" technology and displacing Japan as an industrial power. The two countries were increasingly seeing each other as competitors rather than partners.

The literature on a "China threat" came from many sides in Japan. On the right wing, those who had formerly targeted the Soviet Union as a threat and those looking for an excuse to revise the constitution and increase the military budget found Chinese actions and rhetoric served their needs well. Closer to the center of the political spectrum, many Japanese were aroused in 1996 by the Taiwan straits missile launchings. War guilt, which had never been deeply reinforced by education and the media in Japan, was losing its hold. Politicians who had been sympathetic to China were disappearing from the Diet. China could no longer rely on the Japanese left or a group in the LDP to give their support; indeed, the Taiwan lobby was growing.

Japan's foreign ministry was not prepared, however, to succumb to negative public opinion. In March 1997 Foreign Minister Ikeda's visit to Beijing marked an effort to reinvigorate relations. Loans suspended in 1995 in protest over Chinese nuclear testing were reinstated in recognition of China's pledge to join the global ban on testing. Talk turned to ways to celebrate 25 years of achievement in bilateral relations later in the year, and then in 1998 to recognize the 20th anniversary of the peace treaty between the two countries. Yet doubts lingered that China would take any action to buttress the symbolism of such remembrances.

Giving an optimistic slant to the prospect of stabilizing Sino-Japanese relations, Tanaka Akihiko wrote in early 1997 that the end of the Cold War brought a period of "confusion." He argued that the transitional period first saw U.S.-Japanese and Sino-U.S. tensions, and then the tension spread. Only by stabilizing triangular relations will the Sino-Japanese relationship be secure. He predicted that as U.S.-Chinese relations improve, China will be reassured and see that it overreacted to the April 1996 reinterpretation of the U.S.-Japanese security agreement. No matter how accurate he is in stressing triangular rather than bilateral relations, Tanaka was too optimistic in predicting an upswing in Sino-U.S. relations. If, as he concludes, societal forces more than governmental ones are dragging down relations, then the solution is likely to be more difficult than he suggests.[21] In the fall of 1998 Tanaka looked ahead to Jiang Zemin's visit to Japan. Although he recognized progress since Hashimoto had visited China in September 1997, he worried that Bill Clinton's visit to China in the summer of 1998 and new weakness in the Japanese economy left Japanese policy isolated.[22]

Russo-Japanese Mutual Perceptions

While the Japanese public was slow to warm to Russia, from 1993 the Japanese government was striving to improve relations. It fended off criticism in urging more financial assistance. Little that Russia did helped, although Yeltsin's October 1993 visit cleared away a serious obstacle. More concerned about chaos than democracy, Japanese were frightened by what they saw in Russia.

It is widely recognized that the Japanese people have long been driven by deep-seated emotions toward Russia as well as toward China, with contrasting effects.[23] Although the rising military and economic power of China may be reducing the goodwill rooted in guilt, the post-Soviet transition has made little impact. Neither the substance of Russia's actual changes nor the symbols of Russian behavior toward Japan have created a positive impression.

More important than what Russia did to encourage Japan was the juxtaposition of two developments: a loss of self-confidence in Japan and a rise in concern over China. As Sino-Russian relations were improving, the Japanese government grew eager for a breakthrough in Russo-Japanese relations.

The new attitude was on display in the fall of 1996 in meetings and writings marking the 40th anniversary of the restoration of diplomatic relations between Tokyo and Moscow. One article by

Shigeki Hakamada in a Russian newspaper signaled this approach. He observed that Japan was beginning to see normal relations with Russia as necessary for its national interests, for its strategic position in the region. Hakamada called for calm, reducing the role of emotional factors in bilateral relations. Looking back more than 100 years, he noted that Japan and Russia had been able to understand each other and, indeed, Japanese had shown an unusual love for Russian literature as seen in the greater number of translations than elsewhere in the world. Not only did this history offer hope for the present, but current conditions, if honestly recognized, also can be a basis for mutual trust, added Hakamada.[24]

If the Russian government was for a time more receptive to improved relations than the Japanese, it was in any case not in a rush. Even as the impression lingered that Japan's obstinacy was holding relations back, the primary onus was shifting to Russia. The Yeltsin administration chose China over Japan in the fall of 1992, it failed to show gratitude for Japanese assistance, and it made little effort to create conditions that permit normal economic relations. When Tokyo became serious about accelerating normalization, especially economic ties, Moscow delayed. All that the Russian press reported about the visit of Primakov to Tokyo in November 1996 was the possibility of softening mutual dissatisfaction by discussing some bilateral problems, such as joint development of the disputed South Kurile zone and Japanese measures to reduce illegal fishing in the same area.[25]

Japanese authorities consciously sought to transform Russian views of their country. In 1991 to 1993 the focus of a public relations blitz from the cultural affairs office of the Moscow embassy was to inform Russians about the actual history of the disputed territories.[26] This effort backfired, however, as some were angered by Japanese obsession with this issue and others found the coverage too slick and one-sided. Down and out, Russians were ill-disposed to look dispassionately at an issue with such nationalistic overtones. Separately Japan sponsored a glossy journal to inform Russians broadly about Japan and a specialized academic journal to stimulate debate about the relevance of the Japanese experience for Russian reforms.[27] There was no quick payoff as Russian foreign policy experts and officials turned instead to China and economic experts remained for the most part Eurocentric. Without nuclear weapons or a large territory, Japanese did not feel that their country was being taken seriously. They could hope, however, that once Russians gave priority to economic development and long-range planning, Japan would rise to the forefront. Beginning in the fall of 1996 a strategy of patient appeal to common interests gave some Russians, at least, an encouraging message for overcoming the drift in their country.

Ever since the 1980s some Russians had looked on academic experts as too sympathetic to Japan. A number of these experts held Japan up as a model or even proposed a compromise on the territorial question. In the mid-1990s the influence of these experts may have receded before the dual power of the security experts and the nationalist enthusiasts, both of whom claimed to be better at recognizing Russian national interests. But experts continued to urge an integrationist approach. Not only in economic relations, but also in regional security, they encouraged Russia to strive harder to normalize relations with Japan and to develop all-around cooperation aimed at collective security.[28] But even if worries about a Japanese threat were not substantial, it remained far from clear that seriousness about a Japanese opportunity would spread.

From mid-1997 Japanese leaders took the initiative in boosting relations with Russia. As the official atmosphere became upbeat, hope rose in both countries. It created an environment for moving forward. But the fact that Japanese and Russians had very different expectations left the possibility that mistrust would again rise to the fore. Russians who focused on Japan's continued expectations for a quick decision to allow the eventual transfer of the four disputed islands doubted the goodwill would last.[29]

An Overview of Images and Relations

Of China, Russia, and Japan's six images of each other, not one could properly be called positive. Japan's image of China had worsened in 1989 and then, before fully recovering, had fallen again in

1995–96. Whereas remorse over the suffering Japan had caused, admiration for China's rapid economic development, and respect for China's historical civilization provided a foundation for goodwill, it was rapidly dissipating. China's image of Russia also might have developed from a positive foundation. After all, many Chinese regretted the Sino-Soviet split and felt a bond with Russia's late attempts to transform a traditional socialist system quite similar to China's. Yet the Chinese government censored reassessments of Mao Zedong that might have questioned his handling of Soviet relations, led in criticisms of Boris Yeltsin and the collapse of Soviet socialism that tarnished views of Russia, and could do little to reinforce geopolitical partnership with sympathy for a country so blatantly causing its own self-deterioration. The other potentially positive inclination was the Russian outlook on Japan. For approximately two decades prior to intensification of negotiations to normalize relations and the coming of glasnost to the Japan field in 1988, Russian attitudes toward Japan, especially among the Soviet intelligentsia, had been improving.[30] While such attitudes may not have spread widely and may have lost ground to the charge that Japan was unfairly pressuring Russia to return territory when Russia was down, they left behind a residue of goodwill.

Bilateral images in all three cases revealed, at least for a time, a glaring asymmetry. Japan had high hopes for China, while China instead of shaking off memories of wartime horrors was reinforcing them. China insisted that its citizens viewed Russia warmly even as it expressed alarm that Russian sources took an excessively negative view of China. Japanese exaggerated the gap, but were not entirely off the mark in characterizing somewhat more positive Russian attitudes toward Japan as "unrequited love."[31] Such one-sidedness is not likely to be stable. The negative Chinese posture contributed to a downturn in Japanese attitudes toward China. Chinese sympathy toward Russia was too superficial to endure if Russian attitudes did not improve toward China. And Russian sympathies toward Japan would require Japanese encouragement if Russia was to be convinced that Japan sought to relieve Russia's weakness rather than take advantage of it. That, of course, required the Russian government to demonstrate that it was taking the necessary steps to allow foreign investment.

Highly symbolic events helped to justify the misgivings each nation had toward the other. Although Japanese expressed sympathy toward China, the 50th anniversary of the end of the war brought resolution after resolution from local and national parliaments in Japan that reminded Chinese of the callous disregard of the Japanese people for the suffering they inflicted. While Japanese claimed to hold China in special regard, Chinese felt more insulted than grateful. Russians, meanwhile, focused on the behavior of Chinese "suitcase traders," who showed little regard for Russia's laws. In 1992–93 their behavior had outraged Russians, particularly in the Russian Far East, and the impression that Chinese behaved in Russia as if they were masters rather than guests did not go away. On the Japanese side, repeated snubs by Russian leaders sustained ill feelings. Not only did Yeltsin periodically offend Japanese sensibilities, such as with incorrect assertions that Japan gave no humanitarian aid, but other leaders did so too, such as in early 1997 when Deputy Premier Viktor Iliushin gave a flimsy excuse for not traveling to Tokyo as scheduled only to show up at an International Olympic Committee meeting in Western Europe.[32]

Suspicions were also aroused by images of other nations as militarist and criminal. Chinese kept alive such stereotypes of the Japanese, reinforcing them through attention to the close ties between right-wing politicians and the *yakuza*. Russians argued that the Heilongjiang mafia and other criminal organizations supported by the government were dominating cross-border commerce. And Japanese pictured Russian sailors and others deboarding ships in their ports as thieves who stole every bicycle or appliance they could get their hands on. Normal friendly relations did not suffice to supplant these images in the national consciousness.

One strategy for improving goodwill is to concentrate on economic relations first. Many criticized Japan for linking politics and economics in ties with Russia during the late 1980s and early 1990s, and some still doubt that Japan has adequately separated the two because of its frequent references to the importance of making progress on the northern territories problem. In Sino-Russian relations the idea is spreading that only by greatly expanding economic linkages can the two countries guarantee that close political ties will endure. Economics will produce interest groups dependent on good relations, while simultaneously ameliorating public perceptions. Yet in 1992–93, when political relations were relatively cool, the erroneous idea spread that spontaneous cross-border trade would uplift bilateral relations, smoothing the way for closer political ties. The opposite, in fact, occurred, and politics had to rescue the hostile atmosphere left from economic relations. Of course, the primary test of the hypothesis that economic progress transforms public opinion and smoothes the way to political cooperation is the path of Sino-Japanese relations. Despite the unprecedented acceleration of trade, investment, and overall economic ties, Sino-Japanese mutual images in 1996–97 were more troubled than at any time since the 1970s.

At fault for exaggerated suspicions is excessive nationalism. In China this is centrally sponsored nationalism to sustain the power of the Communist Party. Chinese sources convey a one-sided image of Japan consistent with the great power struggle that leaders encourage. Since the public is predisposed to recalling Japan as a brutal aggressor, it is inclined to become more hostile than the leadership desires. Thus, a tension exists between a leadership that encourages negative views of Japan, then discourages public manifestations of anti-Japanese sentiment. Such ambivalence is further fueled when leaders who manage improving relations are accused after their downfall of being soft on Japan, as happened to Hu Yaobang and Zhao Ziyang.

Russia's excessive nationalism is closely intertwined with domestic political strife. In the summer of 1992 the parliamentary attack on a soft policy toward Japan constituted the first successful jab against the Kozyrev foreign policy strategy. In early 1997 three conflicting forces in Moscow were vying to shape policy toward Japan. On one side nationalists eager to discredit Yeltsin continued to look for an advantage in criticizing Japan, and have done their best to prevent large-scale Japanese investment in Russia through terms that might be commercially viable. On the other side Moscow economists charged with planning the development of the Russian Far East were hopeful that the appointment of Boris Nemtsov as deputy prime minister with responsibility for the region and for economic relations with Japan would at last overcome nationalism. In the middle, Foreign Minister Yevgeniy Primakov was walking a tightrope between stirring up multipolar passions against an integrated world order and beckoning to Japan with messages of joint development. Russian nationalism toward Japan as well as China continued to block proposals for regional and bilateral economic cooperation. In 1997–98 the Russian side responded to Japanese overtures and nationalism slipped into the background, but it can reemerge quickly.

Neither is Japan free of the nationalism that interferes with great power relations in Asia. In 1991 and 1992 hesitation to provide humanitarian assistance and in late 1992 and 1993 opposition to aiding a country responsible for rude behavior toward Japan revealed an undercurrent of nationalism toward Russia inconsistent with the international responsibilities of an economic superpower. In 1995 the inability to apologize properly for war atrocities and in 1996–97 the renewed clout of the right wing of the LDP suggested that the periodic outrageous denials on the part of LDP ministers that led to their forced resignations were not an aberration.

While each country in forming an impression of the others exaggerates the danger of nationalism, currents of super-nationalism give some credibility to these reactions. Uncertainty in the domestic politics of each country means that it is too soon to predict a decline in such forms of nationalism.

Closer bilateral economic ties may help, but more direct solutions must also be sought. Four deserve our attention. First, the two countries should act quickly to solve or set aside the most emotional symbols of nationalistic conflict. Completion of the Sino-Russian border demarcation in 1997 with maximum assurances to those who were most worried was a good start. Other islands are still in dispute, but China has postponed its claims. An agreement between Japan and Russia on how to manage their territorial dispute over four islands and between Japan and China on further postponing their dispute over the Senkaku or Diaoyu islands would ease tensions. Second, security issues must not simply be set aside for the indefinite future. A security dialogue including the United States is needed, although it is unlikely until North Korea decides on its strategy toward the region. Third, showcase regionalism that promises gains to all sides could do a lot to assure Chinese, Japanese, and Russians that benefits of cooperation far outweigh the costs. Failure to make progress toward Northeast Asian regionalism, including such projects as the Tumen river delta development, has left an atmosphere of doubt. Finally, entirely new initiatives are needed to foster cultural multilateralism. Instead of criminal groups controlling cross-border contacts on the basis of spheres of influence, multicultural business, educational, and other networks should prove the value of open borders. In all of these ways, trust can be generated in a region that still shows the effects of its absence in the Cold War era.

In all three bilateral relations similar themes arise. There is talk of an "image gap." Analysts and officials alike recognize that relations depend heavily on perceptions, on both public opinion and foreign policy elite understanding. Countries appear to be driven by a desire for respect. Negotiations aim for restoring relations of trust. Apologies matter. In short, national pride has emerged in the post–Cold War era as a powerful force in bilateral relations. Public relations to persuade other nations and one's own nation now warrant a prominent place in the diplomatic arsenal. Ambassadors who show appreciation for the host country's culture and are optimistic about its future are becoming indispensable. Russian ambassadors to China and Japan, Igor Rogachev and Alexandr Panov, China's ambassador to Moscow Li Fenglin, and Japan's recent ambassador to Moscow Koji Watanabe have made their mark by demonstrating such empathy.[33]

It is still unclear which of the three non-Western bilateral great power relations will rise to the forefront. On the basis of economic ties and a shared East Asian Confucian civilization, the Sino-Japanese bond seemed to have the edge in 1992–93. From 1994 to 1996 the Sino-Russian partnership gained prominence, uniting countries reared in communist worldviews and opposed to Western hegemony. There may even be a chance for recently budding Russo-Japanese relations if economic complementarity becomes the driving force and China overplays its hand as the central kingdom in a new regional order. The outcome for triangular relations remains in doubt, but the importance of mutual reassurances cannot be denied. The pair of countries that best convinces each other of their sincerity and goodwill will gain an advantage in this complex competition.

Notes

1. Luo Zhaohong, "Sulian jieti ji qi dui shijie jingji yu zhengzhi gezhu de yingxiang," *Shijie jingji yu zhengzhi,* no. 10, 1992, pp. 1–5.
2. V. Portiakov, "Kitaitsy idut? migratsionnaia situatsiia na Dal'nem Vostoke Rossii," *Mezhdunarodnaia zhizn',* no. 2, 1996, pp. 79–86.
3. Gao Zhongi, "Eluosi jingji shili ji qi zai shijie de diwei," *Dongou Zhongya yanjiu,* no. 1, 1995, p. 9.
4. "'Jinqi Eluosi zhengjing xingshi ji Zhong E guanxi' yantaohui zongxu," *Dongbeiya yanjiu,* no. 2, 1996, pp. 79–81.
5. Zheng Yu, "Daguo guanxi de quanmian zhankai—1994 nian Eluosi waijiao gailun," *Dongou Zhongya yanjiu,* no. 1, 1995, p. 67.
6. Li Renfeng, "Eluosi mianlin kezhi weiji," *Dongou Zhongya yanjiu,* no. 1, 1997, pp. 46–49.
7. *Nekotorye problemy demarkatsii Rossiisko-Kitaiskoi granitsy 1991–1997 gg.,* Moscow: Nezavisimaia gazeta, 1997.
8. V. Larin, "Rossiia i Kitai na poroge tret'ego tysiacheletiia: kto zhe budet otstaivat' nashi natsional'nye interesy? Vzgliad s Rossiiskogo Dal'nego Vostoka," *Problemy Dal'nego Vostoka,* no. 1, 1997, pp. 15–26.
9. Alexandr Chudodeyev, "Russia, China: Summit Long on Rhetoric, Short on Benefit," trans. from Moskva segodnia, *FBIS-SOV-97-079,* April 24, 1997.
10. L. Deliusin, "Sindrom 'veroiatnogo protivnika:' kto I pochemu predstavliaet Kitai kak ugrozu Rossii," *Literaturnaia gazeta,* January 5, 1996.
11. I. Korkunov, "Rossiisko-kitaiskie vneshneekonomicheskie sviazi: itogi I perspektivy," *Problemy Dal'nego Vostoka,* no. 6, 1996, pp. 69–80.
12. Shi Ze, "Lun xin shiqi de Zhong E guanxi," *Guoji wenti yanjiu,* no. 2, 1996, p. 7.
13. "Jiang Zemin Knows Russia Well and Likes Russian Literature; Visit to Yasnaya Polyana," trans. from Rossiiskie vesti, April 22, *FBIS-SOV-97-077,* April 22, 1997.

14. Han Hua, "How Jiang and Yeltsin Engage in 'Small Talk'—Ambassador Rogachev 'Divulges Secrets' in the Air," trans. From Wen Huibao, April 21, *FBIS-CHI-97–111*, April 21, 1997.

15. Gilbert Rozman, "Sino-Russian Relations in the 1990s: A Balance Sheet," *Post-Soviet Affairs*, vol. 14, no. 1 (Spring 1998), pp. 93–113.

16. Sun Yan, "Riben zhengzhi daguo zhanlue dui DongYa de yinxiang," *Dongbeiya yanjiu*, no. 2 (1997), pp. 49–52, 72.

17. Xiao Yong, "Jiage geming yu Riben jingji qianjing," *Riben wenti ziliao*, no. 1, 1995, pp. 1–3.

18. Zhang Dalin, "An Analysis of Japan's Strategy of Returning to Asia," *International Studies*, nos. 4–5, 1994, p. 8.

19. Tian Peiliang, "1996 nian Zhongguo waijiao huigu," *Heping yu fazhan*, no. 1, 1997, p. 7.

20. Sun Honggen, "Shiji zhi jiao de Yatai daguo guanxi yu Zhongguo de xingshi," *Guoji guancha*, no. 2, 1996, p. 28.

21. Akihiko Tanaka, "97 nen, BeiChu wa wakai suru," *Chuo koron*, February 1997, pp. 52–63.

22. Akihiko Tanaka, "Shin seiken wa Jiang Zemin o do mukaeru noka," *Chuo koron*, no. 9 (1998), pp. 60–69.

23. Shigeki Hakamada, "Nihon no kimyo na 'nejire gensho,'" *Foresight*, March 1995, pp. 56–57.

24. Shigeki Hakamada, "Rossiia i Iaponiia sposobny poniat' drug druga: reshenie problem etogo veka ne sleduet otkladyvat' na budiushchee," *Nezavisimaia gazeta*, October 18, 1996, p. 5.

25. "Vizit Primakova v Iaponii," *Nezavisimaia gazeta*, November 15, 1996, p. 2.

26. Akio Kawato, *Roshia ni kakeru hashi*, Tokyo: The Simul Press, 1995.

27. *Znakomtes' s Iaponiei* and *Iaponskii opyt dlia Rossiiskikh reform*.

28. *Iaponiia I problemy bezopasnosti v ATR*, Moscow: Center for the Study of Contemporary Japan, 1996, pp. 305–306.

29. Aleksandr Bovin, "My nichego ne dolzhnyi Iaponii," *Izventiia*, June 3, 1998, p. 3.

30. Semyon Verbitskii, "Russian Perceptions of Japan," in James E. Goodby, Vladimir I. Ivanov, and Nobuo Shimotamai, eds. *"Northern Territories" and Beyond: Russian, Japanese, and American Perspectives*, Westport, CT: Praeger, 1995, pp. 63–69.

31. "NichiRo kokumin 'kataomoi'," *Asahi shimbun*, November 30, 1992, p. 3.

32. Vasilii Golovnin, "Rossiisko-Iaponskie sueveriia: za poslednie shest' let v diplomaticheskikh otnosheniiakh Moskvy i Tokio voznikla svoia mifologiia," *Itogi,* March 25, 1997, pp. 24–25.

33. Koji Watanabe, "Fear Not—Russia Will Rise Again," *The Japan Times,* December 13, 1996, p. 7.

PART 2

MAJOR POWERS' INTERESTS
AND PERSPECTIVES

CHAPTER 3

A PARADIGM SHIFT
IN RUSSO-JAPANESE
RELATIONS

*Tsuneo Akaha**

Introduction

RUSSIA AND JAPAN ARE IN A POSITION to contribute, individually or
jointly, to the establishment of a post–Cold War world or regional
order. The two countries' national identities as great powers compel
them to play global and regional roles commensurate with their
enormous power, both potential and real. Their failure to do so will
be a major source of frustration to them and an important factor in
instability in the post–Cold War world. Further, as geographical
neighbors of global importance, each country is in a position to facilitate or frustrate the other country's global aspirations and regional interests. For example, Russia could support or veto Japan's

*An earlier version of this chapter was published in *Demokratizatsiya*, vol.
6, no. 2 (Spring 1998), pp. 347–362. A part of the article is reproduced here
with permission of the publisher.

effort to obtain the coveted permanent seat on the United Nations Security Council, and Japan could facilitate or frustrate Russia's bid to become a full-fledged member of the Group of Seven (making it a Group of Eight). Tokyo could also endorse or deflect Moscow's efforts to join the Asia-Pacific Economic Cooperation (APEC) forum or the World Trade Organization (WTO), and Moscow could respond favorably or negatively to Tokyo's call to limit the proliferation of arms in East Asia.

Against the background of their expanding ties with the United States and China, Russian and Japanese leaders have acknowledged the need to put an end to the "abnormal" state of their bilateral relations. There are clear signs that the leaders in Moscow and Tokyo have accepted a new premise upon which to build relations between the two countries. In 1997, there was a dramatic turnaround. Japanese Prime Minister Ryutaro Hashimoto put forth a new Japanese policy toward Russia: In his speech to *Keizaidoyukai* (the Association of Corporate Executives) on July 24, 1997, the Japanese leader stated that Japan and Russia should improve their relations on the basis of trust, mutual interest, and long-term perspective. He also called for the development of a "Eurasian policy" in which Japan would expand ties with Russia, China, and other nations. Moreover, Hashimoto and Russian President Boris Yeltsin met in an informal summit in Krasnoyarsk in November and agreed to do their best to conclude a peace treaty by the year 2000 on the basis of the 1993 Tokyo Declaration, which had committed Moscow and Tokyo to settle unresolved bilateral issues, including the territorial dispute, through peaceful negotiations. This commitment was reaffirmed in the Moscow Declaration signed by Yeltsin and Hashimoto's successor, Prime Minister Keizo Obuchi, at their summit meeting in Moscow in November 1998.

What are the sources of the remarkable turnaround in Russo-Japanese relations? This is the central question of this brief analysis. I will first place the bilateral relationship in the broader context of changing relations among the major powers in Asia-Pacific. Second, I will discuss Russia's and Japan's interests vis-à-vis each other. I will then briefly examine domestic factors that impinge on bilateral relations. Fourth, I will review the current state of Russian-Japanese cooperation. Fifth, I will discuss some areas that require further co-operation, namely, Russia's economic reform and development, environmental and resource protection, bilateral military confidence building, and nongovernmental contacts between the two peoples.

The Global and Regional Context

In describing recent global trends, many analysts have referred to "the end of history," "the end of the Cold War," and "the end of geography."[1] It is asserted that the end of the East–West ideological conflict has marked the victory of liberal capitalism over socialism and communism and that the disappearance of the Soviet threat has ushered in an era of global cooperation. It is also claimed that the logic of liberal economics and the imperatives of modern technology are creating a borderless world economy. Unfortunately, however, Northeast Asia—the region of immediate concern to both Russia and Japan—has been slow to adjust to the global changes. The regional powers remain suspicious of each other politically and unable to remove national barriers to international economic transaction. Russia's political system is in a period of uncertain transition from a communist dictatorship to a fragile democracy, with authoritarian tendencies remaining strong at the national and regional levels. In Japan and South Korea, political corruption continues to hamper efforts toward administrative reform and economic liberalization. On the economic front, Russia is mired in the contradictory and disintegrative forces of transition from a planned economy to a market economy. The successful market economies of Japan and South Korea remain integrated with the global economy, with only limited, although gradually increasing ties with the other Northeast Asian economies. Their domestic economies are in recession and the necessary cure, further liberalization and greater internal competition, requires more painful adjustments than most politicians are ready to accept. China is experimenting with a "socialist market economy," with the state sector occupying a major, albeit shrinking, role in the nation's economy. Its dramatic growth since the late 1970s is both a welcome sign of the opening of the previously closed economy and a source of uncertainty for political and security calculations in the neighboring countries. North Korea continues its autarkic path toward economic development despite the visible signs of failure of that system and the resulting human suffering of untold proportions.

The end of the Cold War has raised the specter of a major power shift and realignment in Northeast Asia and consequently heightened the level of uncertainty surrounding Russian and Japanese roles there. Declining U.S. hegemony, rising Chinese power supported by its growing economy, Japan's preoccupation with its domestic agenda and regional ambivalence toward its greater role in regional security, and the uncertain transformation of Russia all complicate the structure of international relations in Northeast Asia. The continued division of both China and Korea also represents explosive possibilities.[2]

Russia has a deepening concern over its declining influence in the region since the dissolution of the Soviet empire and is attempting to shore up its regional profile through bilateral improvements with China, Japan, and South Korea. Russia's economic assets are seriously limited, frustrating Moscow's attempt to establish itself as a legitimate and credible Asian-Pacific power.[3] Nonetheless, Russia remains a major military power and a potential security concern to Japan.[4] Japan watches Russia's improving relations with its Northeast Asian neighbors with a mixture of hope and anxiety.[5] Japan's own future is a source of growing uncertainty to its neighbors. Central to this uncertainty, in addition to the history of Japanese aggression, is the imbalance between Japan's aggressive economic policy and its passive defense policy. Following the adoption of the new Guidelines for U.S.-Japan Defense Cooperation, regional concern is now turning toward the question of the unspecified geographical perimeters of Japan's military role within its bilateral security alliance with the United States.

There is a conspicuous gap between Russia's and Japan's economic presence in the world and in the Asia-Pacific region. Japan's exports represent almost 10 percent of the world's total, and it accounts for 6.5 percent of global imports. The importance of regional trade to Japan is evident in the fact that the nation's trade with the other major Asia-Pacific economies represents over 70 percent of its worldwide trade. In contrast, Russia is conspicuous by its negligible presence in the world economy. Its world exports in 1994 amounted to a mere $49,935 million, or 1.1 percent of the global total, and its imports from the rest of the world stood at $28,135 million, or 0.7 percent of the world's total imports, and Russia's exports and imports have both become smaller since. Russia's trade with the other Asia-Pacific economies is growing but represents only 15 percent of its global trade. As Asian-Pacific economies continue to deepen their interdependence, Russia's economic presence remains marginal.

The global context of Russo-Japanese relations has changed dramatically in the aftermath of the Cold War, but their regional environment remains uncertain and complicates the two countries' policy options. Russia's impact in the Asia-Pacific region stems primarily from its geostrategic position and its military power. To the extent that the end of the Cold War has diminished the importance of global military power in determining the political structure of the Asia-Pacific region, it has also reduced Russia's regional influence. On the other hand, Japan's regional influence continues to grow, both as a result of its enormous economic power and as a consequence of the increasing U.S. reliance on Japanese cooperation in maintaining its regional military presence. The disparate foundations of Russian and Japanese national power do not create a common strategic calculus. Naturally, therefore, differences abound between their domestic, regional, and global priorities.

Bilateral and Domestic Factors

Although ideological conflict is no longer a factor in Russo-Japanese relations and Russia's military power no longer poses a serious security threat to Japan, there are a number of asymmetries in their relations that can frustrate the development of a strong, stable relationship between the two countries. As the legacies of prewar history and the impact of the global Cold War wane, as they eventually will, domestic structures and processes will become a more dominant influence on the external behavior of Russia and Japan. It is important, therefore, that in exploring the possibilities of bilateral cooperation, we pay closer attention to the differences and similarities in the two countries' internal development.

One of the most important asymmetries appears in the perceptions Russians and Japanese have of each other. The Russian view of Japan is informed by the memory of their humiliating defeat in the Russo-Japanese war of 1904–05 and the resulting loss of the southern half of Sakhalin Island and the entire Kurile Islands, as well as by Japan's intervention in Siberia in 1918–20, and the U.S.-Japanese alliance against the Soviet Union during the Cold War. Most Russians continue to believe that Japan's claims to the southern Kuriles are unjustified in view of Japan's unconditional surrender in 1945. In spite of this, many Russians, particularly those in the Far Eastern regions, hold a generally favorable view of Japan. For example, a 1992 survey of public opinion in southern Primorye indicated that Japan was the second most popular country after the United States. Japan was the country with which the local residents most wished to establish close and friendly relations. The same survey also showed that almost half of the respondents named Japan as the country from which they wished to receive experience and assistance in economic development.[6] A more recent survey of residents of Valdivostok and Khabarovsk confirms the Russian people's generally favorable view of Japan, particularly in the area of economic achievements and cultural traditions.[7]

In contrast, most Japanese hold negative views of Russia. The sources of unfavorable views include the Soviet declaration of war against Japan in violation of the Soviet-Japanese neutrality pact of 1941, Soviet/Russian occupation of the Northern Territories since 1945, the inhumane treatment of Japanese prisoners of war in Siberia after the Second World War, and the Soviet military threat during the Cold War era. According to a survey conducted by the Japanese prime minister's office in October 1995, only 9.9 percent of Japanese had friendly or somewhat friendly feelings toward Russia, in comparison with the 86.4 percent who felt either somewhat unfriendly or unfriendly.[8]

Until the demise of the Soviet Union, another major difference existed in the two countries' political systems. The Soviet Union was a dictatorship with a centralized power structure, and Japan was and continues to be a parliamentary democracy with a durable, if not always effective, system of multi-party competition. Today, Russia is a nascent democracy dominated by a powerful president and unruly opposition, often unleashing drastic policy shifts, both domestically and internationally. There is a great deal of uncertainty and unpredictability in its foreign policy. Japan, on the other hand, is a bureaucracy-driven democracy with a weak political leadership, oriented toward consensual policy-making. Its policy is characterized by a stable and predictable trajectory. Its foreign policy behavior is generally conservative, passive, and reactive.

Third, there are myriad differences in the two countries' domestic economic structures and performance. Russia is a transition economy struggling to introduce market principles in its basic operation. Its industrial production has plummeted since the dissolution of the Soviet command economy. The state still controls much of the nation's strategic industries, but the private sector is growing fast, albeit in a rather chaotic manner. Russia's fiscal system is unstable, and its tax system is unevenly developed; its financial system is volatile, with regulatory power unevenly applied; its legal system is also underdeveloped, and law enforcement remains ineffective. There are serious problems with the legal and administrative mechanisms for foreign trade and investment. Japan, on the other hand, is a global capitalist superpower with a highly developed market and a very efficient productive capacity. The country's fiscal, tax, and financial systems are well developed, as are its legal and administrative structures. In terms of the performance of the two economic systems, Russia and Japan are moving farther apart. The real GDP growth rate for the 1991–95 period was 1.3 percent for Japan and minus 9.1 percent for Russia. The two countries' per capita GDP in 1995 stood at $40,897 and $2,461, respectively.[9] Despite the recent economic downturn and financial market problems in Japan, its economy is likely to regain its vigor following the ongoing financial liberalization and market deregulation.

Fourth, it is often observed that the differences in Russian and Japanese economic capabilities and needs, as well as their developmental gaps, render the two economies complementary to each

other. Russia is indeed a source of energy and other natural resources, and Japan a source of capital and industrial technology.[10]
However, the complementarity has not created an economic interdependence between the two. The growing trade between the Russian Far East and Japan is due largely to the former's natural resource
exports to, and consumer and capital goods imports from, the latter, and the exchange is not contributing to the modernization of industrial production or economic restructuring of the Far Eastern
regions.[11]

Russian-Japanese economic relations are a very small part of either country's overall trade activity. The $3,490 million in Russian
exports to Japan in 1994 represented about 7 percent of Russian exports to the world and less than 1.3 percent of Japanese global imports totaling $274,742 million. Russian imports from Japan
amounted to $1,104 million, or 3.9 percent of the nation's global
imports, and less than 0.3 percent of Japan's worldwide exports totaling $395,600 million. Even within the Northeast Asian context,
the $4,594 million in two-way trade between Russia and Japan in
1994 represented a mere 3.9 percent of the intraregional trade totaling $118,109 million. As a result, Russian-Japanese economic re-
lations have little or no impact on the overall structure of regional
trade and investment. As Khabarovsk Krai's governor acknowl-
edges, "Without question, integration of the Russian Far East into
the Asian-Pacific region is in the early stages of development."[12]

Fifth, Japan's postwar economic growth took place in an entirely different international environment than that which Russia
faces today. Japan's export-driven economic growth could be sustained only because of the United States' strategic assistance and its
open market, and the liberal international trade regime. Japan's
membership in the General Agreement on Tariffs and Trade, the International Monetary Fund, the World Bank, the Asian Development Bank, and other multilateral institutions was very important in
the nation's postwar economic development. In contrast, Russian
exports continue to be severely restricted by export controls carried
over from the Cold War era, and Russia's membership in international economic institutions is conditioned on the pace of its domestic economic reform. Moreover, Russia today faces a much more

competitive international market. The global market is much more demanding in terms of cost, product quality, and environmental, safety, and other requirements. There are serious doubts that Russian products can successfully meet those demands.

There are a number of parallel tendencies in Russia and Japan today. They share a degree of similarity in the overbearing power of central administrative bureaucracies. In both countries there are marked disparities in economic development between the highly industrialized and urbanized centers of economic power and relatively neglected provinces. There are growing local and provincial initiatives for bilateral and regional economic cooperation. However, the historical orientation in both countries toward a powerful center is likely to bring their national priorities into the forefront of bilateral economic relations, overshadowing local and provincial interests.[13]

Russia's liberalization of trade and investment policies and consequent exposure to external economic processes is reminiscent of Japan's postwar economic development, in which international trade and foreign investment played a crucial role. Post-Soviet Russia is discovering the growth potential of export activities in its strategic industries, including primary commodities and military production, and becoming dependent on foreign investment and capital goods imports, not to mention the important role international economic assistance plays in stabilizing Russia's economy. In this respect, Russia can learn much from Japan's experience in postwar economic development. Following its disastrous defeat in the Second World War, Japan consistently and persistently followed an industrial policy focused on public investment in basic and strategic industries and export-driven growth. The lesson has not been lost on Moscow, which in February 1997 adopted a "development budget" of over $3 billion and established a Federal Economic Development Agency for the purpose of developing basic and strategic industries.[14]

Given the absence of economic forces strong enough to bring Russia and Japan closer together, it is obvious that major incentives for closer bilateral relations, if they exist at all, must be found in the political-strategic interests of the two countries. In other words, efforts to develop closer economic ties are likely to be driven more by political calculations and strategic motivations in Moscow and Tokyo than by private-sector business interests.

Political and Strategic Interests

During the Cold War, Moscow saw Tokyo in the context of its strategic rivalry and ideological conflict with Washington. From Moscow's vantage point, Tokyo was a docile ally of Washington, and Japan's economic power was of only limited use to Russia's overarching strategic policy against the United States and its allies. Gorbachev's priority in Asia during the last years of the Soviet Union was rapprochement with China. The last Soviet leader was preoccupied with his domestic political agenda and with the redefinition of the strategic relationship with the United States.

Behind Moscow's policy, during the Gorbachev years and since, has been the need to maintain a stable international environment so that Moscow may continue to focus on domestic reform. When Gorbachev found Tokyo unwilling to bend on its territorial claims to the southern Kuriles, he quickly turned to Seoul for political rapprochement and economic exchange. However, Moscow soon realized the limits to Russian-South Korean economic opportunities, particularly in the area of infrastructure development that would require enormous capital infusion. More important, its mishandling of relations with Pyongyang gave Washington an opportunity to replace Moscow as one of the two major influences on the Korean peninsula, the other being Beijing. Moscow's relations with Pyongyang had deteriorated precipitously following Gorbachev's abrupt decision to reach rapprochement with South Korea, which led to the establishment of diplomatic ties between Moscow and Seoul in 1991 and to the termination of the favorable trade terms Pyongyang had enjoyed during the Cold War years, including the "friendship" prices on Soviet exports to North Korea. Those decisions contributed substantially to the virtual political and economic isolation of North Korea. Equally important was Moscow's notification to Pyongyang in 1995 that it was no longer bound by the obligation to render immediate military and other assistance in case of an armed aggression against North Korea.[15]

The U.S.-DPRK Agreed Framework and the four-party peace talks have left Moscow lamenting aloud its loss of influence over the Korean peninsula's political future. On October 21, 1994, Pyongyang agreed that it would forego nuclear weapons development in exchange for Washington's pledge that it would secure international assistance to replace graphite-moderated nuclear reactors in North Korea with light-water reactors. In March 1995, Japan joined the Korean Peninsula Energy Development Corporation (KEDO), the international agency set up to provide nuclear energy assistance, and pledged support toward the estimated $4 billion needed to implement the project. The United States, in close consultation with Japan and South Korea, rejected Russia's well-publicized attempt to have its nuclear reactors used to replace the North Korean reactors and instead secured North Korea's agreement to accept South Korean-made light-water reactors as part of the KEDO project.

Yeltsin's Asian policy has basically been a continuation of Gorbachev's policy, with further removal of bilateral barriers at the top of his priorities vis-à-vis Beijing. The culmination of this policy has been the establishment of a "strategic partnership" between Moscow and Beijing. This notwithstanding, Moscow found itself in the unenviable position of having little or no influence over the course of events surrounding the Korean peninsula.

Russia wants to prevent a U.S. monopoly on regional political and security agendas. Its establishment of a "strategic partnership" with China is aimed in large measure at limiting U.S. dominance in Asia-Pacific, particularly in Northeast Asia. Russia is also looking for economic opportunities in its improved relations with China but is aware of the limits to such opportunities. Moreover, China's economic development and its growing trade and labor flows into Russia's Far Eastern regions have posed and will continue to pose serious problems for the two countries' political relations, as well as, potentially at least, for Russia's territorial integrity.

Moscow is now turning its attention to improving relations with Japan. During the Cold War, Moscow was adamantly opposed to the increasing defense cooperation between Japan and the United States, inasmuch as the defense pact was targeted against the Soviet Union. Moscow now views the U.S.-Japan security alliance as contributing to the stability of the region and expressed its support for the new Guidelines for U.S.-Japan Defense Cooperation announced by Tokyo and Washington on September 23, 1997. The new guidelines spelled out areas of defense cooperation within the framework of the U.S.-Japan security treaty. The envisaged cooperation included contingency planning and operational cooperation in peacetime, in case of an armed attack against Japan, and "in situations in areas surrounding Japan that will have an important influence on Japan's peace and security." The last of these terms is believed to include the outbreak of hostilities on the Korean peninsula and across the Taiwan Strait.

Moscow's support of the new guidelines contrasts sharply with China's critical comments about the unspecified geographical perimeters of Japan's military role under the new guidelines. Russia also sees Japan as potentially an important factor in the evolution of North-South Korean relations, particularly if further U.S.-North Korean improvements lead to the opening of the North Korean economy to foreign trade and investment. Moscow believes Tokyo has a legitimate interest in the resolution of the Korean conflict and has called for the expansion of the four-party peace talks to a six-party framework that will include both Moscow and Tokyo.

To Russia, Japan's economic assets—rich capital, advanced technology, and proven industrial and commercial know-how—are very attractive. Russia also needs Japan's cooperation to enter the dynamic Asia-Pacific economy and to join the World Trade Organization. Russia is aware of Japan's prominence in APEC, its leading role in the Asian Development Bank, and its dominant presence in the ASEAN economies, as well as the important role Japan's official development assistance and direct investment have played and continue to play in the economic development of China and Southeast Asia.

Japan also finds a good deal of value in improved relations with Russia. Following the dissolution of the Soviet Union, Tokyo continued to see its relationship with Moscow primarily from a bilateral perspective. However, Tokyo has recently adopted a more regional view of its relations with Moscow, and this has led to the adoption of a more flexible approach to the dispute over the Northern Territories. Tokyo is also visibly more interested in expanding bilateral economic ties either on their own merit or for the potentially beneficial impact they would have on political relations with Moscow.

Tokyo had long insisted on progress on the territorial dispute with Moscow as a precondition for improved bilateral ties. This position was known as *seikei fukabun,* or the inseparability of politics and economics. As the international community has become increasingly supportive of Russia's participation in the management of global issues, such as nuclear nonproliferation, UN peacekeeping, and the global environment, Tokyo has softened its stance on the territorial issue. It did so first by adopting the policy of *kakudai kinko,* or expanded equilibrium, whereby progress would be sought on both political and economic fronts. Most recently, following Russia's joining the Group of Seven meeting in Denver in 1997, Tokyo has shown an even greater flexibility by announcing the policy of *jusoteki kankei,* or multi-level engagement. The new policy implies that Russian-Japanese ties in economic and other fields may be allowed to grow ahead of progress on the territorial issue. If this interpretation is correct, it represents a paradigm shift in Japan's policy toward Russia.

The new policy was articulated by Prime Minister Hashimoto in his speech to the Association of Corporate Executives in July 1997, as noted earlier. Many observers believe Hashimoto's initiative represents a psychological breakthrough in hitherto strained Russian-Japanese relations.[16] Indeed, Russia's first deputy prime minister Boris Nemtsov hailed Japan's new policy toward Russia.[17] As well, during his meeting with Japanese foreign minister Yukihiko Ikeda in Kuala Lumpur, Russian foreign minister Yevgeniy Primakov said, "Prime Minister Hashimoto's new policy toward Russia is quite positive."[18] Russian ambassador to Japan Alexander Panov told the *Yomiuri Shimbun* that he hoped to see a Japan-Russian peace treaty signed during his term, which was supposed to end in five years.[19]

Hashimoto took his initiative directly to President Yeltsin when the two leaders met in a "summit without ties" in Krasnoyarsk in November 1997. They agreed to do their utmost to conclude a peace treaty by the year 2000 on the basis of the Tokyo Declaration. They also agreed to hold another informal summit in Japan in April 1998. The Russian and Japanese leaders announced a "Hashimoto-Yeltsin Plan," calling for expanded cooperation in the areas of high technology, trade expansion, transport infrastructure development, Russia's preparation for membership in the WTO, private enterprise development and management, energy development, and peaceful use of nuclear energy.[20] Hashimoto also pledged his government's support for Russia's membership in APEC. Yeltsin said Russia supported Japan's bid to win a permanent seat on the UN Security Council. Yeltsin and Hashimoto agreed to promote bilateral dialogue on the security of Asia-Pacific.[21] Finally, the two leaders indicated that Moscow and Tokyo would conclude an agreement on Japanese fishing in the waters surrounding the disputed islands before the year was out.[22] After thirteen rounds of negotiations, the two sides indeed reached agreement in December. The accord would allow Japan to catch up to 2,252 metric tons of fish in the waters around the disputed islands in exchange for a payment of 20 million yen toward the protection of resources in the Russian waters, as well as private aid of equipment worth 15 million yen. In addition, the Japanese government will extend humanitarian and technical assistance worth several hundreds of thousands of yen to Sakhalin Oblast in 1998.[23]

There remains in Russia strong opposition to territorial concessions to Japan. A member of the Our Home Is Russia Party expressed hope that the improving relations would encourage large Japanese investment in his country but maintained that resolution of the territorial dispute would require compromise on both sides. Another moderate member of the State Duma said the opinion of the two peoples must be accurately assessed. A nationalist Liberal Democratic Party member maintained that the two countries should establish a joint investment zone in the disputed islands. Communist Party General Secretary Zyuganov asserted that the conclusion of a peace treaty should not harm Russia's territorial integrity.[24] The

Sakhalin Oblast government has harshly criticized the proposal by Valery Zaitsev, vice rector of the Institute of World Economy and International Relations, to place the four islands under direct presidential rule and subsequently under Russian-Japanese joint administration.[25] A public opinion poll conducted by the *Asahi Shimbun* and *Itar TASS* in the fall of 1998 revealed that a majority of Russians were opposed to territorial concessions to Japan and only 3 percent were in favor of the transfer of all disputed islands to Japan.[26]

President Yeltsin and Prime Minister Hashimoto met in Kawana, Japan in April 1998 and reiterated that they would do their best to conclude a peace treaty by the year 2000. This pledge was formally reaffirmed in the Moscow Declaration signed by Yeltsin and Hashimoto's successor Keizo Obuchi at their summit meeting in Moscow in November 1998. The two sides agreed to set up two committees, one to discuss border demarcation and the other to discuss joint economic activities, including the development of the disputed islands. Obuchi stressed the two committees were like two sets of wheels that needed to operate fully for the vehicle to move forward, but many observers pointed out that Russia hoped the new arrangement would lead to a successful conclusion of a peace treaty irrespective of territorial settlement and allow Russia to reap economic benefits before (or even without) territorial resolution. Many media reports in Russia and Japan indicated that Prime Minister Yevgeniy Primakov, in a delicate balancing act vis-à-vis the communist-controlled State Duma, was assuming more foreign policy authority and that he was the chief architect of Moscow's proposal for joint development of the disputed territories.

Under more normal circumstances, i.e., in a politically stable Russia, one would look to government policy pronouncements for clear indications of Moscow's likely course of action on this and other issues. However, the situation surrounding the Yeltsin government is so unpredictable that it leaves enormous room for speculation and conjecture. One should therefore be cautious about projecting likely scenarios for future Russo-Japanese relations, particularly with respect to such a potentially explosive sovereignty issue. As Yeltsin's power continues to decline along with his health, there is a distinct possibility that the most Tokyo will be able to gain from the Yeltsin government before a new president assumes power in the year 2000 is a peace treaty that simply reaffirms the two sides' commitment to eventual territorial resolution without agreement on the modality or timing of the settlement. In fact, Ambassador Panov confirmed that Russia had proposed that the peace treaty should simply indicate the two sides' commitment to resolve the territorial dispute and that the actual settlement should be left to a separate agreement.[27]

If Moscow insists on a peace treaty in the absence of near-term prospects for agreement on an acceptable formula for territorial resolution, there will be much political frustration among the political elite in Japan. Many Japanese believe that Tokyo has already made an important concession by indicating its willingness to let Russia continue to control the islands in return for Russian recognition of Japanese sovereignty over the territories.

Bilateral Cooperation

If Russia and Japan are to develop their relations on the basis of the three principles put forth by Prime Minister Hashimoto—trust, mutual interest, and long-term perspective—it is necessary to identify areas where their cooperative efforts must be focused. There are at least four such areas: Japanese assistance with economic reform and development in Russia, bilateral cooperation in environmental and resource conservation in the Russian Far East, enhancement of bilateral military confidence-building, and expansion of nongovernmental contacts between the peoples of Russia and Japan.

Japan has been criticized for a seeming lack of interest in assisting Russia in its economic reform. It is rather obvious that Tokyo's interest has been substantially dampened by the lack of progress on the Northern Territories issue. Nonetheless, Japan's assistance to Russia is by no means negligible, nor is its slow process to be blamed entirely on the Japanese side. By January 1996, Tokyo had pledged $4.4 billion in total assistance for Russia, making it the third-largest provider of aid after Germany and the United States. Tokyo has pointed out that the absence of legal and institutional infrastructure and accountability for the disbursement of international assistance in Russia are important obstacles to a more effective and timely transfer of Japanese assistance.

Goals and objectives of Japanese assistance programs are stated as (1) support of Russia's transition to a market economy, (2) support of its democratization, and (3) establishment of diplomatic relations based on "law and justice," a reference to the settlement of the dispute over the Northern Territories.[28] Immediately after the dissolution of the Soviet Union, Japan's assistance was primarily in the form of emergency humanitarian aid. Since then, its focus has shifted toward technical aid for human resources development in support of market economy development. Japan has earmarked $1.2 billion for loans through the Export-Import Bank for various projects to develop telecommunications, energy supply, and small-to-medium enterprises as well as to privatized corporations. Japan has also pledged $2.9 billion for trade insurance to cover major Russian industries. These loans are designed both to assist Russia's effort to modernize its primary industries and to promote trade between Russia and Japan. Japan has also provided assistance for building facilities to store the nuclear materials removed from warheads. In Vladivostok, a plant is being constructed with Japan's assistance for processing liquid radioactive waste.

Russia's Far Eastern regions receive priority attention in Tokyo. Since 1993, Japan has opened consulates-general in Vladivostok and Khabarovsk and a branch of its Khabarovsk consulate general in Yuzhno-Sakhalinsk. Tokyo has pledged $500 million in Export-Import Bank loans in this region, another $200 million in Export-Import Bank loans to support the modernization of communication links between Moscow and Khabarovsk, and $50 million for the establishment of a regional enterprise fund for small- and medium-sized enterprises in Eastern Siberia and the Russian Far East. In addition, Tokyo supports the expansion of local contacts between the two countries. In this context, since 1993, the Japan-Russian Far East Governors' Conference has been meeting annually. In November 1992, local governments and major industries in the Japanese prefectures facing the Sea of Japan set up a Liaison Council for Japan Sea Rim Regional Cooperation with the support of the government in Tokyo. A year later, the Council hosted a Japan-Russian Far East Governors' Conference. The governors of sixteen Japanese prefectures and five Russian Far East regions who attended the conference agreed to meet annually to discuss ways to promote economic and technical cooperation between the two countries with a focus on the development of the Russian Far East.

In addition, Tokyo has disbursed or committed funds for humanitarian assistance in this region. About 60 million yen in humanitarian aid was extended to the residents of the Northern Territories in the aftermath of the earthquake off the Pacific coasts of the islands in October 1994. Tokyo provided additional humanitarian assistance, including setting up a temporary clinic on the island of Shikotan in October 1995.[29] Tokyo also extended 125 million yen in humanitarian assistance to Sakhalin in the wake of the devastating earthquake in the northern area of the island territory on May 27, 1995. In 1996, Japan began technical assistance programs for the governments of Khabarovsk and the Primorskiy region, with a focus on the development of stock markets, local industry, public housing, municipal finance, and energy resources.

Japan has also been willing to extend cooperation and assistance to Russia in curbing environmental problems in the Russian Far East and in the ocean area between the two countries.[30] The most visible program concerns the disposal of radioactive wastes in the Sea of Japan. Following Moscow's acknowledgment in 1993 that from 1959 to 1992 the Soviet Union had dumped radioactive wastes in the North Sea and the Far Eastern seas and the Russian Pacific Fleet had also dumped radioactive waste material in the Sea of Japan in 1992, Russia, Japan, South Korea, and the International Atomic Energy Agency (IAEA) jointly studied the environmental impact of those activities.[31] Japan is cooperating in the construction of radioactive material treatment facilities in Bolshoi Kamen near Vladivostok, as part of bilateral cooperation in nuclear weapons dismantlement. The facilities will have the capacity to dispose of 7,000 cubic meters of liquid radioactive waste. The need to expand bilateral cooperation in the environmental field was made amply clear by the oil spill by the Russian tanker *Nakhodka* off the coast of Shimane Prefecture in January 1997.[32]

In the area of military confidence-building, Russian-Japanese cooperation is at early stages. In 1992, Japanese defense officials began participating in Russian-Japanese policy planning consultations organized by the two countries' foreign ministries. A defense research exchange began in 1993. During President Yeltsin's visit to Tokyo in October 1993, the two countries concluded an agreement on maritime accident prevention. President Yeltsin also announced that Russia would withdraw all military troops other than border troops from the four disputed islands. In March 1996, Foreign Minister Primakov explained to Foreign Minister Ikeda that the current number of Russian military troops on the island territories was 3,500 and that there were no military troops on Shikotan Island. Bilateral defense dialogue also began in April 1996, when the Japanese Defense Agency director general visited Moscow, an event unprecedented during the entire Soviet period and the post-Soviet years. In July 1996, a Japanese Maritime Self-Defense Force escort, the *Kurama*, called in Vladivostok. This was reciprocated by a Russian destroyer's visit to Tokyo in June 1997. Another event of note was Japan's advance notification to Russia of the joint U.S.-Japanese military exercise in the Sea of Japan in November 1996. Moreover, Russian Defense Minister Igor Rodionov visited his counterpart Fumio Kyuma in Japan in May 1997. Rodionov called for expanded defense exchanges with Japan and gave Moscow's blessing to the new Guidelines for U.S.-Japan Defense Cooperation. He even suggested that there should eventually be a mechanism of defense cooperation that included all three countries.[33]

Finally, increased people-to-people contact is an essential part of the equation. In this context, the growing interest in mutual communication and cooperation among many local and provincial communities on both sides of the Sea of Japan is encouraging. Also welcome are the Japanese government's various technical assistance programs—for example, the establishment of five Japan Centers since 1994, the founding of the Regional Venture Fund in cooperation with the European Bank for Reconstruction and Development for small-to-medium private enterprises in the Far East and Eastern

Siberia, the dispatch of Japanese experts and training for Russian experts in Japan in human resources management since 1991, and the initiation of the Ministry of International Trade and Industry's Support Plan for Russian Trade and Industry in 1994, the so-called Hashimoto Plan.[34] Not only will these programs facilitate technology transfer from Japan to Russia, they will also promote the expansion of contacts between professionals of the two countries.

Another indication of bilateral interest in promoting human contact is the agreement announced in March 1997 to expand non-visa mutual visits by the citizens of both countries. By 1996, more than 2,300 people from both sides had participated in the program. The expanded program would involve not only former Japanese residents of the Northern Territories and reporters but also technical experts in agriculture and education.[35] These and other Japanese government assistance programs will contribute to expanded human contact between Russian and Japanese people, as will private-level technical cooperation and nongovernmental humanitarian assistance. Government-sponsored programs under the Hashimoto-Yeltsin Plan have been expanded since the second informal summit in Kawana in 1998.

The Moscow summit in November 1998 advanced the agenda of bilateral economic cooperation. The two sides signed an agreement on the promotion and protection of investments designed to improve the investment environment in Russia. The accord provides for most favored nation (MFN) treatment in admission of investments and in other areas, MFN and national treatment in such areas as all asset investment categories, returns and investment-related business activities and access to the courts, protection against losses to nationalization, expropriation or outbreak of hostilities, subrogation of rights, such as the right to make claims based on investment guarantees, freedom of remittance, and submission of investment disputes to arbitration. The agreement also calls for transparency in government decisions affecting foreign investors, and the prohibition of trade-related investment measures. The two sides also signed a number of agreements to promote tourism and cooperation in environmental protection, posts and telecommunications, science, and technology.[36]

Summary and Conclusions

The foregoing analysis points to many sources of change in the relations between Russia and Japan. They are found at global, regional, bilateral, and domestic levels. First, the end of the Cold War has thrust the major powers into an uncertain global and regional environment. Neither bipolar nor multipolar, the fluid configuration of major power relations forces Russia and Japan to take initiatives to reduce uncertainty by improving bilateral relations with the other major powers, including the United States and China. Second, there is growing consensus among the major powers that improved Russo-Japanese relations will contribute to the stability of the region. The serious nature of remaining obstacles, including the territorial dispute, probably helps to reduce exaggerated expectations on both sides and also allays other regional powers' fear that closer Russo-Japanese relations could threaten their security. Third, Russia wants to establish itself as a credible Asia-Pacific power, but it is painfully aware of its limited resources and sees Japan's economic power as a source of support for its transition to a market economy. Fourth, Japan increasingly wants to play a credible and influential international role, commensurate with its economic capacity, but realizes its strained relationship with Russia is a liability in the post–Cold War world in which the international community accepts Russia as a legitimate partner. Fifth, there is a coincidence of Russian and Japanese interests in developing the Russian Far East, a liability for capital-scarce Russia and an opportunity for resource-poor Japan. Sixth, there is growing local and provincial interest in international cooperation among Russia's Far Eastern communities and their counterparts in Japan.

A new paradigm is emerging. A mutually compatible Russian-Japanese relationship will be a minimum requirement for the stability of the Asia-Pacific region. A mutually supportive relationship will represent an even greater contribution to the construction of a peaceful Asia-Pacific. What is minimally required is bilateral cooperation, not in the sense of "harmony of interests" but in the sense of "mutual adjustment" of policies based on each country's basic interests.[37] Short of reciprocal admiration and overflowing friendship,

Russia and Japan must develop a mutually compatible relationship. This will be possible if and only if Russia becomes a democratic society with a market economy. Russia's successful transformation into a market democracy will enable the two countries to develop bilateral relations at socio-economic levels, beyond official ties that themselves remain limited. Russia, with an open market economy, will be able to take advantage of its natural resources and advanced technology as sources of export earnings, as well as Japan's capital and technological inputs for the economic development and modernization of Russia.

The most important test of the paradigm shift in the Russo-Japanese relations is whether the two countries can effectively cooperate and facilitate each side's attempt to develop a legitimate and credible regional role. There remains a great deal of uncertainty in Asia-Pacific, but improved Russo-Japanese relations will help to remove some of it. Russia and Japan finally appear ready to free themselves from the shackles of history and to develop a mutually compatible relationship.

Notes

1. The "end of geography" refers to the emergence of a borderless world economy through transnational interdependence of national and regional economies.

2. For a detailed exploration of the uncertain balance of power in Asia, see Paul Dibb, *Toward a New Balance of Power in Asia,* Adelphi Paper 295, London: International Institute for Strategic Studies, 1995.

3. See Tsuneo Akaha, "Russia in Asia in 1994," *Asian Survey,* vol. 35 (January 1995), pp. 100–110, and Tsuneo Akaha, "Russia and Asia in 1995," *Asian Survey,* vol. 36 (January 1996), pp. 100–108.

4. Wolf Mendl, *Japan's Asia Policy: Regional Security and Global Interests,* London: Routledge, 1995, p. 61.

5. For Japanese defense analysts' view of changing Sino-Russian security relations, see *Higashi-ajia Senryaku Gaikyo, 1996–97,* Tokyo: The National Institute for Defense Studies, 1997, pp. 102–103 and 114–118.

6. The survey was conducted by the Institute of History, Archaeology, and Ethnography in Vladivostok. Nikolai G. Shcherbina, "The Reac-

tion to the Foreign Presence in the Primorsky Region," a report prepared for the Monterey Institute of International Studies' Center for East Asian Studies, 1994, pp. 7–9.

7. Tsuneo Akaha, "Contemporary Perceptions of Japan in the Russian Far East: A May 1997 Field Survey," paper presented at the conference on Russian-Japanese Relations, September 6–10, 1997, Princeton University, Princeton, New Jersey.

8. Sorifu Kohoshitsu, ed., *Seron Chosa*, Tokyo: Okurasho Insatsukyoku, 1996, pp. 27–34.

9. *Japan 1997: An International Comparison*, Tokyo: Japan Institute for Social and Economic Affairs, 1997, p. 17.

10. See, for example, Kazuo Ogawa and Kinji Hishiki, *Kan-nihonkai Keizaiken to Roshia Kyokuto Kaihatsu*, Tokyo: JETRO, 1994; Kazuo Ogawa and Takashi Murakami, *Mezameru Soren Kyokuto: Nihon no Hatasu Yakuwari*, Tokyo: Nihon Keizaihyoronsha, 1991; Yevgeny B. Kovrigin, "Problems of Resource Development in the Russian Far East," in Tsuneo Akaha, ed., *Politics and Economics in the Russian Far East: Changing Ties with Asia-Pacific*, London and New York: Routledge, 1997, pp. 70–86. For a more cautious view, see Tsuneo Akaha and Takashi Murakami, "Soviet/Russian-Japanese Economic Relations," in Tsuyoshi Hasegawa, Jonathan Haslam, and Andrew C. Kuchins, eds., *Russia and Japan: An Unresolved Dilemma between Distant Neighbors*, Berkeley: University of California International and Area Studies, 1993, pp. 161–186.

11. Tsuneo Akaha, Pavel A. Minakir, and Kunio Okada, "Economic Challenge in the Russian Far East," in Akaha, ed., *Politics and Economics in the Russian Far East*, pp. 49–69.

12. Viktor Ishaev, "Foreword," Pavel A. Minakir, ed., Gregory L. Freeze, ed. and trans., *The Russian Far East: An Economic Survey*, Khabarovsk: Institute of Economic Research, 1996, p. 7.

13. For an exploration of this theme more generally in the entire Northeast Asian region, see Tsuneo Akaha, "Northeast Asian Regionalism: State-directed Economic Interdependence?" *The Sejong Review*, vol. 3 (November 1995), pp. 81–112.

14. *Asahi Shimbun*, February 15, 1997, p. 12.

15. The obligation was provided for in Article 1 of the 1961 Soviet-DPRK Treaty of Friendship, Cooperation and Mutual Assistance. Since 1968, Moscow had interpreted this provision to apply only in cases of "unprovoked attack," but the 1995 notification made Moscow's intentions unequivocal and unmistakable.

16. "Japan and Russia in Northeast Asia: Building a Framework for Co-operation in the 21st Century," Report of the Workshop in Tainai, Niigata, July 29–30, 1997, Niigata, Economic Research Institute for Northeast Asia, 1997, pp. 2–3.

17. *Yomiuri Shimbun,* July 27, 1997, p. 2.

18. *Nikkei Shimbun,* July 29, 1997, p. 1.

19. *Yomiuri Shimbun,* August 8, 1997, p. 2.

20. *Asahi Shimbun,* November 2, 1997, p. 1.

21. *Asahi Shimbun,* November 3, 1997, p. 1.

22. For a background to this issue, see Nobuo Arai and Tsuyoshi Hasegawa, "The Russian Far East in Russo-Japanese Relations," in Akaha, ed., *Politics and Economics in the Russian Far East,* pp. 177–181.

23. *Asahi Shimbun,* December 31, 1997, p. 1.

24. *Asahi Shimbun,* November 5, 1997, p. 2.

25. Vasily Golovnin, "Yeltsin Waits for the Japanese Dragon," *Izvestia,* October 28, 1997, p. 3; *Asahi Shimbun,* November 3, 1997, p. 3.

26. The survey in Russia was conducted by the polling service Vox Populi. Five percent of the Russian respondents said the Habomais and Shikotan should be transferred to Japanese sovereignty. This option was favored by 35 percent of the Japanese respondents, while 28 percent believed all four islands should be returned to Japan. (*Asahi Shimbun,* November 17, 1998, p. 11.)

27. *Yomiuri Shimbun,* November 14, 1998, evening, p. 2.

28. For a full description of Japanese assistance programs for Russia, see "Japan's Assistance Programs for Russia," available at the Japanese foreign ministry's home page: http://www2.nttca.com:8010/info-mofa/jr/assist/index.html. (November 15, 1997).

29. In the aftermath of the October 1994 earthquake off the Northern Territories, Japan set up a temporary medical facility in Shikotan to treat the wounded. Japan sent medical supplies, staff, and tents as part of the humanitarian relief aid.

30. For an examination of the environmental situation in Russia's Far Eastern regions and its implications for international cooperation, see Tsuneo Akaha, "The Environmental Challenge in the Russian Far East," in Akaha, ed., *Politics and Economics in the Russian Far East,* pp. 120–134.

31. Ministry of Foreign Affairs, "Investigation of Environmental Radioactivity in Waste Dumping Areas of the Far Eastern Sea Areas: Re-

sults from the First Japanese-Korean-Russian Joint Expedition 1994," Tokyo, July 1995.

32. It was reported that the tanker was exploded in order to hide the traces of oil products worth about $3 million that had been stolen. Denis Dyomkin, Aleksandr Maltsev, Vadim Bratukhin, and Leonid Berres, "'Nakhodka' Has Left Many Spots," *Kommersant-Daily,* February 4, 1997, p. 6.

33. *Asahi Shimbun,* May 17, 1997, p. 1. China Daily reported that Rodionov even suggested holding tripartite military exercises between Russia, Japan, and the United States as a way to establish military cooperation among the three countries in the Asia Pacific region. *China Daily,* May 19, 1997, p. A11.

34. Ministry of Foreign Affairs, Secretariat of the Cooperation Committee, "Japan's Assistance to the New Independent States," Tokyo, March 1996, p. 5.

35. *Asahi Shimbun,* March 30, 1997, p. 2.

36. A summary of these agreements is available at the Japanese Foreign Ministry's website http://www.mofa.go.jp/region/europe/russia/pmv 9811/index.html (January 20, 1999).

37. For this definition of "cooperation," see Joseph Nye, *After Hegemony: Cooperation and Discord in the World Political Economy,* Princeton, NJ: Princeton University Press, 1984, p. 12.

CHAPTER 4

JAPAN'S VIEWS OF NORTHEAST ASIA REGIONAL ECONOMIC COOPERATION
Bilateral Priorities and Multilateral Experiments

*Stephen J. Anderson**

Introduction

AS A REGIONAL ZONE, NORTHEAST ASIA is only beginning to join in the economic dynamism of the greater Asia-Pacific Basin. While ASEAN has expanded membership among Southeast Asia countries

* This article is based on individual views of the author and reflects research largely completed as a Senior Research Associate at the Institute for Pacific Rim Studies of Temple University Japan. The author is currently a Commercial Attaché, U.S. Embassy, Beijing.

to ten governments, the Northeast Asian countries including Japan remain preoccupied with territorial, ideological, and cross-national disputes. Indeed, the nation-states closest to Japan are most often concerned with bilateral differences rather than with multilateral relations. Opinion leaders in Japan, in particular, are preoccupied with a hard line toward North Korea and persisting bilateral problems with their closest neighbors. Japan has placed limits on the rapid expansion of multilateral regional cooperation.

This paper explores the bilateral priorities and multilateral experiments of Japan in the Northeast Asia region. My central argument is that Japanese leaders have begun cooperative experiments calling for "Asian" views or proposing specific, limited goals through regional initiatives, but the top Japanese priorities remain managing and responding to changes in bilateral relations. In other words, Japan is not exercising broad international leadership and tends to emphasize its bilateral initiatives. As Japan's economic malaise continues, bilateral priorities are becoming even more pronounced. Optimism has faded about autonomous Japanese initiatives. The dominant views that emerge are those of a Japan emphasizing bilateral relations in foreign policy and corporate economic strategies, rather than broad multilateral initiatives.

To prepare for the new millennium, Japanese leaders are exploring solutions to Northeast Asia problems that have some potential for multilateral efforts. Such problems will call for greater cooperation beyond country-to-country agreements, and the first signs of multilateral cooperation emerging from the pressing problems of food relief and nuclear energy for North Korea. A new set of financial proposals offered loans to address the Asian economic crisis, but without guarantee of acceptance or success. These experiments, along with various stalled projects and lingering territorial difficulties, have suffered from continuing skepticism in Japan about the pace of regional cooperation efforts in Northeast Asia. The following review examines the leading bilateral relations and addresses some representative multilateral experiments that are arising in the Northeast Asian region.

Bilateral Priorities in Northeast Asia

In the past decade of change, Japan has maintained an alliance with the United States whose basis is intact and whose scope redefined. This strong alliance in geopolitics influences relations throughout the region and has an impact on the bilateral relations among all actors in this area. The most important relations may be those affected by the 1997 agreements between China and Russia. Still, Japanese priorities for the long term in the economic realm have allowed a broadening of ties with neighboring countries, perhaps especially through the APEC initiatives.[1] Given its umbrella emphasis on security and economic ties to the United States, Japanese actors have attempted to develop bilateral economic relations to an extensive degree with near neighbors.

The United States: Alliance Redefined

In the American relationship, some observers argue that material interests have replaced ideology as rationales for an alliance. The Ministry of Foreign Affairs duly records the high-level visits by the second Clinton administration renewing the partnership. MOFA notes that during the last of the series of visits: "Vice President (Al Gore) reaffirmed that Japan is a key ally of the United States and its closest partner in the Asia-Pacific region."[2] Yet the rationale for this partnership was not developed beyond the statements of the first Clinton administration and its "Nye Report," in which 100,000 troops were committed to the region. Some analysts have raised questions about these troop levels.[3]

A redefinition of the scope of regional security has proceeded over several years. In early 1997, the new secretary of defense William Cohen reasserted the need for these 100,000 troops in Asia. As a justification for this commitment, the material gains of economic vitality have tended to replace the Cold War-era statements about ideology. In April 1997, CINCPAC admiral Archie Clemens emphasized the flow of oil and products from this region.[4] The imminent problems of North Korea and longer-term concerns about

Hong Kong and Taiwan in their relations with the central government of the People's Republic of China have also occupied observers considering possible security threats in the region. Over 250,000 American personnel patrol the area that extends from the east coast of Africa to the west coast of America and stretches from the Arctic Ocean in the north to Antarctica in the south.

The June 1997 report on U.S.-Japan Defense Cooperation has new implications for economic cooperation in the region.[5] Japan committed itself to acting broadly in the region, even outside of Japanese territory. On the question of how to respond to a contingency near Japan, proposed measures include: (1) humanitarian operations; (2) actions to ensure the effectiveness of economic sanctions; (3) operations to evacuate civilians and noncombatants; and (4) Japan's support of U.S. forces' operations. The mobilization of Self-Defense Forces (SDF) personnel is also proposed in connection with logistical support for U.S. forces. Activities will include making available commercial airports and harbors, supplying goods to U.S. vessels and aircraft at SDF or commercial facilities, maritime transportation to and from U.S. vessels on the high seas, patrolling and monitoring by the SDF, and exchanging intelligence related to these activities. On logistical support, the report specifies "using private-sector capabilities in a proper manner" in addition to those of the central and local governments. At the same time it points out, "it is expected that both Japan and the U.S., in their respective judgments, will appropriately reflect this in concrete policy measures," and in effect asks for Japan to prepare appropriate legislation.[6] The report also proposes that Japan and the United States, after the review of the guidelines is complete, proceed with studies on a joint operational plan and a mutual cooperation program.

As defense cooperation is reaffirmed, the economic relationship between Japan and America is reaching maturity. Bilateral trade and investment between the two continue to dwarf other partners; Japan exported 27.3 percent and imported 22.4 percent of its total market through trade with the United States in 1995.[7] However, the rise of Asian partners and regional integration are high on the agenda of MITI and other agencies. The MITI *White Paper on International Trade* emphasizes the increasing proportion of economic growth and trade in East Asia and marks a shift in balance through its emphasis on the region.[8] Thus far this shift has not sought to exclude the United States, despite recent emphasis on security rather than economic issues.

As the relative share of bilateral economic activity with America declines, Japanese officials increasingly seek to emphasize multilateral efforts. MITI writes that "economic effects of regional integration, the aspects such as the promotion of direct investment and international harmonization of systems, as well as trade effects, such as market expansion resulting from economies of scale, are attracting attention."[9] But in all of these moves, an openness to the world and coordination with the United States remains critical. The pressing bilateral relations with Korea have led to KEDO and are addressed below among other similar experiments. From this vantage point, I turn to Japan's bilateral relations with other neighbors.

Greater China in Northeast Asia

Japan and China must overcome historical difficulties in seeking economic cooperation. The two countries have a range of disputes that affect economic interests that they share in the region. Wartime history, domestic instability, and territorial disputes influence the bilateral relationship. As Hong Kong reversion and Taiwan independence movements gained attention, bilateral difficulties arose despite common economic interests. In addition, as fiscal problems have mounted in Japan, growth in foreign aid flows have slowed slightly.

With energy and national sovereignty at stake, the Sino-Japanese territorial disputes have intensified.[10] The disputed islands that lie between Okinawa and Taiwan, called *Senkaku* by the Japanese and *Diaoyu* by the Chinese, first became controversial in 1968 when potential oil deposits were identified. While diplomats sought quiet solutions, radicals built a lighthouse on Uotsuri, a small island in the disputed territory that is jointly claimed but solely patrolled by Japan. The 1996 drowning death of a Hong Kong protester near the islands raised the stakes, and again on May 6, 1997, the dispute became a focus. A group of Japanese politicians including Shingo

Nishimura, a Diet member then of the New Frontier Party (NFP) and now of the Liberal Party (LP), landed on Uotsuri and raised the Japanese flag. The Nationalist author and now govener of Tokyo, Shintaro Ishihara, who accompanied the politicians on their venture, claimed that Japan has sovereignty over the islands and that it is not necessary for Japan to hold consultations with other countries on the issue. In response, on May 26 a group from Hong Kong and Taiwan attempted to land on Uotsuri, but were stopped by Japanese coast guard vessels. In the future, Japanese observers expect further protests.

Officially, Japanese and Chinese diplomats are seeking to settle the issue through negotiations. Japan's Ministry of Foreign Affairs contends that the issue was not raised until the 1970s and that the mainland Chinese (PRC) claim to the Senkaku chain is new.[11] On the other hand, PRC Foreign Ministry spokesman Cui Tiankai has said that the Diaoyu islands have been an integral part of Chinese territories since ancient times. The PRC demands that the Japanese government take measures to prevent the repeat of any infringement upon PRC sovereignty and damage to Sino-Japanese relations.[12] Japan must contend with such claims in the aftermath of a 1998 summit where Chairman Jiang Zemin challenged Japan to make a written apology for its wartime actions equivalent to that offered to South Korea. The PRC is sensitive to any Japanese revision of history, and Beijing is not alone.

Taiwan also has protested Japan's approach to settling wartime accounts. Japanese groups have sought to offer "atonement money" from a government-initiated private fund in order to compensate women from Taiwan who were forced into sexual servitude before and during World War II. Indeed, on May 4, 1997, the Asian Women's Fund ran half-page advertisements in Taiwan's three major dailies inviting those who had been victims of the practice to apply for the money. However, instead of resolving the issue, the Japanese efforts have triggered outrage and protests. Taiwan's foreign ministry, meanwhile, has called "on the Japanese government to squarely face our stance and to speedily take effective measures to enable the victims to obtain reasonable compensation and consolation and to solve this unfortunate issue in history."[13] The settlement of wartime accounts remains difficult for Japan.

Regarding China as a whole, Japan must also face the geopolitical shift that includes closer cooperation with the Russian Federation (RF). In April 1997, PRC chairman Jiang Zemin and RF president Boris Yeltsin signed a PRC-RF Joint Declaration on Multipolar World and Formation of a New International Order. The Russian newspaper *Izvestia* wrote that the multipolar world idea was initially developed by the PRC and now has been adopted by the RF because both countries are concerned with foreign military alliances stepping up their activities near their respective borders, namely NATO and the U.S.-Japan alliance.[14] PRC political scientists are studying alleged U.S. efforts to contain the PRC, while PRC diplomats in private talks with RF colleagues urge them to be tougher on the NATO expansion issue. In *Izvestia*, one analyst observed that the present-day absence of ideological rivalry between the two countries paradoxically makes the development of RF-PRC relations an easier task than in the past.[15] As for Japan, the implications are that relations with China may be countered by balancing in relations with Russia.

Japan continues to place China high on its list of economic partners and foreign aid recipients. In 1995, China accounted for 10 percent of Japan's imports (over 15 percent if Taiwan and Hong Kong are included) and foreign investment reached $8.7 billion or 2 percent of Japan's total. China has long led the list of foreign aid recipients ($1.38 billion disbursed in 1995), but there are signs of decline.[16] As the yen fluctuated relative to the dollar and economic recovery faced delay, Japan's economic tools were limited. Pressure to use aid as a diplomatic tool then increased.[17] On June 3, 1997, the Japanese government announced a 10 percent cut in official development assistance (ODA), which resulted in reduced bilateral aid to China in FY 1998.[18] Though a reduction from $1.5 billion to $1.35 billion reversed the growth of disbursements, the level of loan aid to China remains the largest in the Japanese foreign assistance portfolios.

Coastal special economic zones mark a rise in regions of Japanese involvement in China. As early as September 1992, Yuichiro Nagatomi, acting as an economic diplomat, began to emphasize areas such as Dalian, Shenzen, and Huanan for Japanese investment.[19]

The continued development, especially in the Dalian area where perhaps a third of foreign corporations and a large part of the foreign community are Japanese, shows promise of bilateral economic relations between the two countries.

Russia in Northeast Asia

Japan's relations with Russia are still hampered by the unresolved dispute over the so-called Northern Territories. Since the end of the Cold War, negotiations have continued and a special arrangement has allowed visits without a visa between residents of the Russian Far East and former Japanese residents of the disputed islands and a few others.[20] The difficulties, however, remain formidable.

Japan's diplomats are making efforts to explore options.[21] In 1993, Russian-Japanese relations appeared to turn a corner. Following the summit in October 1993, Russian President Boris Yeltsin and Japanese Prime Minister Morihiro Hosokawa signed the Tokyo Declaration, in which they recognized the need to overcome the difficult past, acknowledged the existence of the territorial dispute over the Habomai, Shikotan, Kunashiri, and Etorofu islands, and pledged to strive for the conclusion of a peace treaty by resolving the territorial question on the basis of law and order. Russia's domestic problems and Yeltsin's health have frustrated Japanese efforts to reactivate Japan-Russia negotiations on fishing and economic exchange in the Northern Territories, but there have been some signs of improvement in bilateral ties. Shortly after the G-7 Summit in Denver in late June 1997, Tokyo became visibly flexible in its approach. Prime Minister Ryutaro Hashimoto issued three principles—trust, mutual benefits, and long-term view—as the basis upon which to improve relations between Tokyo and Moscow. At the informal summit in the Siberian city of Krasnoyarsk in November 1997, Yeltsin and Hashimoto pledged to do their best to conclude a peace treaty by the year 2000. This pledge was reaffirmed when the two leaders met again in Kawana, Japan, in April 1998. Moreover, at the summit between Yeltsin and Hashimoto's successor, Keizo Obuchi, the two sides reconfirmed their commitment to do their utmost to conclude a peace treaty by 2000. At the same time, the sides agreed to set up two committees within the framework of the bilateral committee on peace treaty, one committee to work on border delimitation and the other on joint economic activity.

A number of problems remain, however. Popular perceptions of Russia in Japan remain quite negative, and recent developments have not been helpful in this regard. On the west coast of Japan, a major oil spill affected relations with Russia. On January 2, 1997, the Russian oil tanker *Nakhodka* broke apart in high seas and spilled oil in the surrounding regions of western Japan.[22] Negative publicity surrounded the cleanup. *The Japan Times* wrote: "On Jan. 9, Moscow, which had remained silent over the disaster caused by its tanker transporting heavy oil to Russia from China, offered to cooperate in cleanup operations. Meanwhile, the oil spread to shorelines in five prefectures along the Sea of Japan."[23] Environmental damage spread, and water intake at nuclear power plants required special protection. Skepticism on the Japanese side has grown about overall economic development because compensation for the cleanup and damages must now be settled. The accident added to difficulties in the broader relationship, leading some weekly magazines to suggest a linkage between the return of the Northern Territories and compensation for damages.[24]

On the economic front, a joint Japan-Russian commission, the "Japan-Russian Federation Inter-Governmental Commission on Trade and Economic Problems," seeks progress on broad economic issues. MOFA reports that three groups began meeting in Moscow in 1995, including a sub-commission on economic relations with Russia's Far Eastern region. In March 1996, Foreign Minister Ikeda and First Deputy Prime Minister Soskovets adopted the joint report prepared by the three sub-commission groups, which includes concrete proposals for enhancing the economic relations between the two countries. At a meeting of the full commission, progress appeared possible: "Japan also confirmed its policy of attaching importance to strengthening relations with Russia's Far Eastern region through a number of projects in the region, such as development and production of oil and natural gas on the Sakhalin continental shelf and Far Eastern forestry resources development."[25] At the end of 1998, former prime minister Ryutaro Hashimoto agreed to act as special envoy in dealings with Russia and new prime minister Keizo Obuchi confirmed this position in his speeches to the Diet.

Japanese observers recognize that Russia seeks to join the economic dynamism of the region, but Japan has yet to commit major efforts in support of its participation. From the Vladivostok speech by Gorbachev to current efforts by Yeltsin, Russia's aim has been mainly to increase interactions. RF president Boris Yeltsin and PRC chairman Jiang Zemin, on his official 1997 visit to Russia in particular, produced the joint RF-PRC Declaration on Multipolar World that resists hegemony under America. Russian observers have maintained that the RF just has to break through to the PRC and the other Asia markets the same way as the West expands its presence in Eastern Europe. Two rounds of April 1997 summit talks between China and Russia touched on economic, border, and nuclear energy issues, and in 1998 PRC Chairman Jiang visited President Yeltsin prior to a trip to Japan. According to the Russian presidential press secretary, during the talks President Yeltsin favorably commented on joint projects such as economic and nuclear energy cooperation and the idea of a trans-Asian Tomsk-Shanghai gas pipe-line.[26] However, Japan has yet to announce direct involvement in this type of project.

Regarding Korea, Japanese sources are not vocal about Russian contributions toward maintaining stability on the Korean peninsula. A group of Russian researchers, seeking the development of Siberia and its coastal areas, argue that Russia needs Korean participation and thus reunification of Korea. These analysts believe that Moscow could be very helpful in the transition period to a reunified Korea, where North Koreans will have to adjust to new economic, political, and social realities. But Japan has placed emphasis on first solving the problems of nuclear energy, in line with the United States and the Korean Peninsula Energy Development Organization (KEDO). All Japanese efforts start with KEDO in mind.

Despite criticism from Russia and elsewhere, Japan has largely supported U.S. efforts to approach North Korea. The steps of the Clinton administration aimed at improving relations with North Korea create a certain apprehension in the ruling circles of Russia, because KEDO activities and the four-power talks initiative are perceived as detrimental to Russian interests. According to some reports, Russian officials complain in private conversations that U.S. diplomacy is pushing Moscow aside in a country where the Soviet Union has spent a great deal of time, money, and effort. Russian opposition figures, as well as many scholars and journalists, actively oppose Washington's policies vis-à-vis North Korea. Despite these Russian critics, Japan has been insistent in its effort to resolve the multilateral dilemmas on the Korean peninsula, and seeks consistency in its bilateral relations with both Koreas.

Korean Relations in Northeast Asia

Japan and the Republic of Korea (ROK or South Korea) have overcome recurring problems of history, territory, and economics to seek a new cooperation. Security and economic cooperation is increasing, and the symbolic goal of jointly hosting the 2002 World Cup gives rise to optimism about the future. In May 1997, regarding security in Northeast Asia, ROK vice prime minister Kwon O-kie told Japanese reporters that he proposed a Northeast Asian version of the Organization for Security and Cooperation in Europe (OSCE) as a multilateral security institution, and suggested that Japan's and Russia's participation in the Korean peace talks could provide such a mechanism.[27] While such experiments are being considered, the economic relationship has matured in industries such as the manufacture of semiconductors, consumer electronics, automobiles, and computers.

The Republic of Korea is Japan's second largest export market. Though only a quarter of the U.S. market, ROK imports over $30 billion each year and ranks ahead of Taiwan, Hong Kong, Singapore, and China.[28] In certain areas of technology, Korea has begun to rival Japan and thus shift the competition. At the same time, the problems of technology transfer and the "flying geese" approach used by Japan have left Korean partners at a disadvantage in the economic relationship. Japan faces criticism for not providing adequate openness to new technology and placing all of Asia in a position of dependence in seeking Japan's know-how.[29] The economic relationships are complicated by technological competitiveness.

Economic cooperation between Japan and the Republic of Korea is often focused on their common interest in the north. The problems related to the Democratic People's Republic of Korea (DPRK) have given rise to a common agenda in seeking immediate practical solutions.

Japan's views of the rise of Kim Jong Il in the North fall within a narrowing range. On the one hand, sympathetic writers have long held that the DPRK succession will be stable and Kim Jong Il can retain control. In 1992, after his visit to Korea as a journalist and professor, Tadashi Takahashi wrote that ideological control over the inhabitants north of the DMZ would take a long period to overcome.[30] "But if Japan and the North reach an agreement that differs in the least from that between Japan and the South, Seoul will protest," and in turn Pyongyang will then raise its stakes.[31] This need for balance has led to the use of outside arbiters such as the United States. On the other hand, the evidence of military and espionage cases involving agents from the North has led to growing intransigence and greater fears in Japan. In May 1997, Taku Yamazaki, chairman of the Policy Research Council and a leader of the ruling LDP, called for a quick resumption of Japan-DPRK negotiations, including those on the DPRK's suspected kidnapping of Japanese civilians.[32] The implication was that such problems must be addressed to respond to public protest and domestic critics within Japan.

Japan's views of the Korean peninsula are under scrutiny in the Republic of Korea. Kwon O-kie stated in May 1997 that Japan should be stricter about food aid to the DPRK and that for Japan to provide aid to the DPRK for humanitarian reasons would seem odd in light of the suspected abductions of Japanese civilians by the DPRK.[33] Japanese officials involved with the Tokyo talks have said that the United States and the ROK do not plan to give large-scale food aid to the DPRK until the Pyongyang government agrees to open peace talks, and Japan does not plan to give any aid at all until ties with the DPRK are normalized.

Japan stood firm in May 1997 when it denied famine relief requested by the United Nations' Secretary General. Foreign Minister Ikeda reported to UN Secretary General Kofi Annan that suspicions about the abduction of Japanese nationals and drug smuggling by North Koreans have kept Tokyo cautious about providing such aid. The number of suspected DPRK kidnappings in the 1970s and 1980s stands at seven cases involving 10 Japanese nationals, where kidnap victims may have been used to train DPRK agents to pose as Japanese in operations abroad. Further, two pro-Pyongyang ethnic Koreans were formally charged with smuggling 60 kilograms (132 pounds) of amphetamines on a freighter bound for Japan from the DPRK.[34] Further progress in negotiations is also hampered by contradictory information about the famine.[35]

The improvement of Japanese-ROK relations may assist Japan on the Korean peninsula. The election of President Kim Dae Jung and subsequent efforts by the South to improve relations with the North are in line with efforts in Japanese diplomacy. Even military provocations by parties in the DPRK may have little impact on this long-term trend, although Japan has responded with alarm. Missile firings are dismissed by some Japanese as failed satellite launches, and sinkings of DPRK submarines only underscore the lack of sophistication of the threats posed to regional security. With the Japanese support of theater-missile defense, the freezing of normalization talks, and stoppage of food aid, momentary setbacks have occurred. But signs have appeared that these are anomalies rather than long-term breaks in the efforts to approach North Korea.[36]

Japanese diplomats have been seeking steady confidence-building measures and mutual understanding through DPRK negotiations. Small steps have been taken in humanitarian exchange and in the discussion of visits between Japan and North Korea. Food aid, further visits, and more confidence-building remain on the agenda.

First, food aid is still a possibility. Japanese Prime Minister Ryutaro Hashimoto hinted for the first time to ROK reporters on May 29, 1997 that Japan might end its adamant refusal to provide food aid to the DPRK. Hashimoto's statement indicated that Japan wanted to avoid being isolated from the United States, the ROK, and European countries that had already extended food aid to the DPRK. At the same time, however, Hashimoto cited several obstacles.

Second, visits by Japanese wives began. With about 1,800 Japanese wives in the DPRK, Prime Minister Hashimoto said that he "cannot accept a situation in which only 10 or 20 of those Japanese women are allowed to visit their home country while the rest are forbidden even to write letters home." For the first time in 40 years, the DPRK allowed a limited number of Japanese wives in the DPRK to visit their relatives in Japan in 1998. However, the process was slow and the exact numbers were limited. Many more cases need resolution.

Third, negotiations themselves are a mark of progress. An important element is the confidence-building that is needed to support regular contacts, including the KEDO efforts. Itaru Umezu, KEDO Deputy Executive Director, noted: "North Koreans are seriously learning how things work in international society and transaction" in an educational process pursued daily through negotiations over time.[37] The multilateral experiments of KEDO and similar efforts are critical steps toward realizing today's visions of cooperation.

Multilateral Experiments

Multilateral economic cooperation, as seen from Japan, is an experiment for the countries of Northeast Asia. In contrast to the robust efforts of ASEAN to expand to ten members and to broaden functions from economics to security, all initiatives in regional cooperation in Northeast Asia are new and must start from scratch. Robert Scalapino notes that "natural economic territories" (NETs) are emerging, and Akihiko Tanaka has responded that a reversion to "maritime medievalism" in East Asia may allow for economic activities to reestablish "natural ties."[38] Tanaka notes the successes of APEC and the ASEAN Regional Forum (ARF) in the greater region and is optimistic that the success of KEDO can open itself to China and Russia as the basis of future cooperation in Northeast Asia. Indeed, the "Asian" element (perhaps free of American involvement) in all of these experiments is gaining emphasis among scholars and policy experts within Japan.

Japanese views of multilateral ventures are of at least two types. First, those seeking independence from the United States and leadership in Asian and global affairs (whom I regard as optimists) are proponents of greater autonomy for Japan, whose mission is to assert an era of independence and the start of multilateral governance. Second, those emphasizing the reliance on bilateral relations particularly with the United States (whom I regard as skeptics) are advocates of building on existing alliances and special relationships to advance Japanese national interests. The former point to KEDO and possible precedents in Southeast Asia as areas of increasing Japanese influence, while the latter regard these ventures only as experiments.

KEDO Unique among Governments

KEDO is the most prominent example in Northeast Asia of a working effort toward multilateral cooperation. Built on an agreement reached in Geneva in 1994, KEDO has a specific goal, namely to provide the DPRK with two 1000-megawatt light water reactors and 500,000 tons of heavy fuel oil a year in exchange for a freeze and eventual dismantling of the DPRK nuclear program. KEDO executive director Stephen W. Bosworth noted in 1997 that KEDO was the only effort where three governments dealt with the DPRK and acted jointly in North Asia.[39] In an overview from the Japanese side, ambassador Hiromoto Seki noted that North Korea must be dealt with according to three principles: 1) encouraging the peace and stability of the Korean Peninsula over the long term; 2) keeping North Korea informed of KEDO's intentions to prevent misunderstandings; and 3) encouraging North Koreans who genuinely seek improved relations in the international community.[40]

Through KEDO, Japanese experts have joined the increasingly regular visits to North Korea. Beginning on April 9, 1997, a large-scale delegation comprised of representatives from KEDO as well as government officials from Seoul, Tokyo, and Washington made a week-long visit to the DPRK for working-level talks on the construction of the two light-water nuclear reactors.[41] The 54-member delegation reached the DPRK port of Yanghwa by sea. This was the first time such a delegation had not traveled to North Korea by plane via Beijing. Yanghwa is located in the vicinity of Sinpo, the site for the nuclear power plant. Construction began by late 1997, and the port was crowded with Japanese and ROK engineers and construction equipment ferried to the reactor construction site. But problems remain—construction once halted when North Korean staff found a crumpled newspaper image of DPRK leaders in a trash can. Considerable obstacles remain for the success of this project.

Beyond KEDO

Besides KEDO, the rise of experiments such as nongovernmental efforts and food aid programs lead to optimism about multilateral efforts in the region. Japanese nongovernmental groups, such as the Economic Research Institute for Northeast Asia (ERINA) in Niigata, seek to study the "great positive changes" in the region; such groups are also building on the pioneering first steps under Saburo Okita that led to the formation of the Northeast Asia Economic Forum. Another experiment is the joint team on Energy, Security and Environment in Northeast Asia (ESENA), which has commissioned papers on energy and security links in Northeast Asia.[42] But broad government support is lacking. Governmental efforts to provide food aid to the DPRK have included European involvement, and in 1997 the European Union sent 155,000 tons to meet three-quarters of the request of the United Nations World Food Program for North Korea.[43] In 1999, Japan will launch a "Miyazawa Initiative" of up to $30 billion in loans to overcome Asian economic difficulties. These efforts indicate a gradual expansion of international involvement in the many experiments in assisting the region in general and North Korea in particular.

The Japanese views of these experiments may again be divided into those of the optimistic autonomists and those of the skeptical bilateralists. The interpretations of past attempts at cooperation, such as the Tumen River Project, may also be colored by such perspectives. The pessimists point to planners drawing on the United Nations Development Program and to the lack of support, such as from Japan and other potential major contributors, for the project. The optimists counter with the view that the notions of the Tumen River Economic Development Area (TREDA) are spin-offs from earlier experiments. The glass is either half empty or half full for both of these camps, and outside observers note that the lack of

Japanese investment, as well as inexperience and instability around North Korea, hamper the Tumen River Project.[44] Japan will remain outside of such projects until problems with the DPRK are resolved.

On the one hand, autonomists/optimists see these efforts as areas where Japan can assert Asian or multilateral visions of their independence in world affairs. Japanese diplomats can apply what the ministry of finance spokesman has labeled an era of multilateralism. The MOF has actually been seeking ways to avoid concessions and even to refuse negotiations with former allies who had benefited from bilateral relations, most directly with the United States. In particular, this has meant that trade disputes such as the Kodak-Fuji case or other issues are deflected into multilateral settings. The optimists may someday prevail, but this independence is not official policy and is discouraged by central authorities in business as well.

On the other hand, bilateralists/skeptics see such efforts at multilateral autonomy as areas where Japan can be harmed or isolated in world affairs. Japanese diplomats worry about their limited capacity to gain concessions and support in world bodies that seek to adjudicate the bilateral negotiations of the past. Thus, there may be perils in multilateral strategies, whether with powerful benefactors such as the United States or rising beneficiaries such as Indonesia. In particular cases such as trade in film, transport, or telecommunications with America or automobiles with Indonesia, settlements were difficult to procure from multilateral bodies.

Recent evidence in support of the skeptics was supplied by a simulation publicized in the *Sankei Shimbun*.[45] Yoshihisa Komori, a *Sankei* reporter, participated in a three-day crisis management simulation under the direction of the Massachusetts Institute of Technology (MIT). The simulation addressed Japan's security from 1996 to the year 2008, speculating on Japanese responses to a crisis in Asia if Japan no longer had a security treaty with the United States. About 50 people participated in the games, including academics involved with Japan-U.S. relations and Asian affairs and congressional staffers. The exercise consisted of role playing to represent the heads of specific countries and mock policy setting. The forecast that emerged had Japan, without a security treaty with the United

States, facing threats from China as well as Russia. Although it sought a renewal of the alliance with the United States, America would not oblige, thus forcing Japan to walk a tightrope between building an independent defense and pursuing multilateral security discussions.

As multilateral experiments continue in the region, Japan is also preparing its abilities to act independently in crises. For example, an "intelligence bureau" as well as a "crisis management headquarters" may greatly change the current Cabinet organization.[46] To link and consolidate the functions of "national security," "crisis management," and "intelligence," a full-scale study began in 1997 as part of administrative reforms. Specifically, the main elements included the following: 1) setting up an "intelligence or information bureau"; 2) reorganizing the National Security Office and a part of the Defense Agency and the Foreign Ministry, and then setting up an organ that has an overall coordinating function; and 3) establishing a "crisis management headquarters" (tentative name), which would have a deputy chief cabinet secretary-class "crisis management office" (also a tentative label). The plans also included specific study within the Conference on Administrative Reform (chaired by then prime minister Hashimoto) related to strengthening the cabinet functions in connection with the reorganization of the government bureaucracy.

Even with structural administrative changes, Japan is not prepared to exercise leadership in regional economic cooperation in the near future. A long-time observer of the Japanese political scene has written in regard to both ROK and Japan in East Asia that these countries, either alone or jointly, will not be effective at leadership in wide-ranging areas of international relations. He argues first that these governments will not commit a sufficient amount of resources; second, neither is independent of America and, increasingly, China, and third, these states cannot act jointly with sufficient mutual trust.[47] This viewpoint addresses Japan's limits in seeking broad multilateral initiatives and building institutions to channel such efforts.

Japan seeks regional leadership despite mounting economic difficulties. A late 1998 plan known as the Miyazawa Initiative offered up vast sums for the economic recovery of Asia.[48] Finance Minister

Kiichi Miyazawa proposed loaning an additional $30 billion in funds, with $3.4 billion by March 1999, under the first reports of the plan. But Japanese domestic problems and continued difficulties with economic growth raise questions about the will of a fragile coalition government under Prime Minister Keizo Obuchi. For now, this multilateral experiment in finance will have many pessimistic observers.

In time, the growing autonomy of Japan in world affairs may eclipse the reliance on past bilateral ties. A new regional order of balance of power and economic relations will require more broadly based relationships for all participants. Thus, a tension will likely rise between an emphasis on the newly emerging experiments with multilateral organizations and the still powerful bilateral relations. When grounded in an understanding of their limits as seen from Japan, the multilateral experiments will have a better chance of leading to truly robust institutions that support peace and stability in Northeast Asia.

Notes

Notes in this paper follow "Citing the Sites: MLA-Style Guidelines and Models for Documenting Internet Sources," version 1.3, for reference to Internet resources. <http://falcon.eku.edu/honors/beyond-mla/#citing_sites> (June 11, 1997). The last date in parentheses indicates a visit to the site to confirm the Internet document.

1. The 1995 Osaka meetings were an instance of such efforts. Stephen J. Anderson, "Can Japan Lead? APEC Summit Tests the Rich Man of Asia," *American Chamber of Commerce Journal,* November 1995, pp. 16–19. <http://ifrm.glocom.ac.jp/doc/a01.002.html> (January 11, 1999).

2. The statement continues: (On March 24, 1997, the) "visit of Vice President Al Gore was a vital step to build comprehensive and cooperative relations with the second Clinton Administration in the context of close high-level talks such as visits of Secretary of State Madeleine Albright in February, Secretary of the Treasury Robert Rubin and Secretary of Defense William Cohen in April, as well as the visit of Prime Minister Ryutaro Hashimoto to the United States in

late April. The Government of Japan believes that this visit has produced . . . results to further promote the balanced and cooperative relationship between Japan and the United States under the second Clinton Administration." From the Ministry of Foreign Affairs (MOFA) web site, <http://www.mofa.go.jp/press/c_s/gore.html> (June 3, 1997).

3. See, for example, Mike M. Mochizuki, "Japan and the Strategic Quadrangle," in Michael Mandelbaum, ed., *The Strategic Quadrangle in East Asia,* New York: Council on Foreign Relations, 1994.

4. Pacific Symposium Presentation by Admiral Archie Clemens, April 29, 1997, Honolulu, Hawaii, Commander in Chief, U.S. Pacific Fleet, <http://www.cpf.navy.mil/pages/pacsym40/index.htm> (June 3, 1997).

5. *Nihon Keizai Shimbun,* June 6, 1997, p. 1.

6. Ibid.

7. MITI figures, in *Japan 1997: An International Comparison,* Tokyo: Keizai Koho Center, December 1996, p. 56, Table 4–33.

8. See MITI "White Paper on International Trade." Summary available at web site, <http://www.jef.or.jp/news/wp1996/white1996con.html> (January 11, 1999).

9. Ibid.

10. Territorial disputes get media coverage in various publications; Japanese views are found in *The Japan Times,* including a map of Japan's claims at <http://www.japantimes.co.jp/special/islemap.html> (January 11, 1999).

11. "The fact that China expressed no objection to the status of the Islands being under the administration of the United States under Article III of the San Francisco Peace Treaty clearly indicates that China did not consider the Senkaku Islands as part of Taiwan. It was not until the latter half of 1970, when the question of the development of petroleum resources on the continental shelf of the East China Sea came to the surface, that the Government of China and Taiwan authorities began to raise questions regarding the Senkaku Islands." From Japan's ministry of foreign affairs, "The Basic View on the Sovereignty over the Senkaku Islands," <http://www.mofa.go.jp/region/asia-paci/senkaku/senkaku.html> (January 11, 1999).

12. "Diaoyu Isle an Integral Part of China," *Wen Hui Daily,* Beijing, April 30, 1997, p. A4, as reported by the Nautilus Institute, "NAPSNet Daily Report," May 1, 1997, <http://www.nautilus.org/napsnet/recent_daily_reports/05_97_reports/MAY01.html#item9> (June

4, 1997). The Japanese claims were described in English by The Weekly Post in a May 19 interview with Ishihara Shintaro, "Ishihara Speaks on Senkaku Island Issue," <http://206.217.210.33:80/weeklypost/970519/970519b.htm> (June 4, 1997).

13. *The Japan Times,* Weekly News Roundup, May 3–9, 1997, <http://www.japantimes.co.jp/wnr/wnrindex.html> (June 4, 1997).

14. Yuriy Savenkov, "Moscow and Beijing Urging for Friendly Coexistence," *Izvestia,* Moscow, April 24, 1997, as reported by the Nautilus Institute, "NAPSNet Daily Report," May 1, 1997, <http://www.nautilus.org/napsnet/ recent_daily_reports/05_97_reports/MAY05.html# item10> (June 4, 1997).

15. Ibid.

16. MITI and JICA figures, in *Japan 1997: An International Comparison,* Tokyo: Keizai Koho Center, December 1996, pp. 56, 57 and 64, Table 4–33, 5–11 and 5–13.

17. "Editorial: Time for Japan to Discuss ODA Strategy," *Sankei Shimbun,* June 9, 1997, p. 2, as translated by the American Embassy, Tokyo, Political Section, Office of Translation Services, Daily Summary of Japanese Press. The editor writes: "The importance of the ODA is its diplomatic role. For instance, whether Japan will extend its large scale yen loans (now offering the fourth yen-loan package) to a fifth or sixth term will be closely connected to a possibility that China will become a military threat in (*sic*) East Asia. Because of such a reason, should Japan provide as much aid as possible to China? What will Japan benefit from offering yen-loans, without resolving the territorial issue over the Senkaku Islands, as well as not correcting a Chinese prominent figure's statement interfering (*sic*) the domestic affairs: 'There still exist some militarists in Japan'." The Sankei writer urges greater weight for national interests in ODA decisions.

18. *Yomiuri Shimbun,* June 4, 1997, p. 1.

19. Yuichiro Nagatomi, "Speech at the PECC Plenary Session," September 24, 1992, p. 11.

20. "1,381 Japanese nationals visited the Northern Territories and 1,400 current Russian residents of the Northern Territories visited Japan during the period 1992–1995, which has resulted in an increase of friendship and understanding between the peoples of both countries." From the MOFA web site, <http://www.mofa.go.jp/jr/territory/index.html#IV> (June 4, 1997).

21. This paragraph was added by the editor to update the material on developments in Russian-Japanese relations.

22. See "Oil Spill," *The Japan Times,* Weekly Roundup, January 4–10, 1997, <http://www.japantimes.co.jp/wnr/1997/wnrindex97.html> (January 11, 1999).

23. Ibid.

24. "Editorial: Goldman Sachs Executive Scolds Japan," *The Weekly Post,* January 20–26, 1997, <http://206.217.210.33:80/weekly-post/970120/970120b.htm> (June 10, 1997).

25. Ministry of Foreign Affairs, "Japan's Policy on the Russian Federation," <http://www.mofa.go.jp/region/europe/russia/russia_policy. html > (January 11, 1999).

26. Sergey Makarov, "Russia and China warned the USA," *Kommersant-DAILY,* Moscow, April 24, 1997, p. 1, as reported by the Nautilus Institute, "NAPSNet Daily Report," May 5, 1997, <http:// www.nautilus.org/napsnet/recent_daily_reports/05_97_reports/ MAY05.html#item10> (June 4, 1997).

27. *Nihon Keizai Shimbun,* May 19, 1997, p. 8.

28. MITI 1995 figures, in *Japan 1997: An International Comparison,* Tokyo: Keizai Koho Center, 1996, p. 56, Table 4–33.

29. Walter Hatch and Kozo Yamamura, *Asia in Japan's Embrace,* Hong Kong: Cambridge University, 1996, especially Chapter Six, "Holding Technology," pp. 97–111.

30. Tadashi Takahashi, "A Scholar's Adventures in Kim-Kim Land," translation in *Japan Echo,* vol. 20, Special Issue, 1993, pp. 29–37 from "'Kimmu-kimmu Rando' Homonki" in *Chuokoron,* November 1992, pp. 214–229.

31. Ibid., p. 37.

32. "Japan's Liberal Democratic Party (LDP) Policy Research Council Head Urges Resumption of Japan-DPRK Intergovernmental Negotiations," *Asahi Shimbun,* May 13, 1997, p. 2, as reported by the Nautilus Institute, "NAPSNet Daily Report," May 5, 1997, <http://www.nautilus.org/napsnet/recent_daily_reports/05_97_re-ports/ MAY16.html#item15> (June 10, 1997).

33. "ROK Vice Prime Minister Understands Japan's Careful Stance on Food Aid to DPRK," *Nihon Keizai Shimbun,* May 19, 1997, p. 8.

34. "Ikeda Spurns UN Chief's Plea for Aid to NK," *Korea Times,* May 14, 1997, as reported by the Nautilus Institute, "NAPSNet Daily Report," May 5, 1997, <http://www.nautilus.org/napsnet/recent_ daily_reports/ 05_97_reports/MAY15.html#item10> (June 10, 1997).

35. Hajime Izumi, a professor and policy expert on Korea, argues that the areas of famine vary by region with Hamgyon, Ryanggan, and Chagan on the border with China hardest hit by disaster. ("Is Pyongyang Ready to Wage a 'Suicidal War'?" *The Daily Yomiuri,* May 20, 1997, p. 5.)

36. The Washington Post reported that Japan said it had resumed unofficial contacts with North Korea in a move to improve icy relations between the two countries. According to the report, after North Korea's surprise launch in August of what Japan said was a long-range ballistic missile, Tokyo decided to break off normalization talks with Pyongyang and suspended any food aid to the famine-stricken communist state. ("Japanese Extend Feelers to N. Korea," *Washington Post,* Tuesday, January 19, 1999, p. A14.)

37. "Seoul Hopes for Change of Heart by North Korea," *The Daily Yomiuri,* May 20, 1997, p. 5.

38. Akihiko Tanaka, "Contending Models of International Security in Asia-Pacific," paper for the international conference on "Greater China: Problems, Prospects and Policies," Open Learning Institute of Hong Kong, January 25–26, 1997.

39. "KEDO Only Game in Town," *The Daily Yomiuri,* May 20, 1997, p. 5.

40. "No Easy Way in Dealing with Threat to Peace," *The Daily Yomiuri,* May 20, 1997, p. 5.

41. "54-member KEDO Team to Visit NK via Sea Route for Talks on N-reactors," *The Korea Times,* April 4, 1997, as reported by the Nautilus Institute, "NAPSNet Daily Report," <http://www.nautilus.org/napsnet/recent_daily_reports/04_97_reports/APR07.html#item13> (June 10, 1997).

42. See on-going commissioned papers of ESENA available on the World Wide Web. <http://www.nautilus.org/esena/papers/papers.html> (June 10, 1997).

43. "Strategic Largesse: EU's Food Aid to North Korea Has Broader Political Goals," *Far Eastern Economic Review,* June 5, 1997, p. 21.

44. Daniel Aldrich, "If You Build It, They Will Come: A Cautionary Tale About the Tumen River Projects," *The Journal of East Asian Affairs,* vol. 11, no. 1 (Winter/Spring 1997), pp. 299–326.

45. "MIT-Controlled Simulation: What If There Were No Japan-US Security Treaty? Japan Would Face Threat from China and Russia; Would Be Forced to Walk Tightrope in Strengthening Its Own Defenses," *Sankei Shimbun,* May 29, 1997, p. 1, as translated by the

American Embassy, Tokyo, Political Section, Office of Translation Services, Daily Summary of Japanese Press.

46. "Japan's Establishment of 'Intelligence Bureau' to Strengthen Cabinet Functions; May Also Set up Crisis Management Headquarters," *Yomiuri Shimbun,* March 31, 1997, p. 1.

47. Haruhiro Fukui, "Korean and Japanese Leadership in Early Twenty-First Century East Asia," paper presented at the conference on the Leadership of East Asia in the 21st Century, Seoul, Republic of Korea, April 25–26, 1997.

48. "Help Yourself: Japan Plans to Spend $30 Billion to Assist Its Asian Neighbors," *Far Eastern Economic Review,* December 31, 1998 and January 7, 1999, p. 12–13.

CHAPTER 5

ECONOMIC AND SECURITY COOPERATION IN NORTHEAST ASIA
A Chinese Perspective

Weixing Hu

Introduction

CHINA'S PERCEPTION OF INTERNATIONAL cooperation has slowly evolved since its opening up twenty years ago. For a long time, Beijing showed little interest in regional cooperation and economic integration; however, as economic development and modernization become the driving force for Chinese foreign policy, Beijing has taken a more positive view of East Asian regional economic cooperation. Yet China still regards the degree and direction of interdependence with other countries as a sensitive issue. This is due to the fact that interdependence may eventually limit China's freedom in national economic management and foreign policy choice.

Several themes emerge from a review of Chinese literature on economic and security cooperation in East Asia. First, economic cooperation and regional integration are generally considered conducive to China's economic development and modernization. Second, despite the benefits of regional economic integration, the potential costs should be fully examined and necessary measures should be taken to minimize the negative consequences of regional integration. Third, Asian states should take a common stand on human rights and democratization to balance Western influence and establish a sense of an Asian community in international politics. Fourth, the nature of East Asian international relations is such that security issues are solved bilaterally, not by multilateral regimes. Fifth, no effective multilateral security regime can be formed unless every state in the region accepts its terms.

Beijing's views of East Asian economic and security cooperation are largely driven by its economic interests and regional security concerns. In this chapter, instead of a general discussion of China's policy toward Northeast Asia, I will examine China's evolving perspective on economic and security cooperation in Northeast Asia, highlighting the five themes just noted.

China's Interest in Regional Economic Cooperation

China's current positive position on regional economic cooperation is deeply rooted in its domestic politics and national policy of economic development. During the Deng Xiaoping era, the paramount leader mobilized the nation to focus on economic reforms and modernization. Deng believed that the objectives of rapid modernization should take precedence over all other objectives and that China's future was in successful modernization. In order to achieve a high rate of growth, social and political stability is indispensable, and the leadership has taken an extraordinarily hard line on demands for political liberalization. In the post-Deng era, this legacy still strongly influences Chinese politics and is likely to remain the political consensus shared by the Chinese elite. Jiang Zemin vows to continue

Deng's reforms and open door policy.[1] For most of the Chinese, the question is not whether Deng's reform policy can be carried on, but rather how to maintain the current high economic growth. Economic prosperity and improvement in living standards are extremely important for the current leadership, because it is on these key factors that the governing regime's legitimacy rests.

Based on the domestic political consensus and the need for economic development, China's foreign policy goal is to maintain a peaceful international environment for modernization and domestic stability. This goal has been consistent since the late 1970s. In dealing with other countries, China is now more concerned with economic interests. A prevalent opinion among Chinese scholars and policy advisors is that economic power is both a means and an end of foreign policy. The outcome of any international power struggle will be determined by the nations' "comprehensive national strength" in the world. In order to speed up economic development, China must actively participate in regional and world economic cooperation and integrate the Chinese economy into the global economic system.[2] China's economic ties with other Asian states will expand through economic cooperation.

China now trades more with Asia than with any other region in the world. In Asia, however, China trades mostly with Japan and Newly Industrialized Economies (NIEs). China's top ten trading partners, five of which are Northeast Asian states or entities, are Japan, Hong Kong, the United States, Taiwan, South Korea, the European Union, Singapore, Australia, Russia, and Canada. In 1997, China's total foreign trade reached US$325 billion, with exports of US$182.7 billion and imports of US$142.3 billion.[3] If the United States and Canada are included, more than 80 percent of foreign trade is with the Asian Pacific. If North America is excluded, then more than 60 percent of China's foreign trade is Asian bound, and more than 50 percent of its trade is with Northeast Asia (including Taiwan and Hong Kong).

Sino-Japanese trade reached US$60.8 billion in 1997. For five consecutive years, Japan has been China's largest trading partner and China has been Japan's second largest trading partner, next to the United States. China and South Korea have become each other's third largest trading partner. The trade between the two countries in 1981 was only US$220 million, but by 1997 it had reached US$24 billion following an average annual growth of 40 percent in recent years.[4] South Korea expects China to become its largest trading partner by the year 2000, with an estimated two-way trade of US$56 billion.[5] China's trade with Russia reached US$7.68 billion in 1993, but the following year it dropped to US$5.08 billion. In 1995, it rose again to US$5.46 billion. The 1996 bilateral trade with Russia was US$6.85 billion, a 25.4 percent increase from the previous year.[6] China's trade within the "China Economic Area" (China mainland, Hong Kong, and Taiwan) is growing faster than its trade with other countries. The Hong Kong Special Administrative Region (HKSAR) is the seventh largest trading entity in the world, and more than 80 percent of its trade is tightly linked with the mainland. Across the Taiwan Straits, China's trade with Taiwan grew from a mere US$77 million in 1979 to $17.8 billion in 1994. Despite the political clouds over the straits in 1997–98, the bilateral trade was maintained at the level of US$22 billion.

Foreign direct investment from Asian nations is critical for China's economic modernization. Currently, China receives more foreign direct investment from Asia than from any other region. East Asia's economic restructuring has caused Japan and NIEs to transfer and reorganize production, especially labor-intensive production, on a regional basis. Among the next-tier countries, China is an attractive place for foreign investment. In 1997 China attracted a total of US$45.26 billion foreign direct investment, an increase of 8.47 percent from the previous year.[7] The top five foreign investors in China are Hong Kong, Japan, the United States, Taiwan, and South Korea. Asian investments in China grew faster than U.S. and EU investment before the financial crisis started in 1997. Japan surpassed the United States in investment in China in 1996 and is now the second largest investor in China, after Hong Kong. South Korean businesses have invested more than US$2 billion in China, particularly in China's Shandong and Liaoning provinces. The military exercises in the Taiwan Straits in March 1996 did not scare away Taiwanese investors, and Taiwan's mainland investment amounted to US$3.48 billion in 1996.[8]

Over the last two decades China's economic reforms have paved the way for its integration with the Asian economic system. China's opening up to the outside world kept pace with the region's economic restructuring and integration. In the last decade, the East Asian economy enjoyed a higher growth rate than any other region in the world. This made regional economic restructuring possible. East Asia industrial restructuring was mainly driven by Japan and the Asian NIEs' rapidly increasing labor costs, currency appreciation, and growing transnational production networks. Moreover, trade liberalization and capital flow in regional countries (except North Korea) created a favorable environment for regional reorganization. After 1989, most Asian countries did not join the U.S.-led sanctions against China; rather, they seized the opportunity to quickly expand business in China. Businesses from Taiwan, Hong Kong, South Korea, and even Japan rushed to the Chinese market as Western countries continued economic sanctions against Beijing.

China's economic integration with the regional economy is promoted by both government policy and market forces. In 1979, Deng Xiaoping's open door policy created four Special Economic Zones (SEZs). Since then, China's opening has gradually spread from southern China to northern China and from the coastal provinces to inland provinces. This controlled opening up to the international market provided development opportunities for China and created several growth triangles along its coast. China's coastal manufacturing has been integrated with the regional division of labor. In many cases, Chinese labor is used to manufacture products from imported material with imported machinery and under foreign management. In the Pearl River Delta, Guangdong acts as Hong Kong's workshop and Hong Kong as Guangdong's shop window. Hong Kong's unique liberal trade policies provide a gateway for foreign access to southern China's rapidly growing market. A similar production pattern has emerged across the Straits between Taiwan and the mainland's Fujian province. Currently, there is a large growth triangle between Southern China, Hong Kong, and Taiwan. All three parties benefit from the system: Taiwan receives the orders, the mainland manufactures the goods, and the products are transferred through Hong Kong. South Korea and Japan have developed a similar cooperative pattern with China's Shandong and Liaoning provinces, a fast growth area called Yellow Sea Economic Circle by Chinese scholars.[9]

Cross-border trade with the Russian Far East is also growing. The two sides share a common interest in transforming the area into a "highly developed economic complex" in the future.[10]

Economic reforms have transformed China from a centrally planned economy to an economy largely driven by market forces. The decentralization in economic decision-making has fundamentally changed the nature of the central government's economic relations with local areas and interregional economic relations. There is an explosion of subnational economic decision making units, such as SEZs, coastal open cities, core cities with quasi-provincial-level economic authority (*jihua danlieshi*), and high-technology zones with economic policy privileges. These subnational units control most private or semi-private enterprises, covering nearly 170 major cities. Many government functions and resources have been shifted downward and outward. Economic transaction is conducted more and more through local and private sector initiatives than by formal government mechanisms.[11] Although the state still plays a large role in economic planning and regulation, roughly 80 percent of commodities in China are now distributed through market channels at market prices. China's opening to the world economy exposed the country to advanced product standards and technologies. It also created competition for domestic producers. In this sense, China's integration with the world economic system in general and the Asian economy in particular has greatly increased productivity and efficiency and changed China's view on regional integration.

Over the past few years, the benefits of regional economic integration that China has experienced have caused Beijing to hold a more positive attitude toward regional multilateral trade regimes. Chinese leaders see integration with the world economy as inevitable and beneficial. International multilateral trade regimes provide secure and stable trade relationships with major trading partners. Although Beijing still insists that it be admitted to the World Trade Organization (WTO) as a developing country, its policy on trade liberalization measures within the framework of Asian Pacific Economic Cooperation (APEC) shows more flexibility. After China joined APEC with Taiwan and Hong Kong in 1992, Beijing took a series of unilateral measures to break down its trade barriers. President Jiang Zeming made a bold move in the 1994 APEC summit in Indonesia by accepting and committing China to the goal of establishing an Asian Pacific free trade area by the year 2020. Many economic and foreign trade officials in Beijing privately complained that China may not be ready.

Many Chinese scholars are concerned that an Asian Pacific free trade area may give Washington the leadership role in pushing harsh liberalization measures over countries like China, whose economic structure and trade system are still in transition.[12] Prior to China's economic reforms, its economy was largely closed to the international market. Today, its economic growth is heavily dependent on external trade, foreign investment, and technology transfer from abroad. In the post-Deng era, the reversal of the open-door policy would risk dire consequences, but commitment to free trade would severely reduce the government's control over external economic relations. Beijing's concern is reinforced by the concept of "New Pacific Community," proposed by President Clinton. After assessing the U.S. blueprint of "Asian Pacific Free Trade Area," some Chinese scholars have concluded that this new concept is an attempt to expand NAFTA to Asia. They contend that a possible U.S. dominance of APEC or expanding APEC to security affairs would give Washington more leverage to impose its will on Asian states.[13]

Costs and Benefits of Economic Integration

China's integration with the Asian economy has made the nation more dependent on or interdependent with the world economy and in particular, with the regional economic system. In the Chinese political and academic community, the costs of integration have become a focal point in the debate on foreign economic strategy.[14] Although most people agree China has received remarkable benefits from participating in regional economic integration, they also share concerns over the costs of integration.

The first concern in weighing the costs and benefits of integration is how dependent China has become on the world economy. Most Chinese scholars and analysts use the traditional measures of trade dependence, but some argue that the price and exchange rate have greatly distorted the traditional calculation. China's trade dependence was a tenth of its GDP in 1978, but by 1996 it had grown to 36 percent. This compares with 20 percent for the United States, 27 percent for Japan, 63 percent for Germany, and 66 percent for South Korea.[15] Since the late 1970s, foreign direct investment in China has totaled more than US$170 billion.[16] The huge amount of foreign investment in China makes for a large export-oriented portion of China's GDP, and thus the degree of dependence on the international market has dramatically increased. Another indicator of dependence is the degree to which foreign-funded enterprises in China contribute to the nation's total foreign trade. The State Bureau of Statistics' figures indicate that in 1996 US$137.1 billion of foreign trade was related to foreign-funded enterprises. Their share in China's overall foreign trade rose from 39 percent in 1995 to 48 percent in 1996.[17]

In purely quantitative terms, it seems that China is becoming highly dependent on foreign trade. However, if statistical distortion caused by exchange rates and the low price level in China are removed, the economy is not as dependent as these numbers suggest. The degree of a country's dependence on the world economy must include how much foreign trade empowers the whole economy. Although it is difficult to measure the empowering effect of foreign trade, one can generalize that the vast inland areas in China have only limited foreign economic contact, and the rural population engaged in non-agricultural production is still relatively small. It is fair to argue that even though the coastal area is becoming economically dependent on the outside world, the entire country's dependency on the world economy is still far below the level of Japan or Germany.[18] Yet another measure of international economic dependence is a country's foreign borrowing. By the end of 1996, China's international loans had reached US$116.3 billion.[19] Unlike many other third world countries, however, the structure of China's loans and the debt service ratio against its export and GDP is relatively low and safe.

Whatever measures are used, one thing is clear for the Chinese policy makers: Beijing must consider the possible negative effects of trade dependence. Looking at China's total export market, it is obvious that the country is becoming over-dependent on U.S. and Japanese markets. Although Hong Kong is the second largest export market, the majority of Hong Kong-bound goods are re-exported. In addition, after Hong Kong was reverted to Chinese sovereignty on July 1, 1997, the role of Hong Kong is no longer a political concern. The political implication for market dependence is that market access can be used as a political weapon in bilateral relations. Trade surplus with the United States now is not only a hot bilateral trade issue, but it also provides Washington with a big stick in U.S.-China relations. From Washington's perspective, if China is involved in a network of international economic ties, it will make Beijing vulnerable to political pressures from the West due to the fear of losing foreign market access, especially in those markets on which Chinese exports are heavily dependent. Beijing also realizes the vulnerability caused by trade dependence and wants to diversify its external trade relations and change its export composition. Unfortunately, the room to maneuver is limited due to the regional trade relations and production patterns in East Asia.

The second issue in the debate concerns the internal disparity that has resulted from integration with the Asian economy. Economic prosperity in the coastal areas has dramatically widened income and growth disparities between these areas and inland provinces. From 1985 to 1992, real income in Guangdong and Fujian grew about 110 percent, whereas inland provinces like Shanxi, Hubei, and Anhui experienced income growths of less than 30 percent. The gap in GDP per capita between coastal and inland provinces increased from 1.7:1 to 2.1:1 during the same period.[20] Some Chinese scholars argue that the disparity problem will take care of itself over time. As the opening up moves from the coast to the inland, the low-income areas will eventually follow the suit of the coastal provinces as their ability to attract foreign investment increases.

The political ramifications of domestic economic disparity are a serious issue for the central government in Beijing. The problem may create social instabilities and large labor flows across the country. Politically, prevailing regional economic trends, combined with changes in the provincial and central leadership, suggest that the regrouping of political forces is evident in the system. The increasingly rich and quasi-autonomous southeast coastal regions are more pro-reform and favor a moderate policy toward Taiwan and Hong Kong. The less developed inland regions that depend on assistance from Beijing, on the other hand, are more conservative in their views of reforms and international economic integration because they enjoy only limited benefits from these policy objectives. In order to reduce regional disparity, leaders in Beijing have to balance demands from the coastal and inland regions. Currently, inland and northeast regions are allowed to share some of the policy privileges previously reserved for the southeast coast. The open-door policy will not be reversed, but the future policy will be more balanced and allow the disadvantaged regions to enjoy greater benefits from the open-door policy and regional integration.

The third debated issue relates to the political impact of regional integration on the changing relationship between the central and local governments. When the reforms started, the central government's intentions were to delegate more financial and economic decision-making power to local governments and enterprises to stimulate the initiatives of localities. But the political repercussion of this policy is that the central government is losing its fiscal capacity and political control over the provinces, especially the southeast coastal provinces. The realignment of fiscal resources and decision-making power has resulted in a decentralized system in which Beijing has to consult with regional "warlords" before making any major foreign economic decisions. Meanwhile, Guangdong and Fujian provinces are demanding still more autonomy in economic policy and regulation. The inland provinces have to fight for more favorable treatment from the central government. In 1996, after a long debate and repeated demands from the inland provinces, some of the special policies ("perks") directed toward the southeast coast and SEZs were suspended.

Lastly, Chinese scholars are engaged in heated debate over what the strategic vision of Beijing should be toward participation in regional economic division of labor. The regional economic restructuring promotes regional integration on both the vertical and the horizontal level. However, the current East Asian economic structure is characterized by a vertical division of labor that has been developed through Japan's and the NIEs' overseas investment and production transfer. This "flying geese" structure places Japan in the lead position, with the NIEs in the middle of the pack and the ASEAN and other emerging economies behind them. Some Chinese scholars argue that the flying geese pattern perpetuates the inequality and disparity in Asian economic development.[21] As the leader, Japan benefits the most from this structure. Tokyo attempts to maintain this vertical division of labor through investment and production networks and to create different economic circles around the Japanese economy. This regional production pattern preserves a core-periphery structure in the Asian economy. It is argued that China's integration with this regional structure will put the country in an inferior position in economic competition and development. According to this view, it is not in China's long-term interest to integrate with a vertical division of labor in Asia. Although in the short run, the vertical division of labor brings economic prosperity to China, in the long run it will force China to assume a peripheral position and leave limited chances for China to upgrade its technological level.[22]

The majority of Chinese scholars, however, argue the opposite. They believe that the Chinese economic structure is diverse enough to fit into different levels of regional integration. China can participate in the vertical structure of economic integration to accumulate capital and management expertise. As the coastal areas complete the import-substitution phase of industrialization, the depth and scope of the opening up will expand to inland areas. The more developed the coastal areas become, the more capital and technology they can transfer to the inland areas. As the coastal areas become highly developed, they can attract more advanced technology and industries to China. For China to upgrade its technology level, according to the dominant view, China needs to use "market for technology" and "market for capital" (yi shichang huan jishu; yi shichange huan zijin).[23] China's market size is its biggest bargaining chip, and it should be used to attract more capital and technology from industrialized countries as well as NIEs.

Regional economic integration is a complex phenomenon in international relations, as people have witnessed in Europe and other parts of the world. Naturally, it generates a great deal of debate on the impact of interdependence. Chinese leaders today view interdependence and regional integration more positively than they did ten years ago. Most people accept that interdependence is a fact of life in international relations and that China's modernization requires its integration with the regional economy. Economic integration would create an international division of labor, internationalized production, free flow of resources, and close interaction between national economies. The question for Beijing is not whether to integrate but rather how to integrate. It is in China's interest to maximize the benefits of integration and to minimize its costs. However, achieving the balance between growth and interdependence is not an easy task.

Establishing Asian Political Identity

The collapse of communism and the Tiananmen Square incident created a period of isolation for China in the world. This period, however, was used by Beijing to adjust its foreign policy strategy. One of the adjustments was to refocus on Asia. Instead of playing the role of a global power, Beijing pragmatically opted to behave as a regional power. China concentrated on building good-neighborly relations, cultivating economic cooperation, and consolidating its power base in Asia.[24]

As the only major socialist power left after the collapse of East European and Soviet communist regimes, Beijing found itself in a "new Cold War" with Western powers led by the United States. Washington's policy of pressuring China on human rights and democratization is seen as a severe threat to the nation's stability and national security. Thus, Beijing focuses on winning over the third world, especially the Asian states, to counter Western pressure in the international arena. Beijing began to participate actively in the Asian community and to engage in frequent exchanges with Asian leaders.

A major battlefield on human rights has been the annual meeting of the UN Human Rights Commission in Geneva. The Chinese government mobilized all its international resources to block the Western sponsored resolutions that condemn Beijing's human rights records. For seven consecutive years, Beijing has successfully blocked or gathered enough votes to reject the Western campaign against its human rights policy. The Chinese strategy is to fight the battle in a North-South context. Beijing argues that there is a great degree of diversity and difference in the world's social and political systems and, naturally, countries follow different practices and standards in the protection of human rights. The concept of human rights is shaped by a nation's cultural tradition, value system, and historical backgrounds, and the West should not impose its concepts and standards on other societies.[25]

Beijing's strategy for fencing off Western pressure on human rights also involves mobilizing Asia on the issue. This strategy has met with some success. China mobilized an Asian coalition on the Most Favored Nation (MFN) issue. Most Asian nations share the same economic interest in a normalized and stable Sino-U.S. trade relationship. Some Asian leaders have publicly supported Beijing's stand that MFN trade status and the issue of human rights should be separated. Some of them have even distanced themselves from Washington by criticizing the American policy on China's human rights record. Singapore's senior minister Lee Kwan Yew and Malaysian prime minister Mahathir are two of the most outspoken Asian leaders on this issue. The two strongly reject the notion that Asia should follow the example set by the United States, a nation that has the highest murder rate, gun ownership, and per capita incarceration in the world.

Chinese leaders understand that Asian political cooperation should be founded on common values and interests. Since there are conflicting interests in many different areas, Beijing argues that Asia's unique cultural and historical backgrounds should lead to an Asian way toward democracy, which may provide grounds for the political cooperation among Asian countries in international politics. The Asian way toward democracy and human rights is distinct from Western notions of individual rights and liberal governance. This argument appeals to many developing countries in Asia, because most of them share similar development paths toward economic growth and political stability. Domestically, many Chinese scholars argue that Deng Xiaoping's neo-authoritarianism is a Chinese version of the development path experienced by South Korea, Taiwan, and some of the Southeast Asian states. China's current development path, in many ways, resembles those of Singapore and Taiwan.

Security Cooperation:
Bilateralism vs. Multilateralism

Compared to its policy on economic cooperation, Beijing's views on regional security cooperation are less optimistic and less favorable. President Jiang Zemin has argued that regional security cooperation should be built on economic cooperation and that Asia should not copy other regional political organizations.[26] In Beijing's view, regional economic cooperation is the driving force that changes international relations, and it will eventually improve the prospects for peace in Asia. It is in every nation's best interest to concentrate on economic development and domestic stability. This is the best safeguard for regional peace and stability. The current East Asian security environment is closely tied to regional economic cooperation. The flourishing economic cooperation will strengthen regional security and improve political relations between countries.

Despite the liberalist rhetoric on regional security cooperation, the crux of Chinese foreign policy rests on the balance of power theory. In important international documents, Chinese leaders prefer the term "multipolarity" to "multilateralism."[27] These two terms represent two different perceptions of the international system. After the Cold War a new structure of big power relations emerged in Asia as well as in world politics. Although Asian Pacific security still depends on the bilateral security ties established during the Cold War, the present power structure in East Asia is moving toward a multipolar system. This system is based on a more diffuse distribution of power. In considering future regional structure, Chinese scholars argue that the major power relationship in Asia is in a process of realignment. Future regional security structure will be built on a multipolarity of the United States, Russia, China, and Japan. U.S. hegemonic dominance in the Asia-Pacific is diminishing. Constrained by domestic economic problems, Moscow is less interested in Asian affairs at the present time. The declining Russian role and the strained Sino-U.S. relationship have accentuated Tokyo's role in East Asian politics.[28]

East Asia is such a vast area that it is difficult to classify it as a region.[29] Asia's complex culture, ethnicity, and the region's territorial disputes pose major difficulties in efforts to design a regional political and security organization. In organizing East Asia, national leaders must solve the problems of political and territorial disputes among themselves and decide what role outside powers would play in regional organization. They have to take into account the balance of power among the major countries and foster appropriate links between economic cooperation and security structure. For this exact reason, Beijing strongly believes the best way for security cooperation in Northeast Asia is to build and manage healthy bilateral relations in the region. In Beijing's view, there is no need for a multilateral institution because Northeast Asian security problems are predominantly bilateral problems: North and South Korea, the Sino-Japanese rivalry, Sino-Russian relations, mainland China and Taiwan, and Sino-U.S. relations.

A key concern for China on the Korean peninsula is the management of the peaceful transition of the North Korean regime and the reunification of the two Koreas. This must be accomplished without disrupting peace and stability in Northeast Asia.[30] After the Cold War, Russia and China established formal diplomatic relations with Seoul. In addition, Pyongyang began direct talks with Washington and Tokyo for the normalization of bilateral relations. The Cold War bipolar structure has been replaced by cross-bloc major power relations with the two Koreas. The new pattern of multilateral international relations on the peninsula is conducive to peace and stability in Northeast Asia. Beijing tends to take a balanced approach toward managing its bilateral relations with North and South Korea. China opted to take a moderate stance during the North Korean nuclear weapons problem and not to push Pyongyang too harshly. In doing so, Beijing tried to achieve two parallel objectives: denuclearization and maintaining stability on the peninsula.[31] Beijing's long-term interest on the peninsula is stability and mutually beneficial economic exchanges with both Koreas. As Beijing's trade relations with the South are prospering, however, its economic ties with Pyongyang are strained. It is not in China's interest to see a sudden collapse of the North Korean regime. Any instability and chaos in North Korea will immediately affect China's Yanbian area, where most of the nation's Korean minority live. Given Beijing's troubled relations with Pyongyang, China has agreed to participate in the four-party peace talks but with a low-key role. Beijing is willing to facilitate a peace agreement, but it insists the key for peace is direct North-South dialogue.

Although Beijing's economic ties with Japan are expanding steadily, political troubles in their bilateral relations frequently appear. Beijing thinks the right-wing forces in Japan keep making trouble in the bilateral relationship, as exemplified by the recent incident on the Diaoyudao (called Senkaku Islands by Japan), the textbook controversy, and the refusal to apologize for Japanese war crimes. In the long run, the alarming factor for China is the growth of Japanese military capabilities and the redefinition of the U.S.-Japan security alliance. Beijing closely monitors developments in Washington and Tokyo regarding the Guidelines for U.S.-Japan Defense Cooperation. Any attempt to extend the geographical scope of defense cooperation to the Taiwan Straits and the South China Sea is viewed as a direct threat to China's security. In the words of the Chinese foreign ministry spokesman, "[China] hopes the bilateral defense arrangement between Japan and the United States will not go beyond its bilateral nature and will not touch on any third party. Any attempt to have a security arrangement going beyond its bilateral character would certainly be a cause for vigilance and concern by other Asian nations."[32]

Relations across the Taiwan Straits have had twists and turns in recent years. Although economic ties are flourishing, political relations between Beijing and Taipei have not improved. On the contrary, they have worsened. Although economic integration has spillover effects on political decisions regarding bilateral trade and personnel exchanges, the two sides are each acting in a way designed to defeat the other diplomatically. In Beijing's view, Lee Teng-hui's visit to the United States in June 1995 was a clear break from the "One China" principle. Beijing sees Taiwan as following a "creeping" course toward *de jure* independence. Recent political

changes on the island (presidential election, constitutional reforms, multiparty system, and the abolishment of the province status) are institutionalizing Taiwan's pursuit of independence. After
Beijing froze bilateral talks on substantial issues, it started a strategy of coercive diplomacy toward Taipei. China attempted to use
economic relations and military threats to compel the Taiwanese
leadership into political negotiation with the mainland.[33] During
the crisis of 1996, Beijing's leadership repeatedly stated that it
would use force if Taiwan pursued *de jure* independence. The
cross-strait relations will remain uncertain in the foreseeable future. Any conflict in the Taiwan Straits will immediately affect
major power relations in East Asia. This was demonstrated by
Washington's March 1996 deployment of two aircraft carriers to
the waters off Taiwan's coast.

In contrast to the Taiwan Straits and the strained Sino-U.S. relations, Beijing and Moscow are enjoying a new "honeymoon." Beijing and Moscow are getting closer to each other due to frequent
high-level exchanges, increased border trade, and, more importantly, mutual antipathy toward U.S. dominance in the international
system. Although the two sides have defined their cooperation as a
"strategic cooperation partnership toward the 21st century,"[34] the
new relationship is far from the alliance they had in the 1950s. In a
sense, the partnership is more like a marriage of convenience. The
two countries are drawn together by mutual economic needs: Russia needs Chinese consumer goods, while Beijing needs Russia's
transfer of advanced weapons systems and military technology. In
the long run, if Russia regains economic and military power, it will
pose a security threat to China. In addition, China's rising military
power is perceived as a potential threat to Russian security.

Multilateral Security Cooperation: On Whose Terms?

Beijing's reluctance to embrace multilateralism is closely related to
its foreign policy dilemma in East Asia. As an extension of China's
consensus on domestic economic development, it has consistently

pursued a peaceful foreign policy in Asia since the late 1970s. The goal is to maintain a stable international environment for its domestic economic development. Another foreign policy objective, however, requires the country to reunify all its territorial claims, including Taiwan, Hong Kong, Macau, and the territories under dispute with Asian neighbors. These two policy objectives have often run into conflict with each other.

Chinese leaders do not view these two goals as contradictory. As China modernizes, it will become stronger in regional politics, making the goal of reunification easier. But the more Beijing emphasizes the goal of reunification, the more alarmed other Asian states feel. They fear China will become more assertive over territorial disputes. What makes them even more fearful is the rise of nationalism in China. They see that the Chinese leadership is fanning the flames of nationalism among the Chinese people. Following the collapse of Marxist ideology, Beijing needs a new unifying force to mobilize the nation in pursuit of a common course. The "glue" is nationalism. More assertive nationalism creates uneasiness in regional international relations.[35]

There are basically two schools of thought concerning future Chinese security policy in East Asia. The first school argues that it is in China's best interest to continue on the path of peaceful foreign policy and participation in regional economic integration. Beijing should use peaceful means to solve bilateral problems with its regional neighbors and not allow territorial disputes to disrupt economic relations and stability in East Asia. Although China's economic power has dramatically increased over the last 20 years, it remains a poor third-world country. It cannot afford to fight major wars as it strives for economic modernization. Without dropping China's territorial claims, this school argues that the solution of territorial disputes should be postponed.

The other school, more militant and assertive, sees a great urgency in the territorial problems and the Taiwan issue. They argue that if no action is taken to stop the encroachment of some of the Spratly Islands by Asian neighbors, China will have difficulty securing a favorable solution to the Spratly dispute. By the same token, if no action is taken on Diaoyudao, Japan will obtain the title of the islands by prescription.[36] Proponents of this school argue for a quick buildup of long-range power projection capability and the use of military force, if necessary, to stop any provocative action against China. The military exercises in the Taiwan Straits in March 1996 were a showcase for these people. They favor coercing Taiwan militarily and using coercive diplomacy against other Asian neighbors in territorial disputes.

Walking a fine line between these two schools, Chinese leaders have to make foreign policy decisions with great caution. They do not want to jeopardize relations with their Asian neighbors, but neither do they want to lose face.

Chinese leaders oppose the idea of establishing an Asian multilateral security organization similar to NATO or CSCE in Europe. They argue that there is no common security threat in Asia after the Cold War. They believe there is a Western conspiracy promoting the idea of a "China threat" among Asian countries. In East Asia, there are security problems and territorial disputes, but China believes the problems should be and can be solved on a bilateral basis rather than in a multilateral venue. East Asia lacks the tradition of multilateralism in regional politics. Asian states prefer informal means of security organization, rather than elaborate institutional frameworks. Any attempt to institutionalize regional security organization would be counterproductive, and it is almost impossible to build a state-centric multilateral security organization in East Asia. This is the dominant view in China.

In recent years, a proliferation of nongovernmental dialogues and conferences on security issues in Northeast Asia has taken place, and many Chinese officials have attended in a private capacity. To date, there has been no serious attempt to form a Northeast Asian multilateral security forum similar to the ASEAN Regional Forum (ARF). ARF is an extension of ASEAN's post-ministerial conference that involves all major regional powers in political and security dialogues with ASEAN. It is a successful example of small states engaging big powers in security dialogues and multilateral diplomacy.

ARF's objective is to discuss confidence building, transparency, and reassurance measures and to suggest solutions for issues of common security concern, such as territorial disputes, refugees, drug trafficking, and piracy on the sea. ARF is a useful venue for regional countries to discuss their security concerns; Beijing, however, was reluctant to participate in ARF or any multilateral dialogues under ARF's auspices. However, at the 1995 ASEAN conference in Brunei, Beijing agreed to establish comprehensive multilateral dialogues with ASEAN. Beijing's distrust of multilateral security dialogues is based on its fear that it might complicate China's efforts to solve territorial disputes bilaterally. China engages in multilateral security dialogues with ASEAN states not because it may result in a multilateral negotiation over the Spratly dispute but because it does not want to alienate ASEAN states or be isolated in regional politics. If relations with Washington grow tense, Beijing needs international support from the ASEAN states. When China uses military threats to intimidate Taiwan, it wants ASEAN to adhere to the "One China" policy. When Beijing agreed in 1996 to engage in multilateral political dialogues on the Spratlys with ASEAN using the 1982 UN Convention on Law of the Sea as the basis for discussion, the ASEAN countries saw this as a major breakthrough. To them, China's agreement to participate in the discussion implies Chinese acceptance of the legitimacy of other claimants on the Spratlys. For Beijing, the multilateral dialogues do not mean negotiation on the sovereignty of the Spratlys, though the parties can exchange opinions based on the principle of "shelf disputes" and "common development." From Beijing's perspective, the multilateral dialogues are multidimensional, including economic, trade, science, and technology cooperation, not just political dialogues.[37]

Conclusion: Economic-Security
Nexus in Northeast Asia

The prospects for Northeast Asian regional economic cooperation improve as "natural economic territories" create a complex interdependence among the region's nations.[38] But regional security relations are still fragile. Regional security cooperation is still at an immature stage. Transnational market forces are integrating regional economies across political borders, but Northeast Asian governments still lack the political will for regional political organization. The region lacks the tradition of multilateralism, and alliances are formed under bilateral frameworks. The success of regional multilateral organization will depend on healthy bilateral relations, especially good relations between major powers. Regional multilateral security institutions will take shape slowly. East Asian nations, including some Northeast Asian nations, have participated in ad hoc cooperation on regional conflict resolution, but the nations have yet to find acceptable terms for a regional multilateral security forum, like CSCE.

Economic dynamism and political fragility are both facts of life in Northeast Asia. What is important is to study how economic interdependence can change political relations in the region. An example is China mainland-Taiwan relations. Economic ties across the Taiwan Straits are rapidly expanding, but this development gives little stimulus to Taipei and Beijing's political dialogues and no major political breakthrough is anticipated in the near future. From Beijing's point of view, economic interdependence between the mainland and Taiwan may eventually help to reunify the two areas. But the asymmetrical interdependence between the mainland and Taiwan does not mean the big side is always the winner. Taiwan's democratization process, instead of facilitating unification, has created political instability and made the bilateral relationship more complicated.

Generally, as economic relations flourish, regional cooperation will progressively affect mutual perception and lead to political discussion on problems of common concern. As regional economic interdependence increases, incentives for cooperation are likely to increase. This should result in greater policy coordination on common regional security goals. Most Northeast Asian governments encourage regional and subregional economic integration. Economic cooperation increases the costs of conflict, and thus the nations are reluctant to go to war against each other. It remains to be seen, however, how the growing economic interdependence and integration will affect political and security relations in Northeast Asia.

Notes

1. See, for example, Ambassador Liu Shan's speech in a conference on China's foreign relations after the reform, *Waijiao Xueyuan Xuebao* (Journal of the Foreign Affairs College), April 1994, pp. 7–8.

2. Ibid.

3. *Beijing Review,* March 30-April 5, 1998, p. 13.

4. *Beijing Review,* November 30-December 6, 1998.

5. See "New Direction of Sino-Korean Economic Cooperation," *East Asia Daily* (Seoul), April 15, 1994.

6. Xinhua, April 22, 1997, cited in *Renmin Ribao,* April 23, 1997.

7. Speech by Ms. Wu Yi, Minister of Foreign Trade and Economic Cooperation at the National Foreign Economic and Trade Working Conference in February 1998, *Beijing Review,* March 30-April 5, 1998, p. 11.

8. Cited in Tao Shi-an, "Efforts to Slow Down Are Bound to Be in Vain," in *Renmin Ribao,* April 8, 1997.

9. Chinese scholars like to use the term "economic circle" (*jingjiquan*) to describe China's economic integration with different subregional growth triangles. Economic circle, in their views, is a loose form of multilateral economic cooperation based on the natural division of labor and trade ties across borders. See Liang Zhanpin, ed., *Huantai Diqu Jingji Keji Hezuo Jingguan* (The landscape of economic and technological cooperation in the Pacific rim), Beijing: Kexuejishu Wenxian Chubanshe, 1993, Chapter One.

10. The term is used by Alexander Nemets in *The Growth of China and Prospects for the Eastern Regions of the Former USSR,* Lewiston, Wales: Edwin Mellen Press, 1996, p. 6.

11. For discussion on the changing central-local relations, see Hao Jia and Zhimin Lin, eds., *Changing Central-Local Relations in China: Reform and State Capacity,* Boulder, CO: Westview Press, 1994; and Dali L. Yang, "Reforms and the Restructuring of Central-Local Relations," in David S.G. Goodman and Gerald Segal, eds., *China Deconstructs: Politics, Trade and Regionalism,* London & New York: Routledge, 1994, pp. 59–97.

12. Song Yuhua, "U.S. New Strategy Toward the Asia Pacific: the Concept of a 'New Pacific Community'," *Shijie Jingji* (Journal of World Economy), December 1994; and Li Junjiang, "U.S. New Economic Strategy toward the Asia Pacific and the Sino-American Relations," *Shijie Jingji,* August 1995.

13. See Wang Jisi, "The United States as a Global and Pacific Power: A View from China," *Pacific Review*, vol. 10, no. 1 (1997), pp. 5–6; Song Yuhua, op. cit., and Li Junjiang, op. cit.

14. The debate involves scholars, government think tanks, and policy advisers to the leadership. While the majority of people take the position that further integration with the regional economy would be beneficial for China, a small group of people take a relatively negative view of the integration into regional economy. Important writings include: China Institute of Contemporary International Relations and Zhejiang Institute on Asian Pacific Studies, *Shijie Jingji Quyi Jituanhua Yu Yatai Jingji Hezuo* (Regionalization of the world economy and Asian Pacific economic cooperation), Beijing: Shishi Chubanshe, 1992; Han Zhenshe, ed., *Yatai Jingji Fazhan Qushi Yu Quyu Hezuo* (Asian Pacific economic development trends and regional cooperation), Beijing: Zhongguo Wujia Chubanshe, 1992; Cheng Jimin, ed., *Yatai Diqu Jingji Huanjing Yu Zhongguo Dongbu Diqu Jingji Kaifa* (Asian Pacific regional economic environment and the economic development of China's east coast), Nanjing: Jiangsu Renmin Chubanshe, 1990; Ma Chaoxu and Duan Jianfan, *Taipinyang Shidai: Zhongguo Mianlin de Tiaozhan yu Quanze* (The Pacific century: Challenges and choices for China), Harbin: Heilongjiang Renmin Chubanshe, 1988; and Jin Zhenji, *Dongbeiya Jingjiquan Yu Zhongguo de Xuanzhe* (Northeast Asian economic circle and China's choice), Beijing: Zhongyang Dangxiao Chubanshe, 1992. There is a comprehensive study funded by the National Foundation for Natural Sciences (fund item #79070074), and the report was later published as Liang Zhanpin, ed., op. cit., 1993.

15. The trade dependence figure is calculated by dividing foreign trade value (US$) by the GDP value (converting Renminbi value into US$ value or vice versa). There exists a big distortion due to price level differences and exchange rates, and a more accurate method (presumably, purchasing power parity) needs to be developed.

16. Premier Li Peng's address to the 32nd World Congress of the International Chamber of Commerce (ICC) in Beijing, April 9, 1997. *Renmin Ribao*, April 10, 1997.

17. PRC State Bureau of Statistics, "1996 Statistical Report on National Economic and Social Development," *Renmin Ribao*, April 7, 1997, part 6. For an English translation, see *Beijing Review*, April 28–May 4, 1997.

18. Two American scholars offer some interesting discussion on this issue. See Wendy Frieman and Thomas W. Robinson, "Costs and Benefits of Interdependence: A Net Assessment," in Congressional Joint Economic Committee, ed., *China's Economic Dilemmas in the 1990s: The Problems of Reforms, Modernization, and Interdependence,* Armonk, New York: M.E. Sharpe, 1992, pp. 723–725.

19. Released by the PRC State Bureau of Foreign Exchanges on April 28, 1997, in *Renmin Ribao* (overseas edition), April 30, 1997.

20. Ding Jingping, *China's Domestic Economy in Regional Context,* Washington, D.C.: Center for Strategic & International Studies, 1995), pp. 15–17. Nicholas R. Lardy states that "[China's] overall income inequality exceeds that in Taiwan and South Korea and is comparable to that observed in several South and Southeast Asian countries." (Lardy, *China in the World Economy,* Washington, D.C.: Institute for International Economics, 1994, p. 24.)

21. See, for example, Ma Chaoxu and Duan Jianfan, *Taipinyang Shidai: Zhongguo Mianlin de Tiaozhan yu Quanze* (The Pacific century: Challenges and choices for China), Harbin: Heilongjiang Renmin Chubanshe, 1988.

22. Ibid.

23. Liang Zhanping, op. cit., pp. 404–408.

24. For a good discussion, see Qu Xing, "Shilun Dongou Jubian he Sulian Jietihou de Zhongguo Waijiao Zhengce" (Chinese foreign policy after the dramatic changes in east Europe and the disintegration of the Soviet Union), *Waijiao Xueyuan Xuebao,* April 1994, pp. 16–22.

25. See Jiang Zemin's interview with CNN on April 9, 1997 (an excerpt is published in *Renmin Ribao,* April 10, 1997), and Foreign Minister Qian Qichen's speech to the Council on Foreign Relations on April 29, 1997 (*Renmin Ribao,* April 30, 1997).

26. Jiang Zemin's interview with German reporters, *Renmin Ribao,* July 17, 1995.

27. Jiang Zemin signed a joint declaration with Russian President Yeltsin in Moscow on April 23, 1997. In the document, the two reiterate their interest in promoting "multipolarity in world politics" and opposing "hegemony and power politics." The statement promoting the transition from bipolarity toward multipolarity in world politics was again inserted in the Sino-French Joint Declaration, signed by Jiang Zemin and French President Chirac in Beijing on May 16, 1997.

28. Chen Qimao, "An Inquiry into New Political Order in the Asia Pacific," *Guoji Wenti Yanjou* (Journal of International Studies) (Beijing), Winter 1992; Wan Guang, "Some Issues about the U.S. Foreign Strategy Adjustment," *Xiandai Guoji Guanxi* (Contemporary International Relations), no. 1, 1996; and Wang Shu, "Analyzing the Changing World," *Guoji Zhanwang* (International Outlook), no. 14, 1994.

29. For a good discussion, see Norman D. Palmer, *The New Regionalism in Asia and the Pacific*, Lexington, MA: Lexington Books, 1991, pp. 21–22.

30. Lu Zhongwei, "Diplomatic Interactions and Future Directions of Northeast Asian Countries," *Xiandai Guoji Guanxi*, March 1993.

31. Weixing Hu, "Beijing's Defense Strategy and the Korean Peninsula," *Journal of Northeast Asian Studies*, vol. 14, no. 5 (Fall 1995).

32. Foreign Ministry spokesman Shen Guofang's remarks on April 18, 1996.

33. See Weixing Hu, "The Taiwan Strait and Asian Pacific Security," *Journal of East Asian Affairs*, vol. 11, no. 1 (Winter/Spring 1997), pp. 149–182.

34. Sino-Russian Joint Declaration (April 23, 1997, Moscow), see *Renmin Ribao*, April 24, 1997.

35. For the discussion on the two types of nationalism, see Allen Whiting, "Chinese Nationalism and Foreign Policy after Deng," *China Quarterly*, no. 142 (1995).

36. In international law, the principle of prescription is accepted as a constituent element of territorial sovereignty if a nation can display continuous and peaceful functions of state within a given region (*The Island of Palmas Arbitration*, the Permanent Court of Arbitration, 1928).

37. Foreign Minister Qian Qichen's press conference on March 8, 1997. China and ASEAN have political consultation at the deputy foreign minister level once a year. The third round took place in Anhui, China on April 17–18, 1997.

38. Robert A. Scalapino, "The United States and Asia: Future Prospects," *Foreign Affairs*, Winter 1991/92, p. 21.

CHAPTER 6

SINO-JAPANESE RELATIONS
The Economic Security Nexus

Peggy Falkenheim Meyer

Introduction

THE FUTURE OF NORTHEAST ASIA WILL BE profoundly affected by the evolution of relations between China and Japan. Recently, there has been growing concern about the possibility of a Sino-Japanese rift. The perception is that the disappearance of the Soviet threat has removed a major incentive for Sino-Japanese cooperation. The anticipated decline in U.S. involvement and influence in East Asia will make competition between China and Japan for regional leadership inevitable. This competition will be fueled by growing nationalism in both countries, by their expanding military power projection capabilities, and by their conflicting needs for energy, food, and other scarce resources. As China's economic and military power grows, it may be tempted to take steps to revise the current unsatisfactory territorial status quo in the South China Sea and across the Taiwan Strait in ways that Japan will perceive as inimical to its own interests.

A rift between China and Japan would fragment Northeast Asia and impede subregional cooperation with profoundly destabilizing effects. Is a rift between these two Asian giants inevitable? This chapter argues that it is not. Despite growing strains in their relationship, there are strong incentives for China and Japan to exercise restraint.

Economic Ties

Economic interaction between China and Japan is very large and important to both countries. Since 1993, Japan has been China's largest trading partner, accounting for approximately 25 percent of China's rapidly growing foreign trade. China has become Japan's second largest export market after the United States. Their two-way trade has grown from US$39 billion in 1993[1] to US$47.89 billion in 1994, US$57.47 billion in 1995, and US$60.06 billion in 1996. In 1996, China exported US$30.88 billion worth of goods to Japan, more than to any other country, and imported US$29.18 billion worth of goods from Japan, largely machinery and electronic products. One-third of the Chinese imports from Japan was equipment for foreign-funded enterprises in China.[2]

Japan has become an important source of direct investment in China. By the end of 1995, Japan had invested a total of US$10.5 billion in Chinese manufacturing and services. Japanese cumulative direct foreign investment in China is lower than that of Hong Kong, Taiwan, and the United States. But it has been concentrated in a few places, particularly the cities of Dalian, Beijing, and Shanghai, where it has constituted a significant portion of the total.[3]

Japan also has been the most important source of aid for China. One-third of China's development assistance comes from Japan. Part of this aid has been provided in the form of long-term credits at attractive rates from Japan's Overseas Economic Cooperation Fund. Between 1979 and 1996, Tokyo provided Beijing with three packages of low-interest credits totaling 1.55 trillion yen. It extended another 580 billion yen (US$5.8 billion) for the three years from 1996 to 1998 and is providing an additional 390 billion yen

(US$3.2 billion) for the 1999–2000 period.[4] These credits have been targeted at projects designed to improve China's environment and agriculture and to help China build up its transportation, communications, and power infrastructure, which enhances China's ability to absorb foreign manufacturing investment.[5]

Although economic interaction between China and Japan has been steadily growing, there have been some underlying strains. In the 1980s, when Japan had a trade surplus with China, Chinese students more than once demonstrated against the "invasion" of Japanese products into China. The Chinese also resented the low level of Japanese investment in China in comparison to trade and Japanese firms' reluctance to invest in high-tech industry in China for fear of creating an economic competitor.

These particular concerns have dissipated in the 1990s, since China now has a trade surplus with Japan, and there has been a marked increase in Japanese high-tech investment in China. However, new points of friction have arisen. China's trade surplus with Japan has induced the Japanese to use quotas, higher tariffs, quarantine restrictions, and other means to limit the flow of Chinese goods into Japan. These measures have caused some Chinese resentment.[6] The rising yen has significantly increased the cost to China of paying back its loans, but Tokyo has refused to renegotiate them.[7]

Despite these frictions, the Sino-Japanese economic relationship is seen by both sides as mutually beneficial. Japanese investment, advanced technology, and marketing skills help China modernize its economy and develop priority industries. In 1993, China's Vice Premier Zhu Rongji said that Japan ranked first in the transfer of foreign technology to China, accounting for almost 30 percent of China's technology imports.[8]

Japanese industrialists are eager to establish production facilities in China and other low-cost Asian countries because the high yen has increased production costs at home. Japan's direct investment in China is likely to increase as China opens up its increasingly affluent domestic market.[9] There is some asymmetry in Sino-Japanese economic relations. Japan's stake in its economic relations with China is less than China's stake in its economic ties with Japan. Trade with China still constitutes less than 5 percent of Japan's total foreign trade. China's heavy dependence on Japanese investment and on the Japanese market makes it vulnerable to a downturn in the Japanese economy. This vulnerability is reflected by the impact of Japan's current financial crisis, which has reduced both Japanese investment in China and Japanese imports from China. Chinese leaders repeatedly have urged Tokyo to assume greater responsibility for dealing with its own domestic financial crisis and with the broader Asian financial crisis by reforming its economy, opening up its markets to imports from other Asian countries, and avoiding further devaluation of the yen.

Japan's economic dependence on China may be limited, but the Japanese perceive that they have a large stake in China's prosperity and stability. China is viewed in Japan primarily as an unconventional security threat. Japanese policy makers are concerned about economic dislocation, political instability, and environmental degradation in China. Air pollution in China is so severe that it negatively affects not only public health and agriculture in China itself but also air quality in South Korea and Japan.[10]

While the Japanese private sector's main motivation is to seek profits in China, the Japanese government has fostered Sino-Japanese economic relations as a means of contributing to China's economic growth and political stability. Economic growth in China is seen as furthering Japan's own economic and security interests. A serious economic downturn in China would negatively affect the profits of Japanese firms. It also could have a negative security impact on Japan and other countries if it produced a large outflow of refugees.

Japanese aid is directed in part toward dealing with these unconventional threats from China. One of the primary causes of Chinese air pollution is the heavy reliance on coal as a source of heat and fuel. So Japanese assistance has been used to help Chinese industry become more energy-efficient in order to reduce sulfur emissions.[11] Japan requires the installation of desulfurization equipment in Sino-Japanese joint venture factories constructed in China.[12]

Another focus of Japan's current aid program is on improving economic conditions and agricultural production in China's poor, interior provinces.[13] Japanese assistance to Chinese agricultural development makes it less likely that competition for scarce food resources will become a source of tension between China and Japan in the twenty-first century. Japan now relies on imports to meet more of its food needs because it has been forced by international trade rules to abandon its policy of agricultural self-sufficiency. Shinkichi Eto, one of Japan's leading China specialists, has argued that it is in Japan's interest to help China expand its food production to make sure that there is enough grain available on the world market to meet its own needs.[14]

Still another goal of Japan's aid program is to gain leverage over China. Japanese policy makers have been inclined to believe that the best way to gain influence is to remain engaged in China. In their view, efforts to influence China by isolating her or imposing sanctions are likely to be ineffective and even counterproductive, inducing Beijing to become more hostile and assertive. For this reason, Tokyo was reluctant to impose sanctions on China after the June 1989 Tiananmen massacre and did so only under U.S. pressure. The sanctions imposed were quite limited, and Japan took steps to end them as soon as possible.

Under U.S. pressure, Tokyo adopted an Overseas Development Aid Charter in 1992 in which it pledged to review aid toward countries with unacceptable policies in the areas of human rights, the environment, arms exports, and the development of weapons of mass destruction. However, when talks were held to discuss Japan's 1996–2001 aid program, these principles were not invoked as a reason to deny aid to China. Japanese policy makers were reluctant to take such a step because they feared that it could undermine the political leadership in Beijing at a time when China was experiencing serious economic problems.[15]

The substantial economic relations between China and Japan have provided a strong incentive for mutual restraint. Both Japan and China attach a high priority to promoting domestic economic growth and modernization. This has given them a stake in a peaceful international environment and an incentive to cooperate to avert potential crises on the Korean peninsula, in Cambodia, and elsewhere in East Asia. Recently, China used some of its growing foreign exchange reserves, which totaled US$131.6 billion by

September 1997,[16] to cooperate with Japan and other countries in an international effort to deal with Thailand's severe currency crisis.

There are other motives as well for Sino-Japanese cooperation. Tokyo needs Beijing's support for its bid to become a permanent member of the United Nations Security Council.[17] China has perceived good relations with Japan as a means of restoring its own international legitimacy after the Tiananmen crisis and of reducing its vulnerability to U.S. pressure and sanctions.

Changing Japanese Security Perceptions

Despite these incentives for cooperation, tensions between China and Japan are increasing, and their perceptions of each other are changing in a negative direction. Although China still is viewed in Japan primarily as an unconventional security threat, there is growing concern that China might one day pose a conventional threat to Japanese interests. This concern has been provoked by China's growing air and naval power projection capabilities and by its increasingly assertive behavior in the South China Sea near critical sea routes linking Japan with the Middle East and Europe. Tokyo reacted critically to China's 1992 Law on Territorial Waters and Their Contiguous Areas, in which Beijing asserted its sovereignty over disputed islands in the South China Sea and also over the Diaoyu (Senkaku) islands in the East China Sea currently held by Japan. China's nuclear tests in 1995 and 1996 produced a sharply negative reaction in Japan. The 1996 Taiwan Strait crisis also provoked an adverse reaction in Japan, where it was interpreted as evidence of China's willingness to use military force as an instrument of intimidation.

The growing Japanese concern about China is most often expressed in private because of the sensitive nature of the Sino-Japanese relationship. But more and more frequently, it is being voiced in public. A 1995 report by the Japan Forum on International Relations warned that "China's emergence as a major power through economic development will encourage its aspirations for regional hegemony." The report added, "The lack of transparency in China's defense policy and its increased military expenditures have compelled other countries in the region to view China as a threat." This report was endorsed by 73 Japanese international relations scholars.[18] In an October 1995 statement to the Japanese Diet, then Foreign Minister Kono Yohei said that China's military modernization and territorial policies could constitute a threat to stability in Asia.[19] Early drafts of Japan's National Defense Program Outline depicted China's military modernization, nuclear tests, and expansionist policies in the South China Sea and around the Senkaku (Diaoyu) islands as a threat. But this language was removed from the final draft under pressure from then prime minister Murayama's Social Democratic Party.[20] The Japan Defense Agency White Paper released in the summer of 1996 acknowledged that China's military modernization was expected to proceed "gradually." But it warned that "the situation must be watched with caution in terms of promotion of nuclear weapons and modernization of the navy and air forces, expansion of naval activity, and heightened tensions in the Taiwan Strait."[21]

It is important to recognize, however, that even those Japanese analysts who stress the growing conventional threat from China realize that it will take a long time, at least two decades, for China to overcome its current military obsolescence.[22] Most Japanese analysts are more concerned about the potential threat that China's military buildup poses to Japanese interests rather than to Japan itself. However, some analysts express concern about the potential nuclear threat to Japan posed by China's new medium-range ballistic missiles. China now is taking steps to increase the precision of these ballistic missiles, which have the range to reach Japan and other targets in East Asia.[23] Japanese policy makers are also concerned about the proliferation threat posed by China's willingness to sell ballistic missiles and other weapons to countries in South Asia and the Middle East.

Growing concern about China was a primary motivation behind Tokyo's decision to support multilateral security dialogue in the Asia-Pacific region. Tokyo was a strong supporter of the process that led to the 1994 establishment of the ASEAN Regional Forum, the Asia-Pacific region's first multilateral security framework. Japanese policy makers hoped that incorporation of China into this framework would increase the transparency and predictability of

Chinese foreign policy behavior. Japan's own participation in an Asia-Pacific multilateral security dialogue would give it an opportunity to dispel other East Asian countries' historically rooted mistrust and to seek tacit allies among ASEAN (Association of Southeast Asian Nations) countries in an effort to balance China's growing power.[24] To combat the proliferation threat from China, Tokyo has encouraged Beijing to sign the Nuclear Nonproliferation Treaty, to adhere to the Missile Technology Control Regime, to agree to the establishment of a United Nations arms sales registry,[25] and to issue a Defense White Paper.

Growing Japanese concern about a potential conventional threat from China was one motivation behind Tokyo's decision to reaffirm and redefine its security relationship with the United States. In April 1996, U.S. president Bill Clinton and Japanese prime minister Ryutaro Hashimoto signed the Japan-U.S. Declaration on Security: Alliance for the 21st Century. This declaration expanded the sphere of U.S.-Japan security cooperation from the Far East to the Asia-Pacific region. It was widely understood in Japan that this new security declaration was directed at China as well as North Korea, but care was taken not to say this in public.

In support of this new Declaration on Security, Tokyo and Washington agreed to issue new guidelines for U.S.-Japan defense cooperation. On September 23, 1997 the foreign and defense ministers of Japan and the United States, meeting in New York, issued these new guidelines to replace ones adopted in 1978. The new guidelines provide for Japanese support for U.S. military operations in defense of Japan or "in situations in areas surrounding Japan that will have an important influence on Japanese peace and security."

Japan's defense responsibilities have been expanded. The new guidelines state that Japanese forces will cooperate with U.S. forces not only in "relief activities and measures to deal with refugees" and "search and rescue operations" but also in the evacuation of noncombatants "from a third country to a safe haven," and measures to ensure "the effectiveness of economic sanctions" including "information sharing and cooperation in inspections of ships based on United Nations Security Council resolutions." The guidelines also commit Japan to "provide rear area support to those U.S. Forces that are conducting operations for the purpose of achieving the objectives of the U.S.-Japan Security Treaty." Such services will be provided "primarily in Japanese territory" but also "on the high seas and international airspace around Japan which are distinguished from areas where combat operations are being conducted." Japan's self-defense forces "will conduct such activities as intelligence gathering, surveillance and minesweeping, to protect lives and property and to ensure navigational safety."[26] Although the guidelines may not breach Japan's prohibition on engaging in collective defense, they certainly are a move in that direction.

Washington and Tokyo deliberately avoided defining in geographic terms the area covered by their new defense guidelines. By not specifying whether the new guidelines covered Taiwan, they wished to avoid antagonizing China and to preserve the ambiguity necessary for effective deterrence.

Unfortunately, the Taiwan issue became embroiled in Japanese domestic politics in a way that proved harmful to Sino-Japanese relations. Even before the new defense guidelines were published, Japan's chief cabinet secretary Kajiyama Seiroku issued a statement in mid-August 1997 declaring that the new guidelines would allow Japanese ships to support U.S. military operations in the Taiwan Strait.[27] It was reported that Kajiyama's intention was to embarrass his rival in the Liberal Democratic Party, Kato Koichi, who had recently returned from a trip to China, where he explained to Chinese officials that the new guidelines were intended to facilitate Japanese logistical support to U.S. troops dealing with an emergency on the Korean peninsula.[28] Although Kajiyama later lost his post as chief cabinet secretary, the damage had been done.

Changing perceptions of China are beginning to have an impact on other aspects of Japanese behavior. There is growing disillusionment with Japan's aid program to China, which seemingly has given Tokyo very little leverage. Although Japan has been the largest aid donor to China, Beijing has ignored strongly felt Japanese views on nuclear testing and other issues. China feels no special obligation to adapt its policy to meet Tokyo's objections because it views Japanese aid as compensation for past Japanese aggression. Tokyo's severe budget deficit has undermined the domestic consensus among politicians, bureaucrats, and big business in support of Japan's large foreign aid program.[29]

Tokyo reacted to China's 1995 nuclear test by freezing part of its grant aid.[30] The Japanese government acted in response to domestic public opinion, which was highly critical of China's nuclear tests. Ninety percent of the respondents to an opinion poll conducted by the *Asahi Shimbun* in October 1995 expressed resentment about China's nuclear tests. Forty-five percent supported the suspension of grant aid, and an additional 44 percent would have preferred an even tougher Japanese response.[31] The aid suspension lasted until February 1997, when Japan announced the resumption of aid after China had stopped nuclear testing and signed the Comprehensive Test Ban Treaty.[32]

Tokyo has shortened the term of its concessionary credits to China and reduced the amount. China is the only country that has received multiyear aid from Japan rather than support for specific projects. This formula was adopted after Beijing and Tokyo signed a Peace and Friendship Treaty in 1978. Tokyo granted China multiyear aid as a payoff for Beijing's willingness to drop claims for compensation for war damage inflicted by Japan.

When Japan's concessionary loan program for 1996–2001 was being negotiated, Tokyo wanted to set aid commitments annually. Beijing pressed for a five-year commitment. China sought 1.5 trillion yen (around US$15 billion at the 1994 exchange rate) for this five-year period, almost double the amount (810 billion yen or US$5.95 billion) allocated for the previous six years. In the end, Japan was willing to commit only 580 billion yen (US $5.2 billion) for a three-year period (fiscal 1996–1998). Japanese concern about China's military ambitions was cited as the reason for the smaller amount and shorter time period.[33] From 2001 on, Japan plans to give China aid on an annual basis.[34] Despite official denials,[35] it seems plausible that these shorter terms are intended to increase Japanese leverage over China.

There are even some dissenting voices in Japan who are beginning to depict aid to China in more realist, zero sum terms, as contributing to the economic and military power of a potential adversary. For example, a May 1996 article in *Sapio,* a popular news magazine, called for an end to Japan's concessionary loan program to China. The author argued that at a time when Japan has a large budget deficit, it is "abnormal" to loan taxpayers' money to "a major power that would use economic growth as a means to attain military supremacy." He observed that while Lenin ridiculed capitalists for selling rope to their enemy, Japan has gone even farther by "giving" it away.[36] This realist argument is a minor refrain in a chorus that still depicts China largely as an unconventional, not a conventional, threat and views economic relations with China in positive-sum terms. But this kind of realist thinking may gain in influence.

The Japanese have become less susceptible to Chinese efforts to use war guilt as a means to manipulate them into giving more aid. Chinese leaders often make public statements stressing Japan's failure to properly acknowledge and atone for its past aggression in China and elsewhere in Asia. These statements presumably are intended to gain domestic political support for the Chinese communist leadership by playing on strong, historically rooted mistrust of Japan and to shame Tokyo into extending additional soft loans and grants to China. Japanese today are less willing to be pressured in this way. Generational change has had an impact. Japanese born after the Second World War, who now constitute much more than half the population, are less likely to be motivated by a sense of guilt and more inclined to be assertive about pressing Japan's own international identity and interests.[37] The Japan Socialist Party's declining electoral fortunes have weakened a formerly strong voice pressing for Japan's acknowledgment of its war guilt.

Growing Japanese reluctance to apologize to China was evident during Chinese president Jiang Zemin's November 1998 visit to Japan. Jiang came to Japan to commemorate the twentieth anniversary of the signing of the 1978 Sino-Japanese Peace and Friendship Treaty. Originally, his visit was supposed to take place in September 1998. It was postponed ostensibly because of the massive floods in China.[38] Because of the postponement, Jiang's visit took place after a visit by ROK president Kim Dae Jung. In the joint communiqué issued during Kim's October 1998 visit, Japanese Prime Minister Keizo Obuchi expressed "deep remorse and heartfelt apology" for the "tremendous damage and suffering to the people of the Republic of Korea" caused by Japan's "colonial rule." After Kim's visit, Beijing made it clear that it expected a similar apology in the joint communiqué issued during Jiang's visit. But Tokyo refused. During Jiang's visit, Obuchi made an oral statement in which he expressed "deep remorse and heartfelt apology for Japan's colonial rule and aggression" in China. But Tokyo refused to include the word "apology" in the joint communiqué, using instead the phrase "deep remorse." The joint statement, negotiated after a tense five hours, was not signed by either leader.

When asked to explain why Obuchi was not willing to make a written apology to China comparable to the one made to Korea, Japanese officials explained that a written apology to China was not necessary because Japan had never colonized China and because Japan had apologized to China a number of times in the past. This explanation was not credible. There were indications that the real reason for Tokyo's reluctance was twofold: pressure from veterans' groups and from conservative forces in the Liberal Democratic Party who opposed an apology and Japanese leaders' perception that unlike Seoul, Beijing did not really want to resolve issues from the past in order to move forward in their relationship.[39]

Changing Chinese Security Perceptions

Beijing has reacted negatively to recent changes in Japanese security policy and the U.S.-Japan security relationship. During the Cold War, there was a *de facto* alliance among China, Japan, the United States, and other countries to contain the Soviet threat. At the height of the Cold War, China supported the U.S.-Japan alliance and the buildup of Japan's Self-Defense Forces as necessary to counter the Soviet threat.

Chinese perceptions began to change, however, in the 1980s in reaction to the declining Soviet threat and to Tokyo's 1987 decision to lift the one percent of GNP limit on defense spending. From this period on, Chinese security analysts became increasingly concerned about Japan's growing economic power and military buildup. They

saw Japan emerging as a new power center in an increasingly multipolar world in which both superpowers were in decline. While
concerned about Japan's rising power, Chinese security analysts
continued to support the U.S.-Japan alliance, which they saw as a
useful constraint on Japan.[40]

Recently, there has been increasing concern in Beijing about
Japan's growing military capabilities and about the expansion of
Japan's security responsibilities implied by the April 1996 Japan-
U.S. Declaration on Security. In a meeting with U.S. defense secretary William J. Perry, China's minister of defense Chi Haotian
described the "redefining of the Japan-U.S. Security Treaty" as "an
unfriendly move with the goal of encircling China."[41] An article in
Peace, a journal published by the Chinese People's Association for
Peace and Disarmament, described the U.S.-Japan declaration as
part of an attempt by "certain big powers to readjust the security
legacy left from the Cold War in order to gain a favorable strategic
position."[42]

Even before the new U.S.-Japan defense guidelines were published, Chinese analysts expressed concern that the United States
and Japan would expand their security responsibilities to cover Taiwan. The author of a January 1997 article in a Beijing journal,
Guoji Wenti Yanjiu (International Studies), noted that the Taiwan
government considered the Japan-U.S. Joint Declaration on Security
"very important to Taiwan's security." The article cited an increase
in contacts by major military officials from Japan and Taiwan and
Tokyo's open expressions of concern about the "Taiwan crisis" as
evidence that Japan might become involved "not only politically but
also militarily in conflicts between the two sides of the strait."[43]

Kajiyama's August 1997 statement and the new U.S.-Japanese
defense guidelines seemed to confirm China's worst nightmares. An
article in *Beijing Review* called the revised U.S.-Japan defense
arrangement an effort to "contain China in a full scale" and "to get
involved in the imaginary disputes in the Taiwan Straits and the
South China Sea." The article went on to say that the "reasonable-
ness and legitimacy" of the U.S.-Japan alliance relationship was
called into question by its efforts "to poke its nose into other people's business."[44] During his November 1998 visit to Japan, PRC

president Jiang declared that including Taiwan within the scope of U.S.-Japan security cooperation constituted interference into China's domestic affairs.[45]

Chinese officials have expressed concern about the joint theater missile defense system being researched by the United States and Japan. In October 1998, the *People's Liberation Army Daily* warned that the U.S. effort to include Taiwan within the scope of this system was unacceptable interference into China's internal affairs.[46] A Chinese foreign ministry spokesperson warned that the theater missile defense system and Japan's recent decision to deploy four reconnaissance satellites would fuel an arms race in the Asia-Pacific region and undermine global strategic balance and stability.[47]

Ideally, what Chinese analysts would like to see is a U.S.-Japan relationship that is close enough to contain Japan but strained enough to give Beijing leverage over Washington and Tokyo.[48] They dislike the current close U.S.-Japan security relationship, which they see as increasingly directed against Chinese interests. But they also are afraid of a breakdown of the alliance because they believe it would trigger a faster and more extensive buildup of Japan's military forces than is now taking place and that Japan might even decide to acquire nuclear weapons.

Tokyo and Washington have tried to convince Beijing that their new defense guidelines are not directed against China. When former prime minister Hashimoto visited China in early September 1997, he reiterated Tokyo's support for Beijing's sovereignty over Taiwan and maintained that the revised U.S.-Japan relationship was purely defensive.[49] During president Jiang's November 1998 visit to Tokyo, prime minister Obuchi declared that the U.S.-Japan security relationship is purely defensive and does not refer to any specific nation. Obuchi reaffirmed Japan's 1972 statement pledging to "respect" the PRC's position on Taiwan. The Japanese prime minister told Jiang that there was no change in Japan's position on Taiwan and that Japan would not support Taiwan independence.

But Obuchi refused to reiterate what Beijing has called the "three noes" proclaimed by U.S. president Bill Clinton during his June 1998 visit to China. During that visit, Clinton declared that "we don't support independence for Taiwan, or 'two Chinas' or 'one Taiwan, one China' and we don't believe Taiwan should be a member in any organization for which statehood is a requirement." Reportedly, Tokyo had particular reservations about the third no that would bar Taiwan's membership not only in the United Nations but also in other international organizations where Taiwan's membership might be appropriate.[50]

To reassure China and avoid misunderstanding, Tokyo and Washington have pressed for bilateral and trilateral security dialogue with Beijing. December 1993 saw the resumption of the bilateral security dialogue between the Chinese and Japanese foreign ministries that had been interrupted after the 1989 Tiananmen massacre. In December 1994, the Chinese military participated in a multilateral Asia-Pacific Security Seminar in Tokyo, where officers from thirteen countries, including Japan, China, South Korea, Russia, and the United States, discussed regional security problems and confidence- and security-building measures.[51] In 1998, the Chinese and Japanese defense ministers exchanged visits. During his February 1998 visit to Japan, Chinese defense minister Chi Haotian and Japan Defense Agency director general Fumio Kyuma agreed to implement further exchanges of high-ranking defense officials and to discuss an exchange of port calls by Chinese and Japanese naval vessels. During his May 1998 visit to China, Kyuma announced the initiation of an exchange between the PRC's National Defense College and Japan's National Institute for Defense Studies.[52]

Japan, China, and the United States have agreed to hold a trilateral security dialogue among specialists from the three countries. This dialogue will begin at the private level, because Beijing so far has resisted U.S. and Japanese proposals to hold a trilateral intergovernmental dialogue.[53]

Despite these efforts, Chinese leaders still publicly and vociferously complain about U.S. and Japanese support for Taiwan and about the resurgence of conservatism and militarism in Japan. They criticize Japanese leaders for refusing to atone properly for Japan's war crimes and for making annual pilgrimages to Yasukuni shrine, a memorial to Japan's war dead. These statements should be taken with a grain of salt. Some Chinese security analysts may be genuinely fearful about Japan's growing militarism. But a number of others in public statements and in private interviews present a more realistic, nuanced view of Japan. While expressing concern about Japan's military buildup and about the ambiguity of the new U.S.-Japan defense guidelines regarding Taiwan, they recognize that the U.S.-Japan alliance, Japan's peace constitution, and Japanese public opinion limit Japan's military buildup. From their perspective, there is more reason to be concerned about Japan as a potential threat to China's economic development and domestic political stability than about a military threat from Japan.[54]

Evidence of Restraint

Their significant economic ties provide strong incentives for Beijing and Tokyo to cooperate. One example of restraint is the way in which Beijing and Tokyo have handled their conflict over the Diaoyu (Senkaku) islands. The waters around these disputed islands, currently held by Japan, contain rich fishing grounds and potentially large undersea oil and natural gas reserves. The recent rapid growth of China's economy and the depletion of China's easily exploitable onshore domestic energy resources have increased Chinese concern about energy security. Since 1993, China has been a net importer of oil. China's demand for energy is expected to increase exponentially with the rapid growth of its air traffic and its automotive and petrochemical industries.[55] Chinese authorities now recognize that the energy resources in remote, relatively inaccessible Xinjiang province will be difficult to exploit, so they are looking for alternative sources.

Some elements in China's navy have been pressing for more assertive action to protect China's territorial waters and energy resources in disputed areas around the Spratly Islands in the South China Sea and around the Diaoyu (Senkaku) islands in the East China Sea.[56] Despite this pressure, large-scale Chinese military aggression in these areas is unlikely. China lacks the military power projection capabilities to carry out such an action successfully and will lack them for some time. Moreover, Beijing will be deterred from any large-scale aggressive action by its significant economic dependence not just on Japan, but also on the United States, Southeast Asia, and other countries.

When considering the constraints on Chinese large-scale aggression, it is useful to think about China's overall trade dependence, not just about its dependence on any one particular country. In a recent article in *International Studies Quarterly*, John Oneal and Bruce Russett observe that countries are restrained from conflict by their total trade-to-GDP (Gross Domestic Product) ratio, not just by their economic dependence on a potential adversary.[57] China's current trade-to-GDP ratio is quite high. And Chinese leaders are aware that their regime's legitimacy depends on raising popular living standards and that domestic prosperity in turn depends on maintaining good economic relations with Japan, the United States, Taiwan, and Southeast Asia.

On many issues, Beijing's overall trade dependence will not constrain its behavior, because it will not face a concerted reaction by its economic partners. When threatened by a vote censoring China's human rights record at the United Nations or a call for economic sanctions in response to a particular Chinese arms sale that violates international norms, Beijing will be able to play on differences among its economic partners and their competing desire for access to China's vast and growing market. As China's military action against a South China Sea reef claimed by the Philippines has demonstrated, even an act of aggression against a U.S. ally will not induce a strong response, so long as China is careful to limit the scale and duration of its action. So China may be able to get away with sporadic island hopping in the South China Sea, periodic exploratory forays in disputed waters of the East China and South China seas, domestic human rights violations, and arms sales that violate international norms without provoking a strong, unified response.

If China were to launch large-scale aggression in the South China Sea or against the Diaoyu islands, however, then it would risk provoking a unified and far more damaging international response. Beijing is not likely to take that risk to obtain energy resources when alternative means are available. Recently, China started using some of its growing foreign exchange reserves to invest in the development of energy resources in Kazakhstan and other countries.

China has tried to prevent the territorial dispute from aggravating relations with Japan. When a wave of anti-Japanese demonstrations erupted in 1996 in Taiwan and Hong Kong in protest against efforts by Japanese right-wing groups to reaffirm Japanese sovereignty over these disputed islands, a Diaoyu protest movement began to emerge at universities around Beijing. Chinese authorities quickly suppressed this movement both because it was suspicious of any grass roots movement not under its control and because it wanted to avoid damaging the sensitive Sino-Japanese relationship.

The recent Sino-Japanese fisheries agreement is further evidence of restraint. During a November 1997 visit to Tokyo by then Chinese prime minister Li Peng, Tokyo and Beijing signed a fishery agreement which established a temporary sea zone in the East China Sea around the disputed Diaoyu (Senkaku) islands. The UN Convention on the Law of the Sea allows countries to establish 200-nautical-mile exclusive economic zones around their territory. The Japanese and Chinese zones overlapped in the area around the disputed islands. The two governments decided to set this issue aside and to establish a temporary zone under joint control.[58]

Prospects and Conclusions

The relationship between China and Japan is strained by strong, historical mistrust and by the growing concerns each has about the other as a potential long-term conventional threat. Beijing is uneasy about recent efforts to strengthen the U.S.-Japan security relationship and the possibility that it may apply to Taiwan. Tokyo is concerned about China's development of military power projection capabilities and about its growing assertiveness regarding territories in dispute with Japan and other countries.

China and Japan are natural rivals for regional leadership in East Asia. Each country considers itself to be Asia's rightful leader, China on the basis of its historically central role in the region and Japan on the basis of its recent economic strength. In both China and Japan, growing nationalism is creating domestic pressure for a more active and assertive foreign policy with a potential for creating tensions between them on issues where their perceived interests diverge.

Despite these problems, China and Japan have strong incentives to avoid a rift. China is so dependent on Japanese investment and the Japanese market that a rift with Japan would threaten China's economic development and domestic political stability. Japan has a strong stake in avoiding economic dislocation, political instability, and environmental degradation in China. These mutual interests have induced China and Japan to cooperate, as is reflected by their restraint in handling their Diaoyu (Senkaku) conflict.

There are only two scenarios that are likely to produce a Sino-Japanese rift: a military confrontation over Taiwan or a U.S. military withdrawal from East Asia if it led to rapid Japanese remilitarization and Japan's acquisition of nuclear weapons. At the moment, neither of these scenarios seems likely. The United States is committed to maintaining a forward military presence in East Asia. While the U.S. military presence in Japan may be significantly reduced in response to U.S. domestic and Japanese external pressure, a total withdrawal seems unlikely at least in the short and medium term.

If China were to mount an unprovoked attack against Taiwan, using military force to try to reunify the country, then the United States would respond with force. Tokyo would back the United States[59] both because failure to do so would rupture the U.S.-Japan alliance and because of Japan's own interests in Taiwan. Taiwan is Japan's former colony and important economic partner. It has a strategic geographic location next to important sea routes. A strong domestic constituency in Japan supports Taiwan's autonomy.

However, an unprovoked Chinese attack against Taiwan is unlikely, because China would risk too much. If Taiwan declares independence or appears about to do so, then China is likely to respond militarily. Any Chinese regime that failed to take strong steps to block Taiwan independence would risk losing its domestic legitimacy. But it is far from certain that the United States would use force to oppose China if Beijing were reacting to a Taiwanese declaration of independence. Such a unilateral action by Taiwan seems unlikely, since many pro-independence politicians in Taiwan now recognize that Taiwan's interests are better served by maintaining its current *de facto* autonomy.

Barring a crisis over Taiwan or a U.S. withdrawal from East Asia, the incentives for Sino-Japanese cooperation will remain strong. Tokyo is likely to pursue what one analyst has called an accommodative policy toward Beijing[60] so long as China is perceived more as an unconventional than a conventional threat, which gives Japan a stake in China's continued prosperity and stability. Beijing will find that its interests are better served through economic cooperation with Japan and other countries than through military aggression. Sino-Japanese relations will be strained and uneasy, but a rift between them is unlikely.

Notes

1. *Mainichi Daily News,* August 1, 1994, p. 1.
2. "Japan: China's Largest Trading Partner," *Beijing Review,* April 14–20, 1997, p. 28.
3. Robert Taylor, *Greater China and Japan: Prospects for an Economic Partnership in East Asia,* New York: Routledge, 1996, pp. 69–70.
4. *Foreign Broadcast Information Service: Daily Report: East Asia (FBIS: East Asia),* no. 112 (June 10, 1996), pp. 6–7; *China News Digest,* December 2, 1998.
5. Taylor, p. 57.
6. *China News Digest,* January 27, 1995, citing comments by Guo Li, deputy director general of the Foreign Trade Ministry's Asian Affairs Department.
7. *China News Digest,* March 14–15, 1995.
8. *Beijing Review,* March 14–20, 1994, p. 5.
9. Taylor, *op. cit.,* pp. 59–60, 74–78; Eric Harwit, "Japanese Investment in China: Strategies in the Electronics and Automobile Sectors," *Asian Survey,* vol. 36, no. 10 (October 1996), p. 978.
10. R. T. Maddock, "Environmental Security in East Asia," *Contemporary Southeast Asia,* vol. 17, no. 1 (June 1995), pp. 27–28.
11. Taylor, pp. 69–70.
12. Shinkichi Eto, "China and Sino-Japanese Relations in the Coming Decades," *Japan Review of International Affairs,* vol. 10, no. 1 (Winter 1996), p. 30.

13. Charles Smith, "Eager to Please: Tokyo Sets Aside Own Rules in China Aid Package," *Far Eastern Economic Review,* January 26, 1995, pp. 25–26.

14. Eto, pp. 26–28. It is anticipated that China's growing population and changing diet will significantly increase its demand for food. There is disagreement about the seriousness of this problem. Some analysts, for example, Lester Brown of World Watch Institute, have predicted that by the year 2030, China's grain import requirements will exceed the total amount available on the world market. Other analysts paint a less alarming picture. They do not deny the seriousness of this problem, but they are confident that China will be able to deal with it through improved agricultural techniques, better storage and transportation facilities, and other measures.

15. Peter Landers, "Halting Help: Japan's Budget-Cutters Target Foreign Assistance," *Far Eastern Economic Review,* May 22, 1997, p. 77.

16. This foreign exchange reserve figure is based on a statement by PRC vice premier Zhu Rongji. (*China News Digest,* September 26, 1997.)

17. So far, however, Beijing has refused to support Tokyo's bid to become a permanent member of the UN Security Council.

18. Cited by Denny Roy, "Assessing the Asia-Pacific 'Power Vacuum'," *Survival,* vol. 37, no. 3 (Autumn 1995), p. 55.

19. Michael J. Green and Benjamin L. Self, "Japan's Changing China Policy: From Commercial Liberalism to Reluctant Realism," *Survival,* vol. 38, no. 2 (Summer 1996), p. 37.

20. Ibid., p. 44.

21. *FBIS: East Asia,* no. 140 (July 19, 1996), p. 8.

22. See Hisahiko Okazaki, *This Is Yomiuri,* December 1996, pp. 202–11, transl. in *FBIS: East Asia,* no. 245 (1996).

23. This concern was expressed by Professor Shigeo Hiramatsu of Kyorin University in a statement cited by Anatoly Semin, "Chinese-Japanese Relations Put to the Test," *Far Eastern Affairs,* no. 4 (1996), p. 23.

24. Tsuyoshi Kawasaki, "Between Regionalism and Idealism in Japanese Foreign Policy: The Case of the ASEAN Regional Forum," *The Pacific Review,* vol. 10, no. 4 (1997), pp. 480–503.

25. Robert Manning, "Burdens of the Past, Dilemmas of the Future: Sino-Japanese Relations in the Emerging International System." *The Washington Quarterly,* vol. 17, no. 1 (1993), pp. 52–53.

26. USIS Washington File, "Text: Guidelines for U.S.-Japan Defense Cooperation," September 23, 1997.

27. *NAPSNet Daily Report,* September 12, 1997. On August 17, 1997, Chief Cabinet Secretary Seiroku Kajiyama stated: "In case of a Taiwan-China military conflict, how could we flatly refuse a request from U.S. forces for support, even a supply of water?"

28. "Japan's War With China, Revisited," *The Economist,* September 6, 1997, p. 39.

29. Landers, p. 77.

30. Lincoln Kaye, "Politics of Penitence," *Far Eastern Economic Review,* July 6, 1995, p. 23.

31. Yukio Satoh, "Beyond Stability: New Directions for Sino-Japanese Relations," *Harvard International Review,* vol. 18, no. 2 (1996), p. 34.

32. *China News Digest,* February 17, 1997.

33. "Japan: Yen for China," *Far Eastern Economic Review,* January 12, 1995, p. 13; *Vancouver Sun,* October 22, 1994; *China News Digest,* January 8, 1995, *FBIS: East Asia,* no. 212 (November 2, 1994) pp. 6–7.

34. Smith, pp. 25–26.

35. Lincoln Kaye, "No Great Success," *Far Eastern Economic Review,* March 31, 1994, p. 21.

36. Yoshihisa Komori, *Sapio,* transl. in *FBIS: East Asia,* no. 106 (May 31, 1996), p. 7.

37. Satoh, p. 34.

38. Some feel the floods were only a pretext for the postponement of Jiang's visit. The real reason was Tokyo's reluctance to meet Beijing's demands regarding the content of the joint communiqué relating to Taiwan and Japan's wartime aggression.

39. *The Japan Times,* November 4, 1998; *The New York Times,* November 27 and November 30, 1998; Peter Landers and Susan V. Lawrence, "Sorry, No Apology," *Far Eastern Economic Review,* December 10, 1998, p. 21.

40. Manning, pp. 46–48.

41. Tadae Takubo, *Tokyo Seiron,* in Japanese, March 1997, pp. 46–59, transl. in *FBIS: Daily Report: East Asia,* no. 60 (1997).

42. Zhang Dezhen and He Gang, "Detente Continues, Potential Danger Looms: A Review of the 1996 Global Situation," *Peace,* no. 43 (March 1997), p. 7.

43. Lu Guozhong, Beijing *Guoji Wenti Yanjiu* (International Studies) in Chinese, January 13, 1997, no. 1, pp. 39–45, transl. in *FBIS: Daily Report: China,* no. 87 (1997).

44. Li Haibo, "Smell of Gunpowder from Tokyo," *Beijing Review*, September 8–14, 1997, p. 4.
45. *NAPSNet Daily Report*, November 27, 1998.
46. Cited in *NAPSNet Daily Report*, October 22, 1998.
47. *China News Digest*, January 1, 1999.
48. See Manning, p. 50; Banning Garrett and Bonnie Glaser, "Chinese Apprehensions About Revitalization of the US-Japan Alliance," *Asian Survey*, vol. 37, no. 4 (April 1997), p. 385.
49. *NAPSNet Daily Report*, September 8, 1997.
50. Susan V. Lawrence, "Miles to Go," *Far Eastern Economic Review*, November 26, 1998, pp. 21–23; *NAPSNet Daily Report*, November 27, 1998; *Reuters* in *The Vancouver Sun*, November 26, 1998. During a November 1998 interview in Tokyo, a senior Japanese academic reminded me that Clinton had not used the word "opposed" and that the term "three noes" was coined by Beijing.
51. Christopher W. Hughes, "Japan's Subregional Security and Defense Linkages with ASEAN, South Korea, and China in the 1990s," *The Pacific Review*, vol. 9, no. 2 (1996), pp. 233–34 and pp. 241–42.
52. *NAPSNet Daily Report*, February 6 and May 8, 1998
53. *NAPSNet Daily Report*, April 10, 1998.
54. Interviews with Chinese foreign policy specialists, Beijing, November 1998; *FBIS: China*, February 24, 1998.
55. These issues are discussed in Kent E. Calder, "Asia's Empty Tank," *Foreign Affairs*, vol. 75, no. 2 (March/April 1996), pp. 55–69.
56. Allen S. Whiting, "Chinese Nationalism and Foreign Policy After Deng," *China Quarterly*, 1996, pp. 599–604.
57. John R. Oneal and Bruce M. Russett, "The Classical Liberals Were Right: Democracy, Interdependence and Conflict," *International Studies Quarterly*, vol. 41 (1997), pp. 267–294.
58. *China News Digest*, November 14, 1997.
59. Nicholas Kristof correctly pointed out that "no one is suggesting that Japan would actually send troops or ships to Taiwan in the event of war." The question is whether Japan would support the United States by allowing it to use its bases in Japan and by providing spare parts, fuel and other assistance to U.S. troops (*The New York Times*, August 24, 1997).
60. Harvey W. Nelsen, "Japan Eyes China," *Journal of Northeast Asian Studies*, vol. 14, no. 4 (Winter 1995), pp. 89–90.

PART 3

SMALL POWERS' INTERESTS AND PERSPECTIVES

CHAPTER 7

KOREA'S PERSPECTIVE ON REGIONAL ECONOMIC COOPERATION

Kap-Young Jeong and Jongryn Mo [*]

Introduction

IN THE AFTERMATH OF THE ASIAN FINANCIAL CRISIS, regional economic cooperation in Northeast Asia has emerged as an issue critical to the future of regional economic and political development. People of Asia believe that their economic recovery hinges on two regional factors. First, China does not devalue its currency and, second, Japan succeeds in stimulating its economy. In addition, Asian countries are realizing that they need to develop a regional mechanism to spur economic growth and prevent the recurrence of similar crises in the future.

* Research for this chapter was supported by a grant from the Asia Research Fund.

For the debate over regional solutions, Japan has taken the lead and has floated two ideas, the Asian Monetary Fund and the Northeast Asian Free Trade Area. Dissatisfied with the IMF's handling of the Asian financial crisis, Asian leaders are exploring the idea of creating a regional fund to manage regional financial relations. Business leaders in Korea and Japan have been promoting the idea of a regional free trade agreement to expand trade among stagnant regional economies.

It remains to be seen whether these regional efforts will succeed. On the one hand, the economic and political conditions seem to be favorable to further economic regionalization and the institutionalization of regional economic cooperation. Asian governments, disappointed with the levels of Western support during the crisis, are sympathetic toward regional solutions. A crisis environment is also helping them to take bold new initiatives. On the other hand, past experiences are not so encouraging. Despite calls for regional cooperation, Asian governments have so far failed to provide a regionally unified response; nor have they been able to take advantage of existing regional institutions like APEC. The APEC has not played a significant role in managing the crisis.[1]

In this paper, we offer Korean perspectives on the low level of regional economic cooperation. The issue is interesting and challenging, because one would expect to see a much higher level of regional cooperation in view of the large economic benefits that it would bring. Regional economic cooperation is an important issue for South Korea. Since the 1980s, Northeast Asia (NEA) has become increasingly important to South Korean trade and investment. We explain the economic and political forces that have contributed to the regionalization of the Korean economy. We argue, however, that the further integration of the NEA economies is being impeded by the presence of many institutional and cultural barriers. Within Korea, we see lack of regional identity and the strength of protectionist attitudes as the main barriers to regional liberalization and integration. The same problems exist outside of Korea, too. In many parts of NEA, the basic business infrastructure is lacking. Most importantly, we do not see the strong leadership necessary to institutionalize and strengthen NEA economic cooperation.

Economic Regionalism

There are several conditions for the formation of regionalism.[2] As demonstrated in the European Union (EU) and NAFTA (North American Free Trade Area), regionalism is a systematic transformation encompassing both political and economic realms. The main transformational motives in the cases of the EU and NAFTA came from the emergence of Japan and the divergence of existing U.S. interests with those of the Western European countries since the 1970s.[3] As the industries of the major powers became more competitive with severe conflicts of interests, the unified market and a common industrial policy were recognized as one of the more effective mechanisms to protect the regional economies. Naturally, top priority was placed on the creation of a single protected market like the EU and NAFTA. In this sense, the formation of regionalism in Northeast Asia is also required if NEA is to experience such a dynamic transformation of the regional economies. Does the NEA region have such a dynamic toward regional integration?

The NEA region is often called a "natural economic territory." Yet this potential is not likely to be realized in the near future. Many other constraints must be resolved before this weak potential is translated into a feasible practice. Although the NEA countries are physically near each other, the level of formal and informal cooperation has not been sufficient to create any set of regional structures.

A regional economic arrangement can, however, develop as an evolutionary process. The EU and NAFTA have a long history of close relations at systemic, regional, and bilateral levels. In contrast, for the last several decades, ideological confrontations severely limited formal regional economic cooperation in NEA. Such a movement had been limited in Asia. An informal consultative approach has been the norm, as typified by the Pacific Basin Economic Council (PBEC) and the Pacific Economic Cooperation Council (PECC). The more recent formation of APEC may be the first formal intergovernmental approach that includes the major NEA countries Japan, China, and Korea.

While it is likely to take a long time for NEA regionalism to develop, the experiences of the EU and NAFTA suggest that institution building is integral to the formation of a regional arrangement.[4] Expanding economic cooperation itself will unleash forces of cooperation and interdependence that will bring the economies of NEA closer. Yet efforts for cooperation and exchanges should be made at more diversified levels for the formation of a regional identity and economic unity.

Korean Interests in Northeast Asian Regionalism

Since the collapse of the socialist bloc, Northeast Asia has opened up new opportunities for Korea with respect to access to markets, resources, and labor. Although the newly opened economies were serious threats to some industries, the Korean economy as a whole has benefited from the economic transformations of regional economies such as China. In fact, the expanding economic exchanges among the NEA countries have facilitated Korea's efforts to globalize and upgrade its industrial structure.

Since the level of Korean development is midway between that of Japan and other NEA countries, Korea's role has become more important than ever in the 1990s. In fact, Korea's active role in NEA cooperation is regarded as a necessary step in Korea's progress toward becoming an advanced country in the twenty-first century.

As a result of expanded relations with NEA, Korea could secure a more diversified trade and investment structure. It took only a few years for China to take the largest share of Korea's overseas investment. Korea has diversified its trade structure to an unprecedented degree, reducing its dependence on North America. Asia now accounts for over half of Korea's trade; NEA alone accounts for 36 percent of Korea's trade.

The regionalization of Korea's economic activities is characterized by growing intra-regional trade and investment. The share of intra-regional trade has grown steadily, especially since the late 1980s. The share of exports going to Asia rose from 37.7 percent in 1989 to 48.7 percent in 1995 (see Table 7.1). In contrast, the share of the United States declined from 33.3 percent in 1989 to 19.3 percent in 1995. Korean exporters turned to developing Asian markets to make up for the loss of market share in the United States. China's rise as a market for Korea has been extraordinary, jumping to 7.3 percent in 1995 from 0 percent in 1990. Table 7.1 shows that developing Asia, namely China and Southeast Asia, has been largely responsible for Korean export growth.

The regional pattern of Korean imports has not changed as drastically as that of exports. One notable change is China, which has emerged as one of the largest sources of Korea's imports. But the share of imports from Northeast Asia has not changed much, since Japan's share in the Korean market has fallen. Japan, China, and Russia together account for about one third of the Korean market.

Table 7.1 Regional Distribution of Korean Trade, 1989–1995
(in percentage)

	1989	1990	1991	1992	1993	1994	1995
Exports							
United States	33.3	29.8	25.9	23.6	22.2	21.5	19.3
European Union	13.1	15.4	14.7	12.8	12.0	11.3	12.2
Asia	37.7	36.9	39.8	41.8	46.3	46.3	48.7
Japan	21.8	19.4	17.2	15.1	14.2	14.1	13.6
China	0.0	0.0	1.4	3.5	6.4	6.5	7.3
Russia	0.0	0.0	0.0	0.1	0.7	1.0	1.1
Northeast Asia	21.8	19.4	18.6	18.7	21.3	21.6	22.0
Totals exports (in billion US dollars)	60.5	65.0	71.9	76.6	81.7	96.0	125.4
Imports							
United States	25.6	24.2	23.2	22.7	22.1	21.1	22.5
European Union	11.6	13.0	13.1	12.9	13.6	13.6	13.4
Asia	39.5	37.8	42.0	41.4	42.0	40.8	40.1
Japan	28.6	26.6	26.0	24.2	24.7	24.8	24.1
China	0.0	0.0	4.2	4.6	4.8	5.4	5.5
Russia	0.0	0.0	0.0	0.0	1.2	1.2	1.4
Northeast Asia	28.6	26.6	30.2	28.8	30.7	31.4	31.0
Totals imports (in billion US dollars)	60.2	69.9	81.5	80.6	81.0	102.3	135.2

Source: Direction of Trade Statistics, Washington, DC: IMF, various years.

The fact that the regional composition of Korean imports has not changed shows that Korea is dependent on certain countries for their imports.

Northeast Asia is also the largest destination of Korean direct investment. As Table 7.2 shows, Asia attracted 52 percent of Korean direct investments in 1995. Korean investments in Asia are concentrated in China and the four Southeast Asian countries, Indonesia, Malaysia, Thailand, and the Philippines. In terms of incoming foreign direct investment, there has been no significant increase in the share or influence of Northeast Asia or Asia as a whole. The largest foreign investors in Korea are still the United States, Japan, and European countries (Table 7.3).

For Korea there were many forces behind this rapid increase in economic ties with other NEA countries. Some factors may be attributable to the favorable environment posed by the transition of socialist economies toward market economies, but strong government and business initiatives have also contributed. At the business level, Korean firms expanded into NEA in pursuit of higher profits and market shares. The newly opened NEA provides Korean firms with new business opportunities. Korean companies have been very active in entering NEA markets, transferring domestic plants, effectively importing raw materials,

Table 7.2 Outbound Foreign Direct Investment by Region* (in percentage)

	1992	1993	1994	1995	Outstanding as of End of 1995
Northeast Asia	14.2	21.6	30.4	30.0	21.1
China	11.6	20.8	27.4	26.6	18.4
Japan	2.3	0.5	2.5	3.4	2.2
Russia	0.3	0.3	0.5	1.0	0.7
Southeast Asia	26.4	14.5	15.2	22.0	22.5
Total (in million US dollars)	1,218.4	1,260.3	2,305.1	3,059.0	10,224.7

*new investments actually made
Source: Yearbook on Overseas Direct Investment, Seoul: Bank of Korea, various years.

Table 7.3 Inbound Foreign Direct Investment by Region (in percentage)

	1990	1991	1992	1993	1994	1995	Cumulative
United States	39.6	21.2	42.4	32.6	23.6	34.3	29.1
Europe	25.8	59.1	31.5	29.4	30.9	24.5	24.4
Asia	32.1	17.8	19.0	37.5	43.2	40.7	43.4
Japan	29.4	16.2	17.4	27.4	32.5	21.5	36.7
China	0.0	0.0	0.1	0.6	0.5	0.6	0.2
Total (in million US dollars)	802.6	1,396.0	894.5	1,044.3	1,316.5	1,941.3	14,466.4

Source: Ministry of Finance and Economy.

and acquiring firms in NEA. Although it is too early to evaluate their performance in NEA markets, their continuing expansion in the region underscores their high expectations of and commitment to the region.

Korean corporate entry into new NEA markets is part of a globalization strategy. Many Korean firms have already moved their plants to China as part of their strategy to develop a global production base. They can fully utilize cheap labor and resources with a fairly small amount of capital. Local production in NEA guarantees easy access to the host country and paves the way for the world market. The implementation of the globalization strategy began with small and medium investments, but big businesses have since begun to enter NEA markets with substantial amounts of investment. Their goal is to establish the NEA production base as a springboard for expanding export to developed markets.

Changes in domestic conditions have also offered incentives for Korean industries to seek production and other facilities in the NEA region. Rapid increases in wage, rent, and interest are a driving force behind the transfer of production assets. Moreover, there are overseas Koreans who can be employed at lower wages than in Korea. Certainly the availability of employees overseas who share a culture identical to management was a powerful impetus for Korean firms to invest in new markets.

The Korean government has also taken initiatives to promote Korean firms' expansion into new NEA markets. The government, which has been setting ambitious targets of high growth and full employment for over 30 years, sees active cooperation with NEA countries as one of the keys to the future of the Korean economy. The end of the Cold War has also provided Korea with an opportunity to extend its relations with other NEA countries. China, in particular, represents an enormous new market opportunity and natural resources for Korean companies.

Inter-industry cooperation with other NEA countries can be noted as another factor promoting the expansion of regional economic relations. Since Korea is poorly endowed with natural resources, gaining ready access to abundant resources outside of the country has traditionally been an important policy goal. China and other NEA countries have more than enough resources to meet Korea's needs.

Moreover, other NEA countries have endowment structures complimentary to that of Korea. Korea's capital and technology can be traded with labor and natural resources in other NEA countries. Korean-made capital-intensive or high-tech commodities can be traded with the agricultural and labor-intensive products of China. Even in the same industry this type of complimentary cooperation prevails in NEA. For instance, low value-added and labor-intensive parts are made in low-wage countries, while high-end technology-intensive parts are produced in more advanced countries in the region.

Finally, the upgrading of Korea's industrial structure is pushing Korean corporations into NEA cooperation. Korea is attempting to upgrade its industrial structure from highly labor-intensive to capital- or information-intensive industries. As an instrument for this transformation, Korea utilizes cheap labor and abundant resources in the neighboring NEA countries.

The government has also regarded its economic cooperation with NEA countries as a part of its "Nordpolitik." It was believed that the expansion of relations with former socialist bloc countries in Northeast Asia would lead to an improvement of North-South Korean relations. Indeed, NEA cooperation has functioned as a channel to North Korea in many cases.

The Soviet Union was the first target of South Korea's diplomatic offensive in the late 1980s, and economic cooperation was a key component of this policy. When South Korea and the Soviet Union agreed in 1990 to establish diplomatic ties, the former promised $3 billion in economic aid as well as expansion of bilateral trade and investment. Many seem to believe that the Soviet Union's decision to establish relations with South Korea was primarily motivated by economic benefits. The conditions for security and trade linkage were favorable at that time. South Korea had an economic advantage; the Soviet Union, a security advantage. From the Soviet perspective, establishing diplomatic relations with South Korea was hardly a security concession because the new ties did not directly change the Soviet Union's national security. In contrast, the diplomatic relations were of critical security value to South Korea.

When South Korea and China agreed to establish diplomatic ties in 1992, their growing trade and investment relationship was also one of the key facilitating factors. Bilateral trade, begun in the early 1980s, had been growing steadily, but remained indirect through intermediaries such as Hong Kong. The absence of diplomatic ties prevented both countries from receiving the potential benefits of bilateral trade and investment relations. Unlike the case of the Soviet Union, no explicit linkage of trade and security was made during the Korean-Chinese normalization negotiations. Despite rumors of forthcoming South Korean aid to China, they did not announce any agreement on economic aid.

Intentions aside, the expanded cooperation with the Soviet Union (now Russia) and China has yet to produce any substantial improvement in North-South Korean relations. This is mainly due to North Korea's rigid attitudes, although many other factors are involved as well. The disappointing result has now dampened South Korea's hope that improving cooperation with other NEA countries, including the former Soviet Union and China, will be a "short-cut to reach North Korea." One reason why South Korea has been unable to enlist Chinese help in improving inter-Korean relations is that South Korea has derived large benefits from trading with China.[5] The economic reform of China has been so successful that South Korea has not been able to induce the kind of asymmetric economic dependence necessary for political influence. In fact, Korea is now as dependent on China as China is on Korea.

The current trends toward regionalization are likely to continue in the future. The modest progress that East Asia has made so far in spite of high barriers to trade and investment is testimony to the potential for further expansion.

Obstacles to Northeast Asian Economic Cooperation

From Korea's perspective, obstacles to Northeast Asian economic cooperation exist both within and outside Korea. Within Korea, the main problems are the lack of regional identity and the strength of protectionism. The lack of regional consciousness is perhaps the most formidable barrier to the formation of regionalism in NEA. Since most NEA countries have to deal with the negative legacy of colonialism, regional consensus and identity seem to be very difficult to develop in the region. NEA countries still have many disagreements over the past and do not seem ready to bury them.

Public opinion surveys confirm the lingering distrust among NEA countries, especially toward Japan. In a major survey conducted by the Korea Broadcasting System and Yonsei University in 1996, close to 90 percent of Korean respondents felt that the Japanese are either "not very remorseful" or "not remorseful at all" about past aggressions. In China, the ratio of people with such negative attitudes was also high, at 77.1 percent. In contrast, 55 percent of Japanese respondents answered that Japanese do feel remorseful. This perception gap between Japanese and people of other NEA countries has hampered the formation of regional identity and trust in NEA. The data show that the future does not promise an improvement; the attitudes of the young do not vary much from those of the old. A vast majority of young Koreans and Chinese in their 20s do not believe that the Japanese feel remorse for their past aggressions. (See Table 7.4.)

Table 7.4   Opinion about Japanese Remorse

	Fully Remorseful	Somewhat Remorseful	Not Very Remorseful	Not Remorseful at All
Koreans	0.5	9.6	37.3	52.6
20s	0.6	9.6	40.1	49.7
Chinese	0.2	22.7	39.1	38.0
20s	0.4	18.9	39.4	41.3
Japanese	11.3	43.7	35.2	5.8
20s	13.0	38.0	38.9	6.5

Note: The question asked was: "Do you think that Japanese feel remorse for their aggressions against Korea and China during World War II?"
Source: White Paper on Public Opinion Survey in Korea, China and Japan, Seoul, Korea: Korea Broadcasting System and Yonsei University, 1996.

The lack of trust among NEA countries has had adverse effects on economic cooperation. The same survey asked people what they thought about the exchange of popular culture among Korea, China, and Japan. Table 7.5 shows answers given by the overall population in each country as well as by young Northeast Asians.

We can see that most Koreans and Chinese have reservations about importing the popular cultures of other NEA countries. The Japanese are most liberal among the three countries, with more than half of them supporting the complete opening of cultural exchanges. Again, the attitudes of younger Northeast Asians do not deviate much from their older counterparts, although as a group they are slightly more open to foreign cultures. Since the survey did not ask about people's attitude toward foreign culture in general, we do not know how prejudiced they are against other East Asian cultures relative to others beyond the region. But anecdotal evidence indicates that East Asian fear of the influence of foreign culture is stronger when it comes from other East Asian countries, especially Japan, than when it comes from elsewhere. The Korean government has

Table 7.5   Opinion about Cultural Exchange among Korea, China, and Japan

	Unacceptable	No More Opening	Selective Opening	Open if They Import Our Culture	Compete Opening
Koreans	3.1	7.0	59.9	19.7	10.3
20s	1.6	3.5	59.9	21.7	13.4
Chinese	1.2	2.9	54.6	9.6	31.7
20s	1.5	3.8	46.7	13.9	34.7
Japanese	0.5	2.1	24.0	11.6	56.3
20s	1.9	1.9	22.2	9.3	61.1

Note: The question asked was: "What do you think about exchanges of popular culture among the three countries, Korea, China and Japan?"
Source: White Paper on Public Opinion Survey in Korea, China and Japan, Seoul, Korea: Korea Broadcasting System and Yonsei University, 1996.

just begun to allow the importation of some forms of Japanese popular culture.

In the area of trade policy, Korea has discriminated against its NEA trading partners by applying more restrictive measures. Under the import source diversification policy, the Korean government maintains tight control over the importation of Japanese goods. Moreover, most Japanese consumer goods are not allowed in the Korean market. Korea's import policy toward China has also been restrictive and often arbitrary. Because China is not yet a member of the WTO, multilateral discipline has had weaker influence on Korean policy toward China.

Korea's restrictive import policies toward the other NEA countries have their roots in part in its protectionism. Korean industry fears the loss of competitiveness; some industries are already faced with serious competitive threats from other NEA countries. Some Korean businessmen are reluctant to invest in China for fear of a possible boomerang effect from technology transfers. Many express concerns over the Japanese domination of NEA economic cooperation and a consequent increase in the gap between Korea and Japan.

Obstacles abroad include foreign barriers to Korean exports and investment and adverse business conditions in some countries. Lack of infrastructure, unfamiliar customs, and institutional impediments are some of the most common barriers. Uncertainties about the future of transitional economies and the rising costs of business in NEA also discourage Korean firms' activities in NEA markets.

Moreover, Korean exports are subject to the same kind of anti-NEA discriminatory policies that the Korean government is guilty of. The most serious obstacle to the institutionalization of NEA economic cooperation may lie in the lack of leadership. In the NEA region, it is not clear whether any country is interested in or capable of playing a leadership role in regional economic cooperation. Although it is not impossible, a regional economic arrangement is difficult to establish without one or more countries having strong interest in and commitment to it. The cooperation between France and Germany is largely responsible for the successful integration of the European economies. In North America, NAFTA is unthinkable without the United States leading the way.[6] In NEA, there are no natural leaders or leadership coalitions.[7] The three largest countries, Korea, China, and Japan, have had difficulties cooperating with each other in the past, and the situation is unlikely to change in the near future.

Finally, there is no country in the region that is powerful and interested enough in a regional economic arrangement to claim and assume leadership. Japan as a global economic superpower has a global strategy and Northeast Asia is not large enough to occupy its attention. To a lesser extent, Korean interest also spans the globe. China, too, has substantial interests in the global market and the regions other than NEA, so it is unlikely to place NEA cooperation at the top of its agenda.

Conclusion

The foregoing analysis identified a number of cultural, political, and institutional barriers to realizing the potential of NEA economic cooperation. The task of the NEA governments would be straightforward: to remove or reduce those barriers unilaterally and through regional cooperation. As discussed at the beginning of this chapter, the process of regionalization is likely to be slow and uneven in NEA, but there is no disagreement over the existence of powerful economic forces pulling NEA economies together. As long as economic imperatives for regional economic cooperation remain strong, the countries in NEA will, eventually, find a regional economic structure acceptable to them.

At a conceptual level, Northeast Asian countries must agree on what kind of regional structure they want to create in the region. If they want to pursue a full-fledged regional preference system such as a free trade area or a customs union, they must first answer the question: How will they manage Northeast Asian economic cooperation in conjunction with other regional and multilateral liberalization efforts such as APEC and WTO? A regional agreement only makes sense if Northeast Asian countries are willing to deepen or accelerate economic integration beyond what is required by larger agreements. Will they want to discuss political issues?

In the short run, NEA governments will be busy with the more modest task of bringing the level of NEA economic cooperation toward that of inter-regional trade. The pursuit of regional cooperation will not undermine multilateral liberalization efforts, because there exist strong biases against intra-regional trade and investment in this region—biases that stem from the cultural and institutional barriers that we discussed.

All NEA countries may agree on the basic objectives of economic cooperation. However, Korea's priorities may be different from those of others. First, as long as Korea remains divided, Korea cannot pursue economic cooperation independently of its strategic objectives. Therefore, political and security considerations will exert a much more powerful influence on Korean policy than on that of any other country. Second, Korea will try to maximize its national interest by acting as a pivotal player in the region. Because of its size, Korea cannot and does not desire to be a dominant power in NEA. Korea will seek, instead, the role of balancer and mediator between the two largest countries in the region, China and Japan. Korea is in an ideal position to mediate future Sino-Japanese relations. Korea is geographically located in the middle, and has an intermediate level of economic development. Korea is also a legitimate middle power that neither country can ignore. How Korea's status as a middle power will affect the process of regional economic cooperation in NEA remains to be seen. What is clear is that Korea's future position in the region depends critically on how well it performs as a middle power.

Notes

1. Tun-jen Cheng, "APEC and the Asian Financial Crisis: A Lost Opportunity for Institution-Building?" forthcoming in *Asian Journal of Political Science*, 1998.
2. See, for example, Ernst B. Haas, *The Uniting of Europe: Political, Social, and Economic Forces.* Stanford, CA: Stanford University Press, 1958; Edward Mansfield and Helen Milner, eds., *The Political Economy of Regionalism,* New York: Columbia University Press, 1997.

3. Jeffrey Frankel and Miles Kahler, eds., *Regionalism and Rivalry: Japan and the United States in Pacific Asia,* Chicago: University of Chicago Press, 1993.

4. Joseph Grieco, "Systemic Sources of Variation in Regional Institutionalization in Western Europe, East Asia, and the Americas," in Mansfield and Milner, pp. 173–175.

5. See Jongryn Mo, "Implementing Comprehensive Security: Lessons from South Korean Economic Policy," in David Dickens, ed., *No Better Alternative: Towards Comprehensive and Cooperative Security in the Asia-Pacific,* Wellington, NZ: Center for Strategic Studies, 1997.

6. Albert Fishlow and Stephan Haggard, *The United States and the Regionalization of the World Economy,* Paris: Organization for Economic Cooperation and Development, 1992, pp. 17–32; Andrew Hurrell, "Regionalism in the Americas," in *Regionalism in World Politics: Regional Organization and International Order,* Oxford, UK: Oxford University Press, 1995.

7. Donald Crone, "Does Hegemony Matter? The Reorganization of the Pacific Political Economy," *World Politics,* vol. 45, no. 5 (1993), pp. 501–525.

CHAPTER 8

KOREA'S PERSPECTIVE ON ECONOMIC AND SECURITY COOPERATION IN NORTHEAST ASIA

Chung-in Moon and Dae-Won Ko

Introduction

ECONOMIC INTERDEPENDENCE HAS DEEPENED and widened around the world since the 1980s, and the Northeast Asian region has also become increasingly subject to this universal phenomenon. The universal process of globalization has been accelerated by recent scientific-technological progress, the end of the Cold War, the institutionalization of a multilateral, liberal trade order under the World Trade Organization (WTO), and the diffusion of democratic ideas and systems throughout the world. This has fostered the disintegration of the mercantile posture of countries in the region, and the formation of open, liberal economic regionalism framed around Asia-Pacific Economic Cooperation (APEC) has significantly contributed to the enhancement of intra-regional economic cooperation. Equally important is the strengthening of existing bilateral arrangements for economic cooperation among countries in the region. The global, regional, and bilateral changes have shaped a new landscape for economic cooperation in the region.

Along with the economic system, the Northeast Asian security system is also undergoing profound changes. No one would deny that the United States continues to play the role of hegemonic stabilizer in the region. It is so more because the United States has emerged as the sole military superpower in the post–Cold War era.[1] But there are signs of some significant structural realignments in the region: the relative decline of American economic power, the prospective weakening of its will and capacity to maintain its security commitments in the region, Japan's groping for a new international role in the post–Cold War system, China's phenomenal economic growth and stronger assertion of its status as a regional power, and the prospective Sino-Japanese rivalry for regional hegemony. This newly emerging security terrain means that the regional outlook is precarious.

In view of the above, the Northeast Asian region seems to be confronted with two contradictory prospects: economic optimism and security pessimism. Ensuring peace and prosperity in the region through the reconciliation of conflicting regional outlooks has become an important policy task. The pathway to peace and prosperity will be ultimately decided by the evolving nature of regional cooperation, which will in turn be shaped by the dynamic interplay of domestic politics and regional parameters. Against this backdrop, this chapter will explore South Korea's domestic foundation for regional cooperation, examine changing regional economic and security outlooks, and look into viable and desirable options for South Korea's regional cooperation.

Economic Interdependence and Security: Domestic Foundation of Regional Cooperation

A country's attitude toward regional cooperation or conflict is usually manifested through its foreign policy. Its foreign policy is in turn shaped by regional environment and domestic politics. What is critical in this equation of regional foreign policy making is South Korea's perspectives on whether regional cooperation is desirable. In reality, there is no single, unified perspective in the country. Depending on their assessment of potential gains, domestic actors may take divergent perspectives. Three contending perspectives can be identified in this regard. They are liberal, nationalist, and radical perspectives.

The liberal perspective is strongly advocated by the coalition of free market forces in South Korea, which comprises umbrella organizations representing big business and exporters, such as the Federation of Korean Industries and the Korea Traders Association, as well as economic bureaucrats and the majority of economists. They hold that increased economic interdependence and the formation of a global and regional liberal economic order is not only inevitable but also desirable on both economic and security grounds. According to them, economic interdependence would foster South Korea's growth and welfare. Given its dynamic economic structure, South Korea would be able to enjoy benefits relatively greater than or equal to those of the majority of states in the region. The South Korean economy could maintain an adequate level of competitiveness and explore new opportunities in an increasingly interdependent regional economy. South Korea is not likely to encounter any serious setbacks because of relative gains by other actors in the region. No doubt, economic opening could bring about negative boomerang effects, making the South Korean economy vulnerable to external turbulence. But preventive domestic realignments and regional and global frameworks for liberal economic order could minimize such negative effects. More importantly, given its poor natural endowments, Korea has no alternative but to pursue an externally oriented economic policy. Even if there are some transitional difficulties emanating from the liberal economic order, South Korea's gains will be much greater than its costs.

In the security arena, liberals argue that increased interdependence can reduce the potential for physical conflict between states in several ways. First, economic interdependence would increase the opportunity costs of war and thus reduce states' incentives to use physical force in settling conflicts.[2] Second, as is argued by functionalists, economic interdependence and cooperation entail positive spillover effects in the political, social, and cultural realm in such a way as to enhance mutual understanding and trust between states.[3] Moreover, growing interdependence leads to the formation of international and regional regimes, which could play a mediating role in reducing states' incentives to use military force and their fear of threats from economic partners.[4] As the Kantian thesis of capitalist peace underscores, economic interdependence cultivates trans-national alliances through the creation of vested interests in the free market, leading to the incompatibility between the "spirit of commerce" and war. Such alliances would serve as powerful political forces to deter any moves to engage in war.[5] Finally, fierce competition followed by increased economic interdependence helps the states realign their national security objectives from military to economic ones, such as technological innovation.[6]

Thus, the liberal perspective strongly favors regional economic cooperation. According to this view, formation of strong regional economic cooperative ties not only enhances economic gains, but also paves the way to peace and security in the region through the positive spillover effects of economic cooperation. Despite recent emphasis on globalization, however, the liberal perspective remains a minor power in Korean politics. Popular fear of open engagement, which is deeply rooted in mercantile inertia and the collective memory of the history of colonial subjugation, has prevented most Koreans from internalizing liberal ideas and practices.

In our opinion, the most popular perspective is the nationalist one, and it is widely shared among workers, politicians, the general populace, and political scientists. They are quite skeptical about the salience of gain from economic interdependence and international cooperation. Several factors explain their pessimism. First, the South Korean economy is currently faced with threats from two directions, one from China and other developing economies, and the other from advanced industrialized countries. Fear persists that economic liberalization within the framework of regional cooperation could severely undermine Korea's economic position by undercutting both its labor-intensive and its high-tech, capital-intensive sectors, resulting in an asymmetric distribution of relative gains.[7] Second, nationalists are concerned that the intensification of economic interdependence and subsequent economic liberalization could also aggravate South Korea's structural vulnerability by fostering its dependency on foreign capital and technology. In particular, penetration by multinational corporations and their control of strategic industrial sectors, such as finance and telecommunications, could endanger South Korea's economic security.[8] Third, growing economic interdependence could also bring about an unequal distribution of costs and gains across industrial sectors and social classes. Such unequal gains could deepen social cleavages and undermine social harmony.

Finally, nationalists do not concur with the capitalist peace thesis expounded by liberals. According to them, ungoverned economic interdependence could be harmful, rather than beneficial, to regional and national security. They contend that increased economic transactions accompany a concurrent rise in economic conflicts and disputes.[9] They fear that failure to settle them could easily escalate into diplomatic and even military tensions. Nationalists maintain that even if the thesis of capitalist peace is valid, it cannot be applied to the Northeast Asian region. The memory of a bitter history, lasting mutual distrust, and the lingering structure of deterrence based on multiple bilateral alliances in the region would not allow economic interdependence and cooperation to produce any viable peace dividends.[10] Thus, despite rising economic cooperation in the region, conflicts over territorial integrity and collective identity will continue, impeding chances for regional peace and security.

South Korean nationalists possess two faces; a mercantilist face in economic management and a realist face in security management. While their mercantilist sentiments go against the virtues of regional economic cooperation, their realist attitude emphasizes the importance of military self-help within the framework of the existing U.S.-Korean bilateral alliance system. Therefore, the prevalence of the nationalist perspective could easily undermine South Korea's support for regional cooperation in economic and security affairs.

The radical Marxist perspective was popular among militant labor and student activists in the 1980s. But the collapse of the Soviet

Union and Eastern European countries precipitated its downfall in South Korea. Marxists view increasing economic interdependence as a disguised and deceptive expression of the expanding capitalist division of labor.[11] They contend that the intensification of interdependence in production, finance and exchange is an aspect of the "shift towards a neo-liberal, disciplinary world order."[12] They believe such a shift involves the growing power of neo-liberal ideas, the application of these ideas in the practices and organizational forms of key social institutions, including states and international organizations, and the reconfiguration of material power and a redistribution of wealth, all of which lead to the ascendancy of capital over the state and labor, and a deepening of inequality within and between states.[13]

Those who share the Marxist perspective argue that, in the existing international division of labor, South Korea is nothing but a semi-peripheral or a peripheral state and that economic interdependence is nothing more than dependency, of which the key aspect is the transfer of surplus from South Korea to the core world economies, mainly through unequal exchanges. They contend that the deepening and widening of economic interdependence is bound to trap South Korea in a structural dependency, aggravating socio-economic inequality across classes and industrial sectors, as well as undermining its sovereignty and political autonomy. Increased inequality and reinforced dominance-dependency structures within a semi-peripheral or peripheral state, following the ascendancy of the power of capital, could jeopardize social integration and precipitate both domestic conflicts and political unrest in which underprivileged groups would demand that the state break its dependent ties with the core.[14]

Marxist radicals are equally critical of the security consequences of economic interdependence. In the tradition of Lenin, they argue that increased interdependence would lead to the highest stage of capitalism, which would eventually result in hegemonic wars among imperial powers.[15] They maintain that even if such a hegemonic war among the core capitalist countries does not occur, there exists a strong possibility of ideological contentions among different forms of capitalism. Cox foresees that the "hyper-liberal form of capitalism" of the United States and Britain will face challenges from other forms, such as the social-democratic or Japanese brand of capitalism.[16]

According to the radical perspective, regional cooperation is neither feasible nor desirable. It is not feasible because of the conflict of interests and potential and actual rivalry among nations in the region. Neither is it desirable, because regional cooperation will incur greater costs to South Korea. An ideal path for South Korea would be to sever its ties with the capitalist world system and the American hegemonic power, as well as to seek self-reliance in the economic and security domain.

As noted before, of the three perspectives, the nationalist one seems to be shared by the majority of Koreans. A nation-wide public opinion poll conducted in 1995 by the Korean National Defense University shows that 24.4 percent of respondents identified trade conflicts with advanced industrial states as the most serious threat to national security, and 24.1 percent responded that the lack of international negotiation capability is another source of insecurity. According to the same poll, 23.5 percent felt that military threats from North Korea should remain on the top of the security agenda.[17] A more recent survey shows that the majority of respondents (52.3 percent) feel that enhancing international competitiveness should be given the top policy priority.[18] Underlying these public responses is the sense that South Korea is still an insecure country and that in order to cope with the security dilemma, it should not only seek a more assertive mercantile policy in international trade but also prepare for military self-help. This trend can be attributed to several factors: political socialization of the idea of "rich nation, strong army," lingering legacies of the Cold War structure, and the collective memory of colonial domination and subjugation.

Assessing Regional Economic Interdependence: A Nationalist Account

Over the past three decades, the Northeast Asian region has become the most dynamic center of economic growth and trade expansion in the world. As of 1993, Northeast Asia, comprising Japan, South Korea, Taiwan, and Hong Kong, accounted for 20.7 percent of world total income, while the shares of North America (the United States, Canada, and Mexico) and Western Europe were 26.3 percent and 22.5 percent, respectively. A future projection shows that by year 2003, the combined world income share of Northeast Asia, under the medium growth scenario, will be 24.9 percent, exceeding that of North America (24 percent) and Western Europe (19.1 percent).[19] Such a projection is supported by the recent growth performance of the region. Between 1986 and 1990, East Asia, including Japan, East Asian Newly Industrializing Economies, and ASEAN states, maintained an average annual growth rate of 5.4 percent, while those of North America and the EC were 2.8 percent and 3.1 percent, respectively.[20] East Asia's share in world trade almost doubled from 10.8 percent in 1970 to 19.4 percent in 1990, while North America and Western Europe recorded a slight decrease.[21] Despite the recent economic downturn, the East Asian economy is likely to remain at the center stage of the world economy.

The dynamic expansion of the Northeast Asian economy during the past decades can be attributed largely to its growing ties with the North American economy, especially the United States. Most Northeast Asian states have adopted an export-led growth strategy, and have sought their market niches in the United States. For both security and economic reasons, the United States has allowed them to have increased access to its markets.[22] In contrast, the level of economic interdependence within Northeast Asia was relatively low. As Petri points out, until 1986, the remarkable regional growth was accompanied by a steady and substantial decline in the intensity of intra-regional interdependence, as measured by the intensity indexes of East Asian trade.[23] A similar trend can be found in the pattern of cross-investment in the region. Thus, it can be safely concluded that the intensity of economic interdependence in Northeast Asia was low, and the region's economic dynamics resulted largely from the expansion of inter-regional economic transactions. The Cold War system and relatively tense military tensions in the region, ideological as well as political incompatibility, competitive, rather than complementary, nature of development strategies, and weak purchasing power among countries in the region have all impeded the deepening of intra-regional economic interdependence.[24]

Since the late 1980s, however, fundamental realignments in the regional economy have been taking place. The sharp appreciation of the Japanese yen, the dissolution of the Cold War system, socialist economies' shift to open-door policy and structural reform, and increasing economic complementarity have facilitated intra-regional economic interdependence. For example, intra-regional trade in Northeast Asia has shown a remarkable rise since 1989. In 1975, the share of intra-regional trade in East Asia's total trade was 30.6 percent, but it rose to 36.5 percent in 1985 and to 45 percent in 1992. Meanwhile, its trade with North America has shown a minimal increase from 22.6 percent in 1975 to 22.9 percent in 1992. The size of intra-regional trade in Northeast Asia is still small compared with shares of intra-regional trade in North America and the EU, which were 38.9 percent and 59.8 percent, respectively, in 1992.[25] But given the absence of formal regional economic integrative schemes in the region, such increases in intra-regional trade are quite significant. Moreover, a great share of intra-regional trade in Northeast Asia involves intra-firm trade through offshore production, implying the advent of a much more dense form of economic interdependence in the region.

Intra-regional investment in Northeast Asia has also been increasing rapidly since the late 1980s. While Japan, South Korea, and Taiwan have emerged as principal investors in the region, China has become the greatest recipient of foreign investment. Japan's regional investment increased from $234 million in 1985 to $1.94 billion in 1993, of which $1.69 billion went to China. South Korea's share in Japan's regional investment has been steadily declining since the early 1990s. The rise of South Korea's investment in the region has been much more remarkable. In 1985, its investment in the region was only $1.1 million, but by 1993 it had risen to $787 million. As with Japan, more than 70 percent ($639 million) of South Korea's regional investment went to China in 1993.[26] Still, unlike trade, Northeast Asia's share in foreign direct investments by Japan and South Korea is relatively small. A major portion of their foreign direct investment went to other regions, especially North America. However, intra-regional investment in Northeast Asia has been constantly on the rise, adding to the growing regional economic interdependence.

Nationalists in South Korea believe that increasing economic interdependence in Northeast Asia since the late 1980s has brought about little significant, positive effects. On the contrary, it has deepened intra-regional competition and conflict. The East Asian region was traditionally characterized by the flying geese pattern of intra-regional division of labor in which the United States was the innovator and pace-setter and Japan followed the American lead, exploiting lower labor costs and emulating U.S. technological and process innovation.[27] South Korea and Taiwan followed in Japan's footsteps, which in turn were followed by China. Such a pattern of regional division of labor not only facilitated intra-regional economic interdependence, but also minimized sectoral frictions among regional economies. Shifting comparative advantages operated relatively smoothly to allocate investment activities in the region.

The old pattern of regional economic division of labor does not seem to work smoothly any longer, however. The increased speed of product cycles as a result of technological progress, relatively easy access to international capital, and assertive industrial policy have all undercut the traditional pattern of harmonious horizontal division of labor. Through the creation of arbitrary comparative advantage,[28] Northeast Asian states have aggressively moved into more value-added, capital- and technology-intensive industries, such as computer, semiconductor, and other cutting-edge industries, while protecting "sunset" industries such as steel and textiles. In some industrial sectors, therefore, the pattern of the "swarming sparrow" has appeared, making sectoral adjustments difficult and intensifying economic competition among Northeast Asian states.[29] Thus, increasing intra-regional interdependence has not mitigated severe economic competition, imposing on South Korea the difficult task of economic adjustment.

Growing intra-regional economic interdependence has not reduced bilateral trade conflicts either. Disputes over chronic trade imbalances, protectionism, and technonationalism have risen in tandem with intra-regional economic interdependence. While South Korea and Japan have engaged in protracted economic friction, there are also some sources of conflict between South Korea and China. China's growing bilateral trade deficits with South

Korea, which amounted to $3.6 billion in 1995, and its high level of tariffs on South Korea's major exporting products, currently three times higher than South Korea's, are also breeding new tensions between the two countries.[30] If the United States is included as a major actor in the region, the structure of intra-regional economic conflicts becomes much more pronounced. Despite the institutionalization of a multilateral trade regime under the World Trade Organization (WTO), the United States has been intensifying bilateral pressures on its East Asian trading partners by wielding the principle of strategic reciprocity. Sporadic outbreaks of acute trade tension with Japan and South Korea and a major economic collision with China over the issue of intellectual property rights underscore the new trend.

The primary source of nationalist grievance over economic interdependence can be found in South Korea's economic relations with Japan. South Korea-Japanese economic frictions show how asymmetric economic interdependence and trade imbalance between states at different stages of development, in addition to an intensifying intra-regional economic competition, could induce mutual mistrust and conflict in bilateral economic relations. As Bello observes, the economic relationship between South Korea, as well as Taiwan, and Japan follows a typical pattern of vertical integration and structural dependency through technology dependence, hierarchical division of labor, and backward integration.[31] Indeed, South Korea's dependence on Japan for technology, capital and intermediary goods, and parts and components runs deep. South Korea has long suffered from chronic bilateral trade deficits with Japan. The imbalance in bilateral trade has been on the rapid rise since the early 1990s. In 1990, South Korea's trade deficit with Japan was $5.9 billion, but it increased to $8.45 billion in 1993, and to $15.68 billion in 1996. While South Korea's cumulative trade deficits with Japan for 27 years between 1965 and 1991 totaled $66.1 billion, the figure for the five years between 1992 and 1996 was $59.42 billion.[32]

What is problematic is not simply the size of the trade deficit, but its structure. Most of South Korea's trade deficits with Japan are in capital goods, intermediary products, and parts and components.

In 1990, Japan's share in South Korea's machinery imports was 44 percent, and its share in electric-electronic parts and components exceeded 90 percent.[33] Thus, the expansion of South Korea's exports in the 1990s was structurally tied to increased imports of Japanese capital and intermediate goods.[34] South Korea is also heavily dependent on Japan for investment and technology. During the period between 1962 and 1991, Japan accounted for 56.2 percent of total foreign direct investments in South Korea. The accumulative total of Japanese direct investments in South Korea between 1951 and 1990 amounted to $4.14 billion, far exceeding the United States' $2.1 billion.[35] And Japan's share in South Korea's total technology import between 1962 and 1992 was 50.9 percent in the number of cases and 31.8 percent in the amount of payment.

South Korea's structural dependency on Japan and the resulting chronic bilateral trade deficits have been responsible for inciting strong discontent in South Korea as well as straining economic and political relations between the two countries. For South Korea, its trade deficits with, and structural dependency on, Japan have long exceeded a tolerable level. The South Korean government has persistently called for correction of structural dependency and bilateral trade deficits, but Japan has not taken any serious remedial measures,[36] fueling nationalist sentiments in South Korea.

More recently, the economic crisis in South Korea has further strengthened the nationalist posture. The South Korean economy encountered an acute crisis in November 1997, only to be saved through the injection of IMF rescue financing. The crisis dealt a serious blow to the idea of economic gains from increased globalization and economic interdependence. No one would deny that the South Korean economic crisis was a product of excessive investments, dismal corporate strategies, moral hazard and the paralysis of the banking and financial sector, and government failures including foreign exchange rate policy mismanagement. But nationalists argue that the meltdown and placement of the Korean economy under the IMF economic trusteeship were precipitated by exogenous variables such as manipulation by international capitalists, contagion effects, panic behavior by international lenders, and mistakes by international credit rating agencies, all of which were results of increased economic interdependence.[37]

Assessing the Regional Security Environment:
A Realist Account

The above examination reveals that South Korean nationalists are extremely skeptical of the benefits of globalization and regionalization of the Korean economy. In a similar vein, they seem to share a rather pessimistic outlook on the security environment in Northeast Asia. Since the late 1980s, the end of the Cold War and increasing economic interdependence in the region have lowered the level of military tension in Northeast Asia, and in particular the risk of military collision between major powers. However, South Koreans, especially nationalists, believe that those changes have brought about new strategic uncertainties in the region, clouding the future of peace and security on the Korean peninsula. From their perspective, the uncertainty exists precisely because the traditional Northeast Asian security order based on the network of bilateral security arrangements between the United States and its regional allies[38] is on the verge of disintegration. Several factors point to this potential disintegration.

The first is the prospect of changes in the American security role in the region. The United States' continuing regional military engagement is justified in terms of two strategic objectives: to preclude a potential hegemonic competition between regional powers and the rise of a regional hegemonic power, and to retain its "full access to and engagement with" the dynamic Asia-Pacific economy.[39] It is highly uncertain, however, whether the United States will be able to maintain an adequate military presence and bilateral security commitments in the future. Since the end of the Cold War, the United States has been faced with greater difficulties in securing political support for, and sustaining the financial costs of, its military presence in the region. The United States has gradually tailored its military engagement to "affordability, feasibility and reciprocity,"[40] by streamlining its military presence, calling for greater burden-sharing on the part of its allies, and gradually withdrawing from its long-standing opposition to multilateral security arrangements in Asia-Pacific. Any change in the security role of the United States in Northeast Asia would necessarily have a profound impact on the strategic choices of countries in the region and on the overall security environment.

The second source of strategic uncertainties in the region is the possibility of fundamental changes in Japan's security policy, as is epitomized in the recent debates on Japan's future as a "normal great power" versus "civilian power." Japan has various threats and strategic uncertainties to cope with in the post–Cold War era. The fragility of the Russian political system and the presence of strong Russian Far East forces pose a potential threat, and no significant progress has been made in Russo-Japanese talks over the four disputed islands. China has been enhancing its naval and aerial power projection capabilities and asserting its territorial claims over the Spratley, Paracel, and Senkaku islands. The Korean conflict is yet to be resolved, and North Korea's nuclear weapons and missile programs have caused enormous anxiety and concern in Japan.

To cope with these threats and uncertainties, Japan seems to have no feasible alternative, at least for the very near future, but to rely on the United States-Japan security treaty arrangement. Domestic factors also make it difficult for Japan to effect a swift change in its security policies. While remaining in the United States-Japan bilateral security framework and accommodating American demands of increased burden sharing, however, Japan seems to be preparing itself for the eventuality of a more substantial reduction in the American military presence in Northeast Asia and possible deterioration of its security relationship with the United States. In this context, Japan has been gradually improving its defense capabilities so that they could be rapidly converted into effective, actual war-fighting capabilities, both conventional and nuclear, if necessary. Japan has also begun to participate actively in multilateral regional and global security arrangements, which may serve as the foundation for possible strategic independence and diplomatic autonomy vis-à-vis the United States. In short, to cope with the uncertain regional security environment, Japan seems to be keeping alive various long-term strategic options, including remilitarization.

The third factor of regional uncertainty is China's continuing efforts to enhance its own power projection capabilities and assert its autonomy in foreign policies. These efforts have been supported by China's fast-growing economy and recent rapprochement with Russia. In view of its growing economy and the regional strategic uncertainties it faces, China's recent military buildup can be seen as quite natural. If China is to sustain a fast-growing economy and to continue to build up its military capabilities for a long period of time, however, it could pose a serious threat to other regional states, regardless of its intention. Countries in the region are in fact very much concerned over China's increasing assertiveness in the territorial disputes and in its relationship with Taiwan, and over the possible arms race or hegemonic competition between China and Japan.

Finally, the Korean peninsula remains highly fluid with acute military confrontation and tension. There are several different scenarios for the future of North Korea and the peninsula: status quo, economic reform and open-door policy, sudden collapse and unification by absorption à la the German model, peaceful co-existence between the two Koreas, and North Korea's suicidal attack on the South.[41] It is extremely difficult to predict which courses North Korea will take. Despite the anticipation that North Korea will soon implode due to the deepening economic hardship and social discontent, the Kim Jong Il regime in the North remains strong and unshaken. Moreover, recent developments in the North, such as the launching of the Daepodong II missile and suspicion over the underground facilities in Kumchangli, have brought about new tensions between North Korea and regional actors including South Korea. Major international efforts involving North Korea, such as the 1994 Geneva Agreed Framework, the four-party talks, and the KEDO project, have not been able to produce any tangible outcomes, complicating the Korean situation. Under these circumstances, suicidal military provocation by the North cannot be ruled out. Or the United States and South Korea could stage major military actions against the North should it continue to develop nuclear warheads and missiles. The situation on the Korean peninsula seems quite precarious and mercurial.

Neither economic interdependence nor the dissolution of the Cold War system has brought peace and security to the Northeast Asian region. On the contrary, in a sense, the security environment surrounding South Korea has worsened. Military threats from North Korea remain unchanged, and regional security parameters have become more uncertain because of an increased probability of American disengagement from the region and the emerging rivalry between China and Japan. It is for these reasons that South Koreans favor the continuation of the existing regional security arrangement based on American hegemony. This status quo option is risk-minimizing and stability-maximizing. Northeast Asian states also seem to be receptive to that option because they are all troubled by the prospect of a power vacuum emerging in the region and resulting strategic uncertainties.

There are serious questions about the prospects of sustained U.S. engagement in the region. First, no matter how minor and manageable, an increasing frequency of economic frictions could produce negative security consequences. The United States is no longer a benign provider of collective goods. It is also unclear whether it will abide by the WTO system. It has increasingly pursued offensive trade policies, often resulting in tense bilateral trade conflicts. Such conflicts could have serious effects on existing bilateral security relations. Second, the gap between the United States' military and economic power could pose a major dilemma to regional actors. In order to ensure an uninterrupted American military presence in the region, its costs should be borne or shared by regional states, especially Japan and South Korea. In view of domestic political and economic developments in Japan and South Korea, however, it might be difficult, if not impossible, to increase their share of the defense burden. The uncertain coalition politics, diluted regional threats, constitutional constraints, and the current level of defense burden will make it harder for the Japanese government to push for increased burden sharing with the United States. Despite the acute tension with North Korea, the South Korean government will also encounter strong domestic resistance to greater defense burden sharing due to

diminishing public concern about national security, emerging pluralist politics, people's rising economic expectations, and the fiscal aus-
terity in the face of the recent economic crisis. Thus, the status quo
option may be viable in the short run, provided that bilateral economic frictions are minimized and that the issue of burden sharing is
resolved. In the long run, however, American disengagement may be
inevitable because of the United States' own domestic dynamics.

Forging Regional Cooperation: Alternatives and South Korea's Choice

We have so far discussed the nationalist portrait of South Korea's
economic and security environment. The portrait seems quite self-
centered and pessimistic. Its proponents see few benefits in economic interdependence in the post–Cold War era. On the contrary,
things are getting worse as far as the nationalists are concerned.
What viable solutions does South Korea have? The nationalists
favor two options: the continuing pursuit of mercantilism on the
economic front and the strengthening of military capability within
the framework of the ROK-U.S. alliance system. Would these options be feasible? Despite the current strong domestic political support base, the survival of economic mercantilism seems highly
unlikely. The South Korean economy has already crossed the "globalization" river of no return. The economic crisis in 1997 and the
compliance with IMF conditionalities have already forced South
Korea to undergo major institutional reforms, which almost completely dismantled its mercantile edifice. A return to the old mercantile order could mean economic suicide. Military buildup within
the framework of the Washington-Seoul alliance could be viable,
but it cannot serve as the ultimate solution. Nor is the growing uncertainty limited to American engagement in the region; there are
domestic limits to increased defense spending in the face of the economic crisis and growing emphasis on the democratic mandate to
provide for the welfare and quality of life of the Korean people.
Thus, nationalist alternatives to South Korean insecurity seem neither feasible nor desirable.

More realistic and desirable would be solutions in the context of regional cooperation. As the experiences of North Korea vividly illustrate, no country can find all solutions entirely by itself. South Korea should make every effort to cope with the uncertain economic and security environment through mutual cooperation with countries in the region. There are several paths to regional economic and security cooperation. In the section that follows, we will examine alternative paths to regional economic and security cooperation and suggest the most feasible and desirable options for South Korea.

Regional Economic Cooperation

Regional economic cooperation refers to conscious efforts to manage economic interdependence and its consequences through mutual consultation and consensus among countries in the region. Such cooperation can occur either through explicit and formal institutional arrangements, e.g., APEC, or through informal ones such as market transactions and the establishment of less binding consultative mechanisms. Four patterns of regional economic cooperation are discernible in domestic discussion in South Korea. They are bigemony, multilateralism, open regionalism, and closed regionalism.

A bigemonic arrangement would involve the formation of an economic bloc under the collective leadership of the United States and Japan. It would comprise a dollar-yen bloc, a free trade system, and burden-sharing in the provision of regional public goods. Japan has been supportive of such a model, but the United States has been reluctant. The U.S. reluctance stems from concerns about the feasibility of the bigemony, at least in the short run, and Washington's unwillingness to bear the burden of leadership in a new integrative system in Asia. China and Russia would also oppose a U.S.-Japanese bigemony for fear of allowing economic power to concentrate in the United States and Japan. As long as the bigemonic arrangement remains open and inclusive, South Korea does not have any compelling reason to oppose it, since there will be everything to gain in terms of expanded market opportunities and access to capital goods and raw materials. Although the bigemonic order might not lead to the abatement of South Korea's structural dependence on the Japanese economy, active American participation in the regional political economy could mitigate South Korea's fear about Japanese predominance in the region.

Second, Northeast Asian states can seek a multilateral alternative at the global level to cope with both regional and global economic problems. This option is predicated on conscious efforts to sustain and revive the current world economic arrangements defined by such existing international institutions as the WTO and the International Monetary Fund (IMF). Most Northeast Asian states have been supportive of reinforcing these multilateral economic arrangements. Two factors, however, have made regional states reluctant to support multilateral rules. One is mercantilist inertia and the domestic political dynamics associated with it, both of which are prevalent in Northeast Asian states. The other is the hegemonic defection by the United States, which has been increasingly impatient with multilateral solutions and is tilting toward bilateral, and often even unilateral initiatives.

The multilateral option has additional limitations. It can threaten or curtail national economic sovereignty.[42] The prospects for the WTO's effectiveness in addressing bilateral or regional trade problems are still questionable, while economic integration in other regions, including Europe and North America, continues. Northeast Asia also may need regional arrangements that could complement the global ones. Finally, under the multilateral economic regimes, the problem of asymmetric economic interdependence in Northeast Asia could not be effectively addressed. On the contrary, the liberal, multilateral arrangements could aggravate the asymmetric interdependence and unequal division of labor in the region.

On the other hand, the multilateral forms of economic cooperation could be attractive to South Korea, since they could not only deter arbitrary unilateral or bilateral measures by such powerful actors as the United States, but also serve as an ideal fall-back strategy if regional cooperation should not materialize. More importantly, multilateral economic arrangements have been gaining power and influence in enforcing liberal economic norms, principles, and rules.

The third plausible option is open regionalism. This can be seen as a less tight regional organization through which regional actors could coordinate their macro-economic, industrial, and trade policies. In order for it to be viable, several conditions should be met: inclusiveness in the membership, conformity with free market principles, and compatibility as well as complementarity with such multilateral regimes as the WTO. Thus it can make a preliminary step toward greater regional economic integration in line with the existing multilateral trading system. This could be achieved either through a reinforcement of the current APEC model or through its extension in the Northeast Asian region. This option is congruent with the unique features of Asian regionalism, informality and inclusivity.[43]

In the post–Cold War era, such a regional arrangement would be a more desirable and realistic option. It would not only incorporate China, North Korea, and Russia into the capitalist economic sphere but also reduce the costs of creating regional collective goods. Since open regionalism would presuppose the decentralization of economic power and collective management through consensus among members, regional actors would favor it. In particular, South Korea has strongly supported the idea of open regionalism through its active participation in the APEC process.

Finally, closed regionalism could serve as another form of regional cooperation. Given the growing trend toward bloc economies, the formation of a Japan-centered trading bloc under yen hegemony cannot be completely ruled out. As one analyst observes, "Today there is no doubt that Japan has the capacity to create a yen-based regional economic grouping in the Asia-Pacific region and that it has been moving in the direction as a way of responding to the expanded market that the EC will form in 1993, and to the North American Free Trade Zone."[44] Despite the haunting wartime memory of the Greater East Asian Co-prosperity Sphere, some ASEAN states are increasingly supportive of the idea of establishing a trading bloc centered around Japan to counterbalance European and American regionalism. In particular, Malaysian prime minister Mahatir has been its staunch supporter by proposing the strengthening of the East Asian Economic Caucus (EAEC), an Asian trading bloc under Japanese leadership, to counter the emergence of regionalism and protectionism elsewhere around the world. The Asian financial crisis and the Japanese proposal for the creation of an Asian Monetary Fund (AMF) have enhanced the appeal of a closed regionalism in East Asia.

A China-centered economic sphere represents another possible form of closed regionalism in East Asia.[45] China already constitutes a center of economic gravity as a result of its remarkable economic growth. The re-incorporation of Hong Kong into China, growing economic rapprochement between China and Taiwan, and extensive commercial networks among overseas ethnic Chinese suggest that the formation of a Greater China Economic Circle could be simply a matter of time. By the early 1990s, overseas Chinese accounted for about 80 percent of foreign direct investments in China, and they hold an estimated $2 trillion of liquid assets worldwide, excluding securities.[46] It is also known that total production by overseas Chinese equals China's current GNP.[47]

The advent of closed regionalism could place South Korea in a very difficult position. Joining a trading bloc could mean relinquishing the gains offered by multilateralism and open regionalism. Not joining one could also jeopardize South Korea's economic position, because it would isolate the country from dynamic regional economic interactions. As matter of fact, the South Korean government has shown a receptive attitude toward the Japanese proposal for an AMF. But its support was conditioned on the proposed fund not deviating from or conflicting with the letter and spirit of the IMF. Therefore, unless the world economy is fragmented into several exclusive, competing economic blocs and the global institutions of the WTO and the IMF are paralyzed, South Korea is not likely to support closed regionalism.

Regional Security Cooperation

Three major options for South Korea's regional security cooperation are conceivable. First is the bigemonic arrangement, which is premised on a duopolistic management of regional security affairs between the United States and Japan. Given the preponderance of economic and military power held by the United States and Japan, the bigemonic security arrangement can be very effective in managing regional security matters. Under such a framework, the two giants can punish spoilers, discipline free riders, and reward supporters. The new guidelines for Japan-U.S. defense cooperation underscore the possibility of such an arrangement.

A fuller development of the bigemonic arrangement, however, may encounter two major constraints. The first would be its low feasibility. American reluctance to share its power and status, Japanese domestic resistance to its military ascension, and blurred division of labor and disputes over cost sharing between the two could hinder the realization of full-fledged bigemony.[48] Even if the two powers build such a duopolistic alliance, it might not last long. Second, the bigemonic arrangement is premised on Japan's partial or full remilitarization, as well as its substantially expanded international leadership role. Such a move could invite enormous opposition from abroad. All the neighboring states, including China and South and North Korea, would certainly resist Japan's remilitarization. The region's hostile reaction to Japan's international peacekeeping initiatives and Chinese sensitivity to the new Japan-U.S. defense cooperation guidelines are powerful evidence of this. In fact, South Korea is not likely to support any security arrangements that go beyond the current one.

The most desirable option seems to be the consolidation of multilateralism in the security domain. The development of multilateral security management could produce a stable regional security environment by preventing the negative spillover effects of economic disputes into the military domain. It could also pave the way toward comprehensive security cooperation by fostering mutual trust, accountability, and shared values and norms. Moreover, the consolidation of multilateral institutions would be instrumental in realizing the *pax universalis* that President Bush envisioned in the wake of the Gulf War. It would emphasize the importance of the United Nations beyond its role in enhancing regional security in Northeast Asia. The rule of law would prevail over the rule of force, and a system of collective security could be firmly established. Inter-state disputes would be resolved through peaceful means. For these reasons, multilateralism would be the most desirable vehicle for ensuring regional security. However, there is serious doubt about its feasibility. South Koreans find it difficult to believe that the United Nations would be able to resolve problems like the Korean conflict or the region's perpetual insecurity.

Finally, the concept of open and inclusive regionalism could be extended to the security domain. Security cooperation through open regionalism could be accomplished by way of two types of regional security orders. One would be an Asian Concert of Power modeled after the European Concert of Power in the aftermath of the Napoleonic War in 1815. It could aim at achieving regional stability through collective management of security affairs by a powerful few. In the absence of hegemonic leadership, the concert of power among a small number of powerful countries could be a viable alternative. The concept is predicated on the delegation of power and authority on security matters to big powers in the region by other regional powers. However, divergent threat perceptions among the major regional powers, the exclusion of middle and small powers' interests, and the under-supply of collective goods could easily hinder the formation of a concert of power.

The other type of regional security order would be based on regional multilateral security regimes, which could coordinate relations among three or more states in accordance with some generalized principles and rules of conduct. So far several versions of regional multilateral security regimes have been suggested: Gorbachev's 1986 proposal for a Pacific conference on multilateral security cooperation; Australian foreign minister Bill Hayden's 1987 proposal for the creation of a superpower dialogue on security perceptions and concerns; Canadian external affairs minister Joe Clark's 1990 proposal for a Pacific version of the Conference for Security and Cooperation in Europe (CSCE); the ASEAN Post-Ministerial Conference (PMC) involving multilateral dialogue on comprehensive security; South Korea's proposal for a mini-CSCE for Northeast Asia in tandem with an expanded ASEAN-PMC security dialogue; the ASEAN Regional Forum (ARF) as an extension of the PMC; and the ongoing multilateral security dialogue by the Council for Security Cooperation in Asia Pacific (CSCAP).

The multilateral option offers at least two merits: inclusiveness of participation by all regional states and potential spin-off effects on regional security cooperation. However, the prospects of a multilateral security framework in Northeast Asia are limited by a lack of interest among the major powers, especially the United Sates and China, divergent threat perceptions and an often mutually conflicting calculus of interests, and difficulty in steering and enforcing policy among a large number of participants.

In summary, South Korea's choices in regional cooperation are rather limited. In the economic arena, South Korea can combine open regionalism with multilateralism. This choice is very much congruent with the liberal perspective. South Korea is not in a position to retreat to its old mercantilist closet, and closed regionalism would be self-defeating. Thus, its regional economic cooperation needs to be guided by liberal norms, principles, and rules. Domestic political opposition will be fierce, but visible and significant gains from liberal economic cooperation can overcome domestic resistance. On the security front, the combination of the status quo and regional multilateral security arrangements will be beneficial to South Korea. In the short run, security cooperation with the United States seems essential. American troop presence in South Korea could be useful even after Korean reunification given the emerging pattern of hegemonic rivalry between China and Japan. In the long run, however, multilateral security arrangements should be developed in order to reduce tension and build confidence among the countries in the region. South Korea, whether divided or unified, will benefit from such arrangements.

Conclusions

The South Korean case presents several interesting implications concerning regional cooperation. First, deepening intra-regional economic interdependence does not necessarily lead to increased cooperation. Nor does it necessarily have positive consequences for regional security. As much as it has laid the foundation for intra-regional cooperation, it has also produced new patterns of economic conflict. And the liberal thesis of capitalist peace also appears to be irrelevant. Despite increased economic interdependence and the lifting of the Cold War overlay from the security landscape, the regional security situation is still volatile. Finding the positive correlates of expanded economic transactions in the realm of peace and security remains an elusive prospect.

Second, contrary to the conventional wisdom, a greater degree of global and regional interdependence has not been accompanied by the formation of a domestic political coalition to support further interdependence. Even after four decades of an export-led growth strategy and enormous gains therefrom, mercantilist forces remain more powerful than liberal elements. This can be attributed in part to the long-term socialization of mercantilist ideas and practices in South Korea. Equally interesting is the fact that mercantilists are more prone to take the realist perspective on security management. It will be quite difficult to forge regional economic and security cooperation without altering the domestic political foundation. Expanding regional cooperation requires the expansion of liberalism in South Korean society.

Finally, our analysis of the South Korean case indicates that liberal options, such as multilateralism and open regionalism, appear to be more rewarding than closed and exclusive ones. Nevertheless, the liberal alternative faces a serious problem in that it promises few short-term gains. While liberal options are desirable, gains from liberal cooperation are usually very much diffused and require long-term engagements. In reality, however, very few countries would venture into regional economic and security cooperation without expecting visible, short-term gains. A balanced pursuit of short-term and long-terms gains will, therefore, be a major task in fostering regional cooperation.

Notes

1. Barry Buzan, "Third World Regional Security in Structural and Historical Perspective," in Brian L. Job, ed., *The Insecurity Dilemma: National Security of Third World States,* Boulder, CO: Lynne Rienner, 1992, p. 169.

2. Robert O. Keohane and Joseph S. Nye, *Power and Interdependence,* Second Edition, Glenview, IL: Scott, Foresman and Co., 1989, pp. 27–29.

3. Chung-in Moon, "Economic Interdependence and the Implications for Security in Northeast Asia," *Asian Perspective,* vol. 19, no. 2 (Fall-Winter 1995), pp. 32–33.

4. Beverly Crawford, "Hawks, Doves, but No Owls: International Economic Interdependence and Construction of the New Security Dilemma," in Ronnie D. Lipschutz, ed., *On Security,* New York: Columbia University Press, 1995, pp. 157–58.

5. Ibid.; Immanuel Kant, *Perpetual Peace,* translated by Lewis White Beck, New York: Bobbs-Merrill, 1957, p. 32.

6. Crawford, pp. 157–58.

7. Kenneth Waltz, *Theory of International Relations,* New York: Random House, 1979, pp. 129–60; Crawford, p. 157.

8. Crawford, p. 151.

9. Moon, p. 31. Thurow observes that the world is moving toward "head-to-head competition," especially between the individualistic and communitarian models of capitalism. (Lester Thurow, *Head to Head: The Coming Economic Battle Among Japan, Europe, and America,* New York: William Morrow & Co, 1992.)

10. See Dalchoong Kim and Chung-in Moon, eds., *History, Cognition, and Peace in East Asia,* Seoul: Yonsei University Press, 1997.

11. Moon, p. 31.

12. Stephen Gill, "Theorizing the Interregnum: The Double Movement and Global Politics in the 1990s," in Bjorn Hettne, ed., *International Political Economy: Understanding Global Disorder,* London: Zed Books, 1995, p. 69.

13. Ibid., pp. 69–74. See also Robert W. Cox, "Critical Political Economy," in Hettne, ed., pp. 39–41.

14. Moon, pp. 31–31.

15. V. I. Lenin, *Imperialism: The Highest Stage of Capitalism,* New York: International Publishers, 1939.

16. Cox, pp. 36–39.

17. National Defense University, *Bomkukmin Anbouisik Josabunsok (Survey and analysis of pan-national security perception),* Seoul: National Defense University, 1996.

18. Jinhyu Mok, "Kukmin Anbouisik Byunhwa (Changes in people's security perception)," a paper presented at the National Institute of National Intelligence, Seoul, December 1996.

19. Marcus Noland, "The United States and APEC: Foundation for Asia-Pacific Cooperation," presented at the conference on APEC and A

New Asia-Pacific Community: Issues and Prospects, Sejong Institute, Seoul, Korea, October 13, 1994.

20. Ippei Yamazawa, "On Pacific Economic Cooperation," in Ross Garnaut and Peter Drysdale, eds., *Asia Pacific Regionalism,* Pymble, Australia: Harper Educational, 1994, p. 202.

21. Soogil Young, "Regional Integration: An East Asian Perspective," in Jaymin Lee and Young Sun Lee, eds., *Economic Cooperation in the Asia-Pacific Community,* Seoul: Institute of East and West Studies, Yonsei University, 1994, pp. 61–63.

22. Moon, p. 36.

23. Peter A. Petri, "The East Asian Trading Bloc: An Analytic History," in Garnaut and Drysdale, eds., pp. 116–19. For the calculation of the intensity index of trade, see page 122.

24. Ibid.; Moon, p. 36.

25. Masami Yoshida et al., "Regional Economic Integration in East Asia: Special Features and Policy Implications," in Vincent Cable and David Henderson, eds., *Trade Blocs?: The Future of Regional Integration,* London: The Royal Institute of International Affairs, 1994, p. 68.

26. Chang-jae Lee, *The Strategy for the East-Asian Economic Cooperation in the 21st Century,* Seoul: KIET, 1994.

27. See Bruce Cumings, "The Origins and Development of the Northeast Asian Political Economy: Industrial Sectors, Product Cycles, and Political Consequences," *International Organizations,* vol. 38, no. 1 (Winter 1984), pp. 1–40.

28. Robert Gilpin, *The Political Economy of International Relations,* Princeton: Princeton University Press, 1987, pp. 178, 221–23.

29. On the "swarming sparrow" model, see Chung-in Moon, "Conclusion: A Dissenting View on the Pacific Future," in Stephen Haggard and Chung-in Moon, eds., *Pacific Dynamics: The International Politics of Industrial Change,* Boulder, CO: Westview Press, 1989.

30. *Dong-A Ilbo,* June 4, 1997.

31. Walden Bello, "Trouble in Paradise: The Tension of Economic Integration in the Asia-Pacific," *World Policy Journal,* vol. 10, no. 2 (Summer 1993), pp. 34–36.

32. Korea Development Institute, *Major Indicators of the Korean Economy,* May 1997, Seoul: Korea Development Institute, 1997. For an overview of the Korea-Japanese economic relationship, see Woo-Hee Park, "The Economic Relationship between Korea and Japan: Rival

or Partner?" in Il Yung Jung, ed., *Korea in a Turbulent World*, Seoul: Sejong Institute, 1992, pp. 291–316.

33. Park, pp. 295–303.
34. Ibid.
35. Hadi Soesastro, "Implications of the Post–Cold War Politico-Security Environment for the Pacific Economy," in C. Fred Bergsten and Marcus Noland, eds., *Pacific Dynamism and the International Economic System*, Washington, D.C.: Institute of International Economics, 1993, p. 383.
36. Park, pp. 303–04.
37. For an overview of the causes of economic crisis in South Korea, see Chung-in Moon, "In the Shadow of Broken Cheers: Globalization and Its Consequences in South Korea," in Jeffrey Hart and Aseem Prakash, eds., *Coping with Globalization*, New York: Cambridge University Press, forthcoming.
38. The pattern is described as a "hub-and-spoke pattern." (David P. Rapkin, "Leadership and Cooperative Institutions in the Asia-Pacific," in Andrew Mack and John Ravenhill, eds., *Pacific Cooperation: Building Economic and Security Regimes in the Asia-Pacific Region*, St. Leonards: Allen & Unwin Australia, 1994, pp. 111–18.)
39. Jonathan D. Pollack, "The United States in East Asia: Holding the Ring," *Adelphi Paper*, no. 275 (May 1993), p. 73.
40. Ibid.
41. See Chung-in Moon, ed., *Understanding Regime Dynamics in North Korea*, Seoul: Yonsei University Press, 1998.
42. Katzenstein, p. 127.
43. Ibid., pp. 123–129.
44. Chalmers Johnson, "History Restarted: Japanese-American Relations at the End of Century," in Richard Higgott, Richard Leaver, and John Ravenhill, eds., *Pacific Economic Relations in the 1990s: Cooperation or Conflict?* Boulder, CO: Lynne Rienner, 1993, p. 53.
45. See the special issue on the Greater China circle, *Chinese Economic Studies*, vol. 26, no. 3 (Winter 1993/4). See also Harry Harding, "The Concepts of 'Greater China': Themes, Variations, and Reservations," *China Quarterly*, no. 136 (December 1993).
46. Andrew B. Brick, "The Emergence of Greater China: The Diaspora Ascendant," *The Heritage Lectures*, no. 411, Washington, D.C.: The Heritage Foundation, 1992, pp. 1–5, recited in Katzenstein, pp. 134–35.

47. Heeok Lee, "Joonggukgye Jabonui Dong Asia Jibaechonryak (The strategy of greater Chinese capital for dominating East Asia)," in Geukdongmoonjeyunguso, ed., p. 37.

48. Peter J. Katzenstein and Nobuo Okawara, *Japan's National Security: Structures, Norms and Policy Responses in a Changing World,* Ithaca, NY: Cornell University, East Asia Program, 1993.

CHAPTER 9

MONGOLIAN PERSPECTIVES ON NORTHEAST ASIAN REGIONAL DEVELOPMENT

Tsedendambyn Batbayar

The Historical Background

THE 1990S BROUGHT SIGNIFICANT CHANGES to Mongolia and to its relations with the outside world. The Mongolian People's Republic, which was rightfully regarded as the Soviet Union's closest ally in Asia during the Cold War era, terminated its existence after almost 70 years of its history (1924–1992). The new, democratic and open Mongolia was born in January 1992.

Up to 1946, the Mongolian People's Republic (MPR) was recognized only by its protector, the Soviet Union. Its international recognition came with the end of World War II when the great powers established the so-called Yalta system. The Soviet leader Stalin insisted on the preservation of Mongolia's status-quo and its eventual recognition by China as a part of the Yalta agreement in exchange for the Soviet entrance into the war against Japan. After the face-saving plebiscite was conducted in the MPR in October 1945, Kuomintang China recognized the Mongolian People's Republic in January 1946.

The birth of communist China was a profound event for the Mongolian People's Republic in the 1950s. Ulaanbaatar recognized Beijing on October 6, 1949, immediately after the founding of the People's Republic of China. The independent status of the MPR was secured when a Sino-Soviet joint communiqué was issued in Moscow in early 1950 following Mao Zedong's trip to the Soviet Union. For a brief period, the MPR enjoyed its role as an important buffer, a bridge, in a larger Soviet-Chinese cooperative alliance.

By the mid-1960s, the Sino-Soviet split left no choice for the Mongolian leadership. Ulaanbaatar took the Soviet position on every issue that divided Moscow and Beijing and agreed to conclude a bilateral treaty with Moscow in 1966. The twenty-year treaty included secret defense-related agreements and started a massive buildup in Mongolia of Soviet troops and missile bases. The MPR had become a front-line of Soviet defense against China, and this lasted for about twenty years.

Relations with China remained the foremost concern for the MPR leadership. Tsedenbal maintained his own "cold war" with China. Even Mao's death in 1976 did not change his hostility and suspicions. Mongolia doubled the size of its army in response to a request made by Soviet defense minister Ustinov to Tsedenbal, while the latter visited Moscow in 1978. Soviet armed forces in Mongolia reached their peak of 120,000 men in 1979.

There was another important reason why Tsedenbal was so anti-Chinese. Tsedenbal had a very powerful "China card" in his pocket, and he did not hesitate to play it. Each twist and turn in Sino-Soviet relations provided an excellent excuse to ask the Soviet Government to render more economic assistance to Mongolia. Because of the MPR's geopolitical importance, Moscow agreed to unconditionally underwrite Mongolia's two five-year plans for 1971–1975 and 1976–1980. (See Table 9.1.)

During the Cultural Revolution, the Chinese Red Guards charged Tsedenbal with allowing Moscow to maintain Mongolia as

Table 9.1 Soviet Economic Assistance to Mongolia, 1971–1990
(in millions of transferable rubles)

Item	1970–75	1976–80	1981–85	1986–90
Soft loan for capital investment	538.9	1,191.3	2,061.4	2,415.7
Non-repayable aid	73.4	229.5	165.4	204.7
Loan for balancing trade deficits	200.0	260.0	360.0	1,350.0

Source: State Committee for External Economic Relations, Mongolian People's Republic.

a "neocolonial" dependency. Tsedenbal used this kind of allegation as a further excuse to acquire more and more aid from Moscow. For this reason, the Soviet government spent, between 1973 and 1981, 600 million rubles to build a huge copper plant, called Erdenet, in northern Mongolia not far from the Soviet border. This giant joint venture to process copper and molybdenum concentrate was the biggest Soviet economic project ever attempted in Mongolia and became the MPR's largest revenue-generating enterprise.

The Emergence of Open Mongolia in the 1990s

By the beginning of the 1980s major changes were occurring in Sino-Soviet relations. With Deng Xiaoping's reform underway in rural China and Brezhnev's death in Moscow, Sino-Soviet relations began to improve. However, Tsedenbal failed to understand the new developments in Mongolia's external environment and continued to stage anti-Chinese campaigns in the hope of getting more favors from Moscow. New leaders of the Kremlin, including Mikhail Gorbachev, were not pleased by Tsedenbal's old tactics and asked the KGB to prove he suffered from a "critical health condition" in order to remove him from the top position. Tsedenbal was ousted in August 1984.[1]

Gorbachev's Vladivostok initiative, including his offer to remove some Soviet troops from Mongolia, was a surprise for Ulaanbaatar, which could no longer enjoy its almost twenty-year isolation from China. The same was true for Mongolia's relations with major western countries. During Gromyko's time as Soviet foreign minister, the MPR was denied its right to enter into diplomatic relations with the United States. The arrival of Shevardnadze to the Kremlin changed this, and Ulaanbaatar was allowed to enter into direct negotiations with Washington. Shevardnadze's January 1986 visit to Ulaanbaatar gave the "green light," and Mongolia and the United States established diplomatic relations in January 1987.

Encouraged by "new thinking" in Moscow, Ulaanbaatar exchanged visits with Beijing on a vice-foreign minister level and entered into diplomatic relations with the Republic of Korea before Moscow did. The Mongolian foreign minister visited Japan in 1987 and in August 1989 Ulaanbaatar suggested the creation of a "mechanism of political dialogue" in Northeast Asia to discuss non-political issues, aimed at developing effective and mutually beneficial cooperation in the fields of economics, science and technology, culture and education, ecology, and humanitarian developments.

The breakthrough in Mongolia's relations with its southern neighbor, China, came in 1990–1991. P. Ochirbat, Mongolia's newly elected president, went first to Beijing in May 1990, not to Moscow as usual, and this paved the way for a new kind of relations between Mongolia and China and ended the two decades of hostility between them. With the announced schedule of Soviet troop withdrawal from Mongolia due to be completed by early 1992, the Chinese leaders had no reason to refuse high-level visits. Chinese President Yang Shangkun paid an official four-day visit to Ulaanbaatar, during which an agreement was concluded for Mongolia's access to the sea and transit transportation across Chinese territory with the use of Tianjin port. Chinese premier Li Peng visited Ulaanbaatar in April 1994 and signed the new bilateral treaty.[2]

Mongolian president N. Bagabandi paid a five-day official visit to China in December 1998. This demonstrated that high-level mutual visits had become a norm in bilateral relations between Mongolia and China. There is a consensus in Mongolia today that the nation's interests are best served by a China preoccupied with its economic development and committed to the peaceful foreign policy it is currently pursuing.

Since 1990, Mongolia has managed to maintain constructive and business-like relations with western countries, in particular with the United States, Japan, and Germany. U.S. secretary of state James Baker visited Mongolia in August 1990 and again in July 1991 and expressed the U.S. administration's strong support for Mongolia's transition from totalitarian regime to democracy. Japanese prime minister Toshiki Kaifu became the first top leader of a major industrial country to visit Mongolia, and his visit showed the Japanese government's firm intention to organize broad-based economic assistance to Mongolia.

During a visit to Ulaanbaatar in May 1998, U.S. secretary of state Madeleine Albright praised Mongolia as "independent and peaceful, proud and free." The joint statement issued during her visit fulfilled the Mongolian government's long-standing desire for an authoritative statement on bilateral relations and offered explicit support for Mongolian independence, political and economic reform, and shared democratic ideals.[3]

Political and Economic Reform

In 1990 Mongolia held the first free elections in its 80 years of modern history and took important steps toward a multiparty, pluralistic, and democratic society. The Mongolian experience provided an example of peaceful transition toward democratic principles and a market-oriented economy. Being in Asia and situated between two former communist giants, the peaceful character of the Mongolian transition deserves special attention. In my opinion, several factors contributed to this remarkable development in the country.

First, perestroika in the Soviet Union and democratic changes in Eastern Europe helped to create a favorable external environment. The political influence of the Soviet Union in Mongolia had diminished substantially by the late 1980s as the Soviet government had to turn more toward its internal problems than toward its allies. Second, the immediate post-Tsedenbal period, when the moderate leadership of the Mongolian People's Revolutionary Party (the MPRP)—the sole ruling party since 1921—failed to introduce

Soviet-style perestroika and glasnost, indicated an urgent need for radical changes. Third, political changes in Mongolia were demanded by a new generation, trained mostly in the Soviet Union and Eastern Europe and influenced by recent developments in these countries. It should also be mentioned that security forces and the army played virtually no role in the 1990 events. The once central role of the security apparatus has diminished.

It is interesting to note that the first priority for young democrats was how to get rid of Soviet dominance rather than how to introduce democracy. The specifics of Mongolia's transition were brought about by its political and economic status as the closest Soviet satellite country. The uninterrupted rule of the MPRP was seen as a political arrangement for perpetuating Mongolia's inferior political status, and the removal of the MPRP's monopoly on power was seen as an act of political decolonization.

The resignation of the MPRP Politburo in March 1990 led to the constitutional amendments that made possible the first free elections, held in July 1990. The standing legislature, Baga Hural, where the MRPR controlled about 60 percent of the seats and young democrats the remaining 40 percent, became the main parliamentary mechanism for Mongolia's smooth transition. Both the majority MPRP and the democratic opposition in the Baga Hural realized the urgent need for a new constitution that would legitimize the emerging political and economic institutions.

The new political elite was also aware of the dramatically changing international situation. To the south, China was pursuing its politically rigid strategy of "building socialism with Chinese characteristics," and to the north, Russia had been thrown into a political, economic, constitutional, and federal turmoil. A new Mongolian constitution would establish a domestic framework for a continued open foreign policy and a new international orientation.[4]

The 1992 constitution became the first document in Mongolia's history that incorporated individual political rights and freedoms, and an independent judiciary. It declared democracy, justice, freedom, equality, and national unity as the premier goals of Mongolian society, and it recognized all forms of property ownership with legal protection for ownership rights. The constitution made the transfer of power a legal procedure through a parliamentary election held every four years.

The constitution established a quasi-presidential regime, the product of a compromise between the young democrats and the MPRP conservatives. The democrats insisted on a parliamentary system and the conservatives on a presidential type of government. As a compromise, a 76-member parliament was seen as a much better option by democrats than a one-man rule that could easily be manipulated by foreign powers, an experience clearly associated with the history of Tsedenbal rule (1940–1984).

Market-oriented economic reform has been carried out simultaneously with political reform in Mongolia. The coalition government, formed in September 1990 as a result of the July elections, started the implementation of a three-year program directed at dismantling the command economy and laying the foundations of a market economy. Of the two possible options—an evolutionary change or a drastic switch—the coalition government chose the latter. This required some unpopular measures. These measures entailed price increases and a decline in living standards and even led to social disturbances.

During the parliamentary elections of July 1992, the main question was which member of the coalition government should take responsibility for the national budget deficit and the ever-deteriorating living standard. The MPRP election platform called for a two-year program aimed at stopping production decline and achieving macro-economic stabilization. Fragmented democratic forces could not provide an alternative economic program. Instead, the democrats tried to play the "Chinese card" in its election campaign against the MPRP. They accused the MPRP leadership of maintaining close ties with the Chinese Communist Party (CCP), having received a donation of 500 tons of paper from the CCP for printing election flyers, and of planning to train MPRP people in the CCP party schools. *Unen,* the central organ of the MPRP, responded with two articles under very illustrative titles: "Is only the MPRP guilty?" and "Would the MPRP bring the country to international isolation?"[5]

The election results brought the MPRP into office with 71 seats in the parliament, leaving only five seats to young democrats. The decision-making process was dominated by the MPRP and a new administration composed only of MPRP people was formed. During the following four years, 1992–1996, the opposition was effectively removed from governance.

The major priority for the MPRP government in 1992–1996 was macro-economic stabilization. Strict financial policy combined with tight budget discipline brought down the nation's galloping inflation from 320 percent in 1992 to 55 percent in 1995. The GDP registered a positive growth of 2.3 percent in 1994 and 6.3 percent in 1995. Hard currency reserves amounted to US$70 million at the end of 1995, which was equal to nine weeks of imports into the country. However, the MPRP government slowed down the privatization of state assets to a virtual halt and postponed the liberalization of energy prices. Although inflation was more or less brought under control, high interest rates made borrowing impossible for private and public producers, borrowing that was essential for the resumption of domestic production. Bad loans by commercial banks reached critical levels.

The 1996 parliamentary elections brought a markedly different situation with the appearance of the Democratic Coalition. Seventy-five years of unbroken rule by the MPRP came to an end with the landslide victory of the Democratic Coalition. The coalition was made up of the Mongolian National Democratic Party, the Mongolian Social Democratic Party, and others, and together they won 50 out of 76 seats, leaving the remaining seats to the MPRP. As a result, a new government composed of Democratic Coalition representatives was formed. It was determined to pursue more market-oriented economic policy. The government promised to implement tax cuts, energetically carry out privatization, and implement further trade and investment liberalization, including the abolition of all import tariffs. The government set the goals of reducing tax burden by 30 percent by the end of 1999, curbing the annual inflation rate to less than 24 percent by 1989–1999, and carrying out the privatization of 60 percent of all state assets by 2000.[6]

The political turmoil of 1998 brought the government's reforms to a standstill, endangering the core of its economic package—privatization of insolvent banks and major state-owned enterprises, including the Erdenet copper plant. In 1998 alone, factional fighting in the camp of the democrats toppled two successive governments and threatened Mongolia's fragile democracy.[7]

Trade and Investment

The Mongolian People's Republic was used to receiving substantial aid from the Soviet Union, an equivalent to about 30 percent of its GDP. Since 1962, it had enjoyed a "captive" market in the former Council of Mutual Economic Assistance (CMEA) countries for many of its products. Prior to 1990, over 90 percent of foreign trade was conducted with other CMEA countries on the basis of so-called transferable rubles.

The disintegration of the USSR and the breakdown of trade with the CMEA badly affected Mongolia's economy. The volume of exports declined by 38 and 13 percent in 1990 and 1991, respectively, but recovered somewhat in 1992. Imports declined even more, by 41 percent in 1990, 48 percent in 1991, and 17 percent in 1992. The initial shock was compounded by shortages of spare parts and machinery from the former Soviet Union, which were used extensively in Mongolian industries.

Both domestic and international trade regimes have effectively been liberalized since 1990. Former state-owned foreign trade companies have ceased to operate, and both private and public enterprises have won the right to conduct foreign trade freely. With exchange rates liberalized in May 1993, export licensing, which was practiced during the 1990–1993 period, was formally abolished except for livestock export. Moreover, a uniform 15 percent import tax was introduced in 1990.

The initial period of foreign trade decline, especially import contraction, was over by 1993. The country's imports have registered large increases since 1994. According to the latest government statistics, Mongolia's imports stood at US$574.7 million and exports at US$451.5 million in 1997. The increases can be explained by somewhat higher world market prices for Mongolia's traditional export items, including copper and raw cashmere. These two export items still dominate Mongolia's exports, copper making up almost 50 percent and cashmere about 20 percent of total exports.

The most notable change is in broad trade diversification, both in terms of the destination of exports and the sources of imports. Prior to 1990, over 90 percent of foreign trade was conducted with the former Soviet Union and Eastern European countries. By 1997, only 10.6 percent of exports was bound for these countries. In contrast, 46.2 percent of the exports went to Northeast Asian countries and the remaining 43.2 percent to West European countries. (See Table 9.2.)

Trade with neighboring China and some other East Asian countries increased rapidly. For example, trade with China increased from less than 2 percent of Mongolia's total in 1989 to about 24 percent in 1993. Although trade volume decreased to 15.5 percent in 1994, exports to China represented 22.5 percent of Mongolia's total in 1997. There is much room for growth. Mongolia's exports to China mostly consist of animal skins and hides (30 percent), cashmere and wool (38 percent), and copper (17 percent). Booming border trade between Mongolia and Chinese Inner Mongolia, which had declined after 1994, recovered and contributed to this remarkable growth.

Trade with the major traditional partner, Russia, is going through a big adjustment. The volume of trade with Russia and for-

Table 9.2 Trade by Destination (in percent of exports and imports)

	Exports			Imports		
	1989	1993	1997	1989	1993	1997
Total	100.0	100.0	100.0	100.0	100.0	100.0
Former CMEA	90.0	62.4	10.6	93.0	60.6	50.9
Former USSR	73.2	52.6	10.4	82.8	58.4	47.8
China	0.5	31.4	22.5	2.1	17.4	11.0
Japan	3.3	4.5	8.3	0.7	5.5	6.0
South Korea	—	0.3	9.8	—	1.1	3.6
USA	—	1.1	5.6	—	4.5	6.4

Source: Mongolian Statistical Yearbooks.

mer CMEA countries declined from almost 89 percent in 1989 to
about 56 percent in 1993. Russia is the traditional destination of
most of Mongolia's copper export and the exclusive source of Mongolia's petroleum import. Mongolia is also still dependent on Russia for some crucial spare parts for its power plants. Although
Mongolia has started to receive hard currency for its copper, it has
to pay world prices for badly needed fuel and petroleum products.
In 1995, copper accounted for 73.5 percent of Mongolia's exports
to Russia, while petroleum products accounted for 21.4 percent of
its imports from Russia. Barter trade made for about 35 percent of
total two-way trade, a reflection of the hard currency shortages on
both sides.

According to foreign trade statistics of the first nine months of
1998, most of Mongolia's foreign trade was conducted with its
neighboring countries, including Russia and China. The G-7 countries were the next most important trade partners. Trade with
Northeast Asian countries, including South Korea and Japan, is increasing rapidly. Petroleum, chemical products, electricity, metal
products, machinery and equipment, electrical appliances, and all
kinds of transport equipment and their spare parts accounted for
62.3 percent of the country's imports. Mining products, textiles,
leather, hide, wool, and cashmere accounted for 78.6 percent of
total exports.[8]

Since the adoption in 1990 of the Foreign Investment Law—the
first ever such law in Mongolia's history—new favorable conditions
have been created to attract foreign direct investment. From 1990 to
1993, the flow of foreign investment was very modest. However, the
revision of the Foreign Investment Law in 1993 increased foreign investment to US$36.2 million in 1994 and US$52.5 million in 1995.
(See Table 9.3.) The law does not distinguish between joint ventures
and foreign equity investments, eliminating the need for foreign investors to look for domestic partners. The new law also insures the
repatriation of profits for foreign investors.

Foreign investment from 41 countries reached US$123.2 mil-
lion in 1990–1996. Table 9.3 shows the top ten countries that invested between US$2 million and 30 million into Mongolian
economy. Russia and China, our two neighbors, are the leaders.

Table 9.3 Foreign Investment by Top Ten Investors (in millions of US$)

	Total	1990	1991	1992	1993	1994	1995	1996
Russia	26.53	0.00	1.63	1.82	0.76	12.40	9.25	0.61
China	19.23	0.86	1.12	1.50	2.59	2.80	7.83	2.50
Portugal	13.50	0.00	0.00	0.00	0.00	13.50	0.00	0.00
USA	12.77	0.00	0.00	0.00	2.57	0.81	4.46	7.48
Japan	11.77	0.10	0.53	0.06	0.09	1.78	8.49	0.69
Italy	8.53	0.00	0.00	0.00	0.00	0.00	8.40	0.13
Republic of Korea	8.44	0.00	0.00	0.00	0.00	2.40	5.02	1.03
UK	3.47	0.02	0.00	0.48	0.00	0.57	0.41	1.99
Hong Kong	3.06	0.00	0.09	0.00	0.55	1.26	0.40	0.75
Canada	2.80	0.00	0.00	0.00	0.00	0.00	2.70	0.10

Note: Totals do not necessarily match due to rounding errors.
Source: The Ministry of Finance, Foreign Investment Board.

Northeast Asian countries such as Japan and the Republic of Korea are among the first ten investors. Japan started to invest in 1990 and has been increasing its presence since. Particularly, during the last three years Japan has increased its investment significantly. The United States, United Kingdom, Italy, and Canada also started to invest in Mongolia in 1993.

The most attractive sectors for foreign investors are animal raw material processing, gold and minerals exploration and extraction, construction and construction materials, and food and light industry.[9]

The Tumen River Project and Mongolia

Since the Ulaanbaatar meeting in 1991 under the sponsorship of the United Nations Development Program (UNDP), the Tumen River Area Development Program has been successfully developed. China's development plan for this area calls for the construction of an international port at Fanchuang in Hunchun, Jilin Province and the designation of this area as a free trade zone. This plan includes the development of the surrounding area, the "Golden Delta," connecting the prefectural seat Yanji, Vladivostok, and Chonjin in North Korea. The master plan envisages the development of this area as the center of the Japan Sea Rim by combining the resources of the Russian Far East and Mongolia, the labor force of China and North Korea, and the capital and technology of Japan and South Korea.

The Mongolian government has welcomed this idea and drafted its concept on how to integrate Mongolia into the Tumen River Area Development Program. The main objective of the program is to transform the Tumen River Area into an international shipping, trading, and manufacturing base. It will eventually help Northeast Asia to ensure sustainable and environmentally sound economic development. Mongolia and other participant parties signed two legal agreements and a memorandum of understanding on the environment at UNDP headquarters in New York in December 1995.

The implementation of these and other agreements will largely depend on the political will of the governments who signed them to understand each other's needs and to facilitate cooperation between riparian and non-riparian countries. It is equally important that developed countries, like Japan, the United States, the Netherlands, and France, as well as international organizations, especially financial institutions, be made partners in the implementation process so as to promote the flow of financial resources and technological know-how into the area projected for development. Provincial governments and the private sector could be of major help if they took initiatives for cooperation not only in this program but also in other projects.

The Mongolian government has proposed a number of transportation development projects to link its eastern part to the Tumen River area. These proposals include:

1. a feasibility study of the most convenient railway route that can connect Eastern Mongolia to the railway system of Northeast Asia. By implementing this project, Mongolia hopes to gain new access to the sea, have ample opportunities to develop natural resources, and facilitate the flow of people and goods;

2. upgrading of the existing port at Choibalsan City in Eastern Mongolia in order to establish it as an international airport;

3. development of a large deposit of high quality coal at Tavan Tolgoi, Mongolia, as a joint development project within the Tumen River Area Development Program; and

4. consideration of a possible Mongolian route for natural gas and oil pipelines from Russian Siberia to China through Mongolia, and further to South Korea and Japan.[10]

Within the overall scheme for regional cooperation and development, Mongolia has some impressive assets to contribute. They include: abundant natural mineral resources; broad opportunities to utilize solar and wind energy; a young population, with 75 percent under the age of 35; a high literacy rate; a large livestock economy with more than 26 million heads of cattle; an agricultural area totaling 140 million hectares; a continental bridge between Central Asia and Northeast Asia; the location between two huge markets in

Russia and China; a strong commitment to a market economy; and political stability.

On the other hand, Mongolia also suffers from some disadvantages—for example, its landlocked location, its low population density, and its extreme continental climate. Perhaps the most challenging problem facing Mongolia is the poor state of its transportation facilities. Access to Mongolia is possible only through Russia or China. Thus, goods from other Northeast Asian countries are carried to either Chinese or Russian ports and then transported by rail some 2,000 kilometers before they reach Mongolia. This situation must, of course, be improved by greatly expanding the transportation network and seeking additional routes to the sea, perhaps through the Tumen River.

Conclusion

It is interesting to juxtapose Mongolia's position in relation to its external environment in the 1990s with its position early in this century. In 1911 the Manchu dynasty disintegrated, giving Mongolia the opportunity to revive its statehood, which had been under alien influence for several centuries. In the 1990s Mongolia's powerful northern neighbor, the former Soviet empire, disintegrated, giving Mongolia a historic chance to regain its de-facto independence.

It is well known that Mongolia's development prior to 1990 was based on the "non-capitalist way," which theoretically was imposed on the nation to prove that a nomadic country could successfully build socialism by skipping a capitalist stage of development. As a result, Mongolia's economy became highly integrated with other centrally planned economies through the Moscow-led CMEA economic zone at the price of being isolated from East Asian and West European markets. The Mongolian People's Republic was destined to supply livestock and related raw materials and some essential minerals to the CMEA countries in exchange for industrial goods and machinery.

Since 1990, Mongolia has developed into a politically pluralistic society, it has adopted an open and non-aligned foreign policy orientation, and compared to the pre-1990 period, its orientation has turned much more toward Asia, especially Northeast Asia. Following the economic reform and international opening, Mongolia's trade and economic relations have become much more diversified. Foreign direct investment is also coming into the country gradually. Regionalism, not nationalism, is seen as one of the best strategic options for Mongolia in the next century.

From the standpoint of Mongolia's development strategy, it would be much more to Mongolia's advantage to align itself with the Northeast Asian countries or territories. There is a growing consensus in the world that the Pacific region, of which Northeast Asia is an important part, could bring important economic growth in the next century. By linking itself to Northeast Asia, Mongolia will place itself under the "economic umbrella" of technologically advanced countries such as Japan, the United States, and South Korea; it will have improved bilateral relations with the Russian Far East and Chinese Northeast as well as with North Korea. Mongolia's eastern part, where many of the country's mineral deposits are located, can be made easily accessible to the rest of Northeast Asia by road and railway, thus giving Mongolia another access to the sea; and it will give Mongolia the opportunity to serve as a land bridge between Northeast Asia and Europe.

Notes

1. Ts. Batabayar, *Modern Mongolia: A Concise History,* Ulaanbaatar: Institute of International and Oriental Studies, 1995, pp. 73–88.
2. G. Tumurchuluun, "Mongolia's Foreign Policy Revisited: Its Relations with Russia and China," *The Mongolian Journal of International Affairs,* no. 2 (1995), pp. 51–53.
3. Alfonse F. La Porta, "U.S.-Mongolia Relations: Future Is Now," *The Mongolian Journal of International Affairs,* no. 5 (1998), pp. 3–9.
4. H. Hulan, "Mongolia's New Constitutional Regime: Institutional Tensions and Political Consequences," *The Mongolian Journal of International Affairs,* no. 3 (1996), p. 44.
5. Ts. Batbayar, "Mongolia in 1992: Back to One-Party Rule," *Asian Survey,* vol. 33, no. 1 (January 1993), pp. 61–66.

6. "Government Program of Action," *Ardyn Erkh,* November 22, 1996.

7. *The Far Eastern Economic Review,* November 5, 1998, pp. 30–31.

8. "Statistical Bulletin," Ulaanbaatar: National Statistical Office, October 1998, pp. 23–37.

9. B. Bathishig, "Foreign Direct Investment in Mongolia: Present and Future," paper presented at the International Conference on Economic Cooperation in Northeast Asia, organized by the Institute of East and West Studies, Yonsei University, Seoul, November 29, 1996.

10. L. Nyamtseren, "Northeast Asia Tumen Region Economic Cooperation and Mongolia's Participation," *Regional Security Issues and Mongolian-Canadian View,* no. 2 (1997), pp. 56–64.

PART 4

REFORM, CRISIS, AND
DEMOGRAPHIC CHANGES:
SECURITY IMPLICATIONS

CHAPTER 10

RUSSIAN CRISIS
Will Northeast Asia Links Help?

Vladimir I. Ivanov

Introduction

UNLIKE ANY OTHER EUROPEAN COUNTRY, Russia has a Pacific coastline, an immeasurable advantage for developing closer economic ties in Northeast Asia and the Asia-Pacific economic area. However, with the current economic decline, political chaos, and social disorganization, the position of Russia in East Asia is uncertain. That was also the case with the former Soviet Union, but because of the military stand-off with key neighbors, not for domestic reasons. Fortunately for Russia, political tensions in Northeast Asia have dramatically lessened and security threats subsided, making its position in the region heavily dependent on internal developments, particularly the country's endless economic troubles.

Asia's economic crisis and slump in oil prices appeared to be additional sources of pressure and uncertainty with adverse, albeit indirect, implications for the Far East. Economic and political upheavals in Moscow in September-October 1998 pointed to the opening of a new chapter in Russia's economic transition. Moscow's partnership-type relationships with the West were threatened by these developments as well. Some observers even suggested that Yevgeniy Primakov's elevation to power symbolized the end of Yeltsin's era of "economic liberalism" and that his proposed economic policy was not too far from "Gorbachev's communist vision" of the interplay of central power and markets. A question was raised as to whether "Russia is lost," and whether the United States and the other G7 countries, as well as the leading international financial institutions, pursued the wrong policies toward Russia's reform and impeded the country's recovery and transition to a civilized system. Furthermore, the alarm was set off that the West's "liberalistic" approach to "market building initiatives" in Russia may only lead to "authoritarian militarism" paired with an economically controlled and closed Russia.[1]

The roots of the problem, however, are much deeper, transcending possible suspicions, or likes and dislikes, of personalities. As far as Far Eastern Russia is concerned, the devastating financial crisis that unfolded in August-September 1998 threatened the country's rudimentary signs of economic recovery and slim prospects for getting foreign investment. In the context of Moscow's aggravated financial problems, some remote territories of the Far East were swiftly changing their status, becoming a de facto liability for the federal government. Increased transportation costs, the end of an era of cheap energy resources, dependence on sources of investment outside of the region, and sudden loss of economic preferences within Russia put the entire Far Eastern economic region in deep trouble. Far Eastern Russia is "drifting" away under the pressure of new economic realities, inept economic policies, and a large-scale redistribution of economic assets and political power.[2]

Economic Decline

No matter how serious and gloomy the developments of the fall of 1998 may have appeared, what happened was rather logical and anything but unexpected. In 1998 massive non-payments and organized labor protests were on the rise, and by August 1998 the public disapproval rating of Boris Yeltsin's presidency had reached 55 percent. His approval rating fell further to 11 percent in the summer of 1998 and to only 1 percent toward the end of the year. One of the key reasons for this was Moscow's economic policy, which was designed and conducted in such a way that it made the Russian economy progressively poorer, with about half of its population nearing the "poverty line."

Manufacturers were suffering from a shortage of credit, since commercial banks were channeling most of their resources into high-yield treasury bonds. With interest rates well above 20–30 percent, enterprises in the real economy were unable to function or even survive. Capital investment in production dropped by 80 percent, while spending on plants and equipment in the metal-cutting and machine-building sectors declined to 6–7 percent of what it had been in 1990. In 1997, about half of the industrial enterprises in the country reported losses.

In 1990, Russia was among the top five manufacturers of metal-cutting tools. By 1995 its share in the world output of this type of equipment had fallen to a mere 0.78 percent, or less than 10,000 units, including only 230 computerized metal-cutting tools, compared with 16,700 in 1990. Russia's machine-building sector's production continued to decline, by 15 percent in 1992, 16 percent in 1993, 31 percent in 1994, 9 percent in 1995, and about 5 percent in 1996. As a result, heavy equipment manufacturing, tractors, and combine harvesters operated at only 5–8 percent of their full capacity; the output of trucks, railway passenger cars, and electric motors declined to 16–18 percent of capacity; and the production of metal-cutting machine tools and freight railway cars decreased to 19–25 percent of full capacity.

The overvalued ruble facilitated large-scale imports, including food, consumer goods, and durables. Domestic producers, even those engaged in the most profitable sectors with fast returns, were losing their market share vis-à-vis foreign competitors. The output of household appliances and consumer durable goods decreased between 7 and 32 percent compared with pre-crisis levels. Russia's dependency on imported poultry jumped to 99 percent, 99 percent for sugar, 97 percent for frozen fish, 60 percent for milk, 33 percent for butter, and 28 percent for meat and beef.

Investment in the agricultural sector also decreased by more than 90 percent, compared with 1990. By 1996, Russia's agricultural output had contracted by 33 percent, its production of grains by 46 percent, meat and meat products by 40 percent, and milk and dairy products by 29 percent. Russia has practically stopped the import of grain, replacing it with imports of processed food, and this has undermined the domestic food industry and agricultural production.

In June 1998, when Russia's balance of payments and foreign trade figures for 1997 were released, it became clear that Russia was nearing insolvency. The declining prices of raw materials, including oil, natural gas, and petrochemicals had sent the country's energy exports down by 29 percent. Because of the declining prices of metals, Russia's combined exports in this sector had dropped by 11 percent. In January-August 1998, the nation's total exports declined by about 14 percent from the same period a year earlier, while imports increased by 4.5 percent. As a result, Russia's foreign trade surplus for these eight months fell sharply, to $12.5 billion, compared with $21.4 billion a year earlier. Moreover, about 50 percent of Russia's domestic consumer demand was met through imports.

Russia was also losing financial resources through trade in services, particularly in tourism and transportation. In 1997 the country's exports in services were $5.2 billion, substantially lower than the estimated $18.7 billion in imports. The illegal outflow of financial resources, according to the Central Bank of Russia, could have been as significant as $7.3 billion. Delayed repatriation of proceeds from exports was estimated at $4.6 billion, and advance payments for non-delivered goods and services from outside Russia reached $6.9 billion.[3]

In 1997, Russian exports declined by 2 percent, to $89 billion, and imports increased by 6 percent, reaching $71 billion. In addition to oil, other raw materials and intermediary goods exported by Russia, including natural gas, coal, and metals, became cheaper. In 1996–1997, these items constituted about 47 percent of the nation's entire exports. As a consequence, Russia's trade surplus fell to $18 billion, compared with $27 billion in 1996, and its current account balance dropped to its lowest level since 1993, from $12.1 billion in 1996 to $3.3 billion.[4]

In 1996–1997, it was possible to manage both the internal and external debts because of the substantial trade surplus the country enjoyed. Fortunately for Moscow, the repayment of $32.5 billion in external commercial debts in 1997 was rescheduled by the London Club of bank creditors, and a similar deal was reached with the Paris Club for another $40 billion. Internal debts, however, were mounting, and in early 1998, when domestic obligations surpassed the $100 billion mark, the major credit-rating agencies downgraded Russia's rating.[5]

With commercial credits prohibitively expensive and no investment support coming from the federal budget, the non-payments and tax arrears became a survival device for most enterprises, taking the form of "forced credit." Surrogates for monetary payment, such as barter and other "quasi-money" were proliferating. Between 1995 and 1996, the share of barter transactions increased from 25 percent to 40 percent in the total sales of enterprises. In 1997, only 20 percent of the total sales were conducted through regular monetary instruments. The eroding taxable base also complicated tax collection at a time when the government had to allocate about half of its cash revenue to service Russia's domestic debt, thus further contributing to the devastating economic situation in the country.

Financial Deadlock and the 1998 Crisis

Before dark clouds formed over Russian reform, the government proposed, and federal legislature adopted, another unrealistic budget for 1998. Toward the end of his prime-ministership Viktor Chernomyrdin announced "financial stabilization," indicating the modest growth of both the nation's GDP and industrial production. Indeed, in 1997 the inflation rate dropped to about 7–8 percent. However, this was accompanied by the inability of federal authorities to follow the budget and fulfill their financial obligations, growing bad debts among enterprises, non-payment of taxes, and chronic delays in wage, salary, and pension payments.

The Central Bank of Russia avoided printing money to cover the budget deficit. However, the federal government borrowed extensively at home and abroad, and accumulated huge short-term and extremely expensive internal debts. To service those debts and to raise new funds, the bank had no choice but to prop up the ruble vis-à-vis major currencies.

In 1997, the Russian federal government received a total of $7.3 billion in new credit, $4.8 billion of it from international financial organizations and $2.5 billion through bilateral agreements. Both federal and some regional authorities raised an additional $4.5 billion through "eurobond-type" loans.[6] The country's external financial obligations, including the debt of the former Soviet Union, estimated by the World Bank at $67.5 billion, reached $151 billion, making Russia the third largest international borrower in the world after Mexico and Brazil. In 1997 alone, the Russian government spent $6.7 billion on interest payments for its external debt. It paid another $3.4 billion to the foreign holders of treasury bonds.

In 1998, the federal government had to allocate about $10 billion of its budget to internal debt servicing. In total, Moscow needed about $20 billion, or about 25 percent of its budget expenditure, to service both internal and external debts. The poor tax collection and weak tax base limited the budget revenues seriously, raising the burden of debt servicing. Net purchases by non-residents of the short-term treasury bonds, the so-called GKO issued by the Ministry of Finance, was estimated at $10.9 billion, including $8.8 billion in January-June and $2.1 billion in July-December.[7] As a result, the share of non-residents in the GKO market increased from 16 percent to 28 percent, and reached 32 percent by mid-1998.[8]

The share of borrowed funds in the federal budget financing increased from 45 percent in 1996 to 62 percent in 1997. The dependence on about $20 billion in the non-residents' "hot money" had become a major problem. The outflow of these funds put enormous pressure on the Russian hard currency reserves, which had rapidly decreased, from $25 billion in 1997 to $13 billion in July-August 1998. In 1997–1998, individual Russians also continued to buy dollars to protect their savings, their dollar purchases reaching an estimated $13.5 billion in 1997 compared with $9 billion in 1996.

The global economic slowdown in 1997–1998, the Chernomyrdin government's failure to propose a realistic budget, and its inability to collect taxes from ruined and weakened enterprises to service huge short-term borrowings became the main factors behind the "Russian bubble" problem. On August 17, 1998, we saw the ruble's devaluation, de facto default on domestic debt, and a moratorium on foreign debt repayments. Leading commercial banks with huge investment in the state bonds were paralyzed.

The direct fallout from these abrupt decisions, presumably made after consultations with Yeltsin, was four-fold. First, with few exceptions, banks suspended their operations, sending the entire financial system into chaos. Second, Russia's ability to import food and medicines was sharply constrained, such imports dropping 6.6 times from August to September 1998 and exposing the entire population to potential food shortages and health problems. Third, reduced personal consumption, growing poverty, expanding differences between the provinces, and regional economic separatism threatened the federal system. Finally, industrial production also dropped, with output declining by 14.5 percent in September 1998 compared with a year earlier, while inflation surged to 50 percent. These developments further aggravated the federal budget situation and weakened the government's ability to finance anti-crisis measures.

The new government had no choice but to revert to emergency measures, including the procurement of additional food reserves, reduction of value-added taxes for food and medicines, reduction of import duties for most needed food products, and a 50 percent cut in railway tariffs for food transportation. The government proposed to reschedule the repayment of nearly $4 billion owed by agricultural enterprises to the state and suggested that the accumulating debt of the Ukraine and Belarus be repaid in foodstuffs. The securing of reliable supplies of food, medicines, and fuels, which the new government called the nation's "life-supporting systems," were named the top priorities in dealing with the economic crisis. A crisis loomed in Kamchatskaya Oblast and Chukotka as serious food shortages crippled these remote regions of the country, vividly demonstrating the dangerous consequences of breakdowns in the "life-supporting systems."

Problems in the Far Eastern Provinces

Years before the 1998 crisis, the economic status of the Far East was abruptly changed by economic reform. The administrative power and influence of Moscow receded, coinciding with the end of the era of state-led economic development. Fewer federal subsidies were available to cope with the rising costs of living and transportation, badly affecting the population and enterprises alike. Capital investments spiraled down. Significant cuts in defense spending and downsizing of the military force further limited the flow of financial resources to the Far Eastern provinces. Fewer defense contracts caused the collapse of almost the entire machine-building industry of the region. Despite rising salaries and wages, purchasing power had declined due to inflation, chronic delays in payments, and the cost of living, which was much higher than the national average and rising.

In the closing decades of the Russian Empire and during the following seven decades of the Soviet rule, different instruments were applied to support population growth in the Far East, ranging from promises of freedom and economic incentives to forced labor camps and the promotion of the defense industry. The population of Far Eastern and Trans-Baikal regions had grown by 755,200 in 1986–1990, but in 1991–1996, it decreased by 825,000 people.[9] In 1996 alone, the population shrunk by 93,300 people. It is estimated that in 1996, despite significantly higher nominal wages, about 40 percent of people in the region lived under the poverty line, compared with the national average of 22 percent. With unemployment rising (219,000 people in 1997) and only a limited number of jobs (13,500 vacancies) available in these regions, it is difficult to expect that a steady population growth can be easily restored, particularly in the more developed and urbanized areas.[10]

Far Eastern Russia was always a remote outpost serving the purposes of industrial and resource-based development. Nonetheless, as a product of the highly centralized planning system and as the nation's frontier in Northeast Asia, the region was high on the list of priorities for Soviet leaders. During the decades of development policies, the region was shaped economically, industrially, and socially by central planning and under heavy-handed party and bureaucratic control. The decision-making process was based on economic assessments within this framework and on calculations that were hardly relevant to such factors as real market costs and efficiency. The logic of the Cold War and the massive presence of military forces in the Far East during the Soviet era necessitated the expansion of the military infrastructure and related industries in the region.

Huge investments in defense enterprises and main industries were made because of perceived security threats and nation-wide economic plans. Key decisions were made largely independently from any detailed cost-benefit analyses. However, from early 1992, when the new Russian government pursued a uniform approach both to the regions and to industries for the sake of "macroeconomic stabilization," the Far East was the first to lose federal support, and its economic deterioration began. High transportation costs virtually isolated the region economically from the rest of the country. Compared with 1991, railroad tariffs jumped as much as 8,500 times, doubling and tripling the cost of fuel transports to the Far Eastern power plants from other areas of eastern Russia. The region was suddenly cut off from its traditional customers and suppliers in central Russia.

On the other hand, unlike the energy-rich provinces of Siberia, the key Far Eastern provinces are maritime and better positioned for foreign trade. In 1990, the region exported only about 5 percent of its industrial output while the national average was 7 percent. In 1996, the total volume of trade of the Far Eastern region reached $3.9 billion, including $2.3 billion in exports. The regional exports reached 22.3 percent of the total regional output and the share of exports in regional GDP increased from 1.9 percent in 1990 to 7.2 percent in 1996. During the same period, the export quota of the key natural resource industries increased, including timber (from 14 percent of the total production to 56 percent), fishery (from 14 percent to 64 percent), oil products (from 7.4 percent to 64.8 percent), and coal (from 7.4 percent to 15 percent). The export share of rolled steel production increased from 14.2 percent in 1990 to 50 percent in 1996, and reached almost 100 percent in 1997.[11]

Japan and China are the leading trading partners of the Far East, followed by the Republic of Korea and the United States. However, the Japanese market for Far Eastern products declined from 65 percent of the region's total industrial exports in 1990 to 21 percent in 1996. In 1996, Far Eastern enterprises exported to Japan $737 million worth of goods and imported $147 million. American companies are the principle suppliers to the region, including large shipments of food. In 1996, their total sales reached $424 million. Exports to Northeast Asia and the United States reached 60–70 percent of the total regional export. The neighboring countries have also become the major suppliers of food and consumer goods to the Far Eastern provinces.[12] The region's dependence on exports has become more pronounced as its relations with the rest of Russia have weakened. The Far East's international trade reorientation, which is becoming a long-term trend, along with the protests by Siberian coal miners and the blockade of the Trans-Siberian railroad in 1998, demonstrate how fragile the Russian Federation could become under the strains of economic crisis.[13]

The rapid relative decline of prices of raw materials compared with those for manufactured goods, food, industrial equipment, and fossil fuels have made many Far Eastern enterprises inefficient. As noted already, increases in transportation costs in recent years have added to the problem. The declining profitability and lack of financial resources seriously limit the ability of producers to procure components and pay for electricity and heat.

From 1990 to 1996, the share of the Far East in the national output declined in every area except for fish catches and potato harvest. The production of coal decreased by 26 percent, oil by 22.2 percent, petrochemicals by 65.4 percent, lumber by 4 times, cement by 5.4 times, and sawn timber by 10 times. During the same period, capital investment in the industrial sector in different provinces dropped by between a factor of 2 and 6, and housing construction contracted by a factor of 2.8. The traffic volume for commercial cargo decreased by about 70 percent, while the number of passengers decreased by 38 percent. Overall, compared with 1990, the volume of industrial output in 1996 was only 43 percent and fixed capital investment about 34 percent.[14]

The region's agricultural output declined, with the share of private farms not exceeding 4.5 percent. The state farms and collective enterprises suffered from lack of support from the government and competition from imported foods. In various provinces, usable agricultural lands contracted by 11–47 percent. From 1986–1990 to 1991–1995, annual average production of grain decreased by 33 percent, vegetables by 15.5 percent, meat and beef by 21 percent, and milk by 22 percent. The production of beef and other meats, milk, and eggs contracted by a factor of more than two between 1990 and 1996.[15]

On April 15, 1996, the federal government adopted a "Federal Program for Economic and Social Development of the Far Eastern and Trans-Baikal Regions for 1996–2005" to ensure sustainable development of the regions concerned. The program was aimed at combating the economic crisis there in 1996–1997 and then to provide support for the regions' recovery in 1998–2000. The initial two years of the program's implementation were unsuccessful. The cumulative financial base of the program was estimated at $74–82 billion. Other federal plans relevant to the Far East were incorporated into the program at the total projected cost of $51–57 billion. This appeared to be the weakest element of the program, because most of these plans were poorly financed. The net additional funds required for 1996–2005 were estimated at $23–25 billion, including $11–12 billion from the federal budget.[16]

Although the federal program was not entirely neglected, only 4.7 trillion rubles, or 13 percent of the total funding requirement, was allocated to the projects envisaged by the program in 1996. In 1997, of the 40.5 trillion rubles requested by the provinces, only 1.034 trillion rubles was approved.[17] Flaws in the administrative mechanisms were revealed in the process as well. A directorate, as an executive body of the program, was not formed as planned. Nor was any decision taken on the creation of the Regional Reconstruction and Development Fund. Moreover, investments for major regional projects, including key energy facilities under construction, such as the Bureiskaya hydropower station, were neither sufficient nor timely.

Problems of the Energy Sector

In 1997–1998, all Far Eastern provinces were experiencing major difficulties in securing their energy supply and managing their energy production facilities. The energy sector of Far Eastern Russia was built during the decades when prices, tariffs, and wages were centrally controlled. More than 70 percent of the population live in urban areas and depend heavily on central heating systems during the extremely cold and long winters. Therefore, a shortage of energy is of grave consequences. This was indeed the case in 1997–1998, when the provinces suffered a serious shortage of local resources and the rising cost of transportation. Coal production hit a low, oil output slumped, and major hydropower projects were delayed or postponed due to investment shortfalls.

The Far Eastern region has traditionally imported 10–12 million tons of oil products and about 7–8 million tons of crude oil. There are only two oil refineries in the region, one in Khabarovsk and the other in Komsomolsk-na-Amure. These facilities normally supply over 40 percent of the oil products consumed in the Far East, including 75 percent of gasoline and 55 percent of diesel fuel. But the volume of oil processed by these two refineries dropped from 10 million tons in 1991 to less than 6 million tons in 1996. Sakhalin's oil accounted for only 12 percent of all raw materials processed at these two refineries.

The relatively high per capita rate of energy consumption, the higher-than-average energy component in industrial output, and the energy shortages were strongly felt in the more industrialized provinces of Khabarovskiy and Primorskiy krais and Amurskaya Oblast. These three territories typically account for about 60 percent of the gross regional product and 65 percent of the region's consumption of energy.

For several years Far Eastern Russia has seen a drastic decline in energy production. Regional output of electric power dropped from 48 kWh billion in 1991 to 37.4 kWh in 1996.[18] After 1992, when most prices were liberalized, federal and regional authorities were inclined to subsidize electricity and household heat bills for individual customers at the expense of corporate energy users. This and other factors pushed the share of energy in the cost of industrial production to 40–70 percent. Needless to say, this contributed to the decline of production and forced many Far Eastern manufacturers out of business.

Coal production in the Far Eastern and Trans-Baikal regions decreased abruptly from 64 million tons in 1990 to 47.6 million tons in 1996. Coal production in the Far Eastern provinces, not including Buriyatia Republic and Chitinskaya Oblast, fell from 50 million in 1990 to 32.4 million in 1996.[19] In the 1990s, the Far Eastern region became a major "importer" of coal from domestic sources despite a decrease in electric power production. When the local output of coal also declined, Far Eastern provinces suffered severe financial losses by having no choice but to purchase coal from other regions. In 1995 alone, Primorskiy and Khabarovskiy krais and Amurskaya Oblast purchased about 12.4 million tons of coal from other regions. The shortage and high cost of energy intensified social problems.[20]

Coal will remain the backbone of the regional energy supply in the Far Eastern region for decades to come, but the needed restructuring and rationalization of inefficient mines requires huge investments. Although the production of coal appeared to stabilize in 1996–1997, it is unlikely that in the next ten years the total coal production in the region will reach 45–50 million tons. This may not cover the needs of the modernized and newly built thermo-power plants, and the region's dependence on external sources of coal will continue to rise. Primorskiy Krai, the most energy deficient territory in the Far East, is likely to increase its dependence on coal for meeting its energy needs, with its share in total supply expected to rise from the current 55 percent to 62 percent in 2005. The Far East's energy dependency on coal is about 70 percent, which is much higher than the Russian national average of about 30 percent. On a per capita basis, the Far Eastern region's coal use is second only to eastern Siberia and far ahead of the national average.[21]

There is hope that the oil and gas resources of Sakhalin will alleviate the energy problems of the coastal areas of Far Eastern Russia, but this will not take place anytime soon. Although the offshore resources of Sakhalin Island include an estimated 291 million tons of oil, 421 billion cubic meters of natural gas, and 33 million tons of condensed gas, the first shipment of oil is expected in 1999–2000, and the first delivery of gas in 2005–2006. Even if Sakhalin's reserves of natural gas can effectively change the energy balance in the region, the construction of the gas pipeline system linking the production sites to the markets in the region is estimated to cost $2.1 billion, and it may take 7–8 years to supply natural gas to the Khabarovsk and Vladivostok areas.

The dependence of the Far Eastern provinces on the out-of-the-area supplies of oil and oil products is very high.[22] This dependence and long distances from the sources of supply make the price of electricity in Sakhalin twice as high as in Irkutskaya Oblast, while in Kamchatka the difference is four-fold. Although the energy sector of Far Eastern Russia has been given priority by both the federal and regional authorities, key energy development projects have been delayed or stalled due to a lack of funds. The region's high dependency on coal and the inefficiency of many of its local mines necessitate the long-distance deliveries of coal from Eastern Siberia, and that, in combination with other factors, makes the electricity tariffs in the Far East the highest in Russia.

The list of problems also includes massive non-payments by power plants, their suppliers, and customers. This is complicated by the rising cost of energy resources, transportation services, and tariffs for electricity and heat. There are numerous examples of disorganization in the industry, such as long delays in salary and wage payments, labor disputes, power outages, inadequate volumes of fuel in emergency storage, etc. Power plant equipment is aging, and there is a shortage of investment in new equipment and related development projects to expand the resource base. Inadequate financing affects the condition of electric power and the reliability of equipment.

Resources for Economic Recovery?

The irony is that the energy sector could lead in Far Eastern Russia's exports to Northeast Asia, where the demand for energy is fast growing. However, it is difficult to justify the development of Siberian gas fields and Far Eastern energy reserves if the feasibility assessment is not linked to larger neighboring markets and investment funds from external sources. The natural gas fields in eastern Siberian may yield an estimated 40–50 billion cubic meters of natural gas a year, but the Far Eastern region's own need for natural gas would be about 17–21 billion cubic meters at most. Moreover, it is not entirely clear whether the foreign policy fallout of the 1998 crisis in Iraq and the 1999 crisis in Kosovo will eliminate the friendly overtones in Russia's relations with the United States, whose cooperation would be essential for the development and marketing of these energy resources.

If the Russian political leadership sustains the course of positive engagement with the West, Russia can become the only strategic exporter of energy resources in Northeast Asia in the twenty-first century. By 2010 other countries in the region will increase their energy consumption at least by 45–50 percent, covering this increase primarily through imports. By 2010 the annual demand for natural gas in China, South Korea, and Japan is expected to double and may reach the range of 100–150 billion cubic meters.[23]

Eastern Russia's future role as a "fuel tank" for the economies of East Asia is promising, but the key issue is how to manage the transition from the current economic malaise to the export bonanza of the twenty-first century. Default on sovereign debt is another potential threat to cooperative and productive linkages with Northeast Asia. Russia's aggravated trade balance in 1998 is unlikely to allow the replenishment of currency reserves (to the desirable level of $18–20 billion), and Russian exporters now must sell 75 percent of their proceeds in hard currency to the Central Bank. The government's ability to raise new loans overseas has sharply deteriorated, threatening the default on sovereign debt. Moreover, the lack of confidence on the part of foreign investors has led to an outflow of capital and the shutdown and downsizing of operations by many foreign companies.

Under these adverse circumstances, the Sakhalin–1 and Sakhalin–2 projects serve as indicators of both negative and positive developments. The production-sharing scheme in the development of the oil and gas fields on the continental shelf off Sakhalin Island facilitated the mobilization of external finance, and leading transnational corporations became involved in the projects. Some of the world's largest corporations, including Exxon, Texaco, Marathon, Mobil, and Shell, are now at various stages of involvement in four Sakhalin projects. The projects include the construction of large offshore pipelines, drilling platforms, on-shore storage facilities, a transportation infrastructure, and LNG plants. The combined cost of the three fields under the Sakhalin–1 project could reach $20.6 billion, and the total cost of the Sakhalin–2 project is estimated at $15 billion.

Foreign investors are expected to benefit substantially from the Sakhalin projects. The island province and the entire Far East of Russia will be better off as well. After Sakhalin oil becomes available in sufficient volumes, the oil refineries of Far Eastern Russia will be able to switch to this source and Sakhalin's natural gas will supply Khabarovskiy and Primorskiy krais. The development of oil and gas fields off Sakhalin will lead to an increase in the annual production of oil from the current level of 1.6 million tons to 30 million tons. Extraction of gas could reach 28 billion cubic meters annually, compared with the current 2 billion cubic meters. In addition, Sakhalin's inland resources include an estimated 170 million tons of oil and 120 billion cubic meters of natural gas.

China is keenly interested in importing natural gas from Russia. Prospects for development of the Kovyktinskoe gas field near Irkutsk are fairly good, and a working-level agreement has been signed to build a 3,360-kilometer-long gas pipeline from Irkutsk to Ulaan Baator, Beijing, and to Rizhao on the Yellow Sea coast. This project is currently estimated at $7–10 billion and can be expanded further if the gas fields of Yakutia and Krasnoyarskiy Krai are connected to the proposed gas pipeline system, which could be extended to Korea and southern Japan. China's northeastern, central, and southeastern regions are large enough markets to consume all 30 billion cubic meters of the gas that can be exported from eastern

Siberia. Moreover, the Far Eastern and eastern Siberian regions together possess more than 80 percent of the hydropower resources of the Russian Federation and can produce about 450–600 billion kWh of electricity annually in the long term.

Japan, too, will remain dependent on foreign sources of oil and gas and, in view of the growing domestic sentiments against the construction of more nuclear power plants, the potential role of Russia as a supplier of fuel and energy resources for Japan could be quite significant.[24]

Conclusion

Cooperative relationships between Russia and its Northeast Asian neighbors in energy development and trade could lead the economy of the Russian Far East to recovery and energy self-sufficiency and also enhance the energy security of Northeast Asian economies.

Evidently, politicians and diplomats in Northeast Asia have come to understand these long-term opportunities. This was demonstrated during the summit meetings between President Boris Yeltsin and his counterparts from Japan and China in 1997–1998. The two "no-necktie" meetings with Japanese prime minister Ryutaro Hashimoto in Krasnoyarsk in November 1997 and in Kawana in April 1998, as well as Prime Minister Keizo Obuchi's visit to Russia in November 1998, showed that positive relations between the two neighbors are developing faster than expected. If successfully developed, Far Eastern Russia's ties with its Northeast Asian neighbors can help Russia re-emerge as an important player in this part of the world.

It is critically important for Russia and its Far Eastern provinces to hold on until new export-oriented energy projects are realized. The central problem is the investment climate in Russia. It is proposed to establish a state-controlled Development Bank to pool financial resources and provide short-term and long-term credit to the real economy, as well as to establish a state insurance agency to cover investment risks and improve conditions for foreign direct investment in Russia. However, in the future the only remaining sizable source of investment will be household savings that cannot be raised without a boost in the public's confidence in the banking system.

The central issue is whether Yevgeniy Primakov's government, if given sufficient time, will be able to arrest the nation's economic and social decline. Primakov's greatest challenge is the lack of a workable system for combining human and natural resources, an industrial base, and research and development potential. The Russian state is expected to strengthen its economic role. Will the state be strong enough to succeed in such an endeavor?

Notes

1. Steven Rosefielde, "Who Is Losing Russia?," *ERINA Report,* vol. 26 (December 1998), pp. 18–21. Other American analysts also emphasize that "a bailout will support the virtual economy, which is fundamentally not market-based." (Clifford G. Gaddy and Barry W. Ickes, "Russia's Virtual Economy," *Foreign Affairs,* vol. 77, no. 5, p. 54.)

2. Victor I. Ishaev and Pavel A. Minakir, *The Far East of Russia: Realities and Possibilities for Economic Development,* Khabarovsk: Institute for Economic Research, 1998, pp. 6, 8, and 91. See also Pavel A. Minakir and Nadezhda N. Mikheeva, eds., *Economy of the Far East: Five Years of Reform,* Khabarovsk: Institute for Economic Research, 1998.

3. A. I. Potemkin, "Balance of Payments of Russia in 1997," *Finansoviye Izvestiya,* no. 36 (May 26, 1998), p. iv. Potemkin is Deputy Chairman of the Central Bank of Russia.

4. M. Luzhnikova, "Foreign Trade of Russia in 1997," *Ekonomika i Zhisn,* no. 7, February 1998, p. 26. See also Potemkin, "Balance of Payments of Russia in 1997." In 1997, the foreign trade surplus estimated by the Russian customs authorities was $32.3 billion because the volume of imports registered by customs was only $52.5 billion, or $18.5 billion (27 percent) lower than figures provided by the Central Bank of Russia.

5. *Russia. Country Report,* 1st Quarter 1998, London: The Economist Intelligence Unit, p. 37.

6. The debt to the International Monetary Fund increased by $700 million and reached $13.2 billion, while the credit extended by the World Bank totaled $5.1 billion, an increase of $2.7 billion.

7. Potemkin, "Balance of Payments of Russia in 1997."

8. Mikhail Sidorov, "The Debt Counter Is Running Tirelessly," *Economika i Zhisn,* no. 22, May 1998, p. 3.

9. Ya. Ivlev and E. Galichanin, "Economic Reform in the Provinces of the Far Eastern and Trans-Baikalia Region of the Federation, 1991–1996," Supplement to *Economic Life of the Far East,* 1997, vol. 1, nos. 9–10, p. 5.

10. *Regions of Russia 1997,* Moscow: Goscomstat, 1997.

11. Pavel A. Minakir, "Northeast Asian Drift," in Vladimir I. Ivanov and Karla S. Smith, eds., *Japan and Russia in Northeast Asia: Partners in the 21st Century,* Praeger Publishers: Westport, CT, 1999, p. 191.

12. Vladimir Ivanov, Dmitriy Sergachev, and Kazuto Furuta, "Preliminary Assessment of the Implementation of the Federal Program for Economic and Social Development of the Far Eastern and Trans-Baikal Regions, 1996–2005 (An Analytical Overview)," ERINA, Niigata, 1998, pp. 33–35 (Unpublished research report).

13. Zbignew Brzezinski conjured up a future map of the Russian Federation that featured a "Far Eastern Republic" as part of a loosely confederated Russia. See Zbignew Brzezinski, "A Geostrategy for Eurasia," *Foreign Policy,* vol. 76, no. 5 (September/October 1997), pp. 56 and 60 (map).

14. Ivlev and Galichanin, pp. 21 and 63. See also *Russian Statistical Yearbook 1997,* Moscow: Goscomstat, 1997, p. 626.

15. Ivlev and Galichanin, statistical supplement, pp. 17–76.

16. See Alexander G. Granberg, "The Far Eastern Provinces and Moscow," in Ivanov and Smith, eds., *Japan and Russia in Northeast Asia,* p. 177.

17. Ivlev and Galichanin, p. 15.

18. *Russian Statistical Yearbook 1997,* Moscow: Goscomstat, 1997, p. 627.

19. Ibid.

20. *Regions of Russia 1997,* p. 705.

21. Khabarovskiy Krai will be looking for capital funds to develop the Urgalskoe deposit, adding as a result a coal output of 2.8 million tons. Amurskaya Oblast's dependence on coal will increase by up to 80 percent by 2005, and the production of coal has to be doubled to 9 million tons. In Magadanskaya Oblast, the production of coal is expected to reach 3.5 million tons, covering 80–83 percent of all energy production. Buriyatiya Republic plans to increase the production of coal up to 8.7 million tons. Only Sakhalinskaya Oblast will be able

to close down some of its old mines thanks to abundant oil and gas resources under development. However, the overall production of coal is expected to grow by 6.4 million tons in 2000, and by 7.4 million tons by 2005.

22. See *World Energy Outlook 1996,* Paris: International Energy Agency and OECD, 1996, p. 270.

23. Richard Layard and John Parker, *The Coming Russian Boom: A Guide to New Markets and Policies,* New York: The Free Press, 1996, p. 282.

24. "Although nuclear power accounts for 12 percent of Japan's energy supply and 34 percent of electricity supply, there is a mounting public distrust of nuclear energy policies in the wake of the prolongation of nuclear power siting and the Monju accident. Thus, re-examine how nuclear energy should be positioned." (*Energy in Japan,* p. 7, available at the Ministry of International Trade and Industry's website, http://www.miti.go.jp.)

CHAPTER 11

THE NORTH KOREAN CRISIS AND REGIONAL COOPERATION

Alexandre Y. Mansourov

Introduction

IT IS ONE OF THE MOST SHOCKING UNTOLD paradoxes of our times that merciless indiscriminate famine, comparable to the potato famine that ravaged Ireland in the 1840s or the rice famine in China in the early 1960s, is virtually killing the entire North Korean nation while its Asian neighbors are carelessly enjoying the well-deserved abundant fruits of a series of economic miracles that brought decades-long, double-digit growth to their economies and immense wealth and well-being to their populations. This picture of the slowly collapsing North Korean isle of humanitarian catastrophe, isolated amidst an almost totally indifferent Asian zone of prosperity, is mind-boggling.

North Korea, the new sick man of Asia, limps along on a very narrow tight rope. Its southern brethren, sensing the beginning of a tragic end, despite their assurances to the contrary, seek to cut this rope short, not to mention to rattle it in their own interests, in order to make this nouveau malade with poor sense of balance fall as quickly and hard as he may. As one of the last vestiges of the Cold War mentality, North Korea's wealthy and prosperous East Asian neighbors and their Western allies still view it as a dangerous and unpredictable military foe and as a rogue state prone to proliferate nuclear and missile technologies, terrorism and drug trade, one that must be held in a water-proof cage of economic sanctions and treated as one of the major military opponents in the Pentagon's strategy of pursuing two regional wars simultaneously. Even its former doctors and benefactors recently have turned away and display indifference to the fate of this seemingly hopeless victim of socialist command-and-control economics, *juche*-style totalitarian ideology and social controls, boundless personality cult, and a string of unprecedented natural disasters that seem to be indicating that lately the mandate of heaven itself has been withdrawn from the new rulers of the dying dynasty.

This paper addresses one of the obvious but nonetheless little-studied questions as to how the deepening domestic crisis in the DPRK may affect international cooperation among nations in Northeast Asia and general prospects for international stability, war, and peace in the region. First, I intend to review briefly a number of theories of international relations that are aimed at explaining, in general terms, the relationship between domestic crises and international behavior of states, with specific application to the North Korean situation. Second, I will review a number of historical cases from Korean history and attempt to discern some patterns in the behavior of the Korean state and its foreign neighbors in times of domestic crises. Third, I will define the scope, depth, and modalities and analyze the dynamics of the current internal crises in the DPRK, as well as the ways in which they are communicated to and perceived by the international community. Fourth, I will identify and study the ongoing institutional responses by the international community to the unfolding crisis in North Korea. I will seek to determine any impact that the North Korean crisis might have on the Western reaction and to assess the motives and limits of international cooperation regarding the North Korean question, as well as to predict its future prospects. In this paper, I will rely primarily on my interviews with Russian diplomats and international humanitarian workers stationed in the North, Western diplomats dealing with North Korea, the DPRK diplomats stationed abroad, as well as analytical reports prepared by various international and domestic organizations involved in Korea.

Domestic Crises and International Conflict: Theory of International Relations and the North Korean Case

In terms of the definitions used in the contemporary theory of international relations, the modern North Korean state can be defined as a revolutionary, "domestically hard," "internationally weak," "small-size state" with an authoritarian regime undergoing profound negative changes in its reservoir of political legitimacy and economic and military capabilities.

The international relations theory provides area studies specialists with a mixture of somewhat contradictory deductive insights into the possible goals and strategies of international behavior of such a state and likely international responses thereto. On the one hand, two general international relations hypotheses, relating the character of the state and its ruling regime and its likely foreign policy behavior and possible international response, point in the direction of rising tensions and greater conflict in the days to come as a consequence of a worsening malaise in the North Korean state. First, revolutionary states (in terms of their goals and ideology) are said to be inherently expansionist, belligerent, subversive and hostile, always intent on undermining their neighbors by claiming their territory and promoting the fifth column in other nations. In response, other states tend to perceive them as a threat to the status quo, whether their fears are warranted or not; and, consequently, revolutionary states tend to attract predatory preventive attacks from outside in times of weakness. Second, authoritarian states are said to be more aggressive than democratic ones. Authoritarian states suffering from internal turmoil are said to become even more belligerent and to have a tendency to pursue an aggressive foreign policy in order to scare away their foreign rivals and divert the attention of their own public from pressing domestic problems. In response, democracies tend to band together to resist the aggressive behavior of autocracies in trouble.

This deeply seated ideological fear of the DPRK as one of the last revolutionary states and as a formidable authoritarian state, left in the wake of the recent worldwide collapse of communism and allegedly still bent on undermining and taking over its capitalist neighbors, is reflected in the current military doctrines, standing operational plans, periodic war games, and public rhetoric and official statements of governments in Seoul, Tokyo, and Washington. The ROK armed forces and the Japanese SDF view the KPA as their main military adversary, while the Pentagon still considers North Korea one of the two potential major regional hot spots where the United States must be prepared to wage war while simultaneously fighting another regional war elsewhere in the world. Thus, despite the hollowing-out of the KPA's military capabilities and near collapse of the North Korean state, as long as its revolutionary and authoritarian nature remain intact, or is perceived as unchanged by the so-called status-quo democracies surrounding it, they are likely to continue to view it as a common threat to their security interests in the region. Moreover, as domestic crises and the tensions rise and systemic weaknesses of the DPRK get further exposed, its neighbors are likely to be more tempted to pursue a more aggressive policy aimed at eliminating this long-standing revolutionary authoritarian threat altogether, thereby changing by themselves the existing international status quo.[1] In turn, this feeds the paranoia of the DPRK leaders, who fear that the hostile outside world is out to get them and to suffocate their regime. Consequently, in order to mobilize domestic public support for the cause of their own survival and ensure the external security of their regime, they are likely to seek to tighten the screws and strengthen their own revolutionary credentials at home and toughen up their international image abroad. Weakness generates contempt and temptation to attack. Temptation to attack instills fear of attack. Fear leads to belligerence. Belligerence undermines cooperation.[2]

On the other hand, two other general international relations hypotheses, relating the nature of the state and its position in the international system to its likely foreign policy and international response, may indicate that as the DPRK's domestic crisis deepens, more propitious conditions will emerge for greater international cooperation on and around the Korean peninsula. First, the international relations theory expects that domestically "hard states" (in terms of state-society relations) rely on internal resource mobilization for their survival to a greater extent than "soft states." Consequently, for ideological and symbolic reasons, the former are less likely in general to seek international aid. Moreover, efforts by the international community to provide various forms of assistance to such "hard states" are largely frustrated even when the latter find themselves in dire straits (like the PRC during the horrible famine of 1960–1963). However, as the "hard states" "soften up" under pressure from the international system or due to deepening domestic crises, they tend to become more constructively engaged in international cooperation aimed at reducing potential for regional conflict and remedying their own internal crises (for instance, the Soviet Union under Gorbachev). Second, internationally "weak states" (in terms of relative power capabilities vis-à-vis other states) are expected to emphasize external validation rather than external extraction to a greater extent than internationally "strong states." Hence, once an acceptable face-saving formula is found, they may go to the latter (usually the West) to plead for assistance, and, consequently, their foreign policy may become more cooperative and conciliatory, which, obviously, encourages international cooperation.

A brief history of international efforts to provide humanitarian assistance to the famine-stricken DPRK reveals the following. For over a year, not least out of fear of having its image as the "workers' paradise on earth" tarnished, the North Korean "hard state" refused to admit the severity of the humanitarian disaster that had struck the area as a result of the two-year-long unprecedented floods. Then, after it did recognize that the conditions in the flood-hit provinces were "difficult" and asked for international humanitarian assistance, its leadership still put security and political propaganda concerns much higher on its list of negotiating and implementation priorities than urgent issues of humanitarian aid. This demonstrated the lack of political will in Pyongyang to recognize the severity of the problem and to compromise other interests in order to resolve this situation, and, hence, caused considerable delays in finding mutually acceptable solutions and settling on quantities and timetables for food deliveries. Moreover, when the food aid did begin to arrive slowly, first, its deliveries were sabotaged by the DPRK's over-zealous security officials and ideological censors. Then its shipments were allegedly diverted for unauthorized use by third parties, including, perhaps, by the KPA.[3] Furthermore, the North Korean government had long resisted any changes in its administrative practices for admission, transportation, distribution of, and accounting for foreign food donations.

However, because of considerable pressure from the international donor community, and as the famine grew much worse, the North Korean "hard state" began to show some signs of "softening up." Recently, the government has allowed some representatives of foreign donor organizations to visit the famine-stricken areas and witness the severity of famine in the hinterland, as well as to deliver international donations directly to their recipients and personally monitor their distribution among the needy. Obviously, such minor changes in the DPRK's attitude and policies toward international humanitarian assistance are not enough to mitigate foreign frustration and allow the NGOs and international donors concerned to overcome the enormous political and administrative obstacles and high economic costs involved in "penetrating" the North Korean "hard state" and reaching out to its society in need. Nonetheless, tentative "softening" of the North Korean state is an encouraging sign that offers new hope for greater humanitarian cooperation on the North Korean situation, especially since the new leaders of this "weak state" seem to be looking for a way to validate their rule in a new international environment, a way that would preserve their own survival through peace and also allow them to save face domestically.

Finally, the balance of power theory may also offer two insights on the prospect of international cooperation on the Korean peninsula. On one hand, as the DPRK's domestic crises worsen, its military capabilities and will to fight are likely to suffer, thereby causing some changes in outside perceptions of its overall power and the threat it poses. As it becomes weaker, disagreements among other states regarding its status as a military threat may rise, and their common front against the so-called North Korean threat may suffer as a result. Consequently, one could expect greater diversity of policies and less willingness to cooperate on security matters involving the DPRK among major Western powers. On the other hand, in general, small states, especially those under growing pressure from the international system, tend to bandwagon with larger states instead of balancing their power. In turn, large states always prefer to offer cooperation and protection to their small neighbors on a bilateral basis, in order to extend their own security zone and balance the power and interests of other large states in the region, rather than to form an international coalition of large states, aimed at isolating, punishing, and/or even eliminating the small state in question, no matter how offensive and hostile its position in the international system may appear in general. Therefore, one should not be surprised at the DPRK's efforts to "drive the wedge" among its opponents and promote bilateral relations at the expense of multilateral cooperation in the region, or attempts by some major powers to "pass the buck" or strike a separate deal with the North, beneficial primarily to their own selfish security and other interests. Thus, in terms of the balance of power theory, the decline in the perceived North Korean threat and the DPRK's structural predisposition to bandwagon with a stronger power to guarantee its own security are not conducive to fostering multilateral security cooperation in the region.

In sum, contemporary international relations theory is ambivalent regarding the prospects for international cooperation in light of the growing domestic crisis in the DPRK. On one hand, the unbending revolutionary nature of the North Korean state, the authoritarian character of its political regime, and the country's small size vis-à-vis other players in the region dampen incentives for and interest in positive multilateral security, economic, and humanitarian cooperation between the DPRK and its neighbors. On the other hand, the "softening" of the "hard state" and its external image, the weakening of its military capabilities, and the foreign reassessment of its military potential and economic and humanitarian woes seem to be creating more willingness abroad to consider various multilateral government and private cooperative efforts aimed at addressing some of its worst problems.

Déja-vu? North Korean Rendezvous with History

In general, Korean history was merciful to the rulers who mismanaged the Korean state. As a rule, despite their royal ineptitude or character flaws or weak will and poor health, "the system" allowed them to stand up to numerous foreign invasions and hang on through decades of economic stagnation, declining central government revenues, the rising power of the local gentry, waves of popular uprisings, factional strife among ruling elites, and bloody feuds within the royal family. Notwithstanding perpetual internal crises and external challenges to their sovereignty, Korean dynasties can boast an extreme longevity and survivability rarely found in ancient, medieval, or modern world history.

Korean history offers only a few cases when a Korean dynasty collapsed altogether and the Korean state had to be rebuilt from scratch by its successors, and only one case when the Korean state was totally dismantled by foreigners and ceased to exist. The lessons from these few painful historical experiences should be kept in mind while deliberating over the seemingly inevitable collapse of Kim Il Sung's dynasty and ensuing possible disintegration of the North Korean state. These instances include the abrupt fall of Koguryo in 668, the implosion of Silla in the 930s, the collapse of Koryo in the late 1380s, and the slow and agonizing death of the Yi dynasty from the 1870s to 1910.

In the middle of the seventh century, the long years of continuous warfare, economic hardships, and dictatorial rule of Yon Kaesomun seriously weakened Koguryo's highly militarized state and society. After Yon Kaesomun's death, an internecine struggle for the throne broke out between his sons and younger brother, and this power struggle drove Koguryo toward its doom. For when the eldest son, Namsaeng, was driven out of power by the second son, Namgon, he fled to the old capital at Kungnae-song and surrendered to the T'ang emperor, whereas Yon's younger brother, Yon Chongt'o, escaped to Silla. Both Chinese T'ang and Silla, eager to capitalize on such a lucrative opportunity, launched a coordinated offensive, relying on the assistance of high-ranking Koguryo defectors, and defeated the remnants of the dynasty and a local resistance movement in less than two years.[4]

The state of Silla represents the only Korean dynasty that imploded from within as a result of its mounting internal contradictions. It was never toppled by any aggressive foreign forces despite its visibly growing domestic weaknesses. From the last quarter of the eighth century until its final days, the authoritarian power of the Silla throne found itself increasingly challenged by the true aristocracy of the capital, powerful local castle lords who accumulated enormous individual wealth and used their vast economic resources to form personal military forces, arming their slaves and recruiting the landless peasants who roamed the Silla countryside, as well as mighty regional military garrisons that served as sources of military support for the ambitions of powerful local gentry families in the Silla countryside. The growing strength of the castle lords and military garrisons weakened the grip of the central government of Silla over the provinces and made it impossible to collect taxes from peasants or enforce corvée duties, whereas the financial needs of the capital aristocracy indulging itself in a life of opulence and pleasure continued to rise. It did not take much time before the royal coffers were emptied, and fiscal crisis erupted in 889. The king's attempts to use force to collect revenues had a destabilizing impact on the old social order: peasants began to abandon their land en mass and roam the countryside in search of food. A new round of internecine strife at the court and a coup d'etat, unfolding against the background of successive large-scale peasant rebellions, sparked an all-out civil war that finally led to the disintegration of the state of Silla into three Korean states (Later Paekche, Later Koguryo, and Later Silla) in the late 890s–early 900s.[5] Remarkably, at that time, both China and Japan stayed out of the Korean civil wars, probably because this period of internal disorder in Korea coincided with chaotic times in these two countries too and because Silla managed to maintain rather good diplomatic relations with both.[6]

The collapse of the Koryo state in the 1380s resulted from repeated failures of successive Korean military governments to resist the Mongol invasions and the subsequent surrender of the Wang royal house to the Yan suzerainty, which led to enormous destruction of property and life all across the peninsula. Neither the Koryo economy nor its social order managed to recover from the devastation and humiliation of the Mongol invasions and rule. Furthermore, attempts by the late Koryo monarchs to curb the power of private estates and to stem increases in the privately owned slave population proved to be unsuccessful, which yet again severely depleted state revenues. The newly rising class of scholar-bureaucrats who sought to offer workable solutions was ignored and denied participation in government, which made it resentful of the dynasty. In the meantime, a profound fiscal crisis erupted, which was followed by a new cycle of royal attempts at forced collection of taxes and corvée duties, peasant and slave rebellions, factional strife at the court, and garrison mutinies. Finally, Ming China stepped in, assisted Korean military commanders in overthrowing the pro-Yan Wang royal family and forcefully proclaimed its support for the establishment of a new pro-Ming Korean royal house of Yi Song-gye in 1392.[7]

The state of Choson died a slow and agonizing death extending from the early 1870s through 1910. The root causes thereof included decades-long economic stagnation, deepening contradictions between the obsolescent feudal economic system and emerging capitalist markets, the inability of the rigid traditional political order to accommodate demands for greater participation on the part of rising new social classes, the breakdown of law and order in the wake of the Tonghak rebellion, and the repeated failures of the forces of enlightenment to overcome Confucian orthodoxy and promote modernization in response to the challenges to Korean sovereignty and way of life posed by the West. The domestic economic and political crises that rattled the state of Choson in the second half of the nineteenth century exposed its internal structural weaknesses to the outside world and made it subject to predatory encroachments on its sovereignty from abroad. Consequently, major Western powers succeeded in opening up the hermit kingdom with a series of humiliating unequal treaties in the 1870s–1880s. Then, Japan began its imperial ascendancy in the Korean peninsula, successfully fighting for absolute control of the Korean state first against China and a decade later against Russia, respectively in 1894–1895 and 1904–1905. Finally, despite Korean royal pleas for international support, after Qing China decided to abandon the Yi imperial household and all major Western powers called it quits in Korea, Japan dismantled the Korean state altogether and proclaimed its own sovereignty over the Korean peninsula in 1910.

In sum, the fundamental lessons that any Korean leader seems to be taught in Korean history textbooks, both old Confucian and modern nationalist or *juche* ones, are as follows. First of all, a weakened Korean state facing domestic crises tends to invite foreign aggression or provoke international squabbles over the divvying up of Korean spoils, which in time might lead to regime change and partial or total loss of state sovereignty. Second, no Korean state has ever succeeded in its fight for survival when forced to wage a battle on two fronts simultaneously (i.e., internally, to raise dwindling state revenues while suppressing popular unrest or protests of local elite, and externally, to fend off foreign provocation or invasion while its own military forces are rebelling). Third, as long as the political elite remain united around the ruler, the state's coercive apparatus, including the military, is well-fed and kept under the firm control of the king or other supreme leader, and the ruling ideology is strictly adhered to. The ruling class seems to be able to marginalize and suppress the discontented and mobilize the domestic resources and public support necessary to mitigate domestic economic and social crises and resist foreign encroachments on the sovereignty of Korean state. Fourth, the role of China is crucial to the fate of any Korean dynasty. No Korean dynasty facing both internal turmoil and threat of foreign invasion has ever survived yet when "the mandate of Heaven," i.e., the diplomatic, political, economic, and military support of China, has been totally withdrawn from Korean rulers. Historically, China could make or break Korean states. Finally, shrewd diplomacy and friendly alliance-making alone did not suffice to prevent the collapse of a state burdened with severe internal problems. A benevolent external environment should be supplemented with profound domestic reforms in order to ensure the long-term survival of the state.

Diagnosis for the Sick Man of Asia: Hard Landing

Let me begin my analysis with a brief overview of structural developments in the DPRK's economy. They are disheartening in the short term and indicative of more dramatic cataclysms in the long run. Historically speaking, from the mid-1950s to the late 1970s, the economy in the North expanded at high (often double-digit) growth rates: this growth occurred mostly in labor and capital intensive sectors of economy such as heavy industries, construction, and transportation. In the early 1980s, as did all other centrally planned economies, the North Korean economy entered the stage of its secular decline; the government, by and large, failed to reallocate production to more technology-intensive industries, and, consequently, growth rates stagnated throughout the 1980s.[8] Moreover, in the 1990s, instead of soft-landing after almost three decades of rapid expansion, the economy virtually crashed in the aftermath of the disintegration of the former socialist camp, which served as an indispensable material and financial support network for the North. In six years of profound depression, the DPRK's economy contracted by over thirty percent in total, i.e., over a third of its pre-1990 size.[9]

In 1994 some key economic indicators, to the extent of their reliability, hinted that the North Korean economic nose-dive appeared to be bottoming out and the negative dynamics of the GNP growth rates, as estimated by the Bank of Korea in Seoul, appeared to be leveling off (in 1990, the GNP shrank by 3.7 percent, in 1991 5.2 percent, in 1992 7.6 percent, in 1993 4.3 percent, in 1994 1.7 percent).[10] Nonetheless, in 1995 and 1996 the DPRK economy continued to contract due to the devastating impact of floods two years in a row,[11] felt in four out of eight provinces in the North.[12] One could

still expect a pickup in economic activity in 1998, as a new pragmatic leadership in Pyongyang, instead of spending millions of dollars to erect monuments, might concentrate scarce government
spending on rebuilding its western seaboard transportation networks, agricultural facilities, and industrial infrastructure, ruined in
the 1995–1996 floods, and to lay infrastructural foundations for the
implementation of the LWR project on its eastern seaboard, as well
as move more aggressively in developing free economic and trade
zones along its coastline.

The estimates of annual growth rates by sector, published by
the Bank of Korea in Seoul last July,[13] provide helpful, albeit not
perfect, snapshots of sectoral development in the DPRK's economy
in the past six years. Mining, manufacturing, and construction took
the hardest hits, declining by 34.1 percent, 38.4 percent, and 36.2
percent respectively in five years.[14] The electric system is said to be
"in a state of collapse." Chronic power shortages, transportation
bottlenecks, cutoff of the Soviet supplies of energy resources and
spare parts, and cumulative underinvestment are responsible for
the steady decay of the backbone of the North Korean industry. It
appears that the de-industrialization of significant parts of the
economy has been set in motion, with industrial plant capacity
being utilized at under forty percent. Industrial skills are being lost,
and hidden unemployment in heavy and light industries is on the
rise. For example, huge industrial *kombinats* in Ch'ongjin,
Hamhung, Hungnam, Taean, Hich'on, Anju, Ryongsong, and other
industrial centers are reportedly idle, with their equipment and machinery rapidly rusting over, while some workers, unsatisfied with
dramatically reduced rations, have apparently deserted their work-
place in search of other sources of income and food, despite harsh
measures aimed at "deviation control" adopted by the party and
the government.

The electrification of railroads, once a cherished goal and proud
achievement of the DPRK's industrialization drive, has become the
country's worst enemy recently: no electricity—no railroad transportation. At present, primarily because of the lack of electric power,
it takes about a week to deliver cargo, even humanitarian aid, by
train from Pyongyang to Sinuiju, whereas it used to take only five

hours to do so in the past. Lack of gasoline and wood (after an unusually cold winter) brought to a standstill automobile traffic on
highways and local roads. The destruction of hundreds of kilometers
of highway and paved roads, and many railroad and other bridges,
in the course of the recent floods has contributed to this partial
breakdown of the country's transportation system, which has physically immobilized large parts of the civilian economy.

As far as the DPRK's foreign trade is concerned, after dramatic
contraction in exports and imports in 1990, caused by radical
changes in the terms of trade with its former communist allies, primarily the former Soviet Union and the PRC, its external trade remained stagnant for three years in 1991, 1992, and 1993, then
shrank again in 1994, 1995, and 1996.[15] Despite the fact that foreign trade was proclaimed one of three top priorities during the
1994–1996 "adjustment period," its share in the North Korean
GNP declined from more than 15 percent to less than 10 percent. In
light of these changes, one can plausibly argue that despite its major
push aimed at promoting exports and luring foreign investors, lately
the DPRK's economy has become even more isolated than it was in
the late 1960s.

Agriculture, forestry, and fishing made up almost one third of the
DPRK's GDP in 1994. As a rule, this sector's performance fluctuates
with the weather. It also reflects some of the endogenous problems of
North Korean agriculture, i.e., soil exhaustion, poor mechanization,
lack of fuel, and the inherent management flaws of collective farming.
The floods of 1990 and 1993 and heavy hail showers in 1994 resulted
in the agricultural sector shrinking by 10.2 percent and 7.6 percent
and 1.75 percent respectively.[16] Even more dramatic decline occurred
in 1995 and 1996 due to yet another round of devastating floods,
which resulted in a shortfall of grain necessary to feed population and
livestock, exceeding two million tons, for two years in a row.[17] Moreover, there are almost no seeds to plant for the next harvest and no
fuel for tractors. Also, there is an acute shortage of fertilizers and zero
pesticides, a result of the idling of most of the chemical fertilizer
plants due to lack of electricity.

The cumulative effect of these repeated failures of agricultural
production and extremely adverse weather conditions was further

agricultural depression, resulting in widespread malnutrition of the population in 1995–1996, followed by the emergence of pockets of famine registered in the hinterland in 1996–1997. Five government grain distribution centers out of ten are reported to have been depleted lately. As of June 1997, statements of the DPRK government officials and reports of the NGOs present in the North suggest that in the capital the average food rations were cut down to 450 grams a day and in the countryside to a minuscule one hundred grams, far below the normal sustenance level.[18] Reportedly, children and the elderly are affected the worst: they show all the classic symptoms of malnutrition, including wasted bodies, with body fat gone and only skin and bone left; swelling around the eyes, a sign of edema; discolored (even red or brown or blond hair) or the hair falling out, a sign of protein deficiency, etc.[19] According to some eye-witness accounts, "People are dying in North Korea. Death is quite visible everywhere."[20]

With such a dramatic decline in the state's revenue base (which relies mostly on taxing domestic production, which is in a tailspin, and shrinking foreign trade), the state finances must be under increasing strain. Notwithstanding the meager role that money is usually allowed to play in the DPRK's orthodox version of command-and-control economy, at present, the government seems to be inclined to use more voluntaristic monetary tools to prop up its image of caring among its people by pumping the economy with more paper money.[21] In the North, nowadays less goods are being chased with more money, which is a classic cause for inflation. One of the indications that inflation is on the rise is the official exchange rate of the local currency, the won, for the U.S. dollar, which over the past three years skyrocketed from 2.14 won per a dollar in 1995 to 200 won per a dollar in summer 1997.

The social implications of these depressing economic realities are negative as well. Hidden unemployment is said to be on the rise. Obviously, the living standards of the DPRK's "middle class" are on the decline. A trend toward re-ruralization of the North seems to be accelerating: recently some anecdotal evidence has suggested that an increasing number of urban dwellers, especially from industrial locales and mid-size towns, frequent or try to relocate to the countryside, closer to the original sources of food supplies.[22] More people fall out of the social safety net and get marginalized. Eye-witnesses report increasing suffering and loss of life on the fringes of society.

In sum, the experience of past few years indicates that North Korea was unable to tap new markets and sources of international financing in response to the external macroeconomic shocks that resulted from the Soviet and Chinese unilateral cutoff of most of the DPRK's credit lines, shutdown of channels of technology transfer, and provision of cheap fuel, food, and vital spare parts, along with a series of natural disasters, and therefore had to absorb them internally in the form of unprecedented industrial depression, dramatic decline in foreign trade, seriously damaged infrastructure, and much lower living standards. In general, in 1995, the North Korean economy appears to be one-third smaller in size, three-fifths less industrialized, heading for re-ruralization, 50 percent more isolated from the world economy, with hidden unemployment and inflation on the rise and a threat of famine looming over large pockets of the country's most vulnerable social strata. If this predicament is not considered a "hard landing," then what is?!

One may wonder how on earth this "sick man of Asia" can still be alive, with all the above-mentioned grave symptoms, ailments and handicaps, and no readily available modern medicine at hand. Indeed, some long-time observers of the North Korean stage describe its current seemingly "near death condition" as the "state of coma" when all non-essential body systems are shut down and life itself is marginally sustained only by intravenous feeding from the top down. That's apparently what is happening in the country. In economic terms, the traditional "natural self-sustaining economy" of the Middle Ages appears to be revived in the countryside; urban locales are becoming more economically "self-reliant" and autonomous; and pockets of increasingly market-oriented relations and commercial activities, filling in the vacuum left by rapidly disappearing government procurement and delivery services, are sprouting within and around free economic and trade zones in Rajin-Sonbong, Namp'o, and Wonsan, the DPRK-PRC border, KEDO-related areas and projects, areas covered by humanitarian

aid, etc. In socio-political terms, the ruling class, afraid of the looming threat of a hostile takeover by the South and potential mass food
riots, tightened social controls and rallied around Kim Jong Il,
whose leadership most of the elite have never questioned. Yet people in power, including the military and the party, are reported to be
suffering from hunger to some extent, too. Someone who frequents
the DPRK has observed that "95 percent of the population are hun-
gry, and only 5 percent are doing well." Nonetheless, they are still
in better shape than the average citizen. Obviously, Pyongyang is
better off than the periphery, not to mention the hinterland. Marginalized people suffer first and the most. As a rule, those who remain steadfastly loyal to Marshal Kim Jong Il are still better off than
those who express even a shred of a doubt about his leadership. Obviously, the message made known to everyone is "be loyal and you'll
survive the famine."[23]

One may wonder whether this very "sick man of Asia" will
ever walk again, or whether North Korea's days are numbered and
it will inevitably come to an end as a "failed state." Three points of
view expressed so far on this subject are as follows. First, some policymakers and analysts, like insurance agents regarding the DPRK
as a "terminally ill patient," set the clock ticking, make bold hawk-
ish predictions that three to five years from now it will be expira-
tion and funeral time for the North Korean state, and put it on a
suicide watch. Second, the "death penalty specialists" view North
Korea as an inmate on death row in a maximum security prison of
international embargoes, guarded by the UN forces in Korea. The
historical guilty verdict is out, and no matter how much effort and
time the North Korean leaders spend in their pursuit of "appeals,"
their state is doomed in the long run. The international community
will see to it that sooner or later, willy-nilly, the "antiquated North
Korean regime," whose "capital offense" is its refusal to get so-
cialized according to the universal rules of behavior of international
society, will be "terminated." Third, the majority opinion seems to
be that the command-and-control economy of the DPRK is confronted with a number of profound crises of both structural and
systemic nature and in part caused by administrative mismanagement, which, in the long run, may lead to major social dislocations

and bring down its political regime; but in the short run, they tend to agree that the ruling elite centered around Kim Jong Il remains in control of the situation for the time being and is likely to weather the storm this time again, like it has many times in the past.[24] My own opinion is that states fall due to human frailty, not because of inherent terminal diseases. Therefore, as long as "the patient" is still alive and nobody attempts to artificially "expedite" its demise, there is hope for recovery, if treated properly. It may take years or decades for the country to come out of its coma, but wise and deliberate application of traditional, "miraculous" Asian and Western medicine may be the right prescription for the "sick man of Asia" to cure its current ills.

Why Can't We All Get Along?

As I have shown earlier in this paper, both in terms of theory and history, because of the particular character of the contemporary North Korean state, its current unenviable position within the international system, and the peculiar history of its relations with its neighbors, for the DPRK the current major crises at home tend to spell all sorts of troubles abroad. In general, throughout the 1990s, standing solely on its own, the DPRK has been confronted with intensifying pressure from the West, reminiscent of the Western challenges to Yi Korea in the 1870s–1880s.

In order of priority, contemporary Western pressure on the DPRK is strategically aimed at: (1) alleviating Western security and humanitarian concerns vis-à-vis North Korea (including reduction of the nuclear and conventional military threat posed by the DPRK, nonproliferation of nuclear, chemical, and biological weapons and missile technologies, elimination of alleged sponsorship of international terrorism and drug trafficking, prevention of refugee crises and mass epidemics caused by famine, MIA-POW issues, etc.) at the very least; (2) modernizing its society, opening and liberalizing its economy, and democratizing its political system at a minimum; (3) eliminating the North Korean state altogether (through Korean unification of some sort) at a maximum.

These strategic goals guide the international response to unfolding crises in North Korea. Western diplomacy is also shaped by
its changing perceptions of threats and opportunities created by the
current situation in Pyongyang. Originally, a more or less unified
Western approach was driven by fears of the perceived strengths of
the DPRK, primarily its military capabilities and its political resolve
to fight for its way of life to the end. In my view, this fear stemmed
in part from the lack of knowledge about the real situation in the
DPRK's military and in part from a misguided Western belief in the
irrationality of the behavior of the North Korean leadership. The
Western governments' "party line" regarding the state of affairs in
the DPRK was that it was a hostile, closed society, and they did not
know how the system worked and what went on there. As a consequence, North Korea was perceived as a serious threat to Western
security that had to be dealt with jointly and firmly.

Even at present, some Western policymakers continue to plead
ignorance of the situation in North Korea, despite the fact that
after the end of the Cold War in Europe, the U.S. intelligence community was told to concentrate its powerful intelligence-gathering
technical and analytical capabilities, including satellite reconnaissance, signals intelligence, and human intelligence on North Korean targets; despite the fact that recently the North Korean
government has begun to liberalize entry for foreign tourists, labor
and capital and has opened the country up to an unprecedented
extent; despite the fact that at present dozens of foreign representatives of a wide range of NGOs and foreign private organizations
roam the countryside daily, talking to local officials and assessing
the damage done by the recent floods and the needs of starving
population; despite the fact that North Korean diplomats and officials are actively engaged in more substantive multi-level and
multi-track negotiations with the KEDO, U.S., ROK, Chinese,
Russian, and Japanese governments than ever before; despite continuous IAEA monitoring of all of the DPRK's nuclear facilities, including physical presence at the Yongbyon Nuclear Research
Complex, since 1994; despite KEDO's ever increasing presence in
the North; despite a series of high-level visits by U.S. Congressmen
and members of the Japanese Diet and their meetings with the

DPRK's senior leaders; despite a perpetual outflow of North Korean defectors of almost all ranks and ages with plenty of heartbreaking and insightful stories to tell. Notwithstanding all this, due to either bureaucratic inertia, or a certain political agenda, or, perhaps, pragmatic convenience, many policymakers and observers still prefer to plead ignorance of the current situation in North Korea rather than seek to re-evaluate the gravity of the North Korean military threat, to downgrade it, and if necessary deal with it accordingly.[25]

In the meantime, as old fears appear to be slowly subsiding, new fears stemming from the freshly detected North Korean weaknesses are emerging. These include the fear of the KPA's lashing out in a desperate suicidal attempt to save the regime, the fear of massive refugee outflows and the outbreak of uncontrolled epidemics, suspicions of the DPRK government's involvement in illicit cross-border activities like missile proliferation and drug trafficking in order to raise badly needed hard currency, and so on. But these new fears are of a different magnitude and urgency. They appear not to be enough to prop up the declining perception of the so-called North Korean threat.

At the same time, deepening domestic crises are pushing North Korean leaders into more substantive and constructive engagement with the international community in search of foreign cures for their ailing economy and worsening social problems. Their participation in various serious negotiations with the West along multiple tracks and on multiple levels shows that there is no longer a need to persuade them that the benefits of international cooperation far outweigh any gains that might accrue from their isolationist policy and their status as a pariah state. The desire to establish a full scope of relations and learn from the international community exhibited by Pyongyang nowadays opens up previously unavailable opportunities for Western diplomacy to attain its strategic goals vis-à-vis the DPRK through nonconfrontational means. These new opportunities for the West include increasing economic and financial leverage, widening military superiority, Pyongyang's growing need for foreign humanitarian aid and technical expertise, increasing North Korean involvement in various binding international organizations and agreements, the growing success of the KEDO framework, North Korea's stated desire to improve relations with the United States, and so on.

But the West is unlikely to be able to capitalize easily and promptly on these new opportunities. North Korean diplomacy is tough and often toys with brinkmanship. Besides, because of the lack of fundamental trust between Pyongyang and its Western negotiating partners, enforcement and monitoring of agreements reached still linger around negotiation tables, and the right mix of sticks and carrots remains part of the debate among Western allies about their tactics in negotiations with the DPRK. Furthermore, whereas in the past, the West confronted North Korea with a unified and well-disciplined triangular alliance pursuing a well-coordinated deterrence policy, nowadays, as the perceived North Korean threat declines and the Western dialogue with Pyongyang proliferates and intensifies, some tensions are emerging in the anti-DPRK coalition in Northeast Asia. These reflect divergent national interests and growing disagreements between Washington, Seoul, and Tokyo on various issues of strategy and tactics for dealing with the North, as well as the increasing role that domestic politics in the allied capitals plays in the formulation of their Korean policy.

The West has to deal increasingly with policy differences and problems in the coordination of allied policy-making on the Korean question. The fundamental disagreement involves the question of whether the DPRK can and will reform its political and economic systems, or whether this "failed state" will inevitably collapse. Correspondingly, policymakers considering various kinds of aid for North Korea disagree as to whether this aid might be used to prevent the "hard landing" and expedite and ease the unavoidable pain of such reforms, or whether it might be perceived as a reward for North Korea's "bad behavior" and might be used to perpetuate a "bad leadership" that is not interested in domestic reforms.[26]

In terms of strategy, there appears to be some disagreement between U.S., ROK, and Japanese government officials as to whether or not to link the provision of substantial humanitarian assistance to the DPRK to the resolution of a number of difficult bilateral political and military security issues, including North Korea's positive response to the proposed four-party peace talks and general compliance with all outstanding agreements signed between Pyongyang and its Western counterparts so far. In other words, even though nowadays there is official recognition both in Pyongyang and every major Western capital that something is terribly wrong with the current situation in the DPRK, there is still little political will in the international community to detach the North Korean humanitarian situation from all other concerns and address it on its own merits and needs for the sake of saving human lives alone.

Furthermore, on the humanitarian relief issue, one can witness a politically motivated debate under way on the scope and magnitude of the current food crisis in the DPRK and what the West should do about it. Differences in the assessment of the DPRK's food situation have surfaced between the U.S. and UN agencies, on one side, and the ROK, consumed in the politics of competitive legitimization, Japan, preoccupied with the politics of vengeance, and the PRC, driven primarily by economics, on the other.[27] The UN agencies and the Coalition to Stop Famine in North Korea, an independent network of thirteen NGOs involved in international humanitarian relief efforts on the ground in the North, assert that the famine that struck North Korea in 1995–1996 is "genuine and severe," the food situation worsens day by day, and the central government in Pyongyang has almost exhausted its own resources in the fight against hunger and cannot alleviate the plight of its people by itself. In contrast, China, Japan, and the ROK believe that the magnitude of the famine is exaggerated and that Pyongyang is capable of resolving the food crisis on its own. Moreover, some very conservative analysts and officials in the South, driven by the logic of competitive legitimization against the North, even speculate that the ongoing food crisis in the DPRK is just a cunning propaganda ploy orchestrated by the North Korean government in order to deceive naive Western donors and trick them into donating food that would raise the food stocks of the KPA at no cost to itself.[28] They suggest that if the food situation were indeed so dire as depicted by the DPRK government and the alarmist reports of private relief agencies, then the North Korean military should release some of its own food supplies to the general population or spend some of its ballooning military budget on public welfare.[29]

There are also differences over whether grain aid from the outside world is enough to head off a famine this summer. The United States, citing reports by the World Food Program, believes that the DPRK still requires large-scale grain aid to overcome the current food shortages. However, some Asian government donors believe that although the DPRK does suffer from chronic food shortages, enough food aid has already been provided to Pyongyang to enable it to avert a major food crisis. The ROK National Unification Ministry believes that the more than one million tons of grain scheduled to be shipped to the DPRK by the end of August by foreign governments, UN agencies and nongovernmental organizations will be enough to prevent famine.[30] A PRC foreign ministry spokesman also said that the DPRK had averted a major food crisis.[31] Obviously, such policy differences, albeit addressed at various multilateral consultative fora, do not further cooperation and mutual understanding in the region.

Policy disagreements among the allies are exacerbated by problems of coordination between the United States, the ROK, and Japan in the course of their joint or individual negotiations with the DPRK. At present, a number of venues for bilateral or multilateral consultation and problem-solving in Northeast Asia appear to be faltering. The North-South political and security dialogue is in dead waters, and is likely to stay there until after the next presidential election in the South. The lack of progress in intra-Korean dialogue compels the ROK government to put brakes on U.S. and Japanese efforts to normalize relations with the North. The DPRK's normalization talks with Japan remain frozen; and Japan appears to be reluctant to coordinate its stance in these talks with its allies, except occasionally when it is scolded by Seoul for edging ahead of the pack. Despite initial high expectations in the aftermath of the conclusion of the Geneva Agreed Framework and ongoing talks on various issues of bilateral concern, further improvement of DPRK-U.S. relations have been stalled recently. Moreover, continuing U.S.-DPRK contacts in the absence of North-South dialogue have upset Seoul, along with various disagreements on strategic and tactical issues continue to strain the U.S.-ROK alliance. Various suggestions for the format of final talks on peace and security on the Korean peninsula (namely, "two plus two," "four plus two," "two plus one," "six plus one," etc.) have proved to be futile so far. The four-party peace talks proposal appears to be stumbling at the moment because of North Korea's suspicion of this "two plus two" formula as a "three against one" scheme. Alternatively, parallel security talks between the DPRK and the ROK, the DPRK and Japan, and the DPRK and the United States might be converged into a comprehensive tripartite peace settlement that would replace the armistice agreement with a new peace mechanism and lay out a timetable for military demobilization, troop withdrawal, and arms reductions, but this would pose great challenges for coordination of negotiating agendas, policy stances and timing between allies to ensure that their bilateral negotiations proceed in parallel.

As far as Russia and China are concerned, both seem to prefer bilateralism to multilateralism in their respective approaches to Korea. Russia seeks to maneuver its way back into the high politics of the Korean peninsula but so far without much success. It wants to be a balancer of various foreign interests in Korea, but its bottom line is not to be excluded from any possible Korean settlement in the end. The PRC sits on the sidelines and waits patiently until the real game begins. In the meantime, as the North Korean economy becomes ever more dependent on China, Beijing is acquiring increasing leverage in Pyongyang, which the North Korean leaders may not like or may be reluctant to recognize. But as the North Korean state goes through its "hard landing," through measured diplomatic support, timely injections of badly needed grain aid, and palatable economic advice, the current Chinese leadership is likely to seek to ensure that Kim Jong Il's regime will survive its current crises even at the cost of significant civilian loss, and there will be no major geopolitical changes in the Korean peninsula in the near future.

The KEDO framework has proved to be the only successful organizational vehicle for furthering regional cooperation so far. This U.S.-shaped, buffer-like channel of multilateral political and inter-bureaucratic consultations brought together representatives of the

United States, Japan, the ROK, and the DPRK from various government agencies and bureaucracies and is being used to positively address everybody's nuclear security concerns in the Korean peninsula, such as ensuring the DPRK's compliance with NPT requirements; to help the DPRK meet its energy needs, including the supply of two light-water reactors and half a million tons of heavy fuel oil per year; and to fulfill the DPRK's desire for more international respectability and recognition in an amicable and efficient way. Moreover, recently it has been considered as a possible channel for drawing the DPRK into the international community of nations and indirectly furthering bilateral North-South dialogue, North Korean-Japanese ties, and U.S.-DPRK relations. However, it is an open question whether the KEDO formula, based on a nuclear package deal reached between the DPRK and the United States in Geneva in October 1994 and later agreed upon by the ROK and Japan, can be emulated when dealing with the issues of high politics, military security, regional economic cooperation, and humanitarian assistance. In particular, the multilateral management of food assistance, including both emergency food relief and long-term revitalization of the DPRK's agricultural system, might best be performed by coordinated private efforts and nongovernmental organizations or international bodies specifically equipped for such a purpose. And even in this instance, U.S. leadership may become necessary.

Notwithstanding frequent policy disagreements and problems of coordination, in my opinion, in the long run, the United States, South Korea, and Japan will not drift apart on the North Korean issue, thereby inadvertently satisfying one of the main goals of the DPRK's diplomacy, i.e., "driving the wedge" between its major opponents. Instead, I believe that their coalition will survive the current challenges of managing the demise of the North Korean state, and their relations will exhibit greater trust and congruity of interests and will move closer to maturity through their numerous and frequent political and security consultations on issues ranging from the DPRK's nuclear problem and KEDO operations to the future of the armistice agreement and peace settlement to the provision of humanitarian assistance and management of refugee problems, and beyond.

Conclusion

Both in terms of theory and historical experience, international co-operation on the Korean question has always been a problem among major powers in Northeast Asia. The recent aggravation of domestic crises in North Korea both opened new possibilities and created new challenges for its neighbors as they seek the realization of their selfish national interests on the peninsula. Generally speaking, the ongoing international cooperation in the region resulted in increasing Western pressure on the DPRK, aimed at providing radical new "treatment" for the various ills of this "sick man of Asia" at a time of growing prosperity throughout the region. It remains to be seen, though, whether future developments in North Korea, including such contingencies as political and military instability, mass famine, and refugee outflow, might contribute to tearing apart or further solidifying the existing anti-DPRK coalition. Also, as history reminds us, the role of China, still somewhat enigmatic, is crucial to the final determination of success or failure of any major international effort aimed at managing the North Korean crisis and to the ultimate resolution of the fate of the North Korean state.

Notes

1. For instance, even today the ROK military refuses to rule out the possibility of surgical strikes against DPRK nuclear facilities, should Pyongyang resume its clandestine nuclear program.
2. To be fair, despite occasional belligerent statements, the DPRK does not appear to behave more aggressively than in the past. On the contrary, it seems to be applying an extra effort to convince the world that it has no intention of waging a new war.
3. See, for instance, an incident in which the DPRK security officials detained a ROK cargo vessel with rice aid on board in DPRK territorial waters on the east coast and forced its captain to fly a North Korean flag before it was allowed to enter and dock at the North Korean port and unload its humanitarian aid cargo.
4. For a more detailed account of the fall of Koguryo, see Ki-baek Lee, *A New History of Korea*, Cambridge, MA: Harvard University Press, 1984, p. 67.

5. Each new king became the target of revenge among the factions he had defeated. Twenty kings occupied the throne over the course of about 150 years in the later period of Silla, and all of them fell victim to unceasing political turmoil. See Ki-baek Lee, pp. 93–94.

6. See Ki-baek Lee, pp. 95–101.

7. See Ki-baek Lee, pp. 162–165.

8. For an excellent detailed analysis of North Korean economic history, see Eui-gak Hwang, *The Korean Economies: A Comparison of North and South,* Oxford: Claredon Press, 1993.

9. My calculation based on The Bank of Korea Report, *Vantage Point,* Seoul: Naewoe Press, July 1995, p. 25, and BOK statistics for 1996.

10. See "Pyongyang Continues to Rely on Juche Economic Policy," *Vantage Point,* Seoul: Naewoe Press, August 1994, p. 2.

11. One could speculate that had it not been for the floods, 1995 could have become the first year with slight positive growth for the economy since 1990.

12. See a flood damage assessment report prepared by the UN Department of Humanitarian Assistance after it analyzed the results of a survey done by its fact finding mission, which visited the DPRK in early September 1995. For reference, see Nautilus Daily Reports for September 5,6,7, 1995, Nautilus Institute for Security and Sustainable Development, Berkeley, CA.

13. See Bank of Korea Report, *Vantage Point,* Seoul: Naewoe Press, July 1995, p. 25.

14. See Bank of Korea Report, op. cit.

15. The total volume of the DPRK's foreign trade was equal to US$ 4,720 million in 1990, US$ 2,710 million in 1991, US$ 2,660 million in 1992, US$ 2,640 million in 1993, and US$ 2,110 million in 1994. See "EIU Country Report: North Korea," Economic Intelligence Unit, EIU, Ltd., London, 3rd Quarter 1995, p. 51. In the first six months of 1995, the total volume of foreign trade equaled US$ 930 million, which was 6.1 percent less than the corresponding volume at the end of the first six-month period in 1994. See "North Korean Trade Volume Totals US$ 930 million," *The Korea Times Daily,* September 14, 1995, p. 2.

16. The UN Department of Humanitarian Assistance estimates that, in 1994, a severe hail shower that fell on 170,000 hectares of farmland lying in the nation's major agricultural areas including the North and South Hwanghas Provinces and other western coastal regions inflicted upon the country the loss of 1,020,000 tons of grain. See

Nautilus Daily Report, Nautilus Institute for Security and Sustainable Development, Berkeley, CA, September 6, 1995. See also Bank of Korea Report, op. cit.

17. The DPRK government claims that 75 percent of the country's territory and 25 percent of the population were negatively affected by floods in the summer of 1995, with the total damage being estimated at US$ 15 billion. The UN DHA estimates that most of the arable land and infrastructure of at least four provinces were affected, and over 500,000 people were left homeless. It assessed that 1,083,000 tons of rice and 818,000 tons of maize in the fields and 1,053,000 tons of grain in stock had been inundated, washed away, or destroyed. For detailed estimates, see Nautilus Daily Report, Nautilus Institute for Security and Sustainable Development, Berkeley, CA, September 6, 1995.

18. On June 4, the WFP issued a report noting that the DPRK's food crisis was worsening rapidly, and that the last available government ration could run out by June 20. Citing the results of a joint site survey by the WFP and the Food and Agriculture Organization (FAO), the report said that the rationing system was now on the verge of collapse with no alternative mechanism available. The WFP's assessment downplayed the significance of grain aid from the international community.

19. Interview with Andrew S. Natsios, a former director of foreign disaster assistance of the U.S. Government, *New York Times,* June 11, 1997, p. A8.

20. Author's interview with Dr. Stephen Linton, New York, May 22, 1997.

21. For instance, in February 1995, on the eve of the anniversary of Kim Jong Il's birthday, the DPRK government announced 30 percent–40 percent salary raises across the board among the professions and increases in students' stipends. See *Nodong Sinmun,* February 10, 1995, p. 1.

22. Prior to the early 1970s, population in the North moved very rapidly from the countryside to urban areas. However, from then until the late 1980s this process of continuous urbanization ceased almost completely.

23. It is one of the ironies of contemporary inter-Korean politics that by refusing to aid the North, the South inadvertently eliminates, by starving to death, those marginal forces within North Korean society that might be opposed to Kim Jong Il's regime.

24. See, for instance, DCI Mr. Deutch's testimony before a U.S. Congressional committee dealing with intelligence in December 1996. For an academic presentation of these views, see Nick Eberstadt, *Korea Approaches Unification,* Armonk, NY: M.E. Sharpe, 1995.

25. A legitimate question is how can one plead ignorance and depict gloom and predict doom at the same time, as many of these observers do, unless one is either not entirely sincere or is engaged in promoting a specific political agenda?

26. For a detailed analysis of this dilemma, see *A Coming Crisis on the Korean Peninsula?,* Special Report, Washington, D.C.: The U.S. Institute of Peace, 1997, p. 8.

27. Plainly speaking, how many North Koreans should die from starvation before the Japanese government decides to de-link the issue of humanitarian assistance to the DPRK from that of Pyongyang's full accounting regarding the whereabouts of a few allegedly kidnapped Japanese citizens?

28. Dr. Stephen Linton, Chairman of the Eugene Bell Centennial Foundation, who visited the DPRK 21 (!) times in the past three years primarily to bring humanitarian relief to the starving North Korean population (most recently from April 27 to May 3, 1997), stressed that "diversion of food to the KPA is a bogus issue." Author's interview, May 22, 1997.

29. See comments by Mr. Park Soo Gil, ROK Ambassador to the United Nations, in Barbara Crossette, "Hunger in North Korea: A Relief Aide's Stark Report," *New York Times,* June 11, 1997, p. A8.

30. These officials assert that the DPRK obtains more than 500,000 tons of grain from the PRC annually and will receive more than 600,000 tons of grain aid from foreign governments, UN agencies and others by October, a volume that is enough to feed 23 million North Koreans until the autumn harvest, if combined with the North's domestic production of over 3.5 million tons.

31. See "Discrepancy Arises Between Allies on North Korean Food Assessment," *Korea Times,* June 8, 1997.

CHAPTER 12

DEMOGRAPHIC CHANGES IN NORTHEAST ASIA AND THEIR IMPLICATIONS FOR REGIONAL STABILITY

Maurice D. Van Arsdol, Jr.

Introduction

THE NORTHEAST ASIA (NEA) REGION IS now being defined by economic, population, and resource links between NEA countries. NEA has been described as contained within the national boundaries of China, Japan, North Korea, South Korea, Mongolia, and the Russian Federation, and as covering the Helonjiang, Liaoning, and Jilin provinces of China, the Russian Far East, and the entirety of the other nations of the area.[1] As shown in Tables 12.1 and 12.2, NEA nations had a mid-1998 population of approximately 1,594 million persons, which was 27 percent of that of the world, while the NEA region itself had a 1990 population of approximately 298 million.

NEA populations are transitioning from high to low vital rates (fertility and mortality rates), from low to high urbanization, from population homogeneity to diversity, and from low to higher international migration. NEA nations vary widely in their populations, economies, and resources.

The security task for NEA is to achieve harmony between populations, economies, and resources. The discussion of security questions can be facilitated by describing how "ultimate causes" or "root causes," as contrasted with "proximate causes," relate to intra- and international conflict. Following Shaw's distinctions between ultimate and proximate causes of environmental degradation, "ultimate causes" or "root causes" of conflict are defined as failures of the social contracts that bind peoples and nations together in cooperative activity.[2] Such failures can be tinder for flash points that ignite conflicts.[3] "Proximate causes" of conflict apply to specific situations,[4] and can include changes in the size, composition, and distribution of populations.

In this chapter I will describe how population factors might contribute to conflict in NEA. As proximate causes, population changes are relevant to conflict in several ways. First, the links between population and conflict are indirect and reciprocal.[5] Second, population changes, including differential growth rates within and between nations, may undermine supporting stability.[6] Third, environmental changes, including decreasing resources and environmental disruptions, can intensify the effects of population-based proximate causes of conflict.[7] Fourth, population changes, by themselves, do not initiate conflicts.[8] Flawed social contracts appear to be the ultimate conflict determinants. Fifth, implementing population policies can sometimes alleviate economic and resource problems, even while flawed social contracts remain in place. Sixth, gaining control of population stocks and flows can sometimes reduce population pressures and facilitate modifications of flawed social contracts. Nevertheless, changes in population policy, if perceived as violating social contracts, may lead to conflict.[9]

I will suggest answers to three questions concerning how demographic changes affect NEA regional stability. First, how do current demographic and epidemiologic transitions in NEA nations, and their interactions with free market economies and with socialist economies moving to free markets, affect regional stability? Second, how might current demographic and epidemiologic transitions in NEA exacerbate or ameliorate social, economic, and environmentally-based tensions? Third, can NEA countries design and implement population policies that promote regional stability? There are three types of conflicts in NEA.[10] (1) "Cultural-civilizational conflicts," such as Sino-Russian conflict over territories lost by China in the Russian Far East, have long histories. (2) Nationalist clashes may occur within shared civilizations, such as those of Japan with China and Korea. (3) State-to-state conflicts are exemplified by the North-South Korean conflict.

Scholars have yet to fully model and verify how population, economic, and resource factors and social contract failures generate intra- and international conflict. I will not systematically consider how the current economic crisis and environmental degradation in and adjacent to NEA may impact populations and thus affect NEA security. These events, if continuing, can threaten domestic stability and increase tensions between NEA countries. Responses to these events may also strengthen NEA economies and facilitate cooperation.[11] International conflicts are linked primarily to the interests of nations taken as a whole, rather than their constituent parts. I will primarily consider conditions for nations containing NEA populations, but also take into account some subpopulations within the more limited NEA region. Given these conditions, my conclusions will be illustrative rather than definitive.

Demographic Transitions

The first question concerns the connections between NEA stability and changes in NEA demographics and the economic regimes of NEA nations.

Vital Rates and Epidemiologic Transitions

Vital rate changes underlie other changes in NEA demographic and economic regimes and further affect NEA resources. It has been argued that modernization (and accompanying increases in levels of living) produces a multi-stage transition from high to low vital rates.[12] (See Figure 12.1) This transition has been described as accompanied by an epidemiologic transition.[13] During the vital rates and epidemiologic transitions, and in the absence of migration, population growth occurs through natural increase, or the excess of births over deaths. Transitions vary in pattern and speed, but once begun they are normally fixed; interruptions tend to be temporary. One consequence may be a "new equilibrium of births and deaths" by the end of the 21st century.[14]

The following description of the stages of vital rates and epidemiologic transitions is useful for our understanding.[15] (See Figure 12.1.) Stage 1, referred to as "The Age of Pestilence and Famine," describes traditional societies. Population size is generally constant; high birth and high death rates tend to cancel out natural increase, or the excess of births over deaths. In Stage 2, "The Age of Receding Pandemics," birth rates remain high, death rates decline, and population growth is rapid. In Stage 3, "The Age of Degenerative and Man-Made Diseases," birth rates decline, death rates bottom out, and population growth begins to level off. Finally, Stage 4 is

Figure 12.1   Stages of the Vital Rates and Epidemiologic Transitions

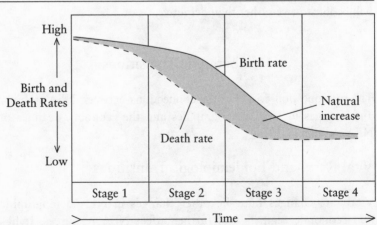

characterized by low and fluctuating birth and death rates of equal magnitude, and population size is again constant.[16] Stage 4 may include higher life expectancies resulting from medical advances and mortality increasingly affected by lifestyle-related causes of death.[17] A new Stage 5 (not shown in Figure 12.1) may reflect increases in deaths from new or re-emerging infectious and parasitic diseases, and increased populations with compromised immune systems.[18] These transitions provide opportunities for policymakers to influence regional stability.

First, the power of a nation reflects, to some extent, the product of population size and the level of living. While some national leaders may delay or slow fertility declines in order to temporarily project power through population increases, larger populations may more rapidly deplete resources, and thus decrease regional stability.

Second, rapid vital rates and epidemiologic transitions can facilitate economic growth by a "demographic windfall effect whereby the demographic transition allows a massive one-time boost in economic development as rapid labor force growth occurs in the absence of burgeoning youth dependency."[19] It has been argued that the economic successes of Japan and South Korea are based on rapid fertility decline and low mortality, which has created "a (demographic) window of opportunity," which includes "a rise in the relative number of working age adults, and later a rise in the relative number of elderly."[20] (The former increases per capita income and facilitates savings and investment.) If labor forces are well educated, and economies are healthy and well managed during these transitions, economic growth (and regional stability) may be enhanced. The 1998 Asian economic crisis may inhibit the benefits of the demographic windfall in China, as well as in Thailand, Malaysia, and Indonesia, and lead to internal repression of some dissident populations, which will negatively impact stability.

Third, countries in Stages 3 and 4 of the vital rates and epidemiologic transitions shift from youth dependency to old age dependency, may experience labor shortages, and may respond by importing migrant labor and by outsourcing production to lower income countries.[21] Japan and to some extent South Korea are examples. These changes may decrease regional stability if governments of affected nations have not maximized the economic benefits of previous labor force expansion and/or if local populations are competing for employment with new immigrants. Further, destabilizing events could occur if the 1998 economic crisis results in the forced return to their homelands of migrants to Japan and Korea.

The vital rates and epidemiologic transitions appear to be complete in Japan and Hong Kong (Stage 4), approaching completion in South Korea (Stage 3), not as far advanced in the rest of China and in Chinese NEA (Stage 3), and less advanced in North Korea and in Mongolia (Stage 2) (Figure 12.1 and Table 12.1). In the Russian Federation (and the Russian Far East or Russian NEA), the recent decrease of life expectancy, particularly for males, makes the near future course of mortality less certain and may be a bellwether for instability.

Urban and Diversity Transitions

Urbanization refers to the economic and social changes that accompany population concentration in urban areas and the growth of cities and their surrounding areas. The percentages of populations termed urban (typically living in cities and towns with populations of 2,000 or more) by NEA countries now ranges from 30 in China to 80 in Japan (Table 12.1). In each NEA country, except China, more than one-half of the population is urban.[22]

NEA populations have great ethnic, geographic, linguistic, and economic diversity. Urbanization may lead to political instability if: (1) poor rural populations expand into surrounding urban areas, increasing environmental degradation and capping agricultural production, (2) urban unemployment increases, (3) urban infrastructures fail, (4) class and ethnic segregation increases, (5) economic and social opportunities decrease and (6) oppositional cultures emerge.[23] The 1998 Asian economic crisis has increased the vulnerability of NEA middle and professional classes, which support stable NEA regimes.[24]

Ethnic antipathies, which stem from economic pressures, are often exacerbated by demographic changes and resource scarcity. They may then take on lives of their own. Recent communal or ethnoreligious conflicts, for example, have occurred in Japan, and nationalistic conflicts have taken place in China, Tibet, and the Russian Federation.[25]

Globalization, including reductions of international trade barriers, intraregional economic integration, transitions from socialist to free market economies, and the establishment of multinational free trade zones, has led to the development of transborder cities and urban systems (TBS's).[26] TBS's, which consist of several central cities and/or adjacent urban aggregations on or near national borders, may be exceedingly diverse, have extensive cross-border economic and social integration, and thus organize transactions between nations. Examples are Hong Kong Guangzhou (China), Singapore-Johor Bahru (Malaysia), and Southern California (USA)-Baja California (Mexico). In addition to raising perplexing questions regarding national sovereignty, TBS's can drive international migration and affect regional stability.

International Migration Transition

The world's foreign-born stock (international migrants) increased from approximately 25 million in 1965 to 120 million in 1990 to perhaps 125 million in 1997.[27] International migration, which may now be surpassing fertility as a topic of global concern (Figure 12.2), raises complex questions regarding the nature of the nation-state, citizenship, ethnicity, and economic activity, as well as cross-border transmission of diseases. Governments increasingly see international migration as affecting their stability and security.

International migration has been described as one of a series of global flows including communications, resources, goods, services, and capital.[28] The interchangeability of some of these flows, their past destabilizing tendencies, and their increasing volatility suggest that migration and other global flows can be linked to conflict.[29] Four major types of current international migration flows have been identified, including labor migration (either permanent or temporary), family reunification, refugee migration and asylee flows, and illegal migration.[30] Much international migration is circular; entries of new migrants are often offset by mi-

Figure 12.2 International Migration Policies of NEA Countries Circa 1993

Country	Immigration Policy			Emigration Policy	Encourage Return of Nationals	Favor Integration of Non-Nationals	Party to Refugee Instruments
	Permanent Settlement	Adult Workers	Adult Dependents				
China	Maintain	Maintain	Maintain	Maintain	No	—	CP
Japan	Maintain	Raise	Maintain	No intervention	—	No	CP
Korea, North	Maintain	—	—	Maintain	No	—	—
Korea, South	Lower	Lower	Lower	Raise	No	Yes	CP
Mongolia	Maintain	Lower	Raise	No intervention	Yes	No	—
Russian Federation	Lower	Maintain	—	Lower	Yes	Yes	CP

Source: United Nations, Population Division, Department for Social and Economic Affairs and Policy Analysis, "International Migration Policies, 1995," United Nations, New York, NY, 1996.

Definitions: C = Party to 1951 United Nations Convention relating to status of refugees.
P = Party to 1967 protocol relating to status of refugees.

grant departures. In addition to the increasing economic ties between sending and receiving countries, international migration is
facilitated by increasing levels of knowledge and experience at
destination, ties between families and friends at origin and destination, and pressures for family reunification.[31]

International migration systems and subsystems are defined by
substantial international migration flows between groupings of nations. These systems are constantly evolving and have been described as including Europe and the Commonwealth of Independent
States, North America, West Asia, Latin America, and Asia.[32] The
NEA subsystem includes migration to Japan and South Korea from
countries with labor surpluses, migration of professionals from outside NEA to South Korea and Japan, and outflows to other regions,
particularly to North America.

Major migration streams originating in NEA are from China,
and flow to the United States and Canada. China had a net emigration of –800,000 from 1990 to 1995.[33] Minor streams origi-
nate in China, the Philippines, and South America and focus on
Japan. Smaller streams flow to South Korea. The most important
migration destinations in NEA countries are the Russian Federation and Hong Kong, which ranked fourth and twenty-third respectively, in terms of the world's total reported net migrants
(in-migrants minus out-migrants) from 1990 to 1995. (These migrants were as follows: Russian Federation—1,800,000; Hong
Kong—228,000.) Percentages of population growth from 1900 to
1995 due to migration for the Russian Federation and Hong Kong
are 120 and 45, respectively.[34]

Feedback mechanisms link international migration and international migration policies. Governments use migration policies to facilitate development, avoid the costs of uncontrolled migration
flows, solidify national identity, and increase international integration.[35] Migration is now subject to increasing government scrutiny
and policy control. In 1976 only 13 percent of all governments reported policies to raise or lower immigration and 17 percent to influence emigration. By 1995 these percentages were 40 and 24
percent, respectively.[36] In 1993 one-third of all governments reported policies to lower immigration; among NEA countries, only

the Russian Federation and South Korea had policies to integrate non-nationals (Figure 12.1). Closing doors to legal immigrants may increase asylum, refugee, and illegal immigration, which may potentially decrease regional stability. Further, refugee migration policies are moving toward repatriation. Moreover, the percentage of countries of origin closing the emigration safety valves is increasing, from 13 in 1976 to 20 in 1993.[37]

International labor migration to NEA countries has recently increased, fueled by rapid economic development in Japan, South Korea, and Hong Kong. There has been a rapid development of immigration management programs involving new international instruments and organizations, and the private immigration industry, to facilitate the recruitment and deployment of labor.[38]

Multinational conflicts, revolutions, state implosions, and environmental changes are increasing refugees worldwide.[39] World refugee population in 1997 was approximately 13.2 million, down from approximately 26 million at the beginning of 1996.[40] These estimates ignore the many millions who have recently lost their homes through development projects. More restrictive migration policies of industrialized states outside of NEA have decreased demands for migrant unskilled labor, yet migration pressures have increased, enhancing undocumented and refugee migrations to NEA, and heightening international security concerns.[41]

Large numbers of current refugees are from economies in transition from socialist to capitalist systems.[42] Many ethnic Russians have returned to the Russian Federation from former south-central and West Asia republics of the USSR. With the exception of the Russian Federation, there are now relatively few refugees in NEA countries. Refugees in NEA countries in 1995 were estimated to be as follows: (1) China—287,000, (2) Hong Kong—1,700, and (3) Japan—9,100. Hong Kong and the remainder of China drew many refugees from the Vietnam War during the 1970s and 1980s.

In recent decades, third-country refugee resettlement has given way to refugee exclusion, or restrictive refugee camps in destination areas, as found in Hong Kong prior to 1997.[43] It has been argued that refugee policies can range from positive to negative depending on how governments assess benefits of international assistance, relations with the sending country, local capacity to absorb refugees, and national security.[44] Temporary policy responses to refugees include (1) exclusion and discouragement, (2) repatriation, (3) using asylum seekers to obtain objectives not linked to refugee issues, (4) containment, and (5) armed prevention.[45] Harsher refugee policies, combined with the repatriation of economic migrants due to the economic crisis in destination countries, and increasing environmental degradation may pose new NEA security problems.

National Cases

My second question is how do current changes in demographic regimes in Northeast Asia affect regional stability?

China and the Hong Kong-Guangzhou Trans-Border City

With 1,243 milllion people in 1998, China has 78 percent of the population of NEA countries. China now appears to be at Stage 3 of the vital rates and epidemiologic transition. Natural increase is one percent/year; and the total fertility rate 1.8 children/woman. China's three northeast provinces contain approximately one-third of the population of the more narrowly defined NEA region. China has declining vital rates, an aging population, rapid urbanization, significant emigration, increasing economic development, medium technological development, and high natural resources. It is assimilating the Hong Kong portion of the Hong Kong-Guangzhou TBS and is exerting lateral pressures to the north, south, and west.[46]

Due to the large size of China's population, the aforementioned trends can strongly impact regional security. Further, population increases in rural China are leading to increased rural-urban migration, more dependence on food imports, and increased resource depletion; they enhance internal economic disparities and may increase current Chinese lateral pressures in NEA and the rest of Asia and the Pacific. Moreover, the implementation of the birth planning program has increased tensions between government institutions and the Chinese population, and between China and other nations. Successful resolutions of population issues in China are prerequisites for successful economic reform in China, which in turn would increase NEA regional stability.

First, China's vital rates transition, which began in the 1960s, has resulted in decreases in fertility, gains in health and life expectancy, and an older population. China's fertility decline is largely associated with the birth planning program.[47] The program was initially based on delayed marriage, larger spacing between births, and fewer children, but was later modified into a "one child policy" in order to more effectively fit population to resources. "Natural changes," including the New Economic Reform, which increase family income, improve women's status, and promote social welfare services, may have decreased desires for children and increased the benefit of having fewer children, particularly in urban areas. But in rural areas, the substitution of the household responsibility system for the commune system may have led some families to prefer more rather than fewer children as agricultural labor.[48] Further, birth quotas and disincentives for unauthorized births may have increased tensions between the rural population and the government, thus placing in doubt the long-term viability of the birth planning program.[49] Chinese planners continue to emphasize guidance by the state as the basis of the birth planning program, but are beginning to give more emphasis to gender considerations and to reproductive choice.[50]

Second, China's family planning program success has led to problems of gender discrimination and an increasing old age dependency burden. Significant numbers of women are missing from the Chinese population—apparently as a result of a son preference and a combination of female infanticide, neglect of female children, under-reporting of female births, and concealment of female infants. While China has been subject to international censure because of these problems, the positive public health consequences of successful family planning have largely been ignored by the international community. China's public health successes also carry a future price. Fertility declines have enhanced infant and child health and life expectancy, thus making China the first developing country with a large population and a serious future old-age dependency burden. This burden may slow the increase in Chinese productivity and inhibit economic development.

Third, there is growing competition between rural and urban areas within China. Residence changes in China may be official or unofficial, depending on whether they are registered. The household registration system or *hukou*, used prior to New Economic Reform to control where the population lived and worked, is still influential today.[51] Traditional labor-intensive agriculture previously anchored most Chinese to rural areas. Technical advances in agriculture, coupled with New Economic Reform and urban development, are now pushing workers (primarily non-*hukou* workers) off the land and pulling migrants to cities.

There appear to be two systems of migration within China—more highly skilled, highly educated and government sanctioned *hukou* migrants and their families, and more free-market-governed non-*hukou* migrants. Approximately 38–48 million rural laborers, many of whom are people who can no longer support themselves or their families in rural areas, are estimated to be part of the "floating populations" of Chinese cities.[52] It is suggested that the remainder of these floating populations, perhaps 30 million in number, consists of temporary urban residents "traveling for business, education, tourism, and to visit relatives."[53] The household registration book defines families as agricultural or urban. Only *hukou* households are entitled to social services.[54] Agricultural families retain their agricultural status when they move to cities, or when there are changes in the rural or urban status of their locales.[55]

One analyst has likened the movement of marginalized, non-*hukou* migrants to Chinese cities to that of illegal Mexican migrants to the United States, and has described it as characterized by maturing migration streams, intensifying regional differences, and fluctuating efforts to control internal movement.[56] It has also been argued that the resulting floating populations of non-*hukou* urban migrants, focused on the coastal and Sichuan provinces, may intensify the effects of deepening social and economic divisions in China as they compete with residentially more stable populations for limited resources.[57] Nevertheless, while the numerical *stock* of Chinese migrants is high in comparison with other countries, China's internal migration *rate* is low, which serves to dampen destabilizing aspects of internal migration. The recent Asian economic crisis may exacerbate problems of stability in urban areas, if increasing unemployment is added to problems resulting from restructuring and downsizing of state enterprises.[58]

Fourth, the overseas Chinese, estimated as more than 36,000,000 in number, have been described as the world's largest "middleman" minority.[59] Some suggest that floating populations from mainland China may soon join this population.[60] Because of its large population size, China has the potential to generate overwhelming emigration, which could have destabilizing effects on migration-receiving countries. The overseas Chinese, who are largely urban, are most concentrated in Asia, followed by the Western Hemisphere. Perhaps because of their middleman position, Chinese have often been the targets of discrimination. In the past the Chinese government has not been able to project sufficient power to protect Chinese overseas. The Chinese government has used emigration as a way of meeting domestic political objectives. The 1989 events at Tienanmen Square led Chinese students to seek asylum overseas, movement facilitated by the Chinese government in order to reduce the number of domestic dissidents.[61] International responses to the refugees, while positive in many cases, may have increased tensions. If the Chinese economy succeeds, many of these refugees may return, resulting in a net gain in human resources.

Fifth, the Hong Kong-Guangzhou TBS also poses questions of regional stability. The transformation of the global economic systems since the 1970s has resulted in the rapid economic development of Hong Kong. Like other TBS's, Hong Kong is based on spatial dispersion and economic integration of populations and coordinates capital accumulation, industry, labor flows and migration.[62] Hong Kong's rise in the 1960s was grounded on cheap labor for labor-intensive manufacturing largely supplied by refugees who might previously have been considered to be "economic migrants."[63] Despite restrictive migration to Hong Kong since 1980, the number of illegal foreign workers (estimated at 130,000) in 1993 was approximately one-third of the total foreign labor force.[64]

The new Hong Kong shares characteristics with other TBS's. It is a separate system from the remainder of China with close links based on economic ties, but with different governments, and a border and immigration control similar to other TBS's.[65] For Hong Kong to facilitate the economic expansion of the rest of China, borders between Hong Kong and the rest of China must be crossed; and questions regarding cross-border refugees, asylum seekers, illegal migrants, and family unification must be resolved to the satisfaction of Hong Kongese and Mainland Chinese. The economic integration of Hong Kong and the rest of China will include more trans-border economic activity, employment, marriages, and households. This, in turn, would facilitate development of the Greater China economic block (China-Hong Kong-Taiwan), and increase China's interdependence with the global system.[66]

Arguments that Hong Kong will cease to link East and West appear unwarranted.[67] Unless fanned by outside forces, consequences of political disruptions that might occur in Hong Kong are likely to be transitory. Experiences of other TBS's, including that of Southern California, USA and Baja California, Mexico, suggest that proximate causes of conflict including social, economic, environmental, and demographically based tensions, are more dangerous in the long run.[68]

Sixth, regional stability is affected by the lateral movement of the Han majority populations into China's northern frontier, including Xinjiang Province in the northeast, the autonomous region of inner Mongolia (in the far north), Heilongiang Province in the NEA portion of China, and the Tibetan Autonomous Region. These areas have been brought into the Han sphere of control by different paths, and for different reasons, Xinjiang to defend the eastern core provinces, and the autonomous region of inner Mongolia and Heilongiang to guard against lateral movements from Russia, Japan, and the West.[69] Water scarcity limits the ability of the periphery to support larger peasant populations, but renewable resources and primary and secondary industry offer avenues for future population support.[70] Recent ethnic conflicts within Xinjiang Province highlight long-standing competition between in-migrating Han population and local Muslims, now focused on control of energy reserves and trade.[71] An analyst argues, "China's very economic vitality has the potential to fuel ethnic and linguistic divisions, rather than further integrating the country as most would suppose."[72] This argument would also apply to Tibet, in which Han population transfer may be leading to environmental degradation and loss of Tibetan culture.

Japan

Compared to China, Japan has a small population, but within the NEA region, its population is relatively large. Japan has a high level of technological development and a low level of natural resources. Since World War II Japan has had to obtain resources by trade rather than by lateral expansion.[73]

The case of Japan illustrates how changing demographics can lead to concerns regarding regional stability. After the loss of occupied territories in Southeast Asia during World War II, Japan undertook a rapid transition from high to low fertility and mortality. As a Stage 4 country in the vital rates and epidemiologic transition, Japan's total fertility rate of 1.4 children per woman in 1998 is the lowest in Northeast Asia, with the exception of the Russian Federation (1.2) (Table 12.1). Japan also has the world's highest life expectancy (80 years in 1998) and next to Finland, the lowest infant mortality (4/1,000 live births/year) (Table 12.1). After World War II Japan transformed itself by economic recovery. Japan is now facing population aging, more focusing of resources on the support of the older population, labor shortages, increasing dependency burdens on the labor force, increasing labor migration, reduced trade surpluses, and possible decreased standards of living.[74] These trends can increase both domestic and international tensions.

The reported aversion of young Japanese to the "3-K" (*Kitanai, Kiken,* and *Kitsui*) or dirty, dangerous, and demanding jobs and Japan's failures, despite low fertility rates, to fully integrate women into the labor force, further aggravated labor shortages and made Japan a labor-importing nation focusing on less-skilled workers. Questions regarding migration are looming larger in Japan.[75]

Foreign workers of other than Korean and Chinese nationality are new in Japan. There is a lack of consensus regarding how to deal with foreign workers, and national migration policies are not in

Table 12.1 Recent Population Data for NEA Countries*

Country	Population Mid-1998 (millions)	Natural Increase (Annual, %)	"Doubling Time" in Years at Current Rate	Infant Mortality Rate	Total Fertility Rate	Life Expectancy at Birth (Years)	Percent Urban	Per Capita GNP, 1995 (US$)
China	1,242.5	1.0	69	31	1.8	71	30	750
China, Hong Kong SAR	6.7	0.4	161	4.0	1.1	79	—	24,290
Japan	126.4	0.2	330	3.8	1.4	80	78	40,940
Korea, North	22.2	0.9	75	39	1.9	66	59	—
Korea, South	46.4	1.0	68	11	1.7	74	79	10,610
Mongolia	2.4	1.6	42	49	3.1	57	57	360
Russian Federation	146.9	-0.5	—	17	1.2	67	73	2,410

Source: Population Reference Bureau, 1998 World Population Data Sheet, Population Reference Bureau, Washington, D.C. © 1998.

Definitions: Mid-1998 Population: Estimates are based on a recent census, official national data, or UN and U.S. Census Bureau projections.

Rate of Natural Increase: Birth rate minus the death rate, implying the annual rate of population growth without regard for migration. Expressed as a percentage.

Population "Doubling Time" in Years at Current Rate: The number of years it will take for a population to double assuming a *constant* rate of natural increase.

Infant Mortality Rate: The annual number of deaths of infants under age 1 year per 1,000 live births.

Total Fertility Rate: The average number of children a woman would have assuming that current age-specific birth rates will remain constant throughout her childbearing years (usually considered to be ages 15–49).

Life Expectancy at Birth: The average number of years a newborn infant can expect to live under *current* mortality levels.

Urban Population: Percentage of the total population living in areas termed urban by that country.

Per Capita GNP: Gross National Product includes the value of all domestic and foreign output.

— = Data unavailable or inapplicable.

*May not be reproduced without written permission from PRB. Contact: PRB, 1875 Connecticut Ave. NW, Suite 520, Washington, DC 20009, attn: Permissions.

place. Illegal immigration has increased rapidly, particularly with respect to the 3-K jobs and jobs for female "entertainers." Illegal foreign workers in 1993 (estimated at 288,000) exceeded legal foreign workers (estimated at 106,000).[76] The recent Japanese immigration law failed to resolve immigration issues, partially because of "side door" mechanisms including the reported issuing of fake passports to Latin Americans falsely claiming to be *Nikkeijin* (individuals of Japanese ancestry), and company trainee programs and student visa programs that serve as mechanisms for importing low-skilled labor.

Japan has yet to articulate fully policy responses to increased migration. Japan has been described as a modern welfare state that is divided along nationality, ethnicity, and gender lines.[77] Suggested policy responses to the need for foreign workers have included (1) admitting foreign workers as a last resort, (2) denying admission to unskilled foreign workers, admitting foreigners on a temporary basis only, (3) setting up more offshore factories and thus reducing discrimination against minorities, including illegal foreign workers, performing 3-K work, (4) restructuring "company trainee" and student visa programs, and (5) making appropriate arrangements with countries supplying labor.[78]

Table 12.2   Area and Population of NEA

Country	Population (million)	Area (1,000) km²
Mongolia	2.2	1,565
Russian Far East	8.0	6,216
Northeast China	99.6	788
North Korea	21.4	125
South Korea	43.7	99
Japan	123.5	361
NEA	298.4	9,154

Source: Hiroshi Kakazu, 1994, "The Possible Organizational Structure and Funding Sources of a NEA Development Bank," *Regional Economic Cooperation in NEA,* Yongpyeong, cited in Lau Sim Yee and Alexander Sheingauz, "National Resources and Environment Management in Northeast Asia," Alexander Sheingauz and Hiroya Ono, eds., *Natural Resources and Environment in Northeast Asia, Status and Challenges, Tokyo, Japan,* Sasakawa Peace Foundation, 1995, p. 18.

It has been reported that the Japanese government is focusing on de facto immigration policies and avoiding an open debate on the question of whether Japan should remain bound to the principle of Japanese ethnicity or should become locked into formal immigration policies.[79] It has also been suggested that an absolute shortage of labor could be prevented by more changes in economic structure and by new applications of technology. The Japanese government may now wish to keep its options open, knowing that technology and more female labor force integration could stave off an absolute labor shortage.[80] (Extending employment for older persons would also help to meet labor force needs.) There is a danger that Japan will put off deciding whether and how to open its doors to permanent migration until its own economy, internal affairs, and foreign relations are damaged. On the other hand, the Japanese government, which has made important contributions to Northeast Asian stability by the successful management of its own vital rates transition and support of fertility and public health programs abroad, will likely attempt to steer a stabilizing course on migration.

North Korea

Within the NEA region, North Korea has a medium level of natural resources and medium size population.[81] North Korea has been experiencing a slower vital rates transition than South Korea. Famine is now affecting its vital rates. North Korea may be at Stage 3 of the vital rates and epidemiologic transition. In 1998, the total fertility rate was 1.9 children per woman, natural increase (the difference between births and deaths) was 0.9 percent/year, and population doubling time was 75 years (Table 12.1). Political issues regarding reunification of the Korean peninsula dominate security concerns in North and South Korea. A worsening political or economic situation and civil strife in North Korea could result in state implosion and/or massive refugee migration to South Korea.[82] On the other hand, increasing emphasis on trade and economic integration with NEA by North Korea could enhance NEA stability. If political conditions warranted, and if well managed, labor flows between North Korea and South Korea could perhaps enhance the economic development of North Korea.

South Korea

South Korea has the third largest population within the NEA region, a rapidly increasing level of technological development, and some resources.[83] South Korea has largely completed the vital rates and epidemiologic transition. In 1998 its total fertility rate was 1.7 children per woman, natural increase was 1.0 percent/year, and doubling time was 75 years (Table 12.1). The country has high life expectancy, is highly urban, and per capita income is estimated to be four times that of Eastern Europe. Educational levels are high, there is low unemployment, and there are labor shortages in low-paying jobs. The government has therefore admitted foreign workers, and South Korea has become a major labor importer and declining labor exporter.[84]

It has been observed that "irregular migration" has become the norm in South Korea, as imported labor is not acceptable to Korean unions.[85] Major labor sources are reported to be the Philippines, Pakistan, Sri Lanka, Bangladesh, and Nepal.[86] Illegal foreign workers are estimated to be 90,000 in number, circa 1993, compared with 5,000 legal trainees and 8,500 legal foreign workers.[87] Along with Japan, South Korea has attempted to limit the settlement of foreign workers. It remains to be seen whether foreign workers will lead to instability in South Korea.

South Korea's efforts to recover from the current economic crisis may contribute significantly to NEA stability. Of concern is the question of how South Korea might respond to intensified North and South Korean economic relations. Such a change would likely lead to extensive labor migration to South Korean cities and increasing demand on South Korean infrastructure.[88]

Mongolia

Mongolia has extensive natural resources and the smallest population in NEA.[89] Mongolia is in Stage 2 of the vital rates and epidemiologic transition. Its total fertility rate of 3.1 children per woman in

1998 was the highest in NEA. Mongolia then had the highest natural increase in all of NEA (approximately 1.6 percent/year). Its life expectancy (57 years) was the lowest, infant mortality (49 deaths per 1,000 live births/year) was the highest, and its percentage of urban population (57) was the lowest, with the exception of China.[90]

The infrastructure in Mongolia for population policy formation and implementation is new. The government still views the birth rate as being at a satisfactory level (Figure 12.2) and wishes to intervene only in order to maintain it.[91] The fertility rate is likely to decrease in the future, as the percentage of married couples using modern forms of contraception (currently 25 percent) approaches that of all couples using all forms of contraception (60 percent).[92] As modernization occurs in Mongolia, there will be pressures for immigration as well as emigration, with attendant hazards and benefits.

The Russian Federation

Within the NEA region the Russian Federation has high natural resources, the next to smallest population, and low development.[93] The Russian Federation is in Stage 4 of the demographic and epidemiologic transition. In 1998 the total fertility rate was 1.2, life expectancy was 67 years, and natural increase was negative. The Russian Federation also has the second largest national population of any NEA country, and high technological development for the nation as a whole. It is in competition with the West, Turkey, and China for access to economic resources of the Commonwealth of Independent States.[94] The Russian Federation has experienced recent declines in production and income and increasing economic uncertainty.

Conflict within the 12-member states of the Commonwealth of Independent States (CIS) led to an estimated 700,000 refugees and 2.3 million internally displaced persons in 1991–1992, declining to an estimated 516,800 refugees and 1.3 million internally displaced persons by early 1996.[95] Further, many thousands of ethnic Russians who were formerly residents of other nations in the CIS have returned to the Russian Federation. Of the reservoir of approximately 25 million ethnic Russians in non-Russian successor states perhaps two million have returned to the Federation. Moreover, there has been extensive migration from the Russian Federation to market economy countries, estimated at 115,900 in 1997.[96] As market economy countries increase their migration restrictions, more migrants from developing countries may be halted "in transit" through CIS countries. Some of these transients may settle within the Russian Federation.

Demographic problems in the Russian Federation have roots in the Soviet era. It has been observed that life expectancy increases first stalled in the 1960s, that the state-run health care system has not successfully adapted to new economic reform, that past world wars, civil wars, and famines have made for unbalanced age structures, and that there are increasing numbers of elderly.[97] According to a 1996 study, "Russia is experiencing unusually high mortality rates from preventable causes (e.g., alcoholism), extremely high induced abortion rates, and fertility rates that are among the lowest in the world."[98] In addition to population aging, there has been a recent decrease in life expectancy, particularly for males. In 1970–1975 life expectancy for Russian Federation males was 63.1 years, compared with 63.2 for the rest of NEA. By 1990–1995 life expectancy for Russian Federation males had decreased to 60.4 years but had increased for the rest of NEA to 67.6 years. The absolute decline in male life expectancy in the Russian Federation for the referenced period was exceeded only in Rwanda, Uganda, and Latvia.[99] A continuation of these trends in the Russian Federation could have negative effects on economic reform and social safety nets.

It has been suggested that stress is linked to the crisis of transformation of the Russian Federation social and economic systems.[100] Stressors in this case would include dislocations in the labor market, family structure, geographic distribution, and inadequate policy action.[101]

Socialist systems, which emphasize equal accessibility to public health and medical care benefits, tend to reduce mortality differentials within societies. The transition to a capitalist econmy has been accompanied by increasing dispersion of levels of loss of life among inhabitants of geographic subdivisions in the Russian Federation.[102] The Russian Far East appears to have a higher level of years of life lost from all (combined) causes of death than Russia for the total male and female populations classified by total rural and urban residence for the years 1989 through 1994.[103]

The specific consequences of current Russian population changes for regional stability are not clear. Decreasing life expectancy can be a threat to the social order. Rapid population shifts, compounded by ethnic changes in the Russian Federation, have destabilizing influences if new populations are competing with established populations for scarce resources. Ethnic rivalries, independence movements, market economy-central planning, related political differences, the fate of nuclear weapons, and environmental problems further compound these questions.[104] Social and economic problems and lack of connection to Moscow are apparent in the Russian Far East. Primorye, in particular, may be a source of future tension with China.[105] Undocumented migration from China may become a serious problem in the Russian Far East. Given that the Russian Federation has extensive natural resources, if the Federation is politically stable the long-term outlook for development may be positive.[106]

Increasing Stability

My final question is can Northeast Asian countries work together to develop population policies that will facilitate international stability? Policymakers in Northeast Asia are aware of the advantages of population stabilization and have created institutions to facilitate an equilibrium of births and deaths. A question remains as to whether nations will be able to adequately support and develop the human resources of their increasingly diverse and increasingly mobile populations given a shrinking supply of nonrenewable resources.

The potential barriers to regional stability presented by NEA country population changes are as follows: (1) China—rural population growth, rural-urban migration, cultural and linguistic divisions, ethnic conflicts, and possible future lateral pressure to the west, north, and south; (2) Japan—settlement of temporary migrants, the end of the economic miracle, aging, unsolved questions of Japanese national identity, and increased international economic tensions; (3) North Korea—potential implosion and potential for mass movement of refugees to South Korea; (4) South Korea—potential refugee migration from North Korea, irregular labor immigration, problems of temporary migrants, increased tensions with labor-supplying countries; (5) return of foreign workers from East Asia to their homelands, and to China, South Korea, and the Russian Federation; (6) Mongolia—any future failure to develop population policy infrastructure; (7) Russian Federation—demographic balkanization, social divisions, public health failures, rivalry with China for access to resources in Central Asia and potential implosion; and (8) all countries—merging sets of population, development, and environmental problems..

A number of issues will affect population-development-environment-stability connections in NEA. In Northeast China, the Russian Far East, and Mongolia the development of resources is tied to population settlement. Japan and South Korea are densely developed. All NEA countries have serious urban environmental hazards, including air, land, noise, and water pollution. China faces coastal erosion and other rising-sea-level problems affecting urban populations, serious air pollution, water shortages and pollution, and loss of needed agricultural land as a result of urbanization and industrialization. The conservation of the forest habitat and cleanup of pollution poses serious problems in the Russian Far East. Japan, North Korea, South Korea, and China have developed extensive fishing industries, but their populations are threatened by ocean pollution. Ethnic and migration issues cross-cut these problems.[107]

The competition of countries for labor on the international market can also be a proximate cause of conflict.[108] A further proximate cause of conflict in NEA may turn out to be the destabilizing potential of some migration streams.[109] There are solutions to such problems. First, Martin and Widgren state that policies that emphasize "trade, investment, aid, and the promotion of peace, respect for human rights—may not immediately eliminate the need for border controls, but they will keep countries on the path of sustained reductions in migration pressures. Abandoning these policies because they work slowly, on the other hand, may invite the very mass and unpredictable migration these countries fear."[110] Second, migration in which migrants send remittances to their homelands helps to sustain the economies of poorer sending countries. Many benefits of remittances filter to households other than those providing emigrants and may help to redistribute income in countries of origin. If demands for goods and services generated by remittances encourage production, increased supplies may lead to higher income and increased employment, facilitate development, and increase stability at origin.[111] Third, migrant integration into the labor forces of migration-receiving countries usually facilitates economic and social changes. It also facilitates cultural adaptability, which enhances stability at destination and establishes "special relations" between areas of origin and destination.[112]

Effective strategies for enhancing NEA security must include population policy components. Inoguchi has put forward five models for "waging peace." These are (1) "balancing realism" (balance of power), (2) "bandwagoning realism" (hegemony as conducive to peace), (3) "institutionalism" (building of mutual confidence), (4) "interdependence" (shared economic interests based on open markets), and (5) democracy (requiring government accountability and responsibility).[113] For each model, I will suggest how population policies can change proximate determinants of conflict and enhance international stability. My assumptions are untested; extensive research is necessary for their verification.

Balancing realism indicates "the more even the power balance the more permanent the peace."[114] From this perspective, peace would appear to be enhanced by demographic stability in Japan, China, Russia, and other Asian nations, and by migration policies that avoid rapid change.

According to Inoguchi, bandwagoning realism assumes that hegemony facilitates peace; hegemony would be enhanced by successful economic activity in Japan and China. Inoguchi states, "The worst scenario is U.S. retrenchment combined with Japanese economic collapse and Chinese mercantilism. The results would almost certainly be some form of assertion and conflict."[115] I assume demographic factors would be included among the proximate causes of conflict for any of these worst cases. Demographic examples are (1) Japanese economic failure reflecting failure to come to grips with Japanese aging, labor shortage, gender, and migration problems, and (2) Chinese mercantilism resulting from a need to expand laterally to draw upon land and other resources abroad in order to support the population at home at its current standard of living. On the other hand, a range of population policies are available for dealing with these issues.

Inoguchi describes the institutionalist view as indicating that institutions can build mutual confidence and lead to peace.[116] I assume that peacemaking is facilitated by increasing the diversity and density of public- and private-sector population policy institutions, including profit-making institutions, that will cope with the vital rates transition, urbanward and international migration, TBS's, aging, and labor force participation.

The interdependence view, according to Inoguchi, is that open markets and shared interests facilitate peace.[117] Nevertheless, fully free markets in population, money flows, and goods and services can sometimes upset the status quo. This would suggest that NEA trading partners could profitably coordinate their population policies, particularly those regarding labor force participation and migration. Government cooperation with private immigration organizations may facilitate more efficient migration management in NEA.

The democratic view assumes that democracy in NEA facilitates peace.[118] Advancing this view would mean arguing for the acceptance of refugees, the promotion of women's rights, and the acceptance of expressions of cultural diversity, while preserving political unity.[119]

Consistent with the view that population factors are proximate but not ultimate determinants of conflict is a finding that population-related conflicts appear to account for a small portion of all conflicts initiated by migration-receiving countries since World War II.[120] There are realistic ways to utilize population policies to wage peace.

New institutions are needed to manage migration and obtain equity between different segments of NEA populations. Changes in demographic regimes offer hope for stability in NEA, as long as policymakers understand them and learn how to guide them and work with their consequences. Much progress has been made; still more remains to be done. Institutional resources are often available. The necessary tasks can be accomplished.

Acknowledgments

Thanks to Dr. Hania Zlotnik, of the Population Division of the Department for Economic and Social Information and Policy Analysis of the United Nations Secretariat, who kindly briefed me on international immigration policies and the quality of current international migration data. The assistance of Marian C. Van Arsdol, Pebble Beach, California, and Fern Price, Price Business Services, Monterey, California, is gratefully acknowledged.

Notes

1. Sim Yee Lau and Alexander Sheingauz, "National Resources and Environment Management in Northeast Asia," in Alexander Sheingauz and Hiroya Ono, eds., *National Resources and Environment in Northeast Asia, Status and Challenges,* Tokyo: Sasakawa Peace Foundation, 1995, pp. 18–19.

2. Paul R. Shaw, "Rapid Population Growth and Environment Degradation: Ultimate Versus Proximate Factors," *Economic Geography,* vol. 1 (1989), pp. 199–279.

3. Michael Dear and Jennifer Wolch, "Learning from Los Angeles," *Environment and Planning,* vol. 24 (1992), pp. 917–920.

4. Ibid.

5. Nazli Choucri, *Population and Conflict: New Dimensions of Population Dynamics,* United Nations Fund for Population Activities, Population Development Series no. 8, New York, NY: United Nations Fund for Population Activities, 1983, p. 25.

6. Ibid. and The Center for Strategic and International Studies, *Population and U.S. National Interests: A Framework for Thinking About the Connections,* Washington, DC: CSIS, 1996.

7. Nazli Choucri and Robert North, *Nations in Conflict: National Growth and International Violence,* San Francisco, CA: W. H. Freeman, 1975, pp. 331–370; Thomas Homer-Dixon, "Population and

Conflict," *International Union for the Scientific Study of Population, Distinguished Lecture Series on Population and Development, International Conference on Population and Development,* Liege, Belgium, 1994; and Gil Loescher, "International Security and Population Movements," in Robin Cohen, ed., *The Cambridge Survey of World Migration,* Cambridge: Cambridge University Press, 1995, p. 559.

8. Choucri, *Population and Conflict,* and Nazli Choucri, "Perspectives on Population and Conflict," in Choucri, ed., *Multidisciplinary Perspectives on Population and Conflict,* Syracuse, NY: Syracuse University Press, 1984, pp. 1–22.

9. Maurice D. Van Arsdol, Jr., "Population Change and Conflict in Los Angeles: 1965 and 1992," in Peter Hedström and Eckert Kühlhorn, eds., *Sociology through Time and Space: Essays in Honor of Carl-Gunnar Janson,* Edsbrula, Sweden Sociologiska Institutionen, 1996, pp. 13–26.

10. Tsuneo Akaha, "International Cooperation in Establishing a Regional Order in Northeast Asia," *Global Economic Review,* vol. 27 (1998), pp. 3–26.

11. Charles E. Morrison, ed., *Asia Pacific Security Outlook 1998,* Cosponsored by Asian Institute for Strategic and International Studies, East-West Center, Japan Center for International Exchange, 1998, p. 10.

12. Kingsley Davis, "The World Demographic Transition," *Annals of the American Academy of Political and Social Science,* vol. 237, no. 5 (1945), pp. 1–11.

13. Abdel R. Omaran, "The Epidemiologic Transition: A Theory of the Epidemiology of Population Change," *Milbank Memorial Fund Quarterly,* vol. 19, no. 4 (1971), part 1, pp. 509–538.

14. Dudley Kirk, "Demographic Transition Theory," *Population Studies,* vol. 50 (1996), p. 387.

15. The description is found in David M. Heer, unpublished program, memorial service for Kingsley Davis, March 22, University of Southern California Population Research Laboratory, Los Angeles, CA, 1997, and Omaran, "The Epidemiologic Transition."

16. Heer, unpublished program, memorial service.

17. Richard G. Rogers and Robert Hackenberg, "Extending Epidemiologic Transition Theory: A New Stage," *Social Biology,* vol. 34, nos. 3–4 (1987), pp. 234–243.

18. Jay Olshansky, Bruce Carnes, Richard G. Robers, and Len Smith, "Infectious Diseases—New and Ancient Threat to World Health," *Population Bulletin,* vol. 52, no. 4, Washington, DC: Population Reference Bureau, Inc., 1997.

19. Edward M. Crenshaw, Ansari Z. Ameen, and Matthew Christenson, "Population Dynamics and Economic Development: Age-Specific Population Growth Rates and Economic Growth in Developing Countries, 1965 to 1990," *American Sociological Review,* vol. 62 (1997), p. 974.

20. Andrew Mason, "Will Population Change Sustain the Asian Economic Miracle?" *Asia Pacific Issues: Analysis from the East-West Center,* Honolulu, Hawaii, no. 34 (1997), p. 3.

21. United Nations, Commission on Population and Development, Thirtieth Session, 24–28 February, Draft, *World Population Monitoring, 1997, Issues of International Migration and Development: Selected Aspects,* ESA/P/WP 132, December 20, 1996, New York, NY: United Nations, 1997, p. 23.

22. Population Reference Bureau, "World Population Data Sheet," Population Reference Bureau, Inc., Washington, DC, 1998.

23. See Douglas S. Massey, "The Age of Extremes: Concentrated Affluence and Poverty in the Twenty-First Century," *Demography,* vol. 33 (1996), pp. 395–412.

24. Charles E. Morrison, ed., *Asia Pacific Security Outlook 1998.*

25. Anthony H. Richmond, *Global Apartheid: Refugees, Racism and the New World Order,* Toronto, New York, Oxford: Oxford University Press, 1994, p. 193.

26. Jane R. Rubin-Kurtzman, Roberto Ham-Chande, Maurice D. Van Arsdol, Jr., and Qian-wei Wang, "Demographic and Economic Interactions in Trans-border Cities: The Southern California-Baja California Mega-City," *Proceedings, XXIInd International Population Conference, International Union for the Scientific Study of Population,* Montreal, Canada, August 24-September 1, 1993, vol. 3, Liege, Belgium, 1993, pp. 131–142.

27. United Nations, Population Division, Department for Economic and Social Information and Policy Analysis, "International Migration Policies, 1995," United Nations, New York, NY, 1996, pp. 8–10.

28. Kevin McCarthy and D. Ronfeld, "Migration as an Intrusive Global Flow: A New Perspective," in *U.S. Immigration and Refugee Policy:*

Global and Domestic Issues, Lexington, MA: Lexington Books, D. C. Heath and Company, 1982.

29. Maurice D. Van Arsdol, Jr. and Naintara Gorwaney, "International Migration, Assimilation and Global Conflict," *Proceedings, XXth International Population Conference, International Union for the Scientific Study of Population,* Florence, Italy, June 5–12, 1985, vol. 3, Liege, Belgium, 1985, pp. 31–42.

30. Philip Martin and James Widgren, "International Migration: A Global Challenge," *Population Bulletin,* vol. 55, no. 1 (1996), Washington, DC: Population Reference Bureau, Inc., p. 19.

31. Douglas S. Massey, Rafael P. Goldring, and Jorge Durand, *Return to Aztlan: The Social Process of International Migration from Western Mexico,* Berkeley, CA: University of California Press, 1994.

32. Graeme Hugo, "The Globalization of Population Movements: Legal Migrants," in Nana Poko and David T. Graham, eds., *Redefining Security: Population Movements and National Security,* Westport, CT: Praeger, 1998, pp. 91–199.

33. United Nations, Commission on Population and Development, p. 27.

34. Ibid.

35. United Nations, Population Division, Department for Economic and Social Information and Policy Analysis, "International Migration Policies, 1995," United Nations, New York, NY, 1996, p. 10.

36. Ibid., p. 9.

37. Ibid., pp. 9–10.

38. United Nations, Commission on Population and Development, pp. 128–129.

39. Charles Keeley, "How Nation-States Create and Respond to Migration Flows," *International Migration Review,* vol. 30 (1996), pp. 1046–1066.

40. United Nations, Population Division, p. 163.

41. Gil Loescher, "International Security and Population Movements."

42. United Nations, Population Division, p. 60.

43. Vaughan Robinson, "Security, Migration and Refugees," in Nana Poku and David T. Graham, pp. 68–90.

44. K. Jacobsen, "Factors Influencing the Policy Reponses of Host Governments to Mass Refugee Influxes," *International Migration Review,* vol. 30 (1996), p. 674; cited in ibid., p. 84.

45. Vaughan Robinson, "Security, Migration and Refugees," pp. 84–86.

46. Alexander Sheingauz and Hiroya Ono, eds., *Natural Resources and Environment in Northeast Asia: Status and Challenges,* Tokyo: Sasakawa Peace Foundation, 1995, pp. 17–31.

47. Peiyun Mme Y. Peng, "China's Experience in Population Matters: An Official Statement," *Population and Development Review,* vol. 20 (1994), pp. 488–491.

48. Haitao Wang, Maurice D. Van Arsdol, Jr., David M. Heer, and Yuhai Wang, "Socioeconomic Determinants of Fertility in Rural China," *Proceedings XXIII International Population Conference, International Union for the Scientific Study of Population,* Beijing, China, October 11–17, 1997, vol. 3, pp. 1387–1404.

49. D. G. Johnson, "Effects of Institutions and Policies on Rural Population Growth: The Case of China," *Population and Development Review,* vol. 20 (1994), pp. 503–531.

50. Peiyun Mme Y. Peng, "Population and Redevelopment in China," *The Population Situation in China, The Insiders View,* Beijing: China Population Association, State Family Planning Association of China, 1996, p. 5.

51. Kam Wing Chan and Yuiyan Yang, "Internal Migration in Post-Mao China: A Dualistic Approach," *23rd IUSSP General Population Conference: Symposium on Chinese Demography,* China Population Association, Beijing, October 1997, pp. 180–181.

52. Kenneth Roberts, "China's Tidal Wave of Migrant Labor: What Can We Learn from Mexican Undocumented Migration to the United States?" *International Migration Review,* vol. 31 (1997), p. 252; A. Terry Rambo, "The Fallacy of Global Sustainable Development," *Analysis from the East-West Center,* no. 30, Honolulu: East-West Center, 1997, p. 6; Chan and Yang, pp. 179–183.

53. Roberts, p. 252.

54. Ibid., and Chan and Yang 1997, p. 181.

55. Sidney Goldstein, "Urbanization in China, 1982–87: Effects of Migration and Reclassification," *Population and Development Review,* vol. 16 (1990), pp. 673–701.

56. Roberts, p. 282.

57. Rambo, p. 6.

58. Charles E. Morrison, ed., *Asia Pacific Security Outlook 1998.*

59. Thomas Sowell, *Migrations and Cultures: A World View,* New York, NY: Basic Books, 1996, pp. 175–233.

60. See, for example, Rambo, p. 6.

61. Ronald Skeldon, "Migration Policies and National Security," in Nana Poku and David T. Graham, pp. 1–14.

62. Jane R. Rubin-Kurtzman, Roberto Ham-Chande, Maurice D. Van Arsdol, Jr., and Qian-wei Wang, "Demographic and Economic Interactions," pp. 1020–1045.

63. Ronald Skeldon, "International Migration and the Escafe Region: A Policy-Oriented Approach," *Asia-Pacific Population Journal*, vol. 7 (1992), pp. 3–22, and Ronald Skeldon, "Hong Kong's Response to the Indochinese Influx, 1975–93," *The Annals of the American Academy of Political and Social Science, Strategies for Immigration Control: An International Comparison*, vol. 534 (1994), p. 92.

64. Philip Martin, "Migrants on the Move in Asia," *Asia Pacific Issues: Analysis from the East-West Center*, no. 29, Honolulu: East-West Center, 1996, p. 7.

65. Frank Ching, "Misreading Hong Kong," *Foreign Affairs*, vol. 76 (1997), pp. 53–66.

66. Cheng-yi Lin, "The Taiwan Factor in Asia, Pacific Regional Security," in Takashi Inoguchi and Grant B. Stillman, eds., *North-East Asia Regional Security*, Tokyo: United Nations University Press, 1997, p. 95.

67. Ching.

68. Van Arsdol, Jr., "Population Change and Conflict in Los Angeles: 1965 and 1992."

69. Rose Maria Li, "Migration to China's Northern Frontier," *Population and Development Review*, vol. 153 (1989), pp. 510–511.

70. Ibid., p. 511.

71. James Dorian, Brett H. Wigdortz, and Dru C. Gladney, "China and Central Asia's Volatile Mix: Energy, Trade and Ethnic Relations," *Asia Pacific Issue: Analysis from the East-West Center*, no. 31, Honolulu: East-West Center, 1997, pp. 1–8.

72. Dru Gladney, "China's Ethnic Awakening," *Asia Pacific Issues: Analysis from the East-West Center*, no. 18, Honolulu: East-West Center, 1995, p. 7.

73. Homer-Dixon, p. 7.

74. Milton Ezrati, "Japan's Aging Economics," *Foreign Affairs*, vol. 76 (1997), pp. 96–105.

75. Wayne A. Cornelius, "Japan: The Illusion of Immigration Control," in Wayne A. Cornelius, Philip L. Martin, and James F. Hollifield, eds., *Controlling Migration: A Global Perspective*, Stanford, CA: Stanford University Press, 1994, pp. 376–410.

76. Martin, "Migrants on the Move," p. 7.

77. Keiko Yamanaka, "Theory Versus Reality in Japanese Immigration Policy," pp. 411–414 in Wayne A. Cornelius, Philip L. Martin, and James F. Hollifield, p. 411.

78. Cornelius et al., *Controlling Migration.*

79. Haruo Shimada, Personal interview; cited in ibid., p. 405.

80. Ibid.

81. Sim Yee Lau and Alexander Sheingauz, "National Resources and Environment Management in Northeast Asia," p. 18.

82. Byung-joon Ahn, "The NPT Regime and Denuclearization of the Korean Peninsula," in Takashi Inoguchi and Grant B. Stillman, p. 127.

83. Lau and Sheingauz, p. 18.

84. Martin, "Migrants on the Move," p. 7, and Graeme Hugo, "Illegal International Migration in Asia," in Robin Cohen, ed., *The Cambridge Survey of World Migration,* Cambridge, UK: Cambridge University Press, 1995, p. 399.

85. R. Isberto, "Illegal Aliens Fill Labour Shortages in Rich Asian Countries," *Bangkok Post,* 5 September, 1993, p. 93; cited in Graeme Hugo 1995: "Illegal Migration in Asia," in Robin Cohen, eds., *The Cambridge Survey of World Migration,* p. 399.

86. Graeme Hugo, p. 399.

87. Martin, "Migrants on the Move," p. 7.

88. Woo Jong and Kyhack Hong, "Regional Labor Flow and International Security in Northeast Asia," *Global Economic Review,* vol. 27 (1998), pp. 102–118.

89. Lau and Sheingauz, p. 18.

90. Population Reference Bureau.

91. United Nations, Commission on Population and Development, p. 277.

92. United Nations, Population Division, 1996.

93. Lau and Sheingauz, p. 18.

94. Charles E. Morrison, ed., *Asia Pacific Security Outlook 1997,* East-West Center, Honolulu, Hawaii, in cooperation with Research Institute for Regional Security, Asean Institute of Strategic and International Studies, 1997, p. 111.

95. United Nations, Commission on Population and Development, pp. 60–61.

96. Ibid.

97. Julie Da Vanzo, "Introduction," in Da Vanzo, ed., with the assistance of Gwendolyn Farnsworth, *Russia's Demographic Crisis,* Los Angeles, CA: Rand, 1996, pp. xiii-xviii.

98. Ibid., p. xiii.

99. United Nations, Commission on Population and Development, pp. 290–294.

100. Judith Shapiro, "The Hypothesis of Stress as a Leading Explanatory Variable," *Beijing 1997 International Population Conference, International Union for the Scientific Study of Population,* vol. 2., Liege, Belgium, 1997, pp. 529–554.

101. Giovanni Andrea Cornia, "Poverty, Food Consumption and Nutrition during the Transition to the Market Economy in Europe," *The American Economic Review,* vol. 842 (1997), pp. 297–302.

102. W. Ward Kinkade and Sergey Vasin, "Mortality by Cause of Death in Russia's Recent Past: Regional Variations Before and After the Breakup," *Proceedings XXXIII International Population Conference, International Union for the Scientific Study of Population,* Beijing, China, October 11–17, 1997, vol. 2, pp. 564–565.

103. Ibid., p. 572.

104. Carl Haub, "Population Change in the Former Soviet Republics," *Population Bulletin,* vol. 49, no. 4, Washington DC: Population Reference Bureau, Inc., 1994, p. 45.

105. Charles E. Morrison, ed., *Asia Pacific Security Outlook 1998.*

106. Haub, p. 45.

107. Sheingauz and Ono.

108. Lars Olsson, "Labor Migration as a Prelude to World War I," *International Migration Review,* vol. 30 (1996), pp. 875–900.

109. Van Arsdol and Gorwaney.

110. Martin and Widgren, 1996, p. 41.

111. J. Edward Taylor, Joaquín Arango, Graeme Hugo, Ali Kovaouci, Douglas S. Massey, and Adela Pellegrino, "International Migration and Community Development," *Population Index,* vol. 62 (1996), pp. 181–214, and 397–418.

112. E. Barth and D. Noel, "Conceptual Frameworks for the Analysis of Race Relations: An Evaluation," *Social Force,* vol. 50 (1972), pp. 333–348.

113. Takashi Inoguchi, "Conclusion: A Peace and Security Taxonomy," in Takashi Inoguchi and Grant B. Sullivan, pp. 183–190.

114. Ibid., p. 184.

115. Ibid., p. 186.

116. Ibid., p. 187.

117. Ibid., p. 196.

118. Ibid.

119. Dru Gladney, "China's Ethnic Awakening," *Asia Pacific Issues: Analysis from the East-West Center,* no. 18, Honolulu: East-West Center, 1995, p. 8.

120. Van Arsdol and Gorwaney.

PART 5

NONGOVERNMENTAL COOPERATION

CHAPTER 13

THE NORTHEAST ASIA ECONOMIC FORUM

Achievements and
Future Prospects

Mark J. Valencia

Concepts and Rationale

THE DRAMATIC SOCIAL AND POLITICAL CHANGES in the late 1980s, cul-
minating in the end of the Cold War, created new opportunities for
broad and bold thinking about the economic development of the
long-neglected parts of Northeast Asia—Northeastern China, Mongolia, North Korea and the Russian Far East. Indeed, the end of the
Cold War has made cooperative economic development in Northeast Asia possible. But it is the region's complementarities that make
it probable.

Northeast Asia is a "natural economic territory."[1] That means
that in one part or another of Northeast Asia one can find all the
complementary ingredients needed—manpower, know-how, natural

resources, technology, and capital—to bring the economically more backward areas to a more equitable level of development.

Clearly, Northeast Asia is one of the world's most promising economic frontiers. But it is also a region that has been riven for centuries by consecutive conflicts involving, at one time or another, all the countries in the region. As recent events demonstrate, these tensions continue to trouble the region. Thus, to realize the region's full economic potential, numerous constraints and obstacles must be overcome—the legacy of 40 years of suspicion and markedly different social and economic systems.

It would be naïve to suggest that region-wide economic cooperation and development can erase or eclipse overnight those ancient enmities. But it is not naïve to suggest that cooperative region-wide economic development could have a leavening effect on the region's stability, if only by raising the ante and reducing the benefits of internecine conflict. Region-wide cooperative development could do even more. It could create a basis for comity, if not confidence and trust, among the concerned nations of the region, which in turn could contribute importantly to the region's stability and security.

But there are several possible economic futures for developing Northeast Asia—not all equally beneficial. In a positive scenario, the necessary infrastructure is provided, open trade prevails, and developing Northeast Asia then follows the lines of comparative advantage. Put broadly, that means initially labor-intensive production and natural resource-based manufactures. Under these circumstances, per capita income would grow more rapidly than the world average, and developing Northeast Asia would begin "catching up" with the higher-income countries. This growth would allow environmental improvement, further raising the quality of life.

In a negative scenario, developing Northeast Asia maintains its present isolation or does not find a way to fund the needed infrastructure, and its share of world trade continually decreases while its resource base becomes progressively irrelevant. Its per capita income would fall farther behind the rest of the world, and the discrepancies between the well-off elite and the rest of the population would at some point lead to social unrest.

A third scenario would see the world closing off into trading blocs with Northeast Asia a de facto or even a formalized bloc. This would be a worrisome outcome, because it could set off competitive protectionism. The major potential problem is that in the process of the inevitable trade battles resulting from regionalization, the possibility of using political power and alignments arises, and, with the aid of resurgent nationalism, this could divide the world into two or three increasingly armed camps leading to self-defeating trade wars or worse. But an increasingly regionalized world could still bring about increased world economic growth and total trade. In this scenario, developing Northeast Asia would still have a symbiotic relationship with the rest of Northeast Asia, the European Economic Community and Eastern Europe, all of which have no really labor-intensive, resource-based advantage.

In sum, then, if the needed reforms are carried out, under all trade scenarios, both developing and developed Northeast Asia will prosper. The developing portion will play a growing role in world trade, especially in exports of labor-intensive and resource-based goods to the rest of Northeast Asia and the world. And these countries and parts of countries will provide a growing market for high-tech capital equipment and producer goods, and for high-tech brand-name consumer goods. With continued growth, international specialization within these product lines will occur. While the greatest relative increases in per capita income from the "opening up" of developing Northeast Asia will come in developing Northeast Asia itself, South Korea and Taiwan will also benefit by maintaining higher growth rates than would otherwise have been possible. To a lesser extent, Japan will benefit as the major trading partner and creditor of developing Northeast Asia.

Which path is taken may be influenced by the relevant government perspectives on the benefits and costs of cooperation. Cooperation may be enhanced when central intellectual players in the region form an epistemic community that coordinates their activities and attempts to translate their beliefs into public policies furthering cooperation.[2] An "epistemic community" is identified by the presence of a broadly shared set of normative and principled beliefs, combined with an internalized and self-validating set of causal and methodological principles and a common policy goal operating within a set of formal, semiformal, and informal institutions and networks that, in a period of dramatic historical change and uncertainty, provide the framework within which to broker a set of policy options drawn from their normative beliefs and amenable to their causal and explanatory principles.

The influence on decision makers of epistemic communities grows under conditions of uncertainty such as pertain in Northeast Asia today. Epistemic communities have value for international and regional organizations because their loyalties are more to the production and application of their knowledge than to any particular government. Through networks and "invisible colleges," they seek to promote cooperation across national boundaries. Often, such epistemic communities are able to introduce values and visions that can capture the imagination of decision makers who, on the basis of their new understanding, may redefine strategic and economic interests so as to enhance collective human interests across national borders. The chances of success of an epistemic community will be enhanced when some of its members are officials, technocrats, or consultants who can affect the political process from within. The Northeast Asia Economic Forum was created to foster an epistemic community that believes that Northeast Asia's human, natural, and capital resources can be cooperatively mobilized to generate dynamic new economies throughout the region.

The History of the Forum

The East-West Center, along with its neutral NGO-spin-off, the Northeast Asia Economic Forum, was one of the first Asian-focused institutions to recognize that the end of the Cold War would bring about a major shift in the region's pre-existing economic and political equilibrium. In an effort to focus the region's and the West's attention on these impending changes, the Center organized a series of regional conferences on cooperative development in Northeast Asia, beginning over a decade ago.

Imagine—and it is not easy—the Northeast Asia of 1985. The Soviet Union is still a solidly communist empire and the outcome of Gorbachev's struggle to end the Cold War is unclear. Most borders are still military exclusion zones, especially the long China/Soviet Far East border. There are no relations between China and South Korea or the Soviet Union and South Korea. North Korea is still a completely sealed hermit kingdom, allied with the Soviet Union. Relations between Japan and China and between Japan and the Soviet Union are tense.

About that time, we decided to embark on the risky venture of bringing together influential persons from these estranged countries. We decided to begin modestly by focusing discussions on an innocuous sector of mutual concern and consequence—the management of shared seas—hoping that such discussions might lead to broader discussion of cooperation in other sectors—like economic development. The idea was that the semi-enclosed seas—the Yellow Sea, the Japan or East Sea and the East China Sea—lap the shores of several countries and that the mutual concern for the environmental condition of these shared seas and their living resources might entice even enemies to talk to each other.

We recognized that leadership is often critical to the formation of successful regimes, because leaders seize opportunities, initiate and structure the bargaining process, set the focus on integrative rather than distributive issues, and facilitate package arrangements. Indeed, the forum was just a concept until key people lent their support. Dr. Saburo Okita, the former foreign minister of Japan, supported such peaceful dialogue among the countries of the Japan Sea rim. Quite independently, Song Jian—China's minister of science and technology and a member of China's Politburo—recognized that Chinese access to the Japan Sea and through the Tumen River would greatly help the economic development of China's Northeastern provinces. Deng Nan, a daughter of Deng Xiaoping and a high official with the powerful State Science and Technology Commission, was also quite supportive. Kim Kihwan, then head of the leading think tank in South Korea and formerly in charge of the South Korean side of the North-South Korea unification talks, supported the concept. And Lee-Jay Cho—knowing almost nothing about the oceans—had the wisdom and the foresight to see that this idea and process might have wider possibilities. He networked with these people and initiated discussions on the cooperative development of the Tumen River area.

We proceeded with an initial meeting in 1987 at the East-West Center—just between China and South Korea, focusing on the Yellow Sea. On the surface, the objective of the meeting was purely technical—to compare scientific data—but the South Koreans were led by a deputy minister of science and technology, and the Chinese by their ambassador for science and technology at the United Nations. The meeting was a success because it produced the realization that each country needed the other—at least in this sector. Both countries' data extended only to the half line of the Yellow Sea and did not match. This ultimately led to the current CORD-SOA joint work on the Yellow Sea funded by the World Bank.

With this under our belt, we decided to work towards a more difficult goal—cooperation among the countries bordering the East Sea. To get the Soviets on board, we approached Victor Ilyichev, a member of the Soviet Academy of Sciences and head of the Pacific Oceanological Institute in Vladivostok. We arranged a meeting with him and his aides in 1988 at the Pacific Science Congress in Seoul. He was suspicious and asked many questions including "Why would anyone want to do this?" "To further mutual peace and prosperity" seemed an insufficient answer. But he took a chance on us.

The Japanese agreed to host the meeting in Niigata. However—and remember it is still 1988—the Soviets failed to arrive on the one flight a week from Khabarovsk. But there was a silver lining in the dark clouds. In their chagrin, the Soviets promised to host a follow-up meeting on the East Sea and the Sea of Okhotsk in 1989. We readily accepted.

To follow up on the Soviet offer, I traveled to Vladivostok in fall 1988. I was told I was one of the first Americans to enter the city since the end of World War II. In late 1989, the Nakhodka-Vladivostok meeting was held. It was a great success and included North Koreans as well as persons from Taiwan. It was at this meeting that the Chinese delegation proposed a subsequent meeting on "cooperative economic development of the coastal zone."

So we organized such a meeting in Changchun in 1990. All entities from the region were there, including, for the first time, representatives of Mongolia. This was the beginning of the Tumen River project. It was a vague proposal at the time and more questions were asked than answered. However, the general concept was endorsed, including by the North Koreans. So we organized a second Changchun meeting in 1991 to get these questions answered. Meanwhile, UNDP had become interested and attended this meeting, which they eventually counted as the first meeting of their regional project. The Center thus played a role as a catalyst, initiator, and honest broker for the Tumen River project.

However, our work was not yet done. We still wanted to fully engage North Korea at the policy level and we needed to institutionalize our effort. So we formed a purely nongovernmental organization called the Northeast Asia Economic Forum—with a network of supporting institutions in many of the countries in the region called Asia-Pacific Institutes.

In 1992, North Korea's Committee for the Promotion of External Economic Relations hosted a major meeting on economic cooperation in Northeast Asia. High-level North Koreans were our hosts, e.g., Kim Dal Hyun, then a deputy prime minister (and who has recently re-entered upper-level government), and Kim Jong U, who later negotiated the nuclear issue in Geneva. We traveled as a group on a special train to the Rajin-Sonbong area to view the then recently declared special economic zone.

The rest, as they say, is history. The forum has held annual conferences around the region on economic cooperation in Northeast Asia—Vladivostok in late 1992 and Yeongbyong in 1993, which marked the beginning of the broad participation of big business from South Korea and Japan.

This effort reached full stride in 1994 in Niigata—where all countries except North Korea were present at a high level. Ambassador Endo, who at the time was responsible for Japan's role in APEC and for Japan/North Korea relations, gave the keynote address. More important was the broad participation of the business sector; leaders of Pohang Steel, Lucky Goldstar, Dae Woo, the Korean Federation of Industries; Keidanren; the export-import banks of China, Japan, and South Korea; and the World Bank, the ADB, and UNDP. The substantive focus was on ideas for economic cooperation; a central information bank to provide companies with market data and advice in technology and finance; a Northeast Asia Development Bank; a central labor bank; a regional transportation and communication committee; a regional energy consortium using a gas pipeline grid linking all Northeast Asia; and the Tumen River project—the crucible of the complementarity concept. All of these ideas are now the focus of research projects by the forum.

The sixth conference was held in January 1996 in Honolulu and was a smashing success, attracting over 150 business persons and government officials from the region including a five-man delegation from North Korea led by Kim Mun Song, then secretary general of CPEEC.

The forum was invited by the prime minister of Mongolia to convene its August 1997 annual meeting in Ulaanbaatar. At that meeting, we added a focus on regional cooperation in telecommunications, and in electricity generation and transmission.

The 1998 annual meeting was hosted by Yonago City and the Tottori Prefectural Government. It was a gala affair keynoted by Taro Nakayama, the former foreign minister of Japan, and Robert Scalapino, a leading American Asian scholar. Significantly, the governor of Tottori, the deputy-governor of Hyogo, and a high government official from Shimane Prefecture were present, as were former governors of Alaska and Hawaii. The central government of Japan was also well represented. The 1999 annual meeting will be hosted by Tianjin, China.

Tasks Ahead

The forum has identified and addressed serious practical impediments to cooperative development in the region and suggested cooperative approaches to their rectification. First, most of developing Northeast Asia's transportation and communications systems are 1950s state-of-the-art. Airports, port facilities, railroads, highways, bridges, and pipelines are far below the standards needed to support commerce and industry in the coming decades. Corresponding conditions exist in the region's communications sector. It is similarly projected that for some Northeast Asian countries, energy generation and distribution will not be adequate to meet long-term economic growth and development requirements. Unless substantial improvements are made, this sector may act as a brake on the region's economic progress. Environmental rehabilitation and safeguards, urban water and waste treatment facilities, reforestation, natural resource management, and a host of other environment-related infrastructure facilities will also require large new capital investments. The forum estimates that developing Northeast Asia could effectively deploy some $7.5 billion a year of external capital to finance regional infrastructure projects. The issue is to identify the source and method of mobilization of this capital. One possibility being studied and discussed by the forum is a separate development bank for Northeast Asia.

Ironically, just when and where there is the most need, there is a conspicuous absence of the West, and even the central government of Japan, from the developing Northeast Asian economic scene. Part of the explanation for this lack of involvement is the West's Eurocentricity, followed faithfully by its Asian allies. And part is due to Japan's Russophobia, and its policy in this case of tying economic assistance to politics, as well as to the pronounced timidity of its central government technocrats in dealing with delicate political problems involving other regional nations. Although some provincial governments in Japan are enthusiastic supporters of "Japan Sea Rim" cooperative development, the central government remains cold and aloof. Consequently, the forum will continue to attempt to generate interest in participation in the economic development of Northeast Asia in the West as well as in Tokyo.

However, absent the kinds of post–Cold War generosity extended by the West to Eastern Europe, the concerned less-developed provinces and states of Northeast Asia, including those in western and northern Japan, are pursuing self-help by whatever avenues are available and feasible. One of the most promising concepts rapidly being adopted in the region is the creation of special "economic zones" that are endowed with a panoply of tax incentives, customs remission arrangements, and other services and facilities intended specifically to attract foreign investors. The leading example in the region is UNDP's Tumen River Area Development Program.

An important spin-off of the Tumen River project is that North Korea has also jumped on the foreign private investment bandwagon. The North Korean Government has created, and is actively promoting, its own Rajin-Sonbong Free Economic and Trade Zone and has earmarked nine industrial estates and some fifty factory sites specifically for foreign private investors. Besides committing scarce foreign exchange to this project, North Korea has enacted some two dozen laws and regulations intended to make it easier for foreign investors to set up and operate plants in this zone. North Korea has been a steady supporter of the forum and has attended most of its meetings. In the absence of other outlets, the forum has provided an opportunity for North Korea to present its views and policies and to learn more about the market system and the needs and behavior of foreign businesses. Russia has also created several special economic zones in its Far East, and Mongolia is planning to follow suit. Thus the forum is helping—and will continue to help—in its own small way in the transition of Russia, China, North Korea, and Mongolia to more open economies and to fuller involvement in the world economic community.

Clearly, much of developing Northeast Asia is not waiting for the kinds of help that the West provided to East European countries. Rather, they are pursuing economic development as best they can, with whatever tools and resources they have. For their part, the Western countries and the central government of Japan may come to regret the fact that they passed up the opportunity to participate more actively in this region's rapidly moving economic development.

Achievements and Future Prospects

The forum has both concrete and intangible achievements. It has helped spawn projects like the Tumen River Area Development Program. It has generated and served as a testing ground for ideas like a Northeast Asia Development Bank, regional transportation and

communication planning fora, and a labor clearing house. It has produced and widely disseminated background research reports on these
and other topics as well as the proceedings of its meetings. Less tangible but more important are the networking it has done and the opportunity it has provided for people to meet and travel across
geographic, political, and ideological barriers. It has exposed and
helped educate policy-makers in centrally planned economies regarding the requirements and vagaries of the capitalist system. Most
valuable, it has helped create and nurture a spirit of optimism, of cooperation, of a vision of a peaceful and prosperous Northeast Asia.

The first step toward the peaceful settlement of international
conflicts is the creation of a sense of international community.[3] The
creation of such a community presupposes at least the mitigation
and minimization of conflict, so that the interests and common
needs shared by different nations outweigh the interests separating
them. Common recognition that even a poor regime is better than
none compels nations to collaborate to the extent of developing a
minimally satisfactory solution. A functional approach can help the
growth of positive and constructive common work and of common
habits and interests, decreasing the significance of boundaries by
overlaying them with a natural growth of common activities and administrative agencies. The challenge for the region then is to develop
a variety of multilateral arrangements that will demonstrate that a
habit of dialogue and working together can build common—and
eventually—cooperative security. In Northeast Asia, continuity and
persistence are critical to advancement of regionalism.

Today, Northeast Asia is almost unique in its lack of regional
institutions.[4] Bilateralism dominates both political and economic
relations. But with the muting of the Cold War, we are witnessing
a transformation of the political system in the region. Most
Northeast Asian governments are now more motivated toward
maximizing wealth than control over territory, and their increasing economic interdependence makes outright conflict too costly.
With the development of political multipolarity and the general
abandonment of Stalinist economic models, economic relationships have begun to develop a more "natural" pattern. These economic relations will concentrate initially in the boundary areas

where adjacent regions have obvious economic complementarities—"natural economic territories"—the Yellow Sea Rim, the Tumen River area, and the Sea of Japan Rim.

Already, economic interaction across ideological and political boundaries is creating a "soft" regionalism in Northeast Asia—one that lacks organizational structure but that is accepted and even encouraged by governments. Apparent is a gradual development of a thin net of regional institutions covering the region in the economic, the environmental, and to a lesser degree the political arenas, but within a broader Asia-Pacific framework—the Pacific Economic Cooperation Council, the Asia-Pacific Economic Cooperation forum, the ASEAN Regional Forum and the "Track Two" Council for Security Cooperation in the Asia-Pacific. And a Northeast Asia Security Dialogue is also likely to emerge, supported by the United States.

Regimes are supplied when there is sufficient demand for the functions they perform.[5] As the regional system becomes more interdependent, multilateral fora and institutions will increase in number and kind to deal with the growing plethora of problems that states cannot resolve unilaterally or bilaterally. Multilateral fora will provide small and medium powers with opportunities for coalition-building among themselves to balance the influence of larger powers within the collectivity. Regionalism will also become more attractive to developing states because of their growing political maturity and the perceived potential of regionalism to promote their economic development, as well as to mitigate their disadvantaged position in the international system. Multilateral institutions will thus be the focus of "middle power" or "niche" diplomacy in setting regional agendas. Regular convening of multilateral fora like the Northeast Asia Economic Forum will help create a "habit of cooperation" among participants. And in multilateral relationships, issue-linkage will create opportunities for creative problem-solving not available in bilateral relationships. Moreover, multilateral norms and institutions will make significant contributions toward stabilizing the peaceful transformation of the international system and will become increasingly important in the management of change at the regional level.

In the economic sphere, the development of such informal channels of communication as the Northeast Asia Economic Forum may play an important role in the process of regime formation and institution building. Habits of consultation and a nascent feeling of regional identity will grow, increasing sensitivities within the governmental elite to each other's interests and developing norms for how to conduct their relations with each other. Eventually, tactical learning, in which the behavior of states toward cooperation is changed, will give way to complex learning, in which values and beliefs about reaching goals through cooperation are changed.[6] At that point Northeast Asia will have attained a regional self-identity, overcome nationalistic constraints, and be well on its way to lasting peace and prosperity.

Notes

1.   Robert A. Scalapino, 'The Post Cold War Asia-Pacific Security Order: Conflict or Cooperation?" Paper presented at the Conference on Economic and Security Cooperation in the Asia-Pacific: Agenda for the 1990s, Canberra, July 28–30, 1993, p. 16.

2.   Peter M. Haas, "Introduction: Epistemic Communities and International Policy Coordination," in Peter M. Haas, ed., *Knowledge, Power and International Policy Coordination, International Organization,* vol. 46, no. 1 (Special Issue, 1992), pp. 31–32; Michel Foucault may have invented the term "epistemic community" in his *The Order of Things,* New York: Random House, 1970. However, as Ernst Haas has argued, Foucault's usage is indistinguishable from what might be called "ideological communities." For the meaning, definition, role, value, and examples of who may or may not constitute an epistemic community, see Burkhart Holzner and John H. Marx, *Knowledge Application,* Boston: Allyn and Baron, Inc., 1979, p. 108; Ernst Haas, *When Knowledge is Power,* Berkeley: University of California Press, 1990, pp. 40–46; Haas, "Introduction: Epistemic Communities and International Policy Coordination," pp. 1–36. The term epistemic community was first applied to international relations by John G. Ruggie, "International Responses to Technology, Concepts, and Trends," *International Organization,* vol. 29, no. 3 (Summer 1975), pp. 569–70. See also Peter M. Haas, "Do Regimes Matter? Epistemic Communities and

Mediterranean Pollution Control," *International Organization,* vol. 43, no. 3 (Summer 1989), pp. 377–403.

3. Hans Morgenthau and Kenneth W. Thompson, *Politics Among Nations: The Struggle for Power and Peace,* New York: Knopf, 1985, p. 559; Robert Scalapino, "Back to the Future," *Far Eastern Economic Review,* May 26, 1994, p. 38.

4. Mark J. Valencia, *A Maritime Regime for North-East Asia,* Oxford: Oxford University Press, 1996, p. 6.

5. Stephen Haggard and Beth A. Simmons, "Theories of International Regimes," *International Organization,* vol. 41, no. 3 (1987), p. 507.

6. Richard Higgott, "Economic Cooperation: Theoretical Opportunities and Political Constraints," *The Pacific Review,* vol. 6, no. 2 (1993), pp. 106–107.

CHAPTER 14

NONGOVERNMENTAL INITIATIVES IN JAPAN FOR REGIONAL COOPERATION

Takashi Shirasu and Lau Sim-Yee

Introduction

THE END OF THE COLD WAR HAS CHANGED the political environment for the economies of Northeast Asia (NEA). As a result, there has been a significant surge of interest in getting Japan to promote regional cooperation in NEA. Particularly, there is a conviction prevailing among the Japan Sea coastal prefectures that the combination of Japanese and Korean capital, technology, and management know-how with the abundant labor and natural resources of the continental part of NEA provides a new dynamism for sustained growth and development.[1] To date, this potential has generated several proposals aimed at creating regional strategies with geographical proximity, economic complementarity, diversification of regional production structure, and policy coordination as the basis for cooperation in NEA.[2]

Undoubtedly, Japan holds the key to regional cooperation in NEA. But, there are many factors impeding the functional cooperation between Japan and the rest of NEA. Historical, social, economic, and political factors in this region are formidable obstacles to Japan's initiation of multilateral engagement with the countries in this region. The historical grievances between Japan, China, South Korea, and North Korea greatly affect the attitude toward regional cooperation. Economic development disparities and differences in economic systems are also serious barriers. Differing security perceptions constitute another hindrance. Similarly, state-to-state relations and territorial disputes impede constructive relations between Japan and certain countries in NEA. For these reasons, despite the growing desire for regional coordination, multilateral cooperation at the official level remains more an elusive goal than a reality in NEA.

Against this background, there is an evolving trend of nongovernmental initiatives in Japan. In large measure, they are a response to what many Japanese citizens view as the rigidity of the national government in fostering regional cooperation as an important means of promoting economic development, political stability, and security in NEA. Our task in this chapter is to discuss the role that nongovernmental initiatives in Japan could play in enhancing regional cooperation in NEA. Our discussion is not comprehensive. Rather, our purpose is to highlight some salient features of Japanese nongovernmental initiatives to promote regional cooperation in NEA.

Definition and General Trends

In our discussion, "nongovernmental initiative" refers to specific actions/activities pursued by nongovernmental organizations (NGOs) that seek to effect qualitative changes in their political, economic, and social environment. An NGO is broadly defined as an organization created by individuals who share and wish to promote a common interest or a common concern. Interests range from social welfare and poverty reduction to peace, religion, human rights, and scientific research. Some NGOs are created to advance a movement, some to administer relief to those in need, some to exchange knowledge and information, and others to promote scholarly contacts and to advance collaborative research. There are also NGOs that are organized to promote the interests of a particular group, industry, or profession. In the widest sense of the term, NGOs include both groups that aim to influence the formation and implementation of public policy and groups that have no concern for the public domain at all. In addition, we note that NGOs refer to all forms of nonprofit organizations that enjoy autonomy from the state and have as one of their important goals to influence the state on behalf of their members.

Nongovernmental initiatives in international cooperation are not a new phenomenon in Japan. The emergence of private international cooperation activities is closely linked to the rise of Japan's economic position in the international community and its internationalization process. Over time, nongovernmental initiatives in international cooperation have been closely related to development activities carried out abroad, such as rural development, health and medical services, education, and environmental protection. In Japan, international cooperation initiatives of many NGOs have revolved around activities related to the assistance of Indochinese refugees in the late 1970s and early 1980s, illegal foreign workers since the mid-1980s, and foreign students and residents in the country.[3] However, it should be noted here that, to date, most NGO initiatives in the area of international cooperation have been confined primarily to relations with developing countries. Japanese NGO activities that have been directed to promote cooperative relations between Japan and the rest of NEA have been relatively rare. However, the last several years have seen a marked increase and progress in NGO activities that foster cooperative linkages among countries in the region. This is particularly the case in the Japan Sea coastal prefectures.

Nature and Scope of NGO Activities

Although interest in promoting regional cooperation in NEA is growing in Japan, the advancement of this movement is often offset by political, diplomatic, and other noneconomic factors at the national level. For this reason, many NGOs in Japan, in their private and autonomous capacity, have made significant efforts to bring together concerned individuals to carry out a broad scope of related activities to cultivate regional cooperation in NEA. Since 1991, particularly, there has been a great proliferation of nongovernmental initiatives devoted to exchanges of people, policy and academic research, and information, as well as activities in environmental protection. It should be noted that these initiatives are mutually self-reinforcing in that they deepen functional cooperative mechanisms.

Exchange of People

During the Cold War, exchanges of people between Japan and most of the continental part of NEA had been strictly constrained by the political and economic orientations in the region. In the aftermath of the Cold War and with the improvement of the general political atmosphere in NEA, however, cross-national exchanges of people in the region have been accelerated. There is no question that regional cooperation is a powerful means to promote economic development, political stability, and security in NEA. In this process, efficient and effective regional arrangements with concrete results are heavily dependent on the harmonious co-existence of people at local, regional, and national levels across national borders.

This recognition has provided strong motivation to numerous grassroots or community-based organizations in Japan, and they have placed particular emphasis on activities to promote and deepen mutual understanding through direct people-to-people exchange. Many Japanese NGOs are now carrying out such varied activities as home-stays for invited foreign visitors, scholarship programs to support foreign students in the country, and student exchange programs in secondary and higher education. Some of these activities are implemented independently by NGOs, while others are administered in collaboration with sister-city programs and international exchange programs initiated by local governments in Japan. Some

Japanese NGOs also participate actively in the dispatch of representatives to exchange activities initiated by their counterparts in China, Korea, Russia, and Mongolia.

The bottom-up approach that Japanese NGOs represent has created many loosely formed networks of citizens both within Japan and across the Sea of Japan. This is a very recent phenomenon that requires further development, but it is a crucial dimension of international relations in this part of the world. Only through improved dialogue and mutual understanding can we create the conditions necessary for an environment conducive to the amelioration of historical, cultural, and social impediments to transnational cooperation in NEA.

Policy and Academic Research

The rich and diversified production endowments in NEA provide an enormous potential for economic development at the regional level. At the same time, however, the diversity in political, economic, social, cultural, and historical contexts presents a formidable obstacle to multilateral cooperation as an approach to development in NEA. For instance, industrial structural adjustment on the basis of comparative advantage is necessary to enhance intra-regional trade but it is a complex and difficult task because of the differences in economic systems that exist in this region. Similarly, the standardization of trade and commercial practices to minimize transaction costs among the countries in NEA is a complicated issue because of contrasting institutional contexts and disparate levels of development.

For these reasons, there is a need to enlarge the common knowledge base of the intellectual communities in NEA regarding how various obstacles may be overcome and what benefits may be derived from expanded international interactions in the region. This points to the need to promote collaboration among the policy and academic research communities in NEA. Fortunately, this need has been widely recognized among academic and other researchers in the region. This has given rise to collaborative initiatives through nongovernmental channels, and the momentum is growing. Several research institutions and academic associations have been established in Japan with a focus on promoting regional cooperation.

Among the most distinguished Japanese research institutes with a Northeast Asian focus are the Economic Research Institute of Northeast Asia (ERINA), located in Niigata City, and the International Centre for the Study of East Asian Development (ICSEAD), located in Kitakyushu City. ERINA and ICSEAD were both established with the joint participation of local government, business and academic circles, and the local community. They are legally autonomous organizations. In addition to these research institutes, several academic associations have been formed in Japan to encourage academic research related to NEA among Japanese scholars. Many of these groups also promote academic exchanges between Japanese scholars and academic communities in other parts of NEA. The most notable among these associations today are the Association for Japan Sea Rim Studies, a nation-wide group, the Association for International Academic Exchange in Japan Sea Rim, comprising scholars from Toyama, Ishikawa, and Fukui prefectures, and the Japan Sea Rim Academic Forum, founded by academics in Kyoto. In addition, there are several loosely organized academic networks dedicated to the promotion of Northeast Asian studies among several universities in the northern part of Japan.

The research areas of ERINA and ISCEAD are mainly confined to the study of industrial development, trade and investment, economic reforms, environmental protection, and modalities of regional cooperative mechanisms/schemes, such as the Tumen River Area Development Program, the Rajin-Sonbong Economic Zone, and the Yellow Sea Rim Economic Zone. In addition, ERINA has put a particular emphasis on the development of a socio-economic data-base, which is useful as a reference source in research as well as for improving the general public's knowledge about the countries of Northeast Asia and their interrelations. In contrast, academic associations have a more broadly defined area of interests, covering historical research, linguistics, cultural studies, international studies, and other humanities and social sciences. Most of

these establishments periodically organize international conferences to encourage constructive dialogues among the intellectual
community in NEA. More importantly, these periodical gatherings
also help to strengthen the intellectual ties among the participants
concerning issues of regional cooperation. Finally, these research
institutes and academic associations publish periodicals, journals,
monographs, and books and disseminate their research findings inside and outside Japan.

Environmental Protection

Environmental issues have become an area of major concern to the
countries of NEA. China, the Russian Far East, North Korea, and
Mongolia are currently facing considerable pollution problems as a
result of their long neglect of their environment, particularly in the
agriculture, industry, mining, transport, and energy sectors. Environmental problems are not confined to a single country, and they
have severe impacts at the regional and global levels. For instance,
air pollution in northeastern China reaches the Korean peninsula
and Japan, and water pollution in the Russian Far East may have
consequences for Japanese coastal waters.

There is no doubt that Japan, with its enhanced economic capability and extensive experience in environmental control, could
contribute enormously to environmentally friendly and sustainable development of its neighboring countries by extending its
know-how to them. Many Japanese NGOs recognize that, individually or collectively, there are many areas in which they can
complement their government in assisting neighboring countries
in this important area. In the last several years, in collaboration
with local governments and governmental agencies, several NGOs
have successfully brought together representatives of local, regional, and national organizations from the countries of NEA to
discuss environmental protection at the regional level in general
and country-specific problems in particular. In addition, several
community-based NGOs have dispatched volunteers to assist
some provinces in China and Mongolia in the restoration of de-
graded soil, such as caused by unsustainable livestock grazing.

These nongovernmental initiatives have generated many ideas that are being discussed in various venues in Japan, including at the local and national levels, some ideas being translated into proposals for funding and technical support projects. Three broad thrusts can be found in these proposals. First, many proposals emphasize the use of existing facilities at the local level workshops to train personnel from neighboring countries in environmental management. Second, there are proposals for the establishment of a regional training facility in NEA to contribute to the development of human resources for sustainable development. Third, some proposals call for the upgrading of on-going multilateral private initiatives into a formal consultative mechanism linking the region's national governments to ensure effective, coordinated implementation of proposed programs in each country involved. Various modalities need to be explored, all with a view to institutionalizing region-wide cooperative mechanisms for sustainable development.

An Example of NGO Activities: The SPF Projects in Regional Cooperation

In this section, we provide several concrete examples of the efforts of the Sasakawa Peace Foundation (SPF) to contribute to the promotion of regional cooperation in NEA. We believe we have played a catalytic role in undertaking specific measures for focusing and strengthening cooperation in NEA. The SPF is a private Japanese grant-making foundation. As an autonomous NGO, the SPF has taken advantage of its independence from any governmental influence and brought together individuals and research institutions from Northeast Asian countries to cooperate on a multilateral basis. We have found a complementary niche between government and the private sector and carried out activities to create and enhance public awareness, build individual and institutional capacity, promote policy research and coordination, and build information exchange networks. These are all essential building blocks for institutionalizing cooperative mechanisms in NEA. Recognizing the various obstacles to regional cooperation noted earlier, the SPF implemented between 1991 and 1995 a program aimed at the enhancement of regional cooperation through three separate projects. We will briefly describe each project.

Northeast Asian Economic Cooperation: International Conference on Economic Development in the Coastal Area of Northeast Asia (NEAEF Project)

"Northeast Asian Economic Cooperation: International Conference on Economic Development in the Coastal Area of Northeast Asia," or the NEAEF Project, had as its overall goal the generation of greater awareness and understanding of the potentials and benefits of regional cooperation in NEA. The central focus of the project was to organize a series of international symposia to bring together scholars, researchers, policy-makers, and government administrators from Japan, South Korea, North Korea, China, Mongolia, the Russian Far East, and the United States to exchange ideas about regional cooperation issues in NEA.

The underlying assumption was that NEA is a region of diversity in terms of the level of economic development, political and economic systems, including the transition economies of China, Mongolia, and Russia, ethnicity, culture, and history. The recognition of diversity immediately leads to the task of increasing public awareness about the myriad obstacles to regional cooperation and ways to overcome the barriers so as to derive benefits from greater interactions between the countries of NEA. In this context, it is most important to create a well-informed and enlightened public who can influence national leaders and policy-makers for the realization of regional cooperation.

With this premise, the SPF organized an international conference in Changchun, China in 1991. "The Changchun International Conference on Economic Development in the Coastal Area of Northeast Asia" was attended by more than one hundred participants with a variety of professional backgrounds, and they discussed emerging issues in economic development and regional cooperation in NEA.[4] The discussion helped the participants realize that the potential gains from regional cooperation are not limited to the solution of problems associated with economic development but also point toward resolving larger noneconomic issues that cloud international relations in this region. The Changchun conference resulted in the inauguration of the Northeast Asia Economic Forum (NEAEF), the subject of review in the preceding chapter. The NEAEF was created to serve as a platform to ensure the continuity of the process of information exchange and research coordination among scholars, researchers, and other specialists interested in the promotion of regional cooperation in NEA. The participants believed (and subsequent developments have proven) that sustained dialogue through such a forum would help to generate specific project proposals for functional cooperation in NEA. In addition, the conference proceedings were compiled and disseminated widely, attracting much media and scholarly attention in Northeast Asia and in the United States.

In 1992, under the NEAEF's auspices, a second international conference was held in Vladivostok, Russia, which until the previous year was a closed city (not only to foreigners but also to most Soviet citizens). The conference, "The Vladivostok International Conference on Regional Economic Cooperation in Northeast Asia," drew more that one hundred scholars and government officials from Japan, South Korea, North Korea, China, Mongolia, the Russian Far East, and the United States. The participants discussed the social, economic, and political environment for regional cooperation in NEA, development strategies for the transition economies in the continental part of NEA, alternative approaches to regional cooperation and their advantages and disadvantages, and multilateral cooperative concepts.

The participants in these conferences agreed that a forum for regular dialogue was essential. Consequently, the NEAEF has been meeting on a nearly annual basis since 1992, with successive gatherings taking on increasingly specific agenda items, as Valencia outlines in the preceding chapter. In addition, the NEAEF has produced a quarterly newsletter that has an international readership of scholars, businessmen, and government officials, providing timely information on the forum's activities and stimulating discussion on issues of regional cooperation in NEA.

Northeast Asia Economic Cooperation Initiative: Capacity Building toward Improved Policy Research and Development Management (NEAEI Project)

"Northeast Asia Economic Cooperation Initiative: Capacity Building Toward Improved Policy Research and Development Management," or the NEAEI Project, was also designed to increase awareness of the importance of regional cooperation in NEA, and we believe the project achieved its goal. More importantly, the project also contributed to the advancement of knowledge about the complex issues involved and potential constraints found in creating a multilateral cooperative framework in the region. The project also responded to the recognition that through increased interaction between scholars and policy-makers in Northeast Asian countries we can improve the quality of policy-oriented research and development management skills in countries with less experience and expertise in these areas. For instance, the SPF program officers and Japanese scholars involved in this project were concerned that the inadequate research and management capabilities in China, Mongolia, North Korea, and the Russian Far East would pose many challenges in the way cooperative policies were designed, formulated, and implemented, with serious implications for policy coordination in NEA. In order to overcome this problem, we decided it was necessary to initiate capacity-building exercises to strengthen the indigenous policy-research and development-management capability in these countries. The subjects chosen for collaborative research were trade and industrial development, foreign direct investment, cross cultural management, and natural resources and environmental management.

The SPF began this project in 1993. The target group for collaboration in capacity-building consisted of more than 30 scholars and researchers representing research institutions in Japan, Korea, China, Mongolia, and the Russian Far East. The participants engaged in a series of joint research activities to examine the selected issues and the prospects for regional cooperation in NEA around those issues.

A review of the publications resulting from this project indicates that the collaborative effort was successful in enhancing the research capacity of the target group, particularly the capacity of the Chinese, Mongolian, and Russian participants. The results of the collaborative research were shared not only among the participants themselves but with their colleagues and others who attended the conferences and seminars that were organized under this project. The publications were also distributed to other interested individuals and organizations. In this way, the project was able to demonstrate to a larger audience the need for enhanced indigenous policy research and development management to ensure effective regional cooperation. One of the most tangible results of these efforts was the establishment in 1994 of the Northeast Asia Development Center (NEADeC) within the Institute of East and West Studies at Yonsei University, Seoul. The center's mandate includes information collection, policy research on issues related to regional cooperation in NEA, training of those involved in policy study and development management, advisory services for those seeking specific answers to specific issues, and publication of relevant information.

Russian Far East Economic Yearbook Project (RFE Project)

One of the main obstacles to the transformation of the Russian Far East economy from its previous structure under central control to a market-oriented system is the lack of published information on basic socio-economic statistics. Without such basic data, it is difficult for agents of market change, including foreign traders and investors, to assist leaders and entrepreneurs in this part of Russia in their reform effort. This problem is compounded by ceaseless and unpredictable changes in the reform policies of the central government, resulting in, among other things, a proliferation of outdated information of little use. The lack of reliable information and the stop-and-go reforms compound the problems the Russian Far East faces in integrating with the economies of Asia-Pacific, a path that should follow naturally from geographical proximity.

In 1991, the SPF proposed to the Institute of Economic Research of the Far Eastern Branch of the Russian Academy of Sciences in Khabarovsk that it assemble social and economic statistics on the Russian Far East to be published in a special volume, *The Russian Far East: An Economic Handbook*. The overall goal of this project was two-fold: to reveal and introduce the realities of this little-known Far Eastern part of Russia to both foreign and domestic audiences, thereby contributing to the region's effort to transform itself into a market-oriented system, and to encourage the development of linkages and co-operation between domestic and international academic communities.

This project ran from 1991 to 1994. More than ten Japanese experts and various public and private agencies in Japan were mobilized to provide intellectual and technical support to the staff of the Institute of Economic Research. In addition, specialists from Korea, Taiwan, the United States, and international organizations were invited to provide advice on various technical and organizational issues in compiling the handbook. The project successfully produced in 1994 a handbook that provides a wide range of social and economic information about the Russian Far East. The volume was published in Russian, English, and Japanese in order to reach a wider international readership. More importantly, the first volume served as a prototype for subsequent issues. Equally impressive, this attempt has become a role model for other regions of Russia, where the need and benefits of publicly available statistical information have been recognized.

Achievements of the SPF Program

The NEAEF, NEAEI, and RFE projects have made several important achievements.[5] First, they have directly contributed to the establishment of an international network of researchers and research institutions in NEA. Second, they have served as an effective way to enhance the research capabilities of the participating researchers and research institutions in China, Mongolia, and Russia. Third, they have contributed to the expansion of a knowledge and information base for the more advanced researchers and research institutions in Japan, South Korea, and the United States. Fourth, the projects have resulted in the publication and dissemination of a rich set of research monographs and reports to members of the international research community concerned with economic development in NEA.

Nongovernmental Initiatives: Opportunities and Limitations

It is increasingly recognized that the development of local and regional economies within Northeast Asia is an important means to promote region-wide economic development, political stability, and security. However, this potential remains largely that: a potential. Much more needs to be done to accelerate the pace of region-wide cooperation. Unfortunately, many historical, social, and political barriers are proving to be quite formidable, despite the growing desire among the intellectual communities in Northeast Asia for generating and sharing economic benefits through closer regional cooperation. Nevertheless, the kinds of nongovernmental initiatives reviewed above are producing some encouraging practical results.

It is important to emphasize that the outcome of regional cooperation initiatives should not be judged solely on the basis of measurable economic results. Rather, our strategy should involve an array of functional cooperation projects that can serve as a vehicle for confidence-building and enhanced mutual understanding. Japanese NGOs' efforts demonstrate that improved information-sharing and dialogues at the grassroots level are a necessary part of our strategy. Timely publication of standardized statistical data and other socio-economic information in the transition economies is another compelling project.

The SPF projects reviewed above show that capacity- and institution-building is a realistic approach to enhancing intellectual cooperation. Improved policy-research capacity in China, Mongolia, and the Russian Far East increases mutual recognition and, it is hoped, will also lead to the adoption of standardized policy practices, which in turn will help to accelerate harmonization on specific policy issues between the countries concerned. We recognize also that the development of human resources in the transition economies can be accelerated if the countries cooperate through joint training programs. Subjects of common interest to these countries include, among other things, international trade and marketing know-how, business management, customs and tax administration, and environmental management.

Our experience also illustrates that the creation of research and academic networks at the local, national, and regional levels can help to improve comparative studies. The resulting research output is added to the shared knowledge base of the research community, and this in turn helps to improve our understanding of the strengths and weaknesses of regional cooperation. Research and academic networks are also useful for harnessing and exchanging research ideas and findings on a more regular basis. It is further hoped that they will help to increase the research community's access to and influence on the policy-making process at the official level.

There are several obvious limitations to nongovernmental initiatives. For example, NGOs may be instrumental in creating incremental qualitative changes, but it is beyond their capacity to create a more sweeping change in the policy environment that would be conducive to accelerated regional cooperation. Another shortcoming relates to financial resources. To ensure nongovernmental initiatives on a sustained basis requires substantial support in the way of financial and technical assistance from public agencies. Therefore, it is necessary to develop a strategy to forge functional collaboration both within NGO networks and between them and the public sector. NGO networks are useful for harnessing the in-depth knowledge of NGOs with respect to specific issues, and cooperation between NGOs and government is very important in addressing the policy problems studied by NGOs. A related strategy would be to establish an effective division of labor between public agencies and NGOs in which the former provide financial support and the latter deliver the services.

Because NGOs represent the opinions, interests, and wishes of the public, their credibility rests on the responsible and constructive role they play in society. To ensure the full realization of their potential will require the most open communication and cooperation possible between NGOs and national government agencies in Japan. Specifically, government agencies should be invited to participate in dialogues with NGOs and to make full use of the networks created by various private initiatives across national boundaries. Unnecessary competition, monopolies on information, and parochial agendas must be avoided if Japanese NGOs are to become effective agents of change. They need to foster cooperation and communication among themselves, domestically and internationally.

Conclusion

In the past, NGOs in Japan have often been viewed by the public sector as an opposition force in the process of policy making and implementation. However, in recent years, donors and government agencies have been offering NGOs a larger role in project execution. It has been realized that the conventional trickle-down (from state to society) approach to development projects often fails to produce satisfactory results or desired changes in society. As an alternative approach, the development community has increasingly emphasized the independence, flexibility, and effectiveness of NGOs in mobilizing cohesive actions at the local, national, and transnational levels.[6]

Today, many private voluntary organizations and community-based organizations constitute perhaps the fastest-growing sector of influence in Japan. Indeed, NGOs have become a mobilizing force for local communities and the public, initiating and supporting action that the national government often fails to deliver effectively. Particularly, volunteerism mushroomed in the aftermath of the Hanshin earthquake of 1995 and in response to the recent oil spill by the Russian tanker *Nakhodka* off the northwestern coast of Japan in 1997. Through their energetic activities, many Japanese NGOs have demonstrated their ability to play a very important role in complementing government programs.

Japanese nongovernmental initiatives play an important role in the development and implementation of specific ideas in forging regional cooperation. One of the major challenges facing NEA today, as it seeks to enhance cooperative mechanisms, is how to generate a sense of common purpose both within and between local and national communities. We hope that the description of our experience and lessons from it will contribute to the broadening of the scope of discussion about the different but complementary roles various actors can play in enhancing regional cooperation in NEA.

Notes

1. Geographically, there are sixteen prefectures facing the Sea of Japan—Hokkaido, Aomori, Akita, Yamagata, Niigata, Toyama, Ishikawa, Fukui, Kyoto, Hyogo, Tottori, Shimane, Yamaguchi, Fukuoka, Saga, and Nagasaki.
2. For example, the Tumen River Development Project (TRDP), the Yellow Sea Rim Economic Zone, and the Pan-Japan Sea Rim Economic Sphere.
3. For an excellent survey of the evolution of Japanese NGOs, see Toshihiro Menju and Takako Aoki, "The Evolution of Japanese NGOs in the Asia Pacific Context," in Tadashi Yamamoto, ed., *Emerging Civil Society in the Asia Pacific Community*, Singapore: Institute of Southeast Asian Studies (ISEAS), 1995.
4. For details, see Won Bae Kim and Burnham O. Campbell, eds., *Proceedings of the Conference in the Coastal Area of Northeast Asia*, Honolulu: East-West Center, 1992.
5. Tsuneo Akaha, "Northeast Asia Project Evaluation—Final Report," The Sasakawa Peace Foundation, Tokyo, 1996 (unpublished).
6. DAC, *1993 Report of Development Cooperation—Aid in Transition*, Brussels: OECD, 1994.

CHAPTER 15

NONGOVERNMENTAL INITIATIVES IN KOREA FOR NORTHEAST ASIAN COOPERATION

Ku-Hyun Jung

Introduction

THE TITLE OF THIS CHAPTER BEGS TWO QUESTIONS. What can best be done at the Northeast Asian regional level and what can be done by nongovernmental organizations to promote cooperation in Northeast Asia? The first question asks why we need to have a regional scheme in Northeast Asia in addition to central and local governments and regional and global organizations. The second question asks about the role of nongovernmental organizations (NGOs) vis-à-vis governments or private enterprises. Given the relative weakness of NGOs in the region, what can we expect from them in promoting peace and prosperity in the region? This chapter will deal with these two questions first and then look at some of the initiatives that are taken by NGOs in Korea to promote Northeast Asian cooperation. In the last section, some suggestions will be made regarding the direction of future NGO activities in the region.

What Can Be Done at the Northeast Asian Level?

For the purposes of this discussion, "Northeast Asia" includes coastal China, Taiwan, Hong Kong, North Korea, South Korea, Japan, and the maritime provinces of Russia. This area is noted for the absence of regional efforts to organize a multilateral governmental organization for regional trade agreement or other forms of economic integration. The World Trade Organization (WTO) reports that there are more than 70 efforts of regional trading agreements (RTAs) worldwide. Almost all of the 200-plus countries around the globe are trying to form an RTA with their neighbors in order to secure peace or obtain a better bargaining position in the globalization process. Yet there is no apparent effort to form an RTA in Northeast Asia. There are several reasons why this is the case. First, the region includes at least two countries, China and Russia, that have huge land masses and thus are difficult to include in a regional scheme. Russia is a former global power with cultural and historical ties to Europe. China is also looking to play a global role. Second, the region was effectively divided into two separate systems during the Cold War, and the countries of the region have only been in close contact with each other for the last decade or so. Third, as noted by many other authors in this book, Northeast Asian countries are so diverse in terms of income, economic development, competitiveness, and economic systems that it is difficult to forge an integration scheme. Fourth, historical animosity and distrust stemming from colonization and war in the first half of this century have not yet been overcome among the countries in the region. For these and other reasons, economic integration of the region is currently being pursued through the broader framework of Asia Pacific Economic Cooperation, or APEC.

Since Northeast Asia is heterogeneous and lacks both a sense of community and an effort to build one, one can ask what can really be done by the countries within the region. This question would be called a subsidiary question in the EU context.[1] The EU divides decision-making on various issues among at least three levels of government (i.e., Brussels, central government, and local government).

The subsidiary principle states that issues requiring collective decisions should be handled at the level where they can be handled best. For example, trade matters are addressed at the EU level, issues of taxation at the national government level, and school-related issues at the local government level. Using the same principle with regard to Northeast Asia, what can usefully be done at the Northeast Asian level that cannot be done at a national or broader level (such as APEC)? The question can be divided into three areas: economics, military security, and nonmilitary security.

In economic areas, little can be achieved at the Northeast Asian level. Trade and investment liberalization can only be handled at the global level. WTO is the proper framework for handling trade-related issues. If WTO functions properly, even APEC will become redundant in trade matters. Investment liberalization can also be handled by either APEC or OECD (the Organization for Economic Cooperation and Development). It is true that intraregional trade and investment relations are expanding very rapidly. One can legitimately ask whether a regional framework is necessary to handle disputes in investment or trade matters. However, it is easier to handle those issues in a global forum than to try to develop a new organization in a subregion such as Northeast Asia. The countries in Northeast Asia or elsewhere play, or should play, by the internationally accepted rules set by global organizations such as WTO and OECD. In this sense, it is desirable for China to join various multilateral organizations, particularly WTO. China is already a member of APEC, ASEM, and UN organizations. Were China to join WTO, a new initiative on trade and investment matters would not be necessary in Northeast Asia.

What about subregional arrangements? In Northeast Asia, the South China economic region, which includes Hong Kong, Taiwan, and two Chinese provinces, is the most vibrant area. Other candidates are: the Tumen River Growth Triangle, the Yellow Sea Economic Region, and the East Sea (or Sea of Japan) Economic Region. What can central governments do to promote cooperation in these areas? Very little. Natural economic territories, or NETs, are driven by private business initiatives. What a central government can do to promote NETs is allow a liberal trade and investment environment.

A central government can also provide an efficient infrastructure and administration aimed at promoting economic development and enhancing the quality of life for its people. For subregional economic cooperation, local governments can work harder to improve their relations with neighboring provinces.[2] For example, Kyushu, Pusan, and Shanghai together are in a better position to promote their economic relations than Seoul, Tokyo, and Beijing. In this respect, in trade and investment matters at least, there is only limited need for a governmental agreement in Northeast Asia.

In traditional security areas, Northeast Asia certainly has many problems. The most immediate danger zone is the Korean peninsula. There are also many territorial disputes between countries in the region. The region certainly needs to discuss security problems and work toward lasting peace. But discussions on security in the region cannot progress very far without the participation of the United States. Meaningful dialogue on regional security requires the participation of all four major powers—China, Japan, the United States, and Russia—as well as smaller countries in the region. After all, geography is not the only criterion for regional cooperation. Country composition can be flexible depending upon the issues. When discussing security, all countries with strategic interest in the region should be involved.

In the area of nonmilitary security, there are some issues which can best be handled regionally. The most immediate problem is that of environmental degradation. Northeast Asia is one of the most populous regions in the world and is fast becoming the most industrialized. As China makes rapid progress in its push toward industrialization, pollution from burning fossil fuels will become critical. Acid rain from China is already a problem for Korea and Japan. One can argue that a richer China will be a better partner in environmental protection for the region. A more reasonable assumption, at least in the immediate future, is that as a country gets richer, the environment will get worse before it gets better.[3] This applies to China. Experiences in Korea show that public concern over the environment becomes serious only after per capita income rises above a certain level, such as US$5,000 or more. Serious efforts to control environmental degradation in Japan only started in the early 1970s. In any case, the region requires an intergovern-mental organization to handle cross-border pollution problems. Energy and food security are also related to pollution problems. It is unclear how possible energy shortages can be handled at the re-gional level. Food problems, on the other hand, should be dealt with at the regional level both for humanitarian reasons and for refugee control.

Another new security issue is illegal immigration. Since income gaps between countries are still very large, there are many people who attempt to enter a richer country by circumventing the proper procedures. So far, the problem of illegal immigration has been kept to manageable levels. There is danger, however, that the famine in North Korea could bring about mass immigration into neighboring countries. At the moment, all three neighboring countries may be working on their own solutions to this potential problem. Coordi-nation between governments could bring about a better response. Other potential problems, such as organized crime and drug traf-ficking, are maintained at reasonably low levels because borders within the region are monitored rather strictly and because North Korea, as a Stalinist regime, maintains very strict control of the movement of both people and goods within its own territory as well as without.[4] The situation could change in the near future if events suddenly triggered mass immigration.

In partial summary, Northeast Asia has not recovered from the legacies of colonialism and the Cold War. Therefore, the preven-tion of war within the region should be the most important item on the agenda for regional dialogue. A broad-based security dia-logue involving the United States and Russia would be the most sensible approach, given the military presence in the region. The issues that can be best handled at an intergovernmental level seem to be nonmilitary security issues such as pollution, food and en-ergy security, and refugee problems. A multilateral governmental body should be set up to discuss and coordinate policy actions on these important problems. Economic liberalization would be best handled at a broader regional or global level. Any actions that cen-tral governments can take to promote subregional economic rela-tions would occur anyway in the context of APEC or overall globalization. Cooperation among local governments may be more effective in promoting growth triangles or NETs in the region.

What Can Be Done by Nongovernmental Organization?

Around the world, there seems to be an increase in organized voluntary activity and the creation of private, nonprofit or nongovernmental organizations. Throughout both the developed and the developing countries, people are forming associations, foundations, and similar institutions to deliver human services, promote grassroots economic development, prevent environmental degradation, protect civil rights, and pursue other objectives formerly unattended or left to the state. In a recent article, Lester M. Salamon described this phenomenon as "a global associational revolution."[5]

Traditionally, Northeast Asian countries have been characterized by the presence of "strong states." Japan and South Korea have been known for the strong role their governments play in economic development as well as in other social areas. At the same time, the economies of both countries have been dominated by large corporations, leaving little room for nonprofit and nongovernmental organizations. Since the democratization process began in earnest in South Korea (about 1987), there has been an increase in public interest in the role of NGOs as a way to counterbalance the almighty government and big business.[6] According to the *Directory of Korean NGOs,* almost three fourths (74.2 percent) of 730 organizations identified as NGOs have been established in the last ten years (1987–1996). This trend shows that the civil society movement has become notable even in a country like South Korea, which was thought to have little room for non-state actors.

The same trend can be observed in Japan. A survey of Japanese NGOs conducted by the Japan Center for International Exchange shows that the number of Japanese NGOs active in international cooperation increased rapidly in the 1980s, especially after 1985.[7] Many Japanese NGOs are targeted toward countries in the Asia-Pacific. According to the survey, 141 out of

186 such organizations, some 76 percent, have programs in Asia. However, their activities are mainly targeted at Southeast and South Asian countries. Countries that Japanese NGOs are targeting include (by order of frequency): the Philippines, Thailand, Nepal, Bangladesh, India, Cambodia, Indonesia, Malaysia, Vietnam, Sri Lanka, and others. Northeast Asian countries are, by comparison, neglected by Japanese NGOs. This can be partially explained by the fact that some of the Northeast Asian countries have not been open to foreign NGOs until very recently. Concerning the overall trend of NGO activities in Japan, the article reported that there is a strong movement toward civil society not only because Japanese people tend to rely less on the government in solving social problems, but also because they have been very disappointed by the corruption and ineffectiveness of politicians. In the future, more active and positive Japanese NGO initiatives can be expected in Northeast Asia.

In socialist countries such as China and North Korea, the private sector did not exist in the past. Most economic entities are still owned by the state in North Korea. Even in China, which has gone through twenty years of economic reform and open-door policy, state-owned enterprises still account for almost one-half of all value added. Actually, in China, the distinction between profit and nonprofit organizations is very vague.[8] For example, armed forces and universities are engaged in various profitmaking ventures. Cooperatives such as township enterprises are a mixture of private and public interests. State-owned enterprises, both at central and local government levels, are public in ownership but are in many cases run like private enterprises. Since the distinction among government, profit-seeking corporations, and nonprofit organizations is very much blurred in China, it is difficult to find a truly nongovernmental organization that is active in regional and international cooperation. In this respect, there seems to be a clear limitation to what NGO initiatives can do to promote Northeast Asian cooperation in China.

China has a different view of the role of NGOs, however. In socialist countries, many social services were originally provided by state-owned enterprises (SOEs). As SOEs have been privatized, these public services have been transferred back to government. But because of the inadequacies of the government budget and personnel, many essential public services are not properly provided. These needs have to be met through nongovernmental organizations. In other words, a transitional economy such as China or Vietnam needs even more nongovernmental organizations to provide them with welfare and other social services. Some observers note that there is thus more room for NGOs to operate in China than in South Korea or Japan.[9]

Overall, the role of NGOs in Northeast Asia is mixed. The region shows a high degree of heterogeneity in terms of the roles of state, business, and volunteer sectors. Geographical proximity alone is not enough to pull countries together to form a community. More important perhaps is the precondition that countries share either values or ideology. It is often said that democratic countries do not start wars. It is important that Northeast Asian countries share a common ideology of democracy and a market economy before they begin to talk about a community in the region. Unfortunately, it is still premature to talk about a common ideology in Northeast Asia. Some countries in the region are still far from democracy or a market economy. China still pursues socialism and also fails to consistently respect basic human rights, and North Korea is a despotic country. Northeast Asian countries are unfortunately too far removed from each other in ideology or values to form a community. This difference in fundamental beliefs and systems makes it difficult for governments to agree on common goals and work toward them. On the other hand, this provides room for NGOs to operate in the region, because NGOs are more diverse in their orientation and thus more flexible than governmental organizations. Until Northeast Asian countries move toward a more homogeneous ideology, NGOs could play an important role in bringing unity to the region. Yet, as NGOs and other private actors are dependent on and influenced by governments, NGO efforts are often frustrated.

The same problem exists in business-to-business exchanges. Although there are private businessmen in China, the Communist Party or government officials are usually also represented in international business meetings. This means that the term "nongovernmental" should be interpreted differently in Northeast Asia than it is elsewhere. Flexibility is required in defining NGOs in Northeast Asia because the distinction between the three sectors is not always clear-cut. In some cases cooperation is achieved through government-organized NGOs or quasi-NGOs. Nevertheless, interactions between various individuals and organizations outside the government, including scholars, research institutions, businessmen, social organizations, and professional organizations, must be expanded.

NGO Initiatives in Korea for Northeast Asian Cooperation

Based on the above premises concerning NGO activities, a survey of Korean NGOs was conducted. Fifteen organizations listed in the *Directory of Korean NGOs,* published by the *Citizen Times,* were identified. This directory is designed to promote cooperation within Northeast Asian countries. Nine of these fifteen organizations responded to a survey regarding their organizational activities and finances. Table 15.1 shows the list of nine responding organizations that are active in Northeast Asian cooperation. These include one government-administered but legally independent foundation. The first characteristic of these nonprofit organizations (NPOs) is that they are basically bilateral organizations. Only one organization, the Korean Northern Relations Council, is multilateral, while all others are bilateral, with partners in Japan, China, or Russia.

Bilateralism is a basic problem in Northeast Asia. There are very few active private organizations that are multilaterally engaged in at least three countries in the region. This demonstrates the lack of community in the region. There is no initiative for organizing a multilateral Northeast Asian association. The first shift of attitudes in Northeast Asia should be a movement toward multilateralism. This does not have to be a governmental effort. A sport or cultural event may be an effective step toward multilateralism. One example of this is the East Asian Games, held in Pusan in 1997, though participants also included some Central Asian countries. A soccer tournament between major East Asian cities would be another effective way to focus attention on Northeast Asia. A *go* competition (a game similar to chess) involving three East Asian countries would also raise the concept of multilateralism by highlighting similarities between cultures. Other multicultural exchanges within the region should be promoted to bring multilateralism to Northeast Asia.

The history of these organizations varies. Organizations dealing with Japan tend to be older than those dealing with China or Russia, thus reflecting a recent normalization of diplomatic relations of those countries with South Korea. A unifying characteristic of these organizations is their concern with economic cooperation. Only one organization is involved in cultural exchanges. As information is only available for the last three years, it is difficult to establish a trend. One short-range trend indicates that South Korean interest in Russia and China has declined since initial relations following normalization of diplomatic relations (in 1989 with Russia and in 1992 with China). However, private-level interactions with China can be expected to continue, principally because China is becoming an important economic partner for South Korea in areas of trade and investment. Interest in Russia, including the Far East, may have weakened in South Korea, reflecting the economic difficulties of Russia as well as personal security concerns. In contrast, Japan-related organizations appear to be stable.

Financially these organizations are on shaky ground. A little more than fifty percent of the operating budget is supplied by interest income from basic assets. Surveyed NGOs said they rely on government support for more than one third of their operating budget. The rest includes membership dues (only 5 percent) and other donations. Civil service organizations require a sufficient supply of financial resources in order to meet new challenges as they arise. Here, private philanthropy, although not so important in quantitative terms, could make a critical qualitative difference by allowing NGOs and research institutes to undertake activities that would not otherwise be possible. However, it should be noted that private philanthropy in Japan and Korea is largely done by corporate foundations. Since corporate foundations are not really independent from sister corporations and are still fundamentally oriented toward domestic issues, they are not likely to contribute

Table 15.1 Korean NGOs Focused on Northeast Asia

NGOs	Fulltime Staff	Membership	Government Registration	Basic Asset*			Budget*		
				1995	1996	1997	1995	1996	1997
Korean Northern Relations Council	12	520	MoFA	—	—	—	—	—	—
Korea-Russia Cultural Exchange Association	3	43	MoCS	0.5	0.5	0.5	1.2	2.3	1.4
Korea-Russia Far East Siberia Association	8	120	MoTIE	4.0	4.0	4.0	3.6	4.4	3.6
Korea-Japan Economic Association	10	105	MoFE	7.3	6.7	4.5	10.2	9.87	6.8
Korea-Japan Cooperation Foundation for Industry and Technology	14	0	MoTIE	10.0	10.0	10.0	47.1	48.3	46.1
Korea-China Economic Council	8	280	MoTIE	—	—	—	2.96	2.62	2.53
Korea-China Friendship Association	3	317	MoFA	—	—	—	2.7	1.8	3.4
Asia Research Fund	1	0	MoFA	—	80.0	80.0	—	7.5	7.5
Korea-Japan Association	5	300	MoFA	1.2	1.2	0.8	1.8	2.1	1.4

Notes: MoFA: Ministry of Foreign Affairs; MoCS: Ministry of Culture and Sports; MoTIE: Ministry of Trade, Industry, and Energy; MoFE: Ministry of Finance and Economy
*Unit of Basic Asset and Budget: 100 million Korean Won

significantly to an international agenda including Northeast Asian issues. Very few private foundations in Korea support international activities. Even in Japan, international funding by private foundations tends to be directed toward the United States. Private foundations in a strict sense do not yet exist in China. This means that NGOs should either have their own assets, solicit contributions from individuals, or turn to government for support. In this respect, flexibility in defining "nongovernmental" efforts is required. As long as an organization has independent governance, it should be considered a private or nongovernmental organization, regardless of government funding.

Expanding funding sources to include governmental support creates an additional funding arena for NGOs. South Korea joined the OECD in 1997 and thus is expected to increase official overseas development assistance. Japan is already one of the largest donors in official development assistance in the world. These two countries could direct some of these funds to the Northeast Asian region. In addition, the World Bank and the Asian Development Bank have recently begun to pay more attention to NGOs in developing countries. They are realizing that NGOs could be good partners in improving living conditions in developing countries. NGOs in developing or transitional economies could receive financial as well as technical assistance from bilateral funds and multilateral development banks.

When asked about their problems, many respondents indicated that the lack of governmental appreciation and support for NGOs creates big obstacles for them in South Korea. It is very important to learn how the relationship between the third sector and government can best be managed. NGOs have historically been viewed with some suspicion by the Korean government because some have been opponents of dictatorial regimes. After the democratization process started in 1987, the attitude of many government offices began to change. They recognize now that NGOs can be helpful in tackling many social problems and are therefore attempting to cooperate with them on some issues, such as the environment, women's rights, youth, and the disabled. The NGO movement must seek to develop cooperative relations with both the government and the private sector without compromising its own social agenda. Direct confrontation with the government is generally not effective. Maintaining independence while receiving financial support from the government and corporations is one of the challenges of nonprofit organizations everywhere, particularly in Northeast Asia.

The *Directory of Korean NGOs* is not comprehensive, as it was only the first attempt to make such a directory in Korea. In addition to the directory, other sources were examined in order to locate nongovernmental initiatives. Many new initiatives were taken by nonstate actors in the areas of military and nonmilitary security. However, many of these initiatives are in the context of Asia-Pacific rather than Northeast Asia. For example, there was an initiative called the Asia-Pacific Civil Society Forum, which held their first meeting in Seoul during August 11–14, 1995. Nineteen countries were represented in the first meeting. They identified key problem areas as follows: "poverty, authoritarian political rule, militarism, social conflict, environmental destruction, and oppression of women."[10] The local organizer is an association of 45 major advocacy-type NGOs in Korea. The meeting touched on very broad areas of interest. There was no special reference to the Northeast Asian region. In relation to the forum, a new South Korean research institute (called the Asian Institute for the Civil Society Movement) was created with the aim of promoting civil society in Asian countries. There seem to be many other initiatives operating within the context of Asia-Pacific, including organizations with specific issues such as women and the environment. These organizations deal with issues specifically related to Northeast Asia.

The Northeast Asia Cooperation Dialogue, or NEACD, is a private initiative conducted by a research unit of the University of California to discuss security issues in Northeast Asia. Participating countries include the four major powers and the two Koreas, although North Korea only participated in the first meeting. NEACD has met five times since 1993 but has not progressed very far in "working out principles governing state-to-state relations."[11] Although NEACD is a so-called track two effort, government officials participate in the meetings in a private capacity.

A brief survey of Korean NGOs concerned with Northeast Asian issues confirms earlier hypotheses about nongovernmental initiatives in Northeast Asia. First, an uneven development of nongovernmental sectors in the region shows that, in general, their activities are at present quite limited. There is little tradition of the private sector in socialist countries in the region. In capitalist Japan and South Korea, which have, until recently, been dominated by government and big business, there has been an increase in the volunteer movement and citizen interest in public issues since the late 1980s. So far the nonprofit sector in these two countries does not have a keen interest in Northeast Asia. NGOs are naturally more oriented toward domestic social issues. Even when they are internationally minded, NGOs tend to look to the west and south rather than to the northeast. Second, there seem to be few NGOs or NPOs that are primarily concerned with multilateral security issues in Northeast Asia.

Conclusion

Northeast Asia has been slow to develop a multilateral security arrangement and a sense of community among its neighbors. Historical animosity and the Cold War legacy linger on in the region. The twentieth century left deep scars. The first half of the century was characterized by Japanese military expansion into the continent, the subsequent colonization of Korea and part of China, and the ensuing wars with neighboring countries. Much of the second half of the century was characterized by the Cold War, which divided the region into two hostile blocs. There was also a bitter war on the Korean peninsula, again reflecting the division of the region. The region has not yet come to terms with its twin legacies of Japanese military expansion and the Cold War. Northeast Asia must look to Europe for a model of the new era. European countries have agreed on a new order in forming a security arrangement to replace Cold War-based NATO.

East Asia should work toward a new multilateral security arrangement. This should include all the major countries in the region as well as the United States. This arrangement could replace the ASEAN Regional Forum but include Southeast Asian countries along with Northeast Asian countries. The second priority of regional cooperation should be in the area of nonmilitary security. There are at least a few areas where a multilateral governmental organization in Northeast Asia could contribute to peace and stability throughout the region. Environmental protection, food and energy security, refugee problems, illegal immigration, and drug trafficking are some of the issues requiring regional cooperation. The governments in the region need to form a regional cooperative body similar to the Nordic Council in Northern Europe. The Nordic Council is not a regional trading agreement. Instead it is a forum for dialogue and for dealing with regional issues.

This will not require exclusive economic integration. In fact, trade and investment issues can best be handled at different levels. Trade issues can be handled by the WTO once China is admitted into the organization. Investment liberalization can be discussed at APEC, as well as in the context of a new OECD initiative called Multilateral Agreement on Investment (MAI). A Northeast Asian Council can confine its discussions to nonmilitary and noneconomic issues. Countries in the region are still very heterogeneous in terms of political, economic, and value systems. Until these converge toward shared values and similar systems, nongovernmental organizations can contribute significantly toward building a community in the region. This is possible because NGOs are more flexible and diverse.

At the current nongovernmental level, there is very little activity in the context of Northeast Asia. The NGO sector in Southeast Asia is much more vibrant, with multiple intraregional networks of collaboration. In Northeast Asia, there are very few NGOs concerned with nonmilitary security issues. There are several reasons why cooperation among nonstate actors is still relatively weak in Northeast Asia. One reason is that socialist countries have quite a different setup of major actors in society. There is no clear distinction between the government, the private sector, and the nonprofit sector. Even in South Korea and Japan, the government's dominant role in society has hampered development of an independent and vibrant nonprofit sector in the past. In addition, Northeast Asian countries are primarily interested in bilateral approaches. International relations are also becoming very complex. In this global era, it is difficult to persuade people to concentrate on Northeast Asian issues. Geographical proximity is just one reason for countries to work together. The United States is the most important ally of both Japan and South Korea. Ideological differences between capitalist and socialist economies are still very large. APEC provides an attractive venue for multilateral collaboration, notably in trade, investment, development, and technology assistance. ASEM provides another opportunity enabling countries in the region to be linked with Europe. Southeast Asia and Oceania provide attractive business and cultural opportunities for Northeast Asian peoples. As a result, it is up to Northeast Asia to demonstrate why nongovernmental actors should turn their attention to the region.

Despite the many obstacles hampering multilateral nongovernmental initiatives in Northeast Asia, there is still a need for new initiatives. In the second section of this chapter, the subsidiary question concerning Northeast Asia was discussed. Security issues, both military and nonmilitary, require a regional approach. In particular, nonmilitary security issues such as the environment, energy, and refugee problems require both governmental and nongovernmental coordination in the region. Until Northeast Asian governments can be persuaded to take action on these issues, NGOs can play a valuable role in bringing various actors together to develop a common approach to such problems.

Notes

1. Gerald Segal, "Thinking Strategically about ASEM: the Subsidiarity Question," *The Pacific Review,* vol. 10, no. 1 (1977), pp. 124–134. Subsidiarity is defined as the "notion that issues should be handled at the most effective level of authority." (p. 125).

2. A new international organization was launched in September 1996, made up of 29 local governments in four countries (South Korea, China, Russia, and Japan). The first meeting was held at Kyungju, Korea and was organized by Kyungsang-bukdo, a province located in southeast Korea.

3. Research on the relationship between economic growth and environmental degradation shows an inverted U-shaped pattern called the environmental Kuznets curve. (Asian Development Bank, *Emerging Asia: Changes and Challenges,* Manila: Asian Development Bank, 1997, pp. 213–214.)

4. Unfortunately, the bankrupt North Korean regime is becoming a source of many illegal activities, such as the production of counterfeit dollars and drug trafficking.

5. Lester M. Salamon, "The Rise of the Nonprofit Sector," *Foreign Affairs,* vol. 73, no. 3 (July/August 1994), p. 109.

6. Hyun Rae Kim, "Civil Society and Non-governmental Organizations in South Korea: Toward Global Governance," a paper presented at the workshop on "How to Help NGO Sector in Korea," organized by the Institute of East and West Studies, Yonsei University, June 4, 1997, in Seoul (p. 3). Based on the *Directory of Korean NGOs* published by Citizens' Times in 1997, Kim identified 730 organizations as NGOs.

7. Toshihiro Menju and Takako Aoki, "The Evolution of Japanese NGOs in the Asia-Pacific Context," in Tadashi Yamamoto, ed., *Emerging Civil Society in the Asia-Pacific Community,* Tokyo: Japan Center for International Exchange, 1995, p. 145. The article utilizes the data compiled by the Japanese NGO Center for International Cooperation (JANIC), which is contained in the Directory of Japanese Non-Governmental Organizations Active in International Cooperation 1994.

8. The most similar structure to NGOs in China is social organizations, or *shetuan.* Among the five types of social organizations, social welfare and public service organizations fit most closely to the model of NGOs. According to Zhang Ye, there has been increasing interest in social organizations in China since the open-door policy was adopted in 1978, reviving some organizations that had existed in the precommunist period. However, since the Tiananmen incident of 1989, regulation of social organizations has become very strict in China. Now a social organization cannot exist without becoming a part of a government department or a state-authorized "mass organization." (Zhang Ye, "Chinese NGOs: A Survey Report," in Tadashi Yamamoto, ed., *Emerging Civil Society in the Asia-Pacific Community,* Tokyo: Japan Center for International Exchange, 1995, pp. 93–108.)

9. This comment is credited to Peter Geithner, formerly a Beijing representative of the Ford Foundation.

10. *Proceedings of First Asia Pacific Civil Society Forum,* August 11–14, 1995, Seoul, organized by the Korea Coalition of Citizens' Movements, 1995, p. 11.

11. *The Korea Herald,* September 11, 1996.

NATIONALISM VS. REGIONALISM IN NORTHEAST ASIA

NATIONALISM VS. REGIONALISM IN NORTHEAST ASIA

Tsuneo Akaha

Summary

THE LONG-HELD STATE MONOPOLY ON FOREIGN policy agendas in Northeast Asia and the historically sustained popular nationalism in each country of the region have long impeded the formation of transnational linkages that could facilitate the development of a regional identity transcending national borders. Institutionalized nationalism at the state level has demanded the loyalty of its citizens in each country, and most public attention has been geared toward domestic concerns. Bilateralism has been the preferred mode of diplomacy. State- and society-level dialogues targeted at regional cooperation within Northeast Asia have been few and far between, with the UNDP-supported Tumen River Area Development Program and the Northeast Asia Economic Forum being two visible exceptions. Northeast Asia remains more a geographical referent than an economic unit, much less a political community. "Northeast Asia" has been an appendix to Asia-Pacific.

However, there are signs of budding internationalism and growing interest in multilateralism among the intellectual and business communities in the region, particularly in its more developed areas. Although their interest is more often directed toward the broader Asia-Pacific region than specifically toward Northeast Asia, momentum is growing at local and subregional levels for both bilateral and multilateral cooperation across the Sea of Japan, the Sea of Okhotsk, the Yellow Sea, and the East China Sea, with bilateral ties also growing across national land borders.

The contributors to this volume have identified myriad reasons why regionalism in Northeast Asia has been a rare commodity. Historical animosity, civilizational and cultural diversity, political and ideological conflicts at the state level, incompatible economic systems, and the paucity of transnational popular movements have been cited as the major obstacles to the development of a regional identity and regional institutions. When it comes to future prospects for regional cooperation, there is a mixture of optimism and pessimism among contributors. Optimistic assessments point to the primacy of economics over politics and the potential for multilateral cooperation to solve problems that transcend national capabilities. Pessimism stems from the recognition that nationalism is still a much more powerful force than multilateral regionalism, and internationalism is only a recent phenomenon in Northeast Asia.

In the preface, Scalapino provided a broad overview of global and regional trends and their implications for Northeast Asia. The picture that he painted is of a region characterized by an uneasy coexistence of forces of change and forces of continuity, an uncertain balance between economic progress and political conflict, and a mixture of growing opportunities for cooperation and outstanding challenges, some new and some old. On the one hand, nationalism represents continuity, sustains conflict, and challenges the region's capacity to solve problems that transcend national borders. Regionalism, on the other hand, represents change, anticipates cooperation, and presents transnational solutions to the common problems facing the leaders of the region's countries. In the end, Scalapino is cautiously optimistic about the prospects for peace and stability in the region.

Buszynski's task in Chapter 1 was to provide an historical perspective on international relations in Northeast Asia. He identified three types of conflicts: cultural-civilizational, clashes of nationalism, and state-to-state conflicts within and across civilizational divides and national boundaries. According to Buszynski, cultural and civilizational clashes are real, but the sharing of common civilizational space or cultural commonalties does not necessarily guarantee peaceful interstate relations. Nationalist clashes within a shared civilization, such as between Japan and China/Korea, have long prevented and continue to prevent the advancement of regional cooperation. While some state-to-state conflicts, such as between Japan and South Korea, may be contained as economic and other necessities bring the two governments into closer cooperation, other conflicts, such as between Pyongyang and Seoul and between Beijing and Taipei, have explosive potential. All is not lost, however. Even these problems may be soluble if there is a strong political push to contain them. Buszynski's analysis points to the urgent need for state-to-state reconciliation and expansion of people-to-people contacts.

In Chapter 2, Rozman emphasized the fluidity of mutual perceptions among China, Japan, and Russia since the collapse of the Cold War structure globally and regionally. He observed important changes that have appeared in their mutual perceptions within very short periods and explained that the unstable political dynamic in post–Cold War Northeast Asia accounts for the instability in mutual perceptions among the big powers of the region. He identified the instability inherent in relations among three great powers sharing the same geostrategic space. Conflict and cooperation between any two powers constrain their respective options vis-à-vis the other great power. Rozman concluded that mutual reassurances are particularly important to prevent the unstable trilateral game from resulting in a major falling out. Clearly the need for multilateralism is indicated. However, trilateral cooperation among China, Japan, and Russia has no historic precedent. The question, then, is What are the prospects that the future will be any different? Again, the fluidity and uncertainty in great power relations in Northeast Asia precludes any definitive prediction. It is likely, however, that if regional cooperation involving all three powers develops, it will not

be an outgrowth of liberal internationalism in pursuit of interdependence but a result of realist calculations based on nationalist interests. We can anticipate an uneasy coexistence of rivalry and
cooperation among China, Japan, and Russia, with the United
States potentially playing a balancing role with each of them.

Part 2 examined bilateral great power relations in contemporary Northeast Asia. In Chapter 3, I reviewed the visibly improving
Russo-Japanese relations since 1997 and pointed out that global,
regional, bilateral, and domestic factors are pushing the two countries toward accommodation. I noted that sustained bilateral improvement will help to ensure the two countries' respective status
as great powers in regional and global contexts. I also observed
that behind the recent improvement in Russo-Japanese relations is
the realization on both sides that their relations have important implications for the broader region, in which they have extensive interests. Particularly at stake are their relations with the other
regional powers, especially China and Korea, as well as the United
States. Clearly the most immediate hurdle Russia and Japan must
clear before they can develop a bilateral relationship that is conducive to their regional interests will be the peace treaty negotiation. The success or failure of bilateral diplomacy over a longer
term will hinge on the resolution of the dispute over the Northern
Territories (southern Kuriles), the legacy of the nationalism and
militarism of the past. Russo-Japanese accommodation will hold
important implications for the other regional powers as well.

In Chapter 4, Anderson outlined Japan's continuing reliance on
bilateralism and its "experimentation" with multilateralism. As
with the United States in Asia during the Cold War, so Japan has
long pursued and continues to pursue a predominantly bilateral
mode of diplomacy, eschewing multilateral initiatives. Even though
Japan participates in two important multilateral processes, KEDO
and APEC, its role in the former is one of support rather than leadership, and its role in the latter has very little to do with Northeast
Asia. As Anderson notes, intellectual preparations are underway for
multilateral engagement, with the expectations of "multilateral optimists" competing against those of the "bilateral pessimists." However, whether Japan will be able to develop a successful multilateral

diplomacy will depend heavily on the willingness of the other major powers, especially the United States and China, to engage in multilateral processes. Prospects for multilateral engagement involving these powers appear much brighter on the economic front than in the security realm.

This observation is supported by Hu's analysis in Chapter 5 regarding China's policy toward international interdependence and multilateral cooperation. He observed that the leaders in Beijing see many benefits in regional cooperation but that they are quite sensitive to the potential costs of cooperation. He noted that PRC leaders are particularly reluctant to engage in cooperation that could limit China's independence and sovereignty, most clearly in the security field but even in the economic arena. He concluded that the success of regional multilateral organization will depend on healthy bilateral relations, especially good relations between major powers. This implies that a balance-of-power system may be a more likely scenario than multilateral regionalism or even a concert of powers. Nationalism remains a very powerful force behind Chinese foreign policy in this region and elsewhere. Territorial disputes, human rights issues, military development, nonproliferation issues—all of them touch the nationalist nerves of the power center in Beijing. Even economic issues, of trade liberalization, investment promotion, and technology transfer, invite nationalist responses when sovereignty and national control are at stake.

In Chapter 6, Meyer presented a balanced assessment of contemporary Chinese-Japanese relations and near-future prospects. As "natural rivals," China and Japan are each particularly sensitive to the expanding power of the other and possible encroachment on their own regional influence. Nationalism is very much a part of the bilateral dynamic between Beijing and Tokyo. However, the two sides also see a growing need to cooperate bilaterally. According to Meyer, how Beijing responds to the aspirations of independently minded leaders of Taiwan will crucially affect Japan's view of and policy toward China. Unfortunately, no multilateral framework is available to address the Taiwan issue—an internal issue as far as Beijing is concerned. Beijing will closely monitor the evolution of U.S.-Japanese defense cooperation for fear that Japan's security role may expand regionally on the basis of the new defense cooperation guidelines. Meyer is cautiously optimistic, however, that barring a crisis over Taiwan or a U.S. withdrawal from East Asia, the incentives for Sino-Japanese cooperation will remain strong.

In Part 3, we examined the interests and perspectives of the smaller powers in the region, Korea and Mongolia. Jeong and Mo observed in Chapter 7 that nationalism in South Korea had long tempered its interest in regional cooperation despite the substantial benefits the country stands to gain from access to the labor, resources, and markets in its neighboring countries, including Japan and China. Nationalist sensitivities are quite strong in South Korea, particularly with respect to Japan's past behavior and its possible cultural influence. Seoul adopted the "Nordpolitik" policy, i.e., normalization with the Soviet Union and China, as a way of finding an opening with North Korea. Results were disappointing, however, with neither the Soviet Union nor China willing or able to exercise its influence over North Korea, as South Korea had hoped. Jeong and Mo reminded us that Seoul's regional policy will remain linked to its strategic concerns vis-à-vis Pyongyang. For South Korea, in other words, regional cooperation is not just a matter of economics but of direct relevance to national security. For the two authors, efforts at economic policy coordination and market integration generally make more sense at the broader Asia-Pacific level than in the Northeast Asian subregion. This view was echoed by Moon and Ko, who also examined domestic debate in South Korea.

In Chapter 8, Moon and Ko noted the dominance of nationalist perspectives in domestic debate in South Korea concerning regional cooperation. They discerned three competing alternative futures for Northeast Asia: a U.S.-Japan bigemony, multilateralism among Northeast Asian countries at both global and regional levels, and integration of Northeast Asia into the broader regional framework of Asia-Pacific under the principle of "open regionalism." In their view, the third scenario is the most promising for most of the Northeast Asian countries, notably for North and South Korea and China. The authors concluded, however, that the fluidity of the current situation in the region does not allow them to forecast with confidence which of the possible futures will eventually materialize.

In Chapter 9, Batbayar analyzed Mongolia's history of dependence on the Soviet Union and the post-Soviet political transformation in Ulaanbaatar. On the one hand, Mongolia has been freed from political domination by the Soviet Union and embarked on a path toward democracy and a market economy. On the other hand, the end of the Cold War support from the Soviet Union has ushered Mongolia into a period of economic uncertainty and political instability. Batbayar highlighted his country's commitment to political and market reform and outlined its pressing domestic economic needs, which can only be met through international cooperation, particularly with the neighboring Northeast Asian countries and the United States. There is a good deal of optimism in Mongolia that the international community will come to its aid. However, the country's influence in the international community is extremely limited. The Mongolians' hopes and dreams for international cooperation may be shattered if their appeal for assistance is lost on the international community.

Part 4 was devoted to the exploration of three very different sources of instability and possible conflicts, the reform in Russia and its consequences for Far Eastern Russia, the North Korean crisis, and demographic changes in Northeast Asia.

In Chapter 10, Ivanov described the downward spiral of the Russian economy since the early 1990s up through the financial crisis in 1998, and its painful consequences for Far Eastern Russia. Fewer federal subsidies, little or no capital investments, and substantially reduced defense contracts have crippled industrial and agricultural production in the region. With much of the Soviet-era social net dismantled, citizens are left on their own to cope with missing or long-delayed wage payments, shrinking purchasing power, and frequent power outages. One glimmer of hope can be found in the region's growing trade with other Northeast Asian economies. Only if Far Eastern Russia can attract international capital for the development of its rich natural resources, including abundant oil and natural gas reserves, may the region be able to raise sufficient capital for reinvestment in its industrial production. This, however, seems a remote possibility in view of the credit crunch under the crippling weight of mushrooming Russian debts and increasingly tight international capital supply amidst the Asian financial crisis. Ivanov believes that the development of a regional energy network of supplies and markets will contribute to the energy security of the entire region. However, whether Northeast Asian countries can agree on a multilateral arrangement for the production, delivery, and marketing of Far Eastern Russia's energy resources remains uncertain.

In Chapter 11, Mansourov reminded us that historically, in periods of major shifts in the balance of power among the great powers in Asia, the Korean peninsula invariably fell victim to the hegemonic rivalry among them. He added that political volatility on the Korean peninsula further exacerbated the great power conflict by inviting interference in the internal affairs of a divided Korea. He compared the current transition period to those earlier periods. He concluded that it remains to be seen whether future developments in North Korea, including such contingencies as political and military instability, mass famine, and refugee outflow, might weaken or strengthen the existing anti-DPRK Western coalition. He also noted the enigmatic yet crucial influence of China in determining the eventual success or failure of international cooperation. The peninsula remains, therefore, at the same time a reason for cooperation and a source of further rivalry among the great powers in Northeast Asia.

In Chapter 12, Van Arsdol discussed potential implications of demographic patterns in each Northeast Asian country for the region's stability. For China, he warned that unchecked population increases could potentially increase rural migration to cities, lead to dependence on food imports, increase resource depletion, and heighten Chinese lateral pressures on other countries in the region. He noted that Mongolia is the fastest growing country in all of Northeast Asia, adding to pressures for immigration and emigration. He also observed that Japan, with its near-zero population growth and fast-aging population, is absorbing increasing numbers of foreign immigrants, but this has had some negative consequences, most notably discrimination against members of national and ethnic minority groups. South Korea is also becoming a major labor importer and declining labor exporter. Van Arsdol warned that a worsening political or economic situation in North Korea could result in state implosion and/or massive refugee migration to South Korea and elsewhere in Northeast Asia. In Russia, he noted, the low fertility rate and decreasing life expectancy are serious challenges, threatening the nation's vitality. These demographic changes may not pose immediate threats to regional security. However, combined with other problems, such as growing income disparity, mounting competition for resources, and a deepening energy crisis, they can exert troubling influences on relations among national and ethnic groups. Therefore, governments of Northeast Asia must develop preventive policies, including effective management of transborder migration and illegal trade.

Finally, Part 5 examined the potential contributions of nongovernmental organizations to international cooperation in Northeast Asia. The consensus among the three studies in this part is that the promotion of human contact and mutual cultural learning through the activities of nongovernmental organizations develops a habit of cooperation among the peoples of Northeast Asia. In Chapter 13, Valencia reviewed the evolution of the Northeast Asia Economic Forum. Since its inception in the late 1980s, the forum has grown into one of the most visible nongovernmental multilateral efforts in Northeast Asia. Most importantly, according to Valencia, the forum has fostered the development of "a spirit of optimism, of cooperation, of a vision of a peaceful and prosperous Northeast Asia." In Chapter 14, Shirasu and Lau reviewed the efforts of the Sasakawa Peace Foundation toward regional cooperation. In their view, the independence (from government), flexibility, and effectiveness of NGOs in mobilizing cohesive action can be a complement to and facilitator of government activity. They acknowledge, however, that attempts at nongovernmental cooperation face some major obstacles, such as historical grievances, disparity in economic systems, territorial disputes, differing levels of development, security issues, and state-level relations that impede cooperation in Northeast Asia.

In Chapter 15, Jung's review of NGO movements in Northeast Asia revealed that nongovernmental initiatives are of recent origin and South Korean NGOs are no exception. He discussed some dilemmas that nongovernmental groups in his country face. He found that financially many organizations are on shaky ground, with many of them requiring or contemplating government or corporate support. Therefore, maintaining independence while receiving financial support is one of the challenges facing them. A related concern is the lack of government appreciation and public support for NGO activities in South Korea. Jung argued that NGOs in Northeast Asian countries should move toward greater multilateralism. He also recommended that they undertake more active cultural exchange as a means of promoting greater understanding, developing a shared vision of the future, and pursuing common interests. An area of potential importance for NGO cooperation is unconventional security issues, such as environmental problems, migration, and economic disparity within and between countries.

Where Do We Go from Here?

What normative generalizations and conclusions can we draw from these analyses of what Northeast Asian countries should do in order to overcome the stifling effects of nationalism and advance the cause of regional cooperation?[1]

At the most general level, Northeast Asian countries must overcome cognitive barriers and build institutional bridges to reach each other. The long history of hostilities from previous centuries through the end of the Second World War and the Cold War division of Asia has prevented the Northeast Asian peoples from openly and directly exchanging their views of history, either ancient or modern, and their contemporary views of each other. In developing international relations they have generally carried state-centered political agendas and worn ideological blindfolds. The end of the Cold War and the technology-driven interdependence of the contemporary world have stripped the peoples of this region of any ideological excuses not to try to reach accommodation and reconciliation with one another. However, nationalism still holds sway over fledgling regionalism.

What should the peoples of Northeast Asia do to overcome nationalist temptations and strive toward regional cooperation? The analyses in this volume offer several important implications.

First, there is a need to identify the sources of conflict accurately and, if at all possible, to develop a common understanding of the sources of conflict. Cultural/civilizational conflicts will be the most enduring, and no short-term solution may be found. To the extent that increased human contact leads to reciprocal understanding and mutual tolerance, the national governments in the region must encourage local authorities and private citizens to develop opportunities to travel and meet people from different cultures. The recent lifting of the South Korean ban on importing various forms of Japanese popular culture demonstrates that Seoul has realized the importance of lifting the cultural blindfolds on its citizens. This development could not have come about if the Japanese government had not publicly and unequivocally acknowledged Japan's past aggression against the Korean people and expressed the remorse the South Koreans had long demanded.

Clashes of nationalism within the same cultural/civilizational sphere can be contained by effective policy promoting transnational contact and economic interdependence. Economic, social, and political grievances can provoke nationalist sentiment and create international tensions. Uncontrolled migration and exploitation of foreign labor are likely to generate nationalist and ethnic tensions within and between countries. Finally, enlightened leadership can control state-to-state conflicts, but this would require the development of a regional system of relations in which a sense of common security prevails, a spirit of openness dominates, and a vision of a common future is shared. Again, this requires expanded contact both at the state level and at the citizens' level.

Secondly, there is much to be done to change the negative and asymmetrical perceptions among the three major powers of Northeast Asia, Russia, China, and Japan. Bilaterally and multilaterally, extensive efforts are necessary to develop open dialogue, to enhance transparency in national policy, and to expand public- and private-level contact. The three governments must mobilize the mass media to educate their citizens about the benefits of expanded economic and social contact. Wherever possible, they should explore multilateralism and limit bilateralism, for the latter breeds suspicion among third parties.

Third, Japan, China, and South Korea have the most to contribute to regional cooperation. Japan must cultivate a multilateral orientation. It has relied too long on its political and security alliance with the United States and it remains reluctant to engage multilaterally with the other Northeast Asian countries. As the richest country in Northeast Asia, it cannot shirk its responsibility for the peace and prosperity of the region. Japan has the most to offer, and it may also gain the most from regional cooperation. Japan's support for Russia's economic reform and development has broader regional and global implications. A democratic Russia with a market economy will be a factor of stability. Its rich natural resources will gain in importance as the other Northeast Asian countries' resource needs grow. Successful military-civilian conversion will help reduce Russia's reliance on military power as a source of influence in regional affairs. Development of effective environmental and resource conservation measures in the Russian Far East will also be in the interest of Japan and other Northeast Asian countries. Japan can also contribute to the peace and stability of the Korean peninsula. Although its influence in North Korea is virtually nil, Tokyo should explore every appropriate avenue of communication with Pyongyang and support Washington's engagement policy and Seoul's "sunshine policy." Japan should also put its own economic house in order so as to contribute to South Korea's and other East Asian countries' recovery from the post-1997 currency and financial crises. Tokyo's proposal for a new Asian Monetary Fund is a welcome sign that Tokyo recognizes its regional responsibility in stabilizing the financial situation in Asia. Financial reform, demand stimulus, and market liberalization, more than anything else, will help establish Japan as the second most reliable market, after the U.S. market, on which other countries can relay to expand their exports and sustain domestic development. In short, Japan's international roles require multilateral, bilateral, and unilateral measures.

China has the greatest potential to either enhance or impede regional cooperation. Given its enormous size and expansive economic growth, no regional cooperation will be effective without Chinese participation or at least Chinese endorsement. Yet, among the regional powers, China is the most reluctant to participate in multilateral cooperation. The other powers must develop incentives to induce Chinese interest. Rather than issuing categorical accusations and condemnations against China's human rights violations and protectionist trade policy, for example, the neighboring countries may be better advised to show an understanding of the enormous challenge China faces in providing for its huge population. They must also offer assistance to promote further economic development in China and to spread the benefits of development in different regions. For the other Northeast Asian countries, environmentally sustainable development in China, particularly in its northeastern provinces, will be advantageous. Japan, South Korea, Russia, and the United States should actively participate in or support multilateral development projects in China. The Tumen River Area Development Program is a test case of the willingness to participate in multilateral cooperation involving China. The project can help develop a habit of cooperation among the wartime and Cold War adversaries.

South Korea has the potential to play a pivotal role in facilitating regional economic cooperation, but it must overcome its mercantilist inertia and nationalist orientation if it is to play this role. The country's geographic location and its intermediate level of development place it in an advantageous position to facilitate relations between China and Japan. South Korea can provide Japan and China with intermediary goods and investment for primary production and semi-finished goods production in China. Japan can supply capital and technology-intensive products to the increasingly sophisticated consumers in South Korea and China. China can offer investment opportunities and supply food and other consumer goods to neighboring markets. South Korea can also expand its presence in the Russian Far East, where the market demand for its manufactured products has grown. South Korea needs to accelerate its domestic economic reform and liberalization and strengthen its international competitiveness. As noted earlier, South Korea and Japan should expand contact at all levels of government and society

and overcome the legacies of a bitter history. They must also cooperate in defusing the tension that results from South Korea's dependence on Japan's economy.

South Korea's effective participation in regional cooperation requires improved North-South relations. Japan, China, Russia, and
the United States should do all they can to facilitate reconciliation
between North and South Korea but at a pace of the Koreans' own
choosing and on terms agreeable to both sides. The United States
has a particularly important role in the four-party talks, as well as
in the KEDO process. Washington, Beijing, Moscow, and Tokyo
should take every opportunity to encourage Pyongyang to open up
to international cooperation, offering humanitarian assistance
where needed and technical and financial assistance when necessary.
Long-term engagement, if challenging, is the only realistic way to increase the probability of gradual changes in North Korea. Further
isolation and military strategies raise the probability of explosion,
implosion, and other destructive scenarios.

Fourth, research communities in the Northeast Asian countries
should engage in collaborative research efforts. Intellectual cooperation will help to develop epistemic communities around pragmatic
issues of mutual concern. Research communities should be mobilized to carry out joint studies of the relationship between economic
development and regional integration on the one hand and regional
security on the other. Defining "security" broadly, we need to inform ourselves better about the security consequences of growing
economic interdependence. Among the issues requiring particular
attention are trade and its effect on income distribution, foreign investment and its impact on wealth distribution, and economic development and transborder environmental pollution. Also needed is
further examination of the bilateral and multilateral intersection of
varied demographic patterns in the region and its transnational consequences. Particularly important is a search for a regional migration policy that is effective in both controlling illegal flows of people
and preventing nationalist clashes and ethnic conflicts. The very
process of collaborative studies among Northeast Asian researchers
will facilitate better communication at the intellectual level and enhance researchers' ability to influence their respective governments'

policies and to raise their countrymen's awareness of the regional consequences of domestic changes.

Fifth, the role of nongovernmental organizations should also be studied and promoted further. Participation of voluntary citizens' groups in national development and international relations should be a welcome development inasmuch as it contributes to the development of civil society and democratization of political processes. Development of civic groups is important, particularly in the transition economies, where citizen participation in voluntary activities has been rare. The growth of nonprofit social groups, educational institutions, environmental organizations, and other kinds of associations will contribute to the diversification and sharing of experiences among the neighboring peoples of Northeast Asia. This region, unlike other parts of Asia-Pacific, has been characterized by state-controlled international relations. States have often exploited and exacerbated nationalist fears and ethnic sensitivities. Although the role of the state generally remains dominant in these countries, further opening of national borders to NGOs will promote the development of trust, elimination of prejudices, and cultivation of a sense of a shared future.

Finally, cooperation in Northeast Asia cannot proceed unless it can take advantage of and follow general trends in the broader Asia-Pacific region. Northeast Asian countries are well advised to discuss whether they need a common agenda and goals to pursue in the APEC forum. The principles on which subregional economic cooperation is based should not ignore or contradict those of such Asia-Pacific regional cooperation efforts as APEC. However, the absence of a conceptual framework for Northeast Asia obscures the rationale and diffuses the momentum for multilateral cooperation at the subregional level. Only when such a framework is in place can Northeast Asian countries develop a shared vision of its future.

Dialogue in Northeast Asia must proceed from the fundamental premise that economic interdependence is in the interest of the whole region but that interdependence has its costs in terms of erosion of national control over decision-making. At the same time, the destabilizing consequences of transnational economic processes must be carefully monitored and contained. Northeast Asia cannot leap to a common vision without the necessary building blocks of cooperation. Issue-focused groups and organizations, at both official and private levels, should be encouraged. Pragmatism must guide the gradual process of building confidence, consensus, and capacity.[2]

Notes

1. I hasten to add that these conclusions do not necessarily represent a consensus among the participants in the Monterey conference. The author alone is responsible for the conclusions drawn here.
2. For a more extensive discussion of regime building in Northeast Asia, see Tsuneo Akaha, "Developing Regional Cooperation in Northeast Asia: Lessons from Europe, North America, Asia-Pacific, and Southeast Asia," unpublished paper presented at the international conference "A Vision for Northeast Asia: International Cooperation for Regional Security and Prosperity," organized by the Center for East Asian Studies, Monterey Institute of International Studies, Monterey, California, June 12–13, 1999.

ABOUT THE CONTRIBUTORS

TSUNEO AKAHA is a professor of international policy studies and director of the Center for East Asian Studies at the Monterey Institute of International Studies, Monterey, California. He received his M.A. and Ph.D. in International Relations from the University of Southern California. Before joining the Monterey Institute in 1989, he taught at the University of Southern California, Kansas State University, and Bowling Green State University (Ohio). He has held visiting positions at Hokkaido University's Slavic Research Center, Seikei University (Tokyo), and the University of Tokyo. He is the author of *Japan in Global Ocean Politics* (1985), editor of *Politics and Economics in the Russian Far East: Changing Ties with Asia-Pacific* (1997), and co-editor of *Japan in the Posthegemonic World* (1993), and *International Political Economy: A Reader* (1991). His other works on Northeast Asian affairs have appeared in *Asian Survey, Brown Journal of World Affairs, Demokratizatsiya, Journal of Asian Studies, Pacific Affairs, Pacific Review, Peace and Change, Peace Forum,* and *Sejong Review,* as well as in numerous books.

STEPHEN J. ANDERSON is a Commercial Attaché at the U.S. Embassy, Beijing and a former director of the Center for Global Communications (GLOCOM) of the International University of Japan in Tokyo. Anderson received his Ph.D. in political science from MIT and has taught at the University of Wisconsin-Madison, University of Virginia, and Temple University Japan. He presently serves as an officer in the U.S. & Foreign Commercial Service, International Trade Administration, U.S. Department of Commerce. He is the author of many articles on public policy, telecommunications, political economy, and international relations, as well as the 1995 Ohira Prize-winning book *Welfare Policy and Politics in Japan.*

TSEDENDAMBYN BATBAYAR is director of the Center of International Studies, Mongolian Academy of Sciences. He received his Ph.D. in regional political studies from the Institute for Far Eastern Studies, Russian Academy of Sciences. He has held visiting researcher positions at Tokyo University of Foreign Studies and Hitotsubashi University of Japan. He is the author of *Modern Mongolia: A Concise History,* and *Mongolia and Japan in the First Half of the Twentieth Century* and editor of *Mongolian Journal of International Affairs.*

LESZEK BUSZYNSKI is professor and dean of the Graduate School of International Relations of the International University of Japan, Niigata, Japan. Previously he was senior research fellow with the Strategic and Defence Studies Centre at the Australian National University, Canberra, Australia. He has also taught in the political science department of the National University of Singapore. He is the author of *Gorbachev and Southeast Asia* (1992) and *Russian Foreign Policy* (1996).

WEIXING HU, an associate professor of political science in the department of politics and public administration, University of Hong Kong, holds an M.A. in International Relations from the Johns Hopkins University School of Advanced International Studies and a Ph.D. in Political Science from the University of Maryland, College Park. He has taught at the University of California, San Diego and the University of Detroit and held visiting positions at the Monterey Institute of International Studies and the University of Georgia. His publications include *Strategic Views from the Second Tier* (with J. C. Hopkins) and articles in *Pacific Review, Journal of Northeast Asian Studies, Journal of Contemporary Asia, East Asia,* and *Journal of Contemporary China.*

VLADIMIR I. IVANOV is a senior researcher at the Economic Research Institute for Northeast Asia (ERINA) in Niigata, Japan, and former head of the department of Asia-Pacific Studies at the Institute of World Economy and International Relations (IMEMO) of the Russian Academy of Sciences, Moscow. He graduated from Moscow State University and received his Ph.D. in political economy from the Institute of Oriental Studies of the Russian Academy of Sciences, where he worked for more than ten years. He has been a visiting scholar at Harvard University and the University of Tokyo, a research fellow at the United States Institute of Peace, a Center for Global Partnership/SSRC Abe fellow, and an adjunct and visiting fellow at the Center for International and Strategic Studies and at the East-West Center. He is the author of *Foreign Investment in Australia After the Second World War,* principal author and co-editor of *Pacific Regionalism: Concepts and Realities,* co-author of *Asia-Pacific Region in the 1990s: Soviet Security Perceptions.* He served as co-editor, contributor, and project director of *"Northern Territories" and Beyond: Russian, Japanese, and American Perspectives,* and *Japan and Russia in Northeast Asia: Partners in the 21st Century.*

KAP-YOUNG JEONG is a professor of economics and director of the Northeast Asia Development Center, Yonsei University, Seoul, Korea. He received his Ph.D. in economics from Cornell University. He has worked in the Korea Institute of Industrial Economics and held a visiting position at Cornell University. He is currently the editor of *Global Economic Review,* the author of *Industrial Organization in Korea,* and co-editor of *Toward New Dimensions of Economic Cooperation in Northeast Asia.*

KU-HYUN JUNG is professor and dean of the Graduate School of Business Administration at Yonsei University. He received his B.A. from Seoul National University, his M.B.A. from the State University of New York at Albany, and his Ph.D. from the University of Michigan. From 1992 to 1997, he served as director of the Institute of East and West Studies at Yonsei. He has taught at the University of Michigan, University of Hawaii, University of Washington, and Chinese University of Hong Kong. He has written more than ten books in Korean and co-authored or edited about a dozen books in English. He recently co-authored *Korean Management: Global Strategy and Cultural Transformation* (1997). Professor Jung has served as advisor to several corporations, economic organizations, and various government agencies. He is currently on the board of directors of the Korea Broadcasting System, Hyundai Construction and Engineering Corp., and a few other profit and nonprofit organizations.

DAE-WON KO, an assistant professor of international relations at Yonsei University, Wonju, Korea, received his Ph.D. in political science from Northwestern University. He specializes in international political economy and foreign policy and has published a number of articles in these areas.

SIM-YEE LAU is the acting director of the Sasakawa Southeast Asia Cooperation Fund, the Sasakawa Peace Foundation, Japan. He is also a lecturer on development economics and development cooperation at Tokyo International University and Aoyama Gakuin University, respectively. He received his Ph.D. from Tohoku University, Japan and specializes in issues pertaining to technology transfer and technology policy.

ALEXANDRE Y. MANSOUROV is currently a research associate in residence at the Korea Institute of Harvard University. He received his Ph.D. in political science at Columbia University in New York. He worked as a diplomat at the Soviet embassy in the DPRK in the late 1980s. He taught Korean foreign policy at the Fletcher School of Government of Tufts University and Korean civilization at Columbia University. He is the author of numerous articles on the domestic politics and economics of North Korea and on various problems of the Korean peninsula. He is the co-editor of *The North Korean Nuclear Program: Security, Strategy, and New Perspectives from Russia* (with James Clay Moltz, 1999).

PEGGY FALKENHEIM MEYER, a professor of political science at Simon Fraser University in Burnaby, Canada (a suburb of Vancouver), received her Ph.D. in political science from Columbia University. She has taught at the University of Western Ontario and the University of Toronto, where she was director of the international office. She is the author of *Japan and Arms Control: Tokyo's Response to SDI and INF.* Her articles on Russia's relations with Japan, China, and the two Koreas, Russian security policy, and Northeast Asian regional relations have been published in *Pacific Affairs, Asian Survey, Demokratizatsiya, The Journal of East Asian Affairs, World Policy Journal, International Journal* and other journals and edited volumes.

JONGRYN MO is a professor and director of the Center for International Studies at the Graduate School of International Studies, Yonsei University in Seoul, Korea and a research fellow at the Hoover Institution, Stanford University. He received his Ph.D. in political economics from Stanford University in 1992 and was a national fellow for 1995–1996 at the Hoover Institution after leaving his position as an assistant professor of government at the University of Texas at Austin. Professor Mo is currently conducting research in the areas of international bargaining theory and the political economy of the Asia-Pacific region. His articles have appeared in *American Political Science Review, Journal of Conflict Resolution,* and *Comparative Political Studies.* Most recently, he co-edited the book *Democracy and the Korean Economy* (Hoover Institution Press, 1999).

CHUNG-IN MOON is professor of political science at Yonsei University. Prior to joining the Yonsei faculty, he taught at the University of Kentucky, the Williams College, and the University of California, San Diego. He has published 12 books and over 110 articles in edited volumes and such scholarly journals as *World Politics, International Studies Quarterly, World Development,* and *Journal of Asian Studies.* His most recent publications include *Democracy and the Korean Economy* (Hoover Press, 1999) and *Understanding Regime Dynamics in North Korea* (Yonsei University Press, 1998).

GILBERT ROZMAN is Musgrave Professor of Sociology at Princeton University, where he received his Ph.D. He is the author of *Japan's Response to the Gorbachev Era: A Rising Superpower Views a Declining One* and editor of *Dismantling Communism: Common Causes and Regional Variations.*

ROBERT A. SCALAPINO, Robson Research Professor of Government Emeritus, University of California, Berkeley, is the founder and former director of the Institute of East Asian Studies at the University of California, Berkeley, where he was also editor of *Asian Survey.* He received his Ph.D. in Government from Harvard University. He has taught at Santa Barbara College, Harvard University, and the University of California, Berkeley, and is recipient of numerous honors and awards for his distinguished scholarly achievements. Among his many published works are *The Last Leninists: The Uncertain Future of Asia's Communist States; The Politics of Development: Perspectives on Twentieth-Century Asia; Asian Communism: Continuity and Transition* (co-editor); and *Asia and the Major Powers: Domestic Politics and Foreign Policy* (co-editor).

TAKASHI SHIRASU is professor of economics at Tokyo International University and program director at the Sasakawa Peace Foundation. He received his Ph.D. in economics from Cornell University. He specializes in development economics and development cooperation. His recent publications include *Macro-Economic Adjustments of Mongolia under Transition, State Enterprise Reform of Vietnam during 1980–1995,* and *NPOs' Initiatives in Japan for Intellectual Cooperation toward Transitional Economies.*

MARK J. VALENCIA is a senior fellow with the Program on Research at the East-West Center. He has a Master's of Marine Affairs from the University of Rhode Island and a Ph.D. in oceanography from the University of Hawaii. Before joining the center in 1977, Dr. Valencia was a lecturer at the Universiti Sains Malaysia and a technical expert with the UNDP Regional Project on Offshore Prospecting based in Bangkok. He has published over 100 articles and books and is a frequent contributor to the public media. Recent relevant works on Northeast Asia economic development include *The Russian Far East in Transition* (editor) (1995); *Regional Transportation and Communication in Developing Northeast Asia: Status, Problems, Plans, and Priorities* and *Regional Economic Cooperation in Northeast Asia* (co-editor) (1993).

MAURICE D. VAN ARSDOL, JR. is adjunct professor, Graduate School of International Policy Studies, Monterey Institute of International Studies. He received his Ph.D. in sociology from the University of Washington. He is professor of sociology emeritus at the University of Southern California, where he was director of the Population Research Laboratory, and has also taught at the University of Washington, the University of Hawaii, and Stockholm University. Professor Van Arsdol has carried out missions for the United Nations Department of Technical Assistance for Development and worked on population research and policy projects with the governments of Bahrain, China, Indonesia, and Mexico. His most recent publications are in *International Migration Review* and *World Resource Review.*

INDEX